Your System at a Glance...

Setting	Computer 1
Processor make, type, and speed	
Math coprocessor?	
BIOS make and version	
Hard disk timeout	
Video power off?	
Hard drive make and model	
Cylinders (drive 1)	
Heads/Sectors	
Cylinders (drive 2)	
Heads/Sectors	
RAM module(s)	
Type	
Number of pins	
Suspend mode	
Video card make and model	
Type	
BIOS version and date	
Sound card make and model	
DMA setting	
Address	
CD-ROM make and model	
Entry in autoexec.bat	
Entry in config.sys	
Dial-up networking provider	
ISP tech support phone number	
Username	
Password	
Dial-up number	
Primary DNS	
Secondary DNS	
SMTP	
POP3	
News server	
COM port assignments:	
COM1	
COM2	
COM4	
COM4	
COM5	
Interrupt assignments:	
IRQ2	
IRQ3	
IRQ4	
IRQ5	
IRQ6	
IRQ7	
IRQ8	
IRQ9	
IRQ10	
IRQ11	
IRQ12	
IRQ13	
IRQ14	
IRQ15	

D0077439

Upgrading & Repairing Your PC

Answers!

Second Edition

Upgrading & Repairing Your PC

Answers!

Second Edition

Dave Johnson and Todd Stauffer

Osborne/**McGraw-Hill**

Berkeley • New York • St. Louis • San Francisco
Auckland • Bogotá • Hamburg • London
Madrid • Mexico City • Milan • Montreal
New Delhi • Panama City • Paris • São Paulo
Singapore • Sydney • Tokyo • Toronto

Osborne **McGraw-Hill**
2600 Tenth Street
Berkeley, California 94710
U.S.A.

For information on translations or book distributors outside the U.S.A., or to arrange bulk purchase discounts for sales promotions, premiums, or fund-raisers, please contact Osborne/**McGraw-Hill** at the above address.

Upgrading & Repairing Your PC Answers!
Second Edition

234567890 AGM AGM 90198765432109

ISBN 0-07-212102-5

Publisher	**Copy Editor**
Brandon A. Nordin	Lori Ash
Associate Publisher, Editor-in-Chief	**Proofreader**
Scott Rogers	Valerie Perry
Acquisitions Editor	**Indexer**
Joanne Cuthbertson	Claire Splan
Project Editor	**Computer Designers**
Nancy McLaughlin	Roberta Steele
	Gary Corrigan
Editorial Assistant	**Illustrators**
Stephane Thomas	Robert Hansen
	Brian Wells
Technical Editor	
John Heilborn	**Cover Design**
	Matthew Willis

This book was composed with Corel VENTURA.

*This book is dedicated to preserving the American
way of life; to the engendering of hope, trust, faith,
freedom, and goodwill worldwide; to life, liberty,
and the pursuit of happiness. Oh—and to my cat, Newt.*

Dave Johnson

*I dedicate my portions of this book to the men and
women of the Boy Scouts of America, without whose
encouragement I would never have bought a Swiss
Army knife, disassembled my mother's bicycle, and
tried to become an engineer in college, only to find
that there wasn't a single train in sight. It was this
attitude that led me to first pry the case off an aging
8086 PC, starting a career that I still would trade in
a heartbeat for a chance to play the dentist in an
off-Broadway rendition of "Little Shop of Horrors."*

Todd Stauffer

ABOUT THE AUTHORS

Todd Stauffer and Dave Johnson have spent the last few years as co-hosts on a variety of different computing call-in radio programs which, for no particular good reason, they have given the blanket name "The Computer Guys." In the course of the show's run, they've heard countless computing questions from novices and intermediate users alike about fixing and upgrading PCs. In addition to co-authoring this book, they've recently written *Small Business Office 2000 for Dummies* (IDG, 1999).

Dave Johnson has been writing about computers since his first book, *The Desktop Studio: Multimedia with the Amiga,* was published in 1990. Since then he's written extensively for such magazines as *Home Office Computing*, *Family PC,* and *PC Computing*. He's helped author such books as Que's *Platinum Edition Using Windows 95* (1997, by Ron Person, Michael Desmond, Robert Voss and Robert Bogue, 1997) and *Special Edition, Using Microsoft PowerPoint 97* (1996, by Nancy Stevenson). His latest books are *Digital Photography Answers* (Osborne McGraw-Hill, 1998) and *How to Use Microsoft Outlook 2000* (with Mark Taber, Sams, 1999). Dave is the mobile computing editor at CMPnet's **PlanetIT.com** Web site.

Dave has flown satellites (making him an official "rocket scientist"), instructed college courses, and driven an ice cream truck (making him relatively unemployed). Currently he's writing a novel and raising a household of dogs and cats.

Todd Stauffer is the author of over 17 computer book titles, including the *Mac Upgrade and Repair Bible* (IDG, 1998), and Que's *HTML Web Publishing 6-in-1* (1997) and *Creating Your Own America Online Web Pages* (1996, with Andy Shafran and Andrew Bryce Shafran). He's also contributed to the Que titles *Netscape Navigator 3 Starter Kit* (1996, by Mark Brown, Steven Burnett, Tim Evans and Heath Fleming), *Platinum Edition Using Windows 95,* and *Special Edition, Using the Internet with Your Mac* (1995, by Mary Ann Pike and Scott Berkun), among others. He's the writer and co-host of the Emmy award-winning "Disk Doctors" show on Knowledge TV and a contributing editor and writer for many regional and national technology publications and Web sites.

Todd has worked as a magazine editor, technical editor, and copy writer. He raises no cats, although there is one in his apartment that occasionally comes out from under the bed and demands tuna.

Contents

Acknowledgments

The whole of every book always seems to end up as more than the sum of its parts. Often, that's because such wonderful people are involved in the project.

At Osborne, we'd like to thank everyone who kept this book on track, on schedule, and the proper shade of blue. That includes Joanne Cuthbertson, Stephane Thomas, Nancy McLaughlin, and all the hardworking folks on the Production staff. Thanks also to editors John Heilborn and Lori Ash.

Dave would like to thank everyone on the home front—especially his ever-vigilant copy-editing wife, Kris. Evan and Marin, thanks for being the best two little kids a dad could ever ask for and generally letting me get my work done, even when you had no school. Kevin and Ann, thanks for the pinochle and Total Annihilation. Do you really have to move to Denver?

Todd would like to thank Donna Ladd, who ever-vigilantly stayed as far away from copy editing this book as possible. ("Upgrading PCs? Yuck!") Thanks for being a great partner and friend, even in the face of adversity, hardship, and a grueling moving schedule.

Todd and Dave also wanted to thank their agent, Neil Salkind, but unfortunately he couldn't be reached by telephone.

xi

Introduction

Over the course of a few years doing call-in computer shows on TV, on the radio and over the Internet, we've heard a lot of questions about computers. We've talked to thousands of folks who simply want to get their systems to do something useful. After all, you bought a PC to process words, make home videos, or play 3-D games. You didn't buy it so you could spend each weekend trying to figure out why your modem stops working when you move the mouse. So we compiled all of those questions—along with other questions that people frequently ask online or on the phone to tech support operators—and created this comprehensive guide to keeping your PC fit, trim, and alert. We doubt you'll find a more complete set of upgrade and repair topics anywhere—this book covers it all, from hard drives and mice to emergency recovery and Windows problems.

We make it a priority to cut through the minutiae and actually solve problems. We really don't like to babble on about motherboards, DIP switches, and BIOS versions unless it helps a listener get back in business. Likewise, this book isn't a gearhead's guide to PC mechanics. It's a solution-oriented book—one that can serve as an encyclopedia of computing answers. Have a question? We can probably answer it—and it won't take a long time to track down the answer, since you don't have to read about the physics of sound waves in order to locate some practical advice on positioning your speakers.

This second edition is divided into 14 chapters. Each one tackles a different part of your PC, such as the motherboard (and everything on the motherboard, including the CPU and memory), the hard drives, and various input devices. Start with Chapter 1, "Top Ten Frequently Asked Questions," to get the answers to commonly asked upgrade and repair questions, and then thumb through Chapter 2, "Tools, the Case, and the Power Supply," for some generic tips on how to open the PC, handle sensitive parts, and keep your system running on a day-to-day basis. You might then want to

thumb through Chapter 13, "Emergency Recovery," and learn just what to do if you're ever faced with a hard disk crash or a BIOS battery failure.

Conventions Used in this Book

Upgrading & Repairing Your PC Answers! uses several conventions designed to help you find the information you need and follow our instructions. These devices include the following:

- **Bold type** indicates text that you should enter using the keyboard.
- Small capitals denote specific keys on the keyboard, such as ENTER and SHIFT.
- Vertical lines separate menu items, as in File | Save or Start | Settings | Control Panel. This helps you make menu selections quickly as you follow along with the instructions in the book.

We also use a few symbols designed to draw your attention to special information:

Note: *Notes are, for the most part, interesting facts that may not signal a major change in your life, but might enhance your understanding of the subject. File these nuggets of knowledge away to impress your friends.*

Tip: *Tips are shortcuts that help you get specific tasks accomplished more easily. We're big fans of shortcuts, because we think computers should work for you—not the other way around.*

Caution: *Take our cautions seriously! We don't have many of them in the book, but when they appear, they signal the possibility of damage to your PC or injury to yourself.*

 ## One Word of Advice

At the front of this book, you'll find an *Instant Answers!* reference card. We highly encourage you to fill out the front with all the little details about your PC. You can get some of the information from the BIOS, and most of the rest from the System Properties box in Windows. (Just right-click on the My Computer icon on your Windows desktop and select Properties.)

Fill out the card and keep it with this book. That way, you'll have the information handy in case you have a problem with your PC and you need to restore its settings or talk to a support technician on the phone. And speaking of tech support, on the flip side of the card we've assembled a handy list of Web sites and contact numbers for the most common PC component manufacturers, along with some sites that provide valuable Windows solutions.

Ready to Get Going?

Enough introduction already! Welcome to the most complete encyclopedia of computing solutions that you're likely to find anywhere. And with that said, if you do have a problem that you can't solve with this book, or by visiting a vendor's Web site, then drop us a line at **questions@radioguys.com** and we'll see what we can do. Be as detailed as you can when you ask your question, and be sure to describe your system to us. For everything else, you can reach us at **dave@radioguys.com** and **todd@radioguys.com**. Good luck, and enjoy the questions and answers!

Chapter 1

Top Ten Frequently Asked Questions

Answer Topics!

Top Ten FAQs @ a Glance

There are some basic questions that are usually on the tongues of nearly every PC upgrader—where do you start, can you upgrade the processor, what's the most important upgrade, and so on. Other questions focus on the very basics of troubleshooting your computer—getting it running again after you encounter a problem. In this chapter, we'll take a quick look at the most common questions—the frequently asked questions—and offer some brief answers. In most cases, more detailed answers are in the rest of the book, but these will get you started and give you an idea of which chapter to turn to next.

1. I'm ready for more speed, but I'm not sure where to start. What's the best part of my PC to upgrade first?

This may be the most common question asked by PC owners who are ready to speed up their systems or get them to work better. The answer can be complicated, but it's based on a simple premise: Find the bottleneck. What operations strain your PC the most? Is it processing power? Graphics within games? Or are you running out of storage space?

In order to determine what to upgrade in your system, you must understand the subsystems within a PC and consider what you use your system for. Then, decide which subsystem is slowing you down the most and upgrade the components of that subsystem first.

Your PC is made up of three basic subsystems—processing, input/output, and storage. *Processing* comprises the central processing unit (CPU), random access memory (RAM), and cache memory, along with other subsystems. These systems work together as the "thinking" parts of your PC. They allow data to be processed and handed back to other subsystems that display the results on your computer screen or accept input from the keyboard. *Input/output* includes your computer monitor, the video interface (and or video RAM) used to display images on your monitor, your printer, your modem, and your upgrade ports (for connecting printers, modems, and other devices). *Storage* refers to your hard drive(s), floppy drives, CD-ROM drive, and removable media such as Zip or tape backup drives.

After you've determined which subsystem most affects the speed of your PC, you can decide if that subsystem is slowing you down enough to warrant an upgrade. The most likely upgrade candidates for increasing your computer's speed (assuming it is only a few years old) are:

- RAM
- Your video card and/or a 3-D accelerator card
- The CPU and/or motherboard
- Modem and/or network interface card

2. Which PC components can I upgrade? And why should I go to the trouble?

There are three basic reasons to upgrade the internal components of your PC: speed, increased quality or capabilities, and storage. Within each reason are a number of actual upgrades you can perform on your computer. The following lists show the type of upgrade and why it will make your PC better.

Speed

- **RAM** If you are running Windows 95 or Windows 98 and you have less than 16MB of RAM, you can upgrade (add more RAM) to increase the speed of your system. Exceeding 64MB will not increase the speed of your system. More memory will, however, enable you to run more programs simultaneously in Windows.

- **Cache memory** Adding this fast memory, used to increase the speed of reading and writing data to and from the hard drive, will eliminate much of the processor's idle time.

- **Video card** Increase the quality (colors and resolution) and the speed of the display for better graphics performance in Windows, multimedia programs, and games; some video cards include 3-D acceleration, while others add 3-D acceleration to a mix of other video functions.

- **CPU**   Upgrade the *central processing unit* for faster computing and to take advantage of more modern software.

- **Modem**   Adding a new, faster modem will increase data transfer speed over the Internet or other online services.

Note: *Be aware that in many instances, the limiting factor(s) in Internet speed can be a faulty or noisy phone line, or traffic on the Web itself—your modem won't always be the culprit.*

- **Hard drive**   Adding a new hard drive will increase your data storage capacity as well as the speed at which stored programs and data are accessed, especially if you step up to an Ultra-DMA hard drive.

- **Drive interface**   Adding a new type of drive interface will add higher-speed hard drives and CD-ROM drives for multimedia and other drive-intensive applications.

Quality and New Capabilities

- **Printer**   Upgrade for higher speed, better quality, and/or color output.

- **Monitor**   Upgrading to a larger monitor enables you to see more of a document without scrolling, to see better image quality, or to increase the size of images for easier viewing.

- **Video RAM**   Increasing VRAM enables you to display more colors and/or produce higher screen resolutions.

- **Audio cards**   Add better sound cards for higher-quality input and output of digital sounds.

- **AV cards**   Adding an audio/visual card enables you to capture video from a camcorder or TV tuner.

- **Network card**   Generally used for connecting you to local area networks for file sharing and printing, network cards are also useful for linking a home or small business PC to high-speed Internet access devices such as cable modems, satellite connections, and Digital Subscriber Line (DSL) technology.

- **Upgrade interface card**   If your PC doesn't have Universal Serial Bus (USB) or FireWire (IEEE 1394) ports, you can add them via an upgrade card. USB ports allow you to add USB devices such as printers, scanners, and modems. FireWire ports are used for high-speed connections, such as FireWire-equipped camcorders that support the DV (Digital Video) standard.

Storage

- **Hard drive**   Adding a new hard drive enables you to store more documents and applications on your computer.
- **Removable drive**   Adding a new removable drive allows you to store more documents and applications on media that can be transported and stored elsewhere.
- **CD-ROM/CD-RW drive**   This drive adds the ability to access modern software, multimedia titles, and games; CD-R and CD-RW drives additionally offer the capability of writing data to CD media, which offers an inexpensive means of storing, archiving, or shipping data to others.
- **DVD-ROM, DVD-RAM**   Digital Versatile Disc (DVD) technologies allow computers to play back DVD movies and retrieve massive amounts of data. CD-ROMs can contain about 650MB of data, while DVDs can hold as much as 17GB of data in the same space—more than 28 times the capacity of a CD-ROM. DVD-RAM technology allows your computer to write data to the discs, making it possible to archive many gigabytes of data on a single disk.

3. Do I really need to upgrade my CPU?

Upgrading your CPU can be a cost-effective way to increase the performance of your computer. CPUs come in many varieties, depending on the type of processor and main system board—or motherboard—your PC contains. CPUs tend to be reasonably inexpensive, and such an upgrade is usually less costly than buying a new computer system.

But while replacing your CPU is often a good idea, it's more important to consider the overall system before investing in a new processor. If you've determined that processing is the only subsystem creating a bottleneck in your system, then opt for the upgrade. (We'll discuss bottlenecks more thoroughly in Chapter 3.) You might decide to upgrade the processor if your computer is aging and your work focuses on computer-aided design (CAD), image manipulation, animation, or video production. You could also upgrade the processor if you have noticed that your machine is taking a long time to recalculate spreadsheets or create tables in your word processor.

If, instead, you know that your video interface, RAM, and cache RAM are also contributing to the slowdown, you may be better served by upgrading those components first; they tend to most affect the performance of computers used for creating graphics, working with multimedia educational software, or playing 3-D games. You may also find, once all your needs have been categorized and the costs have been calculated, that you're better off upgrading the entire motherboard (which might include a faster processor, more cache RAM, and better video circuitry) or buying a new computer.

Tip: *Create a cost/benefit list of possible upgrades to your system. If your PC has enough bottlenecks, it may be cost effective to upgrade the motherboard or buy a new computer.*

4. Do I have enough RAM?

Probably not! Most computers, even those that are six months or a year old, have less RAM than is optimum for good performance using Microsoft Windows.

RAM usage depends on your operating system and the way you work. Up to a point, RAM can increase the performance of your operating system and applications. After that minimum is reached, additional RAM allows you to work with larger documents and with more applications at one time.

Although the official requirement from Microsoft may vary, you should generally abide by the following RAM recommendations, in megabytes, for optimum performance:

- **DOS-only**   If you use only Microsoft DOS and DOS-based applications, then 4MB of memory will suffice, while 8MB will allow you to run games. Some advanced games require 16-32MB.

- **Windows 3.1**   At least 8MB is necessary for satisfactory performance, with 16MB recommended for multitasking, gaming, and multimedia applications.

- **Windows 95/98**   Although a minimum of 32MB is required for decent performance, we recommend that you have 64MB for the best performance. No less than 128MB is recommended for Web designers, graphics professionals, and anyone dealing with multimedia (audio/video) creation.

- **Windows NT**   A minimum of 64MB is necessary for decent performance using advanced operating systems such as NT; 128MB or more is recommended for content creation and multimedia tasks. Many NT applications require 48 or 64MB of RAM, so you should consider that a minimum requirement for NT.

- **Linux**   Linux is a popular alternative to the Microsoft operating systems listed above. If you're interested in working with Linux, you'll find that 16MB or less is sometimes enough to run a text-only Linux session. If you plan to use a graphical interface, like XWindows, then requirements escalate, often requiring 32 to 64MB for a well-running Linux installation.

 5. I want to add a cool new device to my system...or trade up to an even cooler one! Should I upgrade internally or externally?

While many PC upgrades are interface cards that must be installed internally, other types of upgrades offer options. For instance, both internal and external modems are available; external modems simply plug into the serial port on the back

of your PC. Similarly, removable media drives, CD-ROM drives, image scanners, and other peripherals can often be added using the ports on the back of your computer, or via internal interface cards.

Each type of upgrade has its advantages:

- Internal upgrades often perform better because they're designed to interact directly with the motherboard, instead of through an external port.

- Internal components are often cheaper, because they don't require a specially designed case, power connector, or other parts.

- Internal components generally don't prevent you from using the external ports for other upgrades, allowing you to add more components to your system.

- External upgrades are usually easier to perform and require less expertise to install.

- External components can offer more feedback in the way of digital displays, lights, and sounds that tell you how well they're functioning.

- External components (in the case of hard drives, CD-ROM drives, and removable media drives) don't require an open drive "bay" or room in the computer case to be installed.

- External components are more easily portable and can be used with other desktop or notebook computers.

6. I've got a system problem. Do I need to reformat my hard drive or reinstall Windows?

No! Most problems can be solved through much less destructive means—see Chapters 13 and 14 for details. There is rarely a reason to reformat your hard drive after a problem, and doing so may not produce the result you intend. If you have a virus, for example, some boot-sector viruses can survive a hard drive format. (That said, there are some low-level formatting techniques that can be effective in fighting viruses—we'll discuss those in Chapter 13.) That means you're putting your data at risk and not killing the root problem. Likewise, reinstalling Windows over itself may not solve a Windows problem—Windows doesn't overwrite every file, and you may find you've lost your personalized settings and special drivers, but not solved the root problem.

Bottom line? Reformatting or reinstalling Windows should be the very last option you consider, akin to abandoning ship in the middle of the ocean.

7. Is there a painless way of upgrading to Windows 95 or Windows 98? How about Windows 2000 or Windows NT?

Stepping up to a newer version of Windows isn't the nightmare that many people make it out to be. In reality, it's a painless few hours for the vast majority of users. To make the transition as smooth as possible, make sure you take these preliminary measures:

● *Back up your data.* Don't use the Windows 3.1 backup utility, because it isn't compatible with the backup program provided in Windows 95. Instead, use a third-party utility that you can install in Windows 95 if you need to recover lost data. It's also a good idea to copy truly essential data to floppies to have instant access to them.

Note: *In general, don't worry about backing up all the applications on your hard drive. By "data," we mean the documents and files that comprise your unique work. If you still own the original diskettes or CD-ROMs for your applications, you can reinstall them if you have any trouble.*

● *Find new Windows drivers for all of your expansion devices, such as video cards, modems, and scanners.* That way you'll have them handy when Windows asks you for them.

● *See if your existing hardware is supported under the newer version of Windows.* Check the setup.txt file on the Windows CD-ROM for a list of supported hardware. If your hardware is particularly old or obscure, you may need to use generic drivers that don't take advantage of special features in your hardware.

● *Disable everything in the autoexec.bat and config.sys files that isn't essential.* Leave your CD-ROM drivers intact, for instance, but kill virus checkers, sleep-mode timers, and other terminate and stay resident (TSR) programs that might interfere with the installation. (Chapter 14 details how to edit these files.)

Tip: *Your first and best source for new drivers is always the manufacturer's Web site.*

If you're upgrading to Windows NT, you may need to prepare a little more carefully. Most importantly, you'll need to upgrade you hardware drivers to Windows NT-compatible drivers. Windows NT, unlike Windows 98, won't work in "real" mode with older hardware and drivers—you either have the driver or it probably won't work on your PC. And remember that while things may be different with Windows 2000, right now Windows NT is not a good choice for the average home or small business user. Stick with Windows 98.

Keep in mind that with nearly any advanced version of Windows, you can create a dual-boot system that will allow you to boot into either your old or new version of Windows.

Note: *Dual booting is discussed in Chapter 14.*

8. Uh-oh...I've deleted some files that I really need. Can I recover lost files?

Sure you can. In Windows, you can recover any files you've deleted by checking the Recycle Bin, a storage facility that temporarily holds files you've deleted. The Recycle Bin has no jurisdiction in DOS, however. If you want protection there, you should purchase a utility program like Norton Utilities. Norton's Recycle Bin captures deleted programs in DOS as well as Windows, so you can recover any accidentally deleted files.

You'll also find that Norton Utilities and other similar utilities can sometimes find files that exist on the hard drive but have been deleted in Windows. (Windows doesn't usually wipe the drive clean when it erases the file—it simply no longer recognizes the file, marking its space on the drive as OK for overwrites.) If the file hasn't been overwritten, recovery utilities can often retrieve some or all of the data on that file.

If you're not a Windows user, you can also use some DOS utilities to recover deleted files, but they're less reliable. Because DOS has no native built-in protection for recovering deleted files, anything you do to the hard drive before attempting recovery—saving new files, optimizing the hard drive, and so on—can potentially wipe the file away forever. As soon as you realize you accidentally deleted something, you should stop everything and try to get it back. If you're using a pre-Windows 95 version of DOS, you can try Microsoft's UNDELETE command. Otherwise, use a third-party program like Norton Utilities.

9. What is Windows Safe Mode? How can I make the best use of it?

Windows doesn't always load or exit properly—sometimes it'll freeze halfway, and sometimes you'll have conflicts with a certain file (such as a video driver) that prevents Windows from starting at all. Windows 95 has a special mode—called *Safe Mode*—designed to load Windows in just such a situation. Safe Mode launches without starting any drivers that might cause problems, such as the CD-ROM driver, advanced video drivers, or network connections. Freed from possible conflicts, you can troubleshoot Windows safely.

To get into Safe Mode, press F8 when the "Starting Windows 95" message appears. Choose Start Windows in Safe Mode from the menu. To check for errors in your computer's startup sequence, you can also choose Step-by-Step Confirmation, which allows you to see the effect of every command in the autoexec.bat and config.sys files as they're executed.

10. Sometimes Windows doesn't shut down properly on my machine. What should I do?

Any number of problems can prevent your PC from ever making it all the way to the screen that announces "It is now

safe to shut down your PC." Instead, it'll freeze for all
eternity—or until you simply shut it off—on the screen that
says "Please wait while your computer shuts down."

If this problem plagues you, there's some good news and
some bad news. The good news is that it is, of course, fixable.
The bad news is that any number of problems can cause this
annoying quirk, so you may need to try a number of things to
get it working.

- Start by checking the bootlog.txt file in your C:\Windows
  folder or your main C:\ root folder. It will end with a line
  that says "terminate=" or "EndTerminate=". The last item
  should lead you to the source of the problem. If it says
  "KERNEL," things are proceeding normally. Any other
  item is a warning flag.

- One or more of your applications may not be shutting
  down properly. To test this, remove applications from
  the Windows Startup folder, or start Windows with the
  SHIFT key held down. Also, disable any programs listed
  in the "LOAD=" and "RUN=" lines of the win.ini file. Do
  this by inserting a semicolon at the start of each affected
  line. With all auto-starting programs disabled, start and
  shut down Windows. If the problem goes away, you can
  experiment by adding programs back one at a time until
  you find the culprit.

- A virtual device may be corrupted or causing a conflict.
  Use the semicolon method mentioned in the previous
  paragraph to disable every line in the system.ini that
  starts with "DEVICE=" and ends with a ".386". If that
  solves the problem, remove the semicolons one at a time
  and test the configuration until you find the file that
  causes problems.

- The culprit may also be something in the autoexec.bat or
  config.sys file. Press F8 when the "Starting Windows 95"
  message appears and choose Step-by-Step Confirmation.
  Say yes to the following options:

      Process the System Registry
      Himem.sys
      Ifshlp.sys
      Start the Graphical User Interface

Say no to everything else! If Windows shuts down properly this time, you know the drill: Experiment by enabling drivers and files one at a time.

● It is possible that a corrupt sound file set to play on exit is causing the hang-up. Choose Start | Settings | Control Panel, and choose Sounds. Click on Exit Windows and change the sound to None. If that fixes the problem, delete the sound from your hard drive and/or choose another one for Windows Exit.

● Windows itself may have a corrupted file. Try installing a new copy of Windows to a new directory. (See Chapter 14 for more on installing Windows.)

If none of these solutions work, you probably have defective hardware that is impeding Windows' ability to shut down.

Chapter 2

Tools, the Case, and the Power Supply

Answer Topics!

Tools, the Case, and the Power Supply @ a Glance

Getting your feet wet in the innards of a PC is a daunting task for many people—you might be afraid that just opening your PC voids the warranty or that you might break something. Don't worry! Millions of people perform simple surgery on their computers every day, and they're not PC experts either. It just takes some confidence, the right tools, and a little knowledge about what you plan to accomplish.

Often, the trickiest part of upgrading or repairing your PC involves just getting the case open! You'll need to determine which screws—if any—hold the case closed and which screws hold other parts—like the power supply—in place. You should also know a little about case design, particularly if you want to move your motherboard into a larger housing for more slots or storage bays.

A power supply failure is not a question of if, but rather when. If you keep your PC long enough—and just three or four years is more than enough—the fan in your $100 power supply might fail, rendering your PC inoperable until you get yourself a new fan.

THE BASICS OF COMPUTER UPGRADE AND REPAIR

 Can I really do my own upgrades and repairs, or should I take my PC to the shop?

In general, you can do almost any kind of system repair yourself, armed with only this book as a guide. A repair shop will often charge a considerable amount of money to do simple things you can do yourself—would you pay $100 to have memory installed if you knew you could do it yourself in less than 20 minutes?

You can also replace almost any part of your PC on your own: the hard drive, motherboard, power supply—you name it—but be sure to observe these warnings:

- *Don't change more than one thing at a time.* If you want to install a CD-ROM drive and sound card, power down the PC and install the sound card first. Make sure it works. *Then* power down the PC and install the CD drive. If you do both at once, the installation process becomes significantly more difficult to troubleshoot.

- *Observe all safety warnings.* You can zap your PC with static electricity, killing the circuits or rendering some of your system components useless. Even worse, you can zap yourself! If we say something is dangerous—like opening a power supply casing—please trust us; It Is Dangerous. Don't try it.

- *Keep in mind that there are a few things that you simply can't do yourself.* If your hard drive dies completely, for instance, there's almost no chance that you'll recover the data that was stored on it unless you have a very recent backup, or you send the dead drive to a company that specializes in data recovery. (And unfortunately, that's expensive.) What else can't you do? Well, don't bother trying to fix a monitor that's suffering internal problems, or repairing a chip with a broken pin. A standard PC is filled with user-replaceable parts, not user-*repairable* parts; when a component breaks, there are generally few things you can do to fix it. Think of your PC as a military

airplane filled with black boxes—each box can be removed and replaced easily, but to actually *fix* the box—if it can be fixed at all—you'll need to send it to the factory.

Even so, there are a lot of things that you truly can do yourself. Just keep thumbing through this book for details.

I've read a lot about how it's so important to upgrade my PC. How do I know when that makes sense for me?

You know it's time to upgrade when your PC can no longer run the software you want to use, or it runs new software so slowly that you'd be better off with a stone tablet and lots of little beads.

There's no arbitrary measure for the best time to upgrade your system. Don't listen to people who tell you your system is "obsolete" just because it doesn't have the newest widgets. The fact is, a computer only becomes obsolete when it no longer adequately does what *you* need it to do.

A case in point is DVD (*Digital Versatile Disc*) technology. As we're writing this, DVD players—the high-capacity successor to CD-ROM drives—are becoming more and more common. Your system isn't obsolete without one, however, until the day when you want a program that only comes on DVD. Then—and perhaps only then—should you consider adding DVD to your existing system.

On the other hand, if your PC doesn't have a CD-ROM drive, you're at a serious disadvantage. Because virtually all software is now sold on CD, you may need a CD-ROM drive simply to install and run new programs. You need to upgrade. (See Chapter 8 to get the details.)

Finally, there's a reason to upgrade that goes beyond issues of obsolesce: Certain upgrades make your system more powerful and versatile. This can be an important distinction, because you should let yourself think of such upgrades as investments. The more capable your PC—especially if you use it for business or educational pursuits—the better investment it is.

Take the example of a CD-R or DVD-RAM drive. Both are *writeable* versions of their *read-only* (CD-ROM, DVD-ROM) counterparts. In a nutshell, these writeable drives allow you to create your own CDs and DVDs. If that's of use to you—whether it's for backing up your hard drive, sharing archived information, or creating your own music CDs—then it's worth it to upgrade immediately to make your PC more capable.

Is it cheaper to upgrade my PC or just buy a new one?

It depends on how much upgrading you need to do. If you have a system that's more than five years old—a 386, 486, or even an early Pentium system—you'll probably need to replace almost everything, including the motherboard, video card, and hard drives, plus add new components such as a CD-ROM drive and sound card. The performance of these older systems is affected by more than just the processor speed.

In such cases, it's probably less work to simply get a new system. The advantage to upgrading your system yourself, however, is that you can handpick the components you want. Most PC companies substitute parts whenever a cheaper vendor comes along—so if you buy a prebuilt system, you're not always guaranteed to get the exact hard drive, for instance, that you had in mind. You might instead get a hard drive from a different manufacturer—though the capacity will still be what you originally ordered.

I don't want to just get rid of my older PC. What is a 386 or a 486 good for?

Because you can't play the newest games or run the newest applications on an older PC, you should consider what ancillary roles a second PC might serve. Here are some suggestions:

 Keep it as a backup word processing or spreadsheet station. Your family members may appreciate having a free computer in the house. Even if it can't run the latest versions of Microsoft Office applications, your older system may still be able to run Microsoft Works, ClarisWorks, or other less taxing programs—and you can share the files with the more advanced computer in your house.

- *A full-time fax/answering machine/e-mail system.* None of those applications tax the CPU very much, so you can use a slow PC with a fast modem to receive faxes, answer the phone, and deal with your e-mail.

- *Put it in the kitchen or den and use it for filing recipes, keeping track of financial data, or managing household databases.* If your old 486 can accept a TV tuner card, you can even use it as both a computer and a TV.

- *Give it to the kids.* If your children use PCs for homework or research, a dedicated PC can help them work more effectively, because they won't have to get in line behind mom and dad. (On the other hand, most kids' games play poorly on old computers...but this could be a curse or a blessing.)

- *Set it up to manage your home security system.* Software and hardware combinations like Radio Shack's X-10 or IBM's Home Director allow you to control lights, appliances, and security alarms from the PC screen. It takes little processing power, so an old PC is ideal.

- *Establish a simple home network.* Basically, you can turn it into a small office or family file server. Then you can easily back up the important files stored on your main PC, share applications, and have access to multiple printers. (See Chapter 9 to find out about setting up an inexpensive network.)

Where can I get replacement power supplies, memory, chips, and that sort of thing?

More than likely your town or the closest large town has a number of local PC stores that specialize in upgrade items like memory, motherboards, and CPUs. Another option that we recommend is *Computer Shopper* magazine, which is filled with hundreds of pages of advertisements for just that sort of thing. In fact, if we needed a new motherboard or PC case, *Computer Shopper* is the first place we'd turn to, if only for comparison shopping.

There are other interesting options, though, especially online. The popularity of eBay (**http://www.ebay.com**) and the preponderance of similar auction-oriented Web sites make it possible for individuals to sell used computer components easily and rather cheaply. They're a great way to go "garage-sailing" for computer components.

Can I trust mail-order companies?

Sure, as long as you are smart about it. A local company may be easier to complain to—and you'll have more options for recourse if you have trouble with them. At the same time, though, many name-brand online and mail-order outlets offer more generous return and service policies than smaller, local vendors can or will.

Charge mail-order purchases to your credit card, because it's easier to get satisfaction on a purchase if your credit card company is in the middle. Likewise, try to check out the company before you make a purchase. Many people buy computer parts and entire PCs exclusively via mail order or online and never have a problem.

Note: *Many folks still ask the question, "Is it safe to use your credit card online?" In most cases our answer is, "Just as safe as giving it to an underpaid, out-of-work 'actor' who is 'temporarily' paying the bills as a waiter." In many cases it's as simple as that. But there are two things you should consider. First, read your credit card's policies carefully—some of them are purposefully excluding online sales from their $50 fraud limits and such policies, when they legally can. Second, if you're shopping with issues when using a debit card that's branded as a credit card (say a Visa "checking" card), be aware that they sometimes don't offer the same purchase protection as standard credit cards. Again, read your agreement closely.*

My PC needs surgery. What tools should I have handy?

Well, it takes only a few simple tools to open your PC and perform ordinary maintenance and upgrades. Here's what we recommend:

- *Get a set of small Phillips head screwdrivers.* You can actually get away with just one, as long as it's designed to work with 1/4-inch screw heads. You should also consider shying away from a ratchet-style screwdriver; they can be tough to manipulate in close quarters. Get a few handles of differing lengths for reaching different parts of your PC.

- *Have at least one small, flat-head jeweler's screwdriver available.* If you can find one from a set designed to tighten eyeglass screws, you've got the right size. You won't actually use it on many screws, but it will be useful for manipulating tiny switches.

Caution: *Don't use a powered screwdriver. You can too easily over-torque the screws and damage your PC.*

- *Have a pair of tweezers handy.* You can use them to retrieve lost screws and to separate wires that are closely intermingled.

- *Have a small flashlight.* Even in a well-lit room, you might want to shed some additional light on a motherboard. It'll prove even handier when you need to crawl on your hands and knees under your desk, to check on a cable connection.

- *Have tape.* Use tape and a marker or pen to label the wiring inside your PC. (Keep in mind that the single most important step in most upgrades is good labeling.) You can also use tape to attach and bundle wiring to one side when you need to dig deeper into an open machine.

Tip: *Some computer stores sell little kits of "do-it-yourself" tools. For $20 you can get all kinds of interesting gadgets—chip pullers, for instance. Unless you still have a 486 and are considering removing your math coprocessor, don't waste your money. Get just the tools you need, and skip the pricey kits packed with all the tools they couldn't sell in the '80s. That said, you might find a good deal on a tool kit that just includes the basics; if so, and if you don't already have those tools hanging around the house, go for the kit.*

? **Are there any other tools I might need for more advanced tinkering?**

Perhaps. Depending upon how sophisticated you get, you might want the following:

- **Voltmeter**   You can use a *voltmeter* to see if your power supply is providing the right voltages to the motherboard and peripherals. Voltmeters are readily available at electronics stores. You might want to use one if you suspect trouble with your power supply.

- **Loopback plugs for the parallel and serial ports**   *Loopback plugs* let you test the parallel and serial ports of your PC so you can see if they're passing the proper signals. You can typically purchase loopback plugs (see Figure 2-1) by themselves at electronics stores

Figure 2-1   Loopback plugs allow diagnostic software to perform a comprehensive test of your input/output ports.

and computer shops or as part of a diagnostic software package, like Touchstone's CheckIt Diagnostic Kit. If you get unusual behavior from either of these ports, you might need to invest in a loopback plug—it's very inexpensive.

How do I change the DIP switch settings?

DIP switches are the tiny, tiny, tiny little two-position switches found on motherboards and some expansion cards. And they're a pain in the neck to change, particularly when they're buried deep in the motherboard amongst a lot of wires and other obstructions. Our favorite way to move DIP switches is with a low-tech paper clip, which you can bend to reach odd angles and change the length at will. If you don't have a paper clip handy, very narrow flat-head screwdrivers work just as well.

OK, I've taken my PC apart, but all these little pieces make me nervous. Any tips?

Whenever you take a PC apart, you invariably end up with a lot of screws. You should establish a routine for storing them or you'll end up losing a screw—or at the very least, wasting more time looking for the screws than it took you to install the peripheral to begin with.

We recommend keeping a stack of small paper envelopes or plastic cups with your PC tools and putting the screws in them as you work. (Glass or ceramic will work, too, and they're more environmentally correct—unless you throw them away after every use.) You can even label the cups with stickers or tape to keep track of where each size of screw belongs. That way, you can't get confused. Some people prefer coffee cups or egg cartons, but you get the idea—do what works best for you. Whatever you do, don't just lay them in small piles on the rug. And don't assume you'll be able to remember where you dropped them.

All these wires! What's a good way to keep track of where they all go?

Keep a package of labels or masking tape around. (We prefer Avery's blank return address labels for laser printers.) Write the purpose of each wire on a label and wrap the label on the wire like a flag (see Figure 2-2). This is great for they-all-look-the-same cables, such as audio and video connectors. If you don't want to use labels, a roll of masking tape works fine, too.

! **Caution:**   *Avoid tugging on the wires in your computer to loosen them! Instead, grab them by the plastic housing.*

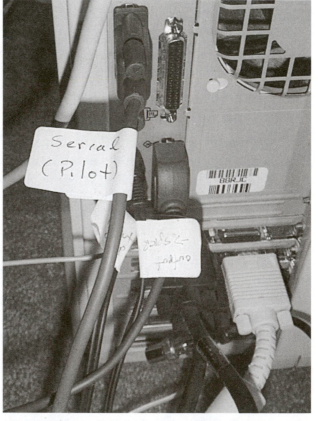

Figure 2-2   If you haven't labeled your wires, as shown here, you'd better start calling your psychic friends.

I'm apprehensive about working on my computer. What precautions should I take?

Most how-to advice includes a generic warning to back up all your data before performing maintenance on your PC. While good advice, it's a bit extreme. If you're careful, changing out a video card won't damage your PC in a way that results in restoring data from backup disks. So, use common sense—if you're working on a hard drive, it might be smart to back up the data first. That said, here are some precautions to keep in mind when working on your PC:

- Back up your hard drive if you're doing anything that might cause the loss of data (like installing a new operating system or adding a new hard drive).

- Create an emergency startup disk for the same reasons. Windows will create one for you, if you choose Start | Settings | Control Panel | Add/Remove Programs | Startup Disk (see Figure 2-3). If you don't mind spending a few dollars, you can make an even better startup and recovery disk using a third-party utility such as Norton Utilities or McAfee Office.

- Ground yourself. Static electricity can kill. Not you, but it can certainly kill your PC. The larger a circuit board is—and the more tracers, transistors, and connections it has—the less susceptible it is to static electricity. But that leaves a lot of vulnerable components in a typical PC, so be careful. You can wear an anti-static wristband (available at most computer stores) or touch a grounded metal surface often, particularly after you move around on a rug. If you leave the power attached, you can ground yourself on the metal chassis of your PC. Some technicians recommend removing the power cable completely, particularly from new Pentium II systems. It's not a bad idea to check with the PC manufacturer to see what they recommend.

Don't force, bend, or push too hard. If you work out, you know the difference between that "good" hurt, which means you're strengthening your muscles, and that "bad" hurt, which means—well, that you've hurt yourself. Whenever you

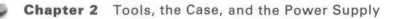

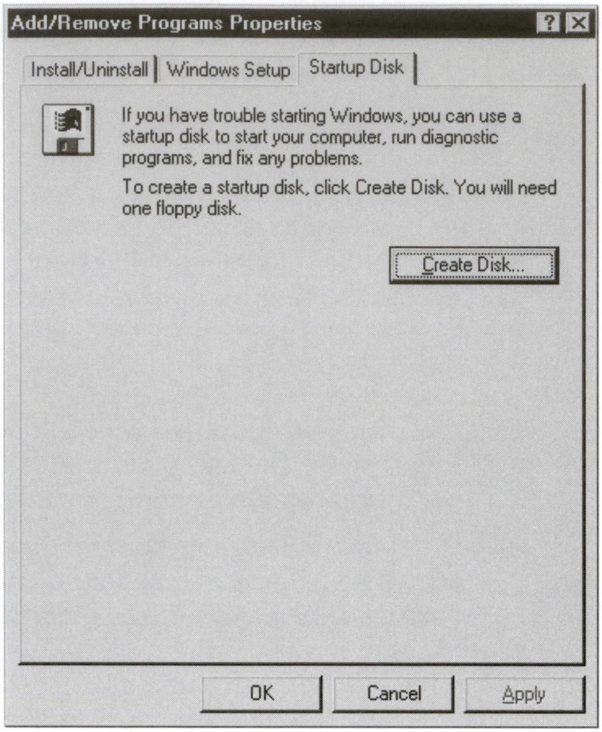

Figure 2-3 Creating a startup disk

need to install something, decisive pressure is okay
(particularly when installing a card for the first time—it'll
slide in easier later if you remove and replace it), but never
use abrupt shoves or excessive force. Even microscopic cracks
in a printed circuit card can break solder joints and tracer
lines. Be careful!

Darn it! I dropped a screw right into the motherboard. How can I get it out? Did I break anything?

You probably haven't broken anything yet, so don't sweat it.
If you left your PC plugged in for grounding purposes, this is
a good time to unplug it. Then try to locate the screw with a
flashlight. Extra light will make it more obvious, and you
may see the glint of the screw from the light beam.

If you can see the screw, try to retrieve it with a pair of tweezers or tape stuck onto the end of a long stick or screwdriver—or sticky tape stuck to your finger.

> **Caution:**   *No matter how you do it, be careful not to grind the screw across the surface of the motherboard as you attempt to get a grip on it. And don't use a magnetized screwdriver near the motherboard or other circuit boards.*

If you can't see the screw, it may have rolled under the motherboard. Pick up the case and rock it gently in one direction or the other until it appears. You can even turn it upside down and let the screw fall onto the floor, but have a spotter handy to watch where it goes—or you'll be back where you started.

What kind of routine maintenance should I perform on my system?

You can often avoid the big problems by performing little maintenance actions every day or week. In fact, many of the things you can do hardly seem like maintenance at all. Try these activities on for size:

● *Don't turn the PC on and off often.* While the jury sometimes disagrees about the best way to treat your PC's power switch, we think it's best to turn it on once in the morning (or the first time you use it) and leave it on all day until you're completely done with it. When you turn a PC on, you're "shocking" the system with a burst of electricity and heat that's much worse than just leaving it on at a fairly steady voltage and temperature all day. It's the repeated stress and expansion that eventually causes motherboard problems, so, don't throw the power switch ten times a day.

> **Tip:**   *If your PC supports the Energy Star option to power down the hard drive, take advantage of it. The hard drive is virtually the only moving part in a PC, and it is susceptible to wearing out.*

● *Turn the monitor off when it's not in use.* A cathode ray tube monitor is a different animal entirely. Rather than leaving the picture tube charged all day, power it down if you'll be away from the system for an extended period of time and turn it back on when you need it. If you have a newfangled flat panel LCD monitor, there are fewer parts to wear out—you can leave it turned on.

Tip: *You can use the Energy Star power-down feature of new monitors to accomplish the same result by forcing the monitor to "sleep" after a predetermined amount of inactive time, as you can see in Figure 2-4.*

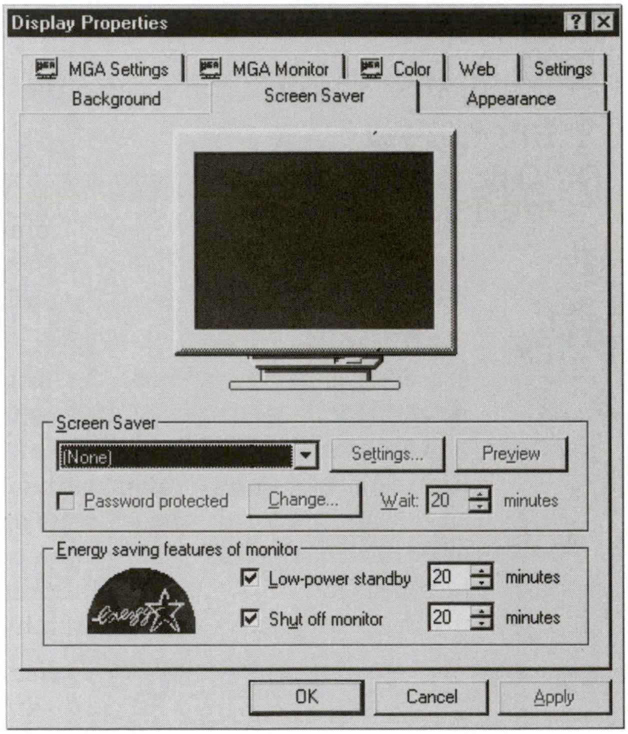

Figure 2-4 The Display Properties dialog box allows you to shut the monitor down after a period of inactivity, extending its lifespan.

● *Use an uninterruptible power supply or a surge suppressor with line conditioning to protect the PC from spikes and brownouts.* Over time, your ordinary power line can kill your PC.

● *Unplug your modem's phone line from the wall outlet during thunderstorms.* A power spike can kill your modem or PC.

Tip: *Get a surge protector that provides phone line protection. While some computers are occasionally lost to power surges, we've seen many modems go bad after thunderstorms that surge power over the phone lines.*

● *Keep your hard drive defragmented.* If your hard drive gets excessively fragmented—that is, data files and applications are scattered in tiny chunks all over the drive—software can run more slowly and, in extreme cases, have trouble running at all. Use Windows' ScanDisk and Disk Defragmenter about once a week to keep the hard drive in top shape. You can get to both of these utilities by opening My Computer and right-clicking on the C drive. Choose Properties then the Tools tab. Use the Check Now and Defragment Now buttons (see Figure 2-5).

● *Use a virus checker.* While Windows 3.1 has a virus checker built in, Windows 95 does not. Almost any commercial virus checker will work fine as long as you keep the virus updates current, usually about once each month. We like Norton AntiVirus and Inoculan AntiVirus, which both offer updates that you can download via the Internet. In fact, some virus checkers automate the update process so you never even have to do this.

● *Open the case of your PC periodically—every few months or so—to eliminate the dust building up inside.* Use a tiny vacuum, not compressed air. (But you can use compressed air to blow out dust from parts of the PC that don't have exposed circuits, like the fan blades.) If you blow air on the motherboard, you're also depositing moisture, which is a bad thing. And don't let the vacuum come in direct contact with the circuit board.

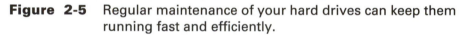

Figure 2-5   Regular maintenance of your hard drives can keep them running fast and efficiently.

● *Get it off the floor.* If you can, raise your PC off the floor, even if it's just a few inches. That can dramatically decrease the amount of pet fur and dust that might get sucked into your PC's case, reducing the frequency with which you need to open and clean the computer.

CONSIDERING THE CASE

 What's with all the different shapes and sizes? How do I know what type of case is best for me?

Essentially, there are two styles of cases: the desktop and the tower. *Desktop cases* lie flat (horizontally) on the desk while *towers* are like desktop cases turned on their sides. Typically, tower cases are bigger, leaving more room for internal expansion and heat dissipation. Towers come in three flavors:

mini, midsized, and full-sized towers. Each size increment offers additional *bays* (installation areas for CD-ROM drives, floppy drives, and other removable media devices) as well as room inside the case for additional internal devices, such as hard drives.

Choose a desktop or tower based on your personal preference and expansion needs. Keep in mind, though, that a desktop case will run out of room rapidly, while a midsized or full-sized tower case can support extensive growth. The desktop case may fit easily in the space you have for a computer, however, while a tower case can require more space under your desk, or a special desk designed to hold the tower in a convenient spot.

Eventually I'm going to want to upgrade my motherboard and other components. Will this be a nightmare if I have the wrong type of case?

In addition to the desktop vs. tower decision, you need to consider whether the case is an AT or ATX configuration. This is important because specific motherboards are designed to fit either the AT or ATX configuration. You should begin by deciding what kind of motherboard you want—or determine what you already have—and get a compatible case. Right now, the biggest issue when purchasing a case involves the Pentium II, because most Pentium II motherboards are designed around the ATX specification. A lesser concern is that the ATX case uses a PS/2 connector for the keyboard, while AT cases often rely on the older, large keyboard connector. It's no big deal, though, to pick up a keyboard converter (they're only a couple of bucks) if you end up with a mismatch.

Note: *True ATX-style motherboards also use a special type of power adapter that's only available in ATX-style cases. Check the power connectors carefully when shopping for a case.*

You may also need to determine if your older computer is an AT-style case or a proprietary design. Some older slim-line Packard Bell systems, for example, have trouble accepting typical baby-AT motherboard form factors. Other manufacturers have offered similar systems. If possible, consult your manual or dealer and determine whether or not your current case can accept a standard-sized motherboard.

Can't I just turn my desktop case into a tower by turning it on its side?

In many cases, yes, you can. Some time ago, there was a concern that hard drives wouldn't operate properly if positioned sideways, and you might find this still to be the case with *very* old PCs—generally, IBM XT or early 286 AT and compatible computers. If you have a hard drive that's old enough to require manual "parking," then you're a prime candidate for keeping the case in its designed-for position. If you don't even know what it means to park a drive, you probably don't have to worry.

Otherwise, if you want to conserve space by standing an ordinary desktop case on its side, you probably won't experience any trouble unless your PC has a CD-ROM drive that insists on remaining in a horizontal position. Check the documentation that came with your CD-ROM drive to be sure. Many new CD-ROM drives can be laid vertically even though they don't use old-fashioned caddies.

Note: *Be careful not to cover any air vents when you lay a case on its side.*

I don't want to void my warranty. Won't that happen if I open the case on my own?

Nope. There used to be PCs so proprietary that you'd void the warranty by opening the case, but thankfully, those days are long gone. Most PCs are now designed to be user-upgradable, so there's nothing wrong with opening the case to add memory, install a hard drive, or perform other routine maintenance. Be careful, though, because if you fry something, any damage you cause probably won't be covered by the manufacturer. In general, though, it takes outright carelessness to damage a PC, and we have faith in your vigilance.

That said, you should read your documentation carefully to see whether performing certain upgrades—such as adding a speed-boosted CPU, installing a new hard drive, or changing your I/O interface—voids the warranty or service agreement.

Some extended warranties and phone support policies are voided if you upgrade certain hardwired components. (Adding a simple expansion card rarely affects a PC's warranty.)

There's an exception to this rule, however: Many notebook PCs are not designed to be opened or worked on by the user. Even to add memory, you're often asked to send the notebook back to the factory, and that's just as well. Notebook machines are generally difficult to upgrade or repair because of their extreme miniaturization and manufacturer-specific design.

Caution: *There are a few other notable exceptions. The Monorail brand of computers, for instance, is designed to be serviced only by authorized dealers. If your PC is an "all-in-one" system, with the monitor and case integrated, you should look closely at your documentation. Also, certain very modern "thin PC" machines are designed to be serviceable only by the manufacturer or qualified dealers.*

Shouldn't I always unplug the PC before opening the case?

Traditional wisdom calls for unplugging the PC completely from the wall, as well as disconnecting peripherals such as the printer and scanner, before mucking around inside. On the other hand, leaving the PC plugged into the wall socket provides a secure path to ground, and that's a good thing.

Most how-to advice tells you to unplug the PC so that there's no doubt whatsoever that power has been removed before you start working inside. If you are sure the PC is turned off, however—and we mean absolutely sure—then you can leave the PC plugged in. That way, you have a good ground and all you need to do is touch the power supply cage to discharge yourself of static electricity.

The best advice we've ever heard on this subject went something like this: If you're more worried about zapping yourself than you are about zapping your motherboard, then unplug the PC and get a grounding strap. A *grounding strap* is a special device, available at most computer stores, that you wrap around your wrist or ankle to ground yourself from static electricity.

> **!**   ***Caution:***   *If you do opt to leave your computer plugged in, be very careful to avoid dropping anything metal onto the motherboard, dragging a metal object or tool across the motherboard, or placing metal objects near the power supply or any of its wiring. Also, you should pull the plug if you'll be working on actual motherboard components—like the CPU, the motherboard wiring, or the power supply itself.*

How DO I open my computer case?

Every case is different, and there's no single set of instructions that'll get you inside all of them. In general, however, follow these steps:

1. Turn off the PC and unplug the power cord (or leave it plugged in for grounding purposes if you follow the advice from the preceding answer). Ground yourself.

2. If you have a traditional case, you'll need to remove a minimum of two (and probably four to six) screws from the back of the PC. Spin the case around so you can see the back and locate the screws that span the outer edges of the case. Be careful not to accidentally unscrew the power supply. The case screws will probably all be the same size—if one is bigger than the others are, you're probably looking at one that does not open the case. Note that the screws will probably secure the case's cover to the back of the case—it will often be very clear which are securing the case's shell and which are for internal elements. Remove the appropriate screws.

3. After the screws are removed, slide the cover off. You'll probably need to pull it upward at the same time, as shown in Figure 2-6.

You might have a tool-free case that requires a little muscle but no screwdriver. Some of these cases are challenging to take apart the first time, and you might want to get a second person to assist you. Look for tabs to press together and pull the cover at the same time, as shown in Figure 2-7. This type of case is more common in tower designs than desktops.

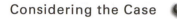

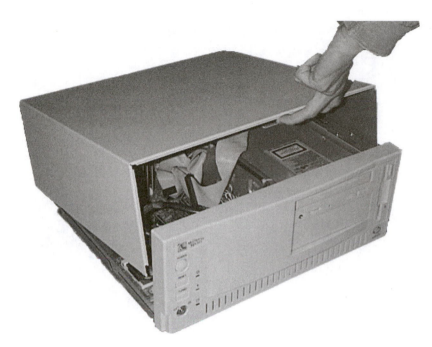

Figure 2-6 Be careful that you don't snag any wires or connectors as you remove the cover from your machine.

Note: *In general, the older the case, the more screws it probably has holding it together. Ease of entry is a welcome feature of modern case design.*

I'm always thinking of something I want to fix inside my machine. Is it safe if I just leave the cover off for good?

No, we don't recommend it. You can certainly leave the cover off for a short period of time, particularly to make sure a new expansion card or hard drive works properly before buttoning everything back up. But people who leave the cover off all the time are asking for trouble:

- The cover is necessary to shield other electronic equipment from radio frequency (RF) interference. The FCC approved your case for use in your home under the assumption that you'd leave the cover on. You won't be

Figure 2-7 This tower case, now lying unceremoniously on its side, is typical of Dell and Micron products. To get inside, you need to press the tabs together and push the cover off at the same time.

arrested on federal charges, but you can interfere with other gadgets in your home.

● The cover provides a closed and controlled temperature environment for your PC. Believe it or not, some PC designs can overheat with the cover off! That's because the path for airflow is determined by the layout of the fans, heat sinks, expansion cards, and other obstacles in the case. If you remove the cover, the air can't follow the engineered path and overheating is possible.

● Dust and other contaminants can collect on the motherboard more easily. That can shorten the life of the PC.

It looks pretty gunky in there...what's the safest way to clean up inside the case?

It's a good idea to get the dust, hair, and pet fur out of your PC every three to six months, or it'll begin to affect air circulation, and in extremely dirty environments even cause a shorting hazard. Although you'll often see compressed air in computer stores, presumably for this task, we prefer that you use a small, low-powered vacuum cleaner for cleaning dust from the inside of your PC. Compressed air sometimes condenses, forming moisture that may be detrimental to circuit boards and other components. (If you do use compressed air, use short blasts of the air and don't use it extremely close to internal components.)

Turn the PC off, remove the case, and follow these guidelines:

- Vacuum contaminants away from vents, the power supply, and the fans.
- Vacuum dust off the motherboard and peripheral cards, being careful not to touch the surface with the vacuum.
- If the PC is very dirty, you can remove the peripherals and gently clean the gold- or tin-plated connectors with a pencil eraser or special cleaners designed especially for this type of cleaning job.

I want to upgrade my case. What kinds of things should I look for?

We've already talked about the critical motherboard issue for deciding between an AT and ATX case. You should also decide between a desktop and tower configuration. We recommend a tower, because you'll have more expansion options and you can get the computer off the desktop and onto the floor, out of the way. Here are some other case features you can consider:

- *The power supply is preinstalled in most new cases.* Match the case to your power needs.

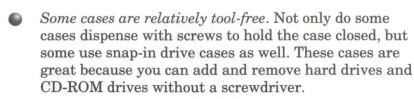

- *Some cases are relatively tool-free.* Not only do some cases dispense with screws to hold the case closed, but some use snap-in drive cases as well. These cases are great because you can add and remove hard drives and CD-ROM drives without a screwdriver.

- *If you have a Pentium or faster motherboard, "turbo" buttons do you as much good as a hood ornament.* The same goes for a digital display that shows the speed at which the PC is running. Save money by avoiding cases with those features. In fact, you might want to avoid cases with any sort of gizmos—smoked glass doors, funny folding bits—and choose a higher-quality case that uses better plastics and offers a logical approach to entry for upgrading.

Tip: *Some motherboards allow you to connect a special cable to the turbo button that allows you suspend the PC— a useful feature.*

- *Some cases come with locks.* Some locks disable the keyboard, while others secure the case itself from being opened. The keyboard lock is ultimately less effective than a password-protected screen saver (and the key is easy to lose as well), so we consider them extraneous. A lock that secures the case is only useful if you're concerned about someone opening your case and making off with your memory chips, such as in a corporate environment.

- *Some cases make the Reset button more difficult to push accidentally.* Either it's recessed or hidden in an obscure location. There's nothing more frustrating than tapping the Reset button with your knee and consequently rebooting a PC, losing hours of data in the process. Our opinion? A good feature to look for.

- *Some cases put floppy and CD-ROM drives behind hinged doors.* It's a useless gimmick in our opinion, because you spend all your time opening and closing the infernal doors to access the drives. Sure, they look nice and suggest that you'll get less dust in the drive slots, but you'll quickly grow to hate them.

● *Some cases look cooler than others.* (We mean aside from the hinged doors.) Don't be afraid to put a few bucks worth of investment into your case, especially if it's attractive and/or makes access to the innards easier. You may end up keeping the case longer than almost any other component in your computer. Splurge a bit.

THE POWER SUPPLY

 Please don't laugh...what exactly does the power supply do?

Hey, this is not a stupid question! Sure, the power supply *supplies power* to the computer. More accurately, the power supply is a transformer that converts wall current into the 5 and 12 volts of direct current (DC), required by the PC's various components. But it does more than that. Built into every power supply is a cooling fan that draws air through your computer's case to keep essential components—like the CPU and power supply—at a reasonable operating temperature. That's what makes the whirring sound you hear when the computer is turned on.

 Where will I find the power supply?

The power supply is easy to find—just follow the AC power cord from the wall outlet back to the PC. The power supply is the metal box that the AC cord feeds into. You'll also notice that the power supply has a fan vent that exhausts air out the back of the case.

 Suddenly my PC's gone very quiet...no more "whir." What's up?

Most likely, your cooling fan has stopped functioning. You need to save any open files and shut down your system immediately. Without a cooling fan, your PC can overheat very rapidly—and expensive components (like the CPU) can be rendered completely and permanently inoperable.

If you suspect that your fan has stopped working, try this simple troubleshooting procedure:

1. Shut down the PC immediately. Allow it to cool for at least 30 minutes.

2. Apply power to the PC and put your hand over the power supply exhaust at the back of the case.

If you feel air blowing on your hand, everything is fine. (Test this repeatedly over time and make sure you continue to hear and/or feel the fan.) If you feel nothing, shut the machine back down until you can purchase a replacement power supply. It's easy to replace, and yes, you can do it yourself. (See the Walkthrough box, "Replacing the Power Supply" later in this chapter.)

Note: *Some power supplies are designed to be nearly silent. Only worry about your power supply if it gets significantly more noisy than usual (a sign of impending failure) or suddenly stops making noise (a sign that failure has just occurred).*

My computer is flaking out. Should I upgrade the power supply?

Even if your power supply seems to be running okay, it may yet be sending voltage spikes or inadequate voltages to the PC's components, affecting your system performance. Here are some things to watch for:

● *CMOS settings keep getting lost.* The CMOS is a small memory chip that remembers essential details about your PC's configuration even when it is turned off. Some of these details include the date and hard drive configuration. Usually, lost CMOS settings are an indication that the CMOS battery has died, and you need to replace it (see Chapter 3). But if the power supply consistently sends an undervoltage to the CMOS, the CMOS can't remember its settings when the battery should be resting. Replace the CMOS battery—odds are good that it's a simple $5 fix. But if the problem persists, it's your power supply.

● *The hard drive fails intermittently.* It isn't unusual for voltage spikes to cause hard drives to overheat after they've been running for a while. If your hard drive starts out fine but experiences problems after it has been running for a while, suspect the power supply.

When I turn on my PC, nothing happens at all. What do I do to revive it?

If this happens, chances are good that the power supply died the last time you switched the system off. Double-check obvious things first, though. Make sure that the PC's wall outlet works by plugging something else into the same socket. Also, be sure that anything that precedes the PC on the way back to the wall outlet—like a power strip or uninterruptible power supply—is working as advertised.

Can I repair my power supply?

No, and don't even try. They're considered remove-and-replace components. A power supply can store a sizable charge internally, so opening the supply itself can cause injury. And because they're relatively inexpensive, there's no point in trying.

I'm shopping for a new power supply. How much power do I need?

As a rule of thumb, the newer your PC or the more peripherals you have installed, the more power your supply needs to be able to deliver.

Here's a guide to calculating your system's worst-case power needs:

Device	Power It Needs
Motherboard	20–40 watts
Floppy drives	5 watts each
CD-ROM	25 watts
Hard drives	10 watts each
Memory	5 watts for each module
Expansion cards	5 watts each
Typical Pentium II machine	210 watts

Of course, older PCs can get away with much less power, and there's no advantage to placing a 250-watt supply in a 386. Notice, though, that a Pentium II will need fairly high wattage, especially if you plan to install many internal drives and/or expansion cards. If you're upgrading to a Pentium II motherboard, bookmark this table and be prepared to replace your older power supply if necessary.

What else do I need to know before I purchase a power supply?

Thankfully, all power supplies conform to the same physical specifications, so they're pretty much interchangeable. Your main concern when purchasing a replacement power supply is how much power it needs to provide. If you have a fairly new Pentium II or Pentium III, purchase a beefy power supply rated for at least 200 watts; 250 watts is a good idea if you plan to include more than one internal hard drive or a combination of disks, removable disks, and other devices.

I want to add a second hard drive, but I've run out of power connectors. Is there anything I can do?

Just make a short drive to the local computer store and purchase a Y-connector. These inexpensive cables plug into any power connector and split the output into two new connectors. You can disconnect an existing hard drive, for instance, add the Y-connector, then use the new cables to reconnect the old hard drive and add a new one to boot. Remember to grasp the cables by the plastic connector and rock them apart gently—never just pull them straight apart. Also, it's best not to split the power between the hard drive and a CD—split your power wires between a floppy disk and a CD.

Caution: *Be sure to get a four-wire splitter, not a cheap two- or three-wire splitter. Also, keep in mind the amount of wattage required for each peripheral, and make sure you aren't overloading your current power supply by adding connectors.*

Walkthrough: Replacing the Power Supply

Replacing a power supply is fairly simple, particularly since the power supply itself is invulnerable to static shock. Here's what you need to do:

1. Turn off the PC and unplug the power supply from the wall outlet. Make sure you have the PC on a workspace large enough to work comfortably.

2. Remove the cover of the case and spin the PC so you're facing the rear of the PC, with the power supply in clear view.

3. Find the two large plugs that are connected to the motherboard itself. Note their orientation and label them accordingly so you'll know how to connect the new supply, as shown here:

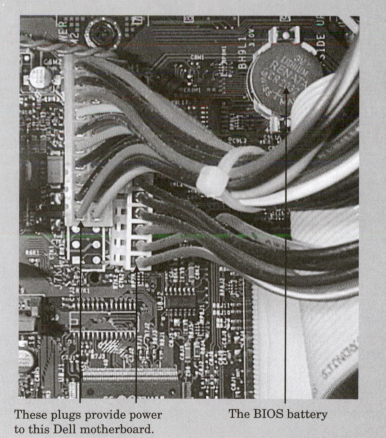

These plugs provide power   The BIOS battery
to this Dell motherboard.

4. Disconnect all the other power connectors—those to the hard disk, CD-ROM, floppy drive, etc. (It can sometimes help to rock these connectors from side to side to work them loose.) It won't matter how you reconnect them later on, because all the connectors of the same size are identical.

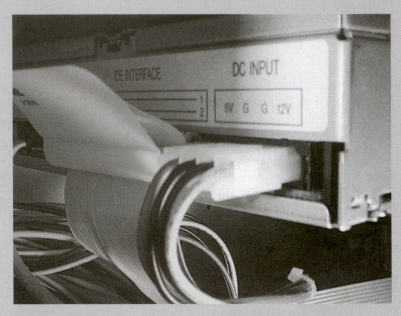

5. Remove the four screws that hold the power supply in place. (Be sure you don't accidentally remove the screws that hold the fan in place in the power supply.)

6. Look for a grounding wire that's connected to the power supply. Not all power supplies have one, but if yours does, disconnect it.

7. Disconnect the power switch wire from the PC's power switch.

8. Pull the power supply out. In some PCs, the layout is so compact that you'll need to move other components—like a floppy drive—to be able to get the power supply out. Be sure to keep track of all the screws if you have to remove anything else.

9. Throw away the old power supply.

10. Insert the new power supply and reconnect all the old power cables.

11. Reattach all the old screws. Be sure to tighten the power supply securely so it doesn't vibrate loose.

12. Make sure that the voltage selector is correctly set to 120 volts for North America or 220 volts as required in other countries. There is usually a switch right on the back of the power supply for just this purpose.

13. Plug it back in and apply power—everything should work. If it does, you're ready to turn off the PC and put the cover back on.

 ## Should I shell out the bucks for an uninterruptible power supply (UPS)?

We recommend it. A UPS is essentially a big battery that protects your PC—and its data—from power failures. It does a lot more than that, though. A typical UPS is designed to perform the following functions:

● **Provide uninterrupted power** A UPS seamlessly transitions to battery power in the event of a power failure.

● **Filter the power going into the PC** The UPS levels out spikes and dropouts so only clean power reaches the sensitive components in your PC.

● **Charge the battery** The battery in the UPS is always ready to provide power in the event of an emergency.

● **Shut down the PC when it's unattended** Not all UPS systems can do this, but it's a handy feature to look for. A UPS is of little value if the PC is left on unattended and then a power loss drains the battery while you're away. The PC will power down abruptly, losing data, whether you have a UPS or not. Thus, some UPS systems have software that powers down the PC after a few minutes, saving any open data files in the process.

Tip: *You can learn a lot about UPS systems by visiting the APC Web site at **http://www.apcc.com**.*

Chapter 3

The Motherboard, CPU, and RAM

Answer Topics!

The Motherboard, CPU, and RAM @ a Glance

The questions people ask most about upgrading a computer tend to center around the motherboard—the main circuit board of any computer—and the central processing unit, or CPU. It's with these two elements that all computational tasks are accomplished, and they can occasionally be the biggest bottlenecks in your system. Plus, some motherboards allow you to spend a few hundred dollars and upgrade only the CPU of your computer, giving you an instant speed boost.

A motherboard upgrade is the most complete replacement you can make without buying a new computer. The motherboard can be a bit daunting, but that doesn't mean you shouldn't know how it works. Even if you're not upgrading the motherboard, knowing more about it can help you make decisions about other upgrades, such as the CPU, expansion cards, and RAM.

The CPU in many systems can be easily upgraded, allowing you to move from, say, a 486 to Pentium technology or from a slow Pentium to a Pentium II or Pentium III. While upgrading the CPU doesn't speed up your entire system, it can speed up some important parts—namely, the speed at which the computer computes data and executes programs. But upgrading the CPU must be done intelligently.

Often the best way to get a speed boost, especially from Windows, is to add random access memory (RAM) to your system. Fortunately, this is also one of the easier upgrades. Simply make sure you buy the right type and quantity of RAM modules for your system.

THE MOTHERBOARD

What's the difference between the motherboard and the CPU?

When you open the case of most any PC, you will see the motherboard right off. It's the largest circuit board in the computer's case, and it's usually anchored to the bottom (in desktop-style cases) or the side (in tower-style cases). It's the circuit board into which all the other boards, controllers, cables, and wires plug into. As the "mother" board, it's responsible for directing traffic within your system. Ultimately, everything plugs into the motherboard and, for the most part, everything has to communicate with the motherboard to work successfully as part of the computer.

On the other hand, the CPU (central processing unit) fundamentally *is* the computer. Also called the *chip* or the *integrated circuit*, it processes all the information that flows through your system. All of the other system components are there to support the CPU.

The CPU plugs directly into the motherboard. (In many cases it looks like the one shown in Figure 3-1.) This arrangement allows the motherboard to control input to and output between your CPU and your video card, sound card, keyboard interface, and other devices. Such input/output components are either part of the motherboard or added to it.

The CPU and the motherboard need one another. Without these two elements, you don't have a functional computer. That said, they are often sold separately for upgrading purposes. When shopping for a replacement or upgrade motherboard, for instance, you'll want to know whether the motherboard includes a CPU or if you need to buy it separately. Most upgraders will opt for a new CPU if they decide to purchase

Figure 3-1   A typical CPU and motherboard for a Pentium system

and install a new motherboard, because motherboards must be designed to work with a given CPU. However, many of the newer motherboards have adjustable voltages and clock speeds so it is possible to buy a replacement CPU and add it to your existing motherboard, as long as the two are compatible.

 ## What kinds of things are built onto the motherboard?

Actually, your motherboard is responsible for managing the input and output for your computer, as well as directing the paths by which data flow between components. In short, your motherboard controls everything from receiving keystrokes from the keyboard to sending those strokes to the processor, receiving the processed results, and passing them on to a

50

video interface for the monitor. Other tasks, such as saving data to a hard drive or receiving sound from an outside source, are also managed by the motherboard. Figure 3-2 shows a complete motherboard and its many components.

As you can see, the motherboard is a complex creature. It can be broken down, however, and its useful bits discussed. Here, then, are the various parts of the motherboard and what they're responsible for:

● **Power receptor** Receives two special power cables from the main power supply for the computer.

● **CPU** The central processing unit resides on the motherboard. The processor is "seated" using either a ZIF (zero-insertion-force) socket—popular for Pentium-style and older chips—or a Slot 1 or Slot 2 edge connector (for

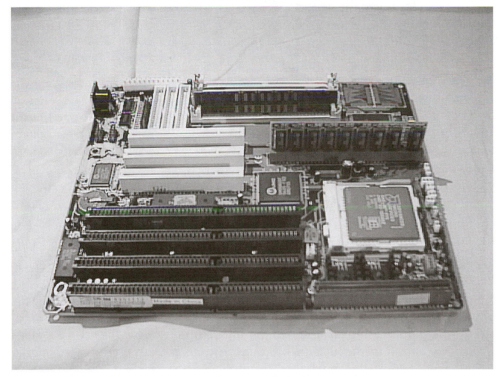

Figure 3-2 Most modern motherboards look something like this one.

Pentium II chips), into which you simply insert the CPU cartridge. Both methods make it easy to remove and exchange the CPU without damaging the motherboard.

- **Memory sockets**   Memory modules can be added to these sockets (in various configurations) to upgrade the amount of RAM available for use. (These sockets can vary in size—standard RAM modules come in 36-pin, 72-pin, and 168-pin versions.)

- **Cache socket**   Some motherboards offer a socket for special cache RAM, which can help to quicken operations by making the CPU work more efficiently.

- **PCI slots**   Not all motherboards have them, but PCI upgrade slots are fairly distinctive. Other upgrade slot technologies generally feature black or gray connectors that are significantly longer than typical PCI slots.

- **ISA slots**   These are the most basic types of upgrade slots for most PCs. The shortest slots can accept 8-bit expansion cards; longer slots are 16-bit versions. Much longer slots usually can handle any type of ISA card or faster VL-bus upgrade cards.

- **AGP port**   The Advanced Graphics Port is a newer, high-speed interface designed for the latest graphics cards and accelerators. While it's based on the PCI interface, this special slot (or, sometimes, built-in circuitry) is designed specifically for accelerating 3-D graphics. It is therefore faster than the typical PCI interface.

- **Power supply connector**   Power from the main power supply in the case is fed to the motherboard and any expansion cards using this slot. (Other connectors go directly from the power supply to hard drives, floppy drives, and similar devices.)

- **Keyboard connector**   Designed to show through an opening in back of the computer case. It connects to a standard keyboard.

- **Battery**   The battery is designed to retain the most basic information when the computer is off. Every reboot requires basic information about the computer itself and

any hard drives attached to the machine so that the operating system can be loaded.

Some motherboards have other elements built onto them—for example, some motherboards include direct hard-drive and floppy-drive interface circuitry, while others don't. Those that don't include this feature require an expansion card designed to handle such interfaces. Figure 3-3 shows the hard drive circuitry that's included on the motherboard.

The following lists the functions of various interface connectors:

● **PCI/IDE hard drive connectors** Connect IDE hard drives to the computer via a ribbon cable. Secondary drives are usually connected using a second connector on the ribbon cable itself.

IDE
connectors

Figure 3-3 The IDE interface on a typical Pentium II-class motherboard

- **Floppy controllers**   Connect one or two floppy drives (3.5- or 5.25-inch drives) to the motherboard.

- **Parallel connectors**   Connect parallel ports to the motherboard via the ribbon cable. The parallel ports are almost always mounted to the inside back of the case so that external devices can be attached to them.

- **Serial connectors**   Connect one or two serial ports to the motherboard using the ribbon cable. Serial ports are also mounted to the case so that external devices can be attached to the computer.

- **USB connectors**   Provide access to new Universal Serial Bus components such as scanners, mice, digital cameras, and more.

What do all the cables and connectors on the motherboard do?

The typical motherboard, even if it doesn't have any interface cards plugged into it, can offer a myriad of cables and connectors that are supposed to be part of the machine. There are essentially three different types of internal connectors that must be connected to the motherboard. These are shown in Figure 3-4.

Each type of wiring and connector is used in a particular range of functions:

- **Ribbon cable**   Individual wires are banded together into ribbons to allow the motherboard to communicate with storage devices such hard drives, floppy drives, CD-ROM drives, and expansion ports.

- **Switch/indicator wiring**   This is typical low-gauge wiring that uses a jumper-style connector for connecting to raised pins on the motherboard. These wires are generally used to wire the motherboard to parts of the case, including any power lights (indicators), digital readouts, disk activity indicators, and the internal speaker.

- **Power connectors**   One pair (usually) of power connectors are connected between the case's power supply and the motherboard, while the rest of the power connectors are available for connecting internal devices.

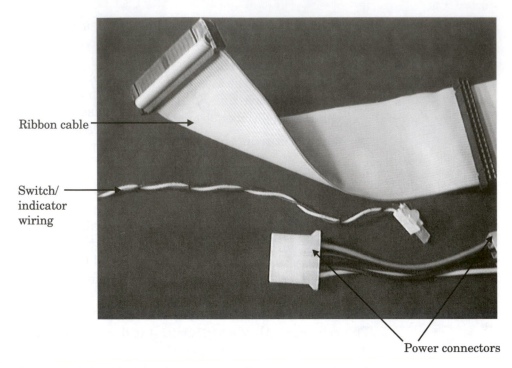

Ribbon cable

Switch/
indicator
wiring

Power connectors

Figure 3-4 Types of internal cabling

 Note: *Power connectors and power adapters are discussed in Chapter 2.*

When removing or upgrading the motherboard, it's best to mark the ribbon cables by their purpose (hard drives, floppy drives, CD-ROM drives, serial cables, etc.). Note that the serial and parallel cables are different sizes from the ribbon cables for storage devices.

Ribbon Cable Purpose	Size of Connector
Hard drives, CD-ROM, CD-R, DVD	40-pin
Floppy drives	34-pin
Parallel port	26-pin
Serial port	10-pin (9 are used)

Each switch/indicator wire has a different purpose, and you'll need to know that purpose if you plan to remove your motherboard for repairs or replace it with a new one. In most cases, it's helpful to have the documentation for both your computer's case and your motherboard on hand. (Some motherboards clearly mark which of the case's switch/indicator wires should be plugged from parts of the case to inputs on the motherboard. Others make it more difficult.)

Why are motherboards and system buses sometimes referred to as "64-bit"?

The number of bits a bus can transmit is called the *width*, as in a *32 bit-* or *64 bit-wide bu*s. Width is important: the wider the bus, the more data that can be transmitted from RAM to the CPU at once. Early 386SX motherboards, for example, had a 16-bit bus, differentiating them from the 386DX processors of the time. Most 486 motherboards had 32-bit buses, and modern motherboards feature 64-bit system buses.

What's All This Talk of Bits?

You may know that *bit* is a term that represents the smallest amount of data that a computer can deal with: A bit is either a 1 or a 0. Added together, eight bits make a *byte* of data, which is roughly equivalent to a single character, like the letter "P." But you might still be confused as to what bits have to do with ISA and PCI buses.

Remember that the ISA bus comes in 8-bit and 16-bit varieties—ultimately, this describes the width of the data path from the expansion card to the motherboard. An 8-bit card has a path that is only 8 bits wide. The latest PCI cards, however, offer 32 bit-wide data paths, allowing four times as much data to pass to the motherboard at once. Coupled with a faster clock speed, this allows PCI-based cards to pass a lot more data more quickly than either type of ISA card.

I've heard about Socket 7, Slot 1, and Slot 2 motherboards. What's the difference between them?

They refer to the kind of socket that the CPU and motherboard use, including the pin spacing and positions. Socket 7 is very common, because Pentium-class chips used it, and many non-Intel CPUs—those from AMD and Cyrix—still use it (or a version of it).

Slot 1, on the other hand, is the connector used by Intel for Pentium II CPUs. A newer spec, called Slot 2, has appeared for even newer Pentium II and Pentium III chips. The bottom line is that you can't upgrade a Socket 7 motherboard with a Pentium II or Pentium III CPU—instead, you'll need a Socket 7-compatible CPU like an upgrade from AMD.

I've lost my manual. How can I figure out who made my motherboard?

Begin by consulting the manufacturer of your system (e.g., Compaq, Packard Bell, Acer); they should be able to tell you. If you have a homegrown or off-brand PC clone, you can sometimes determine what motherboard it uses by watching the BIOS identification when the computer first boots. Then, look up your BIOS at the following Web sites:

- **Wim's BIOS Page**   http://ping4.ping.be/bios/
- **House of Hall's**   http://www.prosystech.com/hohweb/bios.htm

How can I tell whether I should upgrade my motherboard?

There are two main reasons to upgrade the motherboard. The first is that you want to upgrade the CPU, but your motherboard is too old or is incompatible with modern processors. (For example, if you currently own a 486, you can't add a Pentium III processor because of the difference in design of the socket used to plug in the CPU.) The other reason to buy a new motherboard is to increase the speed of your *system bus*, which is responsible for moving data back and forth between the CPU and your computer's memory, or RAM.

This bus directly determines how quickly your PC can get the data it needs to compute. If your motherboard is aging, the speed of your system bus could hamper your ability to upgrade other components in your computer.

System buses are measured in terms of the speed (in MHz) of the bus and the width of the path that data travels to and from the CPU (in bits). Traditionally, the speed of the system bus has been the same as the speed of the CPU. With the advent of the 486 CPU, CPU speeds began to double and sometimes triple the speed of the system bus. This means the CPU runs very quickly, but a lagging system bus can mean the CPU has to wait, occasionally, while more data is fed to it.

When the Pentium and Pentium II processors arrived on the scene, suddenly higher multiples were common—a Pentium running at 266 MHz might have a 66-MHz bus. Over time, motherboard manufacturers (notably Intel) worked to increase the speed of the system bus to support faster processors. Currently, system buses have reached 100 MHz (and in some cases 133 and 200 MHz), providing today's 500- to 800-MHz CPUs a reasonably speedy stream of data from RAM. Table 3-1 shows the slow march of system bus and processor speeds.

The difference between the system bus speeds in earlier models—like the 486 and the original Pentium—made a much more pronounced difference than it does in the Pentium II and Pentium III CPUs. Why? The Pentium II and III use a special CPU that includes high-speed cache memory on the CPU's daughtercard. Data is stored in that cache memory, making it easier for the CPU to get enough data to process quickly. Still, it's important to know what speeds your motherboard supports when it comes time to choose an upgrade CPU, if you decide to buy one. We'll discuss this more in the section, "The CPU and Battery" later in this chapter.

What do I need to know before I buy a new motherboard for my computer?

If you are interested in buying a new motherboard for your existing computer, a few basic considerations will make your

CPU (or CPU Series)	System Bus Speed
8088	4.77 MHz
8086	8 MHz
80286	12 MHz (some 16 MHz)
80386SX/16	16 MHz
80386DX/25, 80486SX/25, 486DX2/50, 486DX4/75	25 MHz
80386DX/33, 80486SX/33, 486DX2/66, 486DX4/100	33 MHz
80486DX/50	50 MHz
Pentium/60, P150	60 MHz
Pentium/100, P166, Pentium II (early models), AMD K5-133, Cyrix 6x86 P166+, Pentium Pro/200	66 MHz
Pentium II (350/400/450), Pentium III	100 MHz
AMB K6/2-300, 400	100 MHz

Table 3-1 System bus speeds for typical processors

purchase go more smoothly. Most importantly, buy your motherboard from a reputable dealer who's willing to help if you run into any snags.

In addition, you should know:

● *What type of case do you have?* (See the discussion of cases in Chapter 2.) The type of case you have dictates the type of motherboard you'll need. It may also limit the types of motherboards you can use to upgrade your computer. Cases and motherboards come in two major form factors: AT and ATX. You'll need a case and motherboard that match. (Some cases can handle multiple motherboard types, but you'll need to know this ahead of time.)

 Tip: *If you can, bring your case to the store when you buy the motherboard. That way, you and the store's technicians can make sure the new board is a good fit.*

● *What's the rating on your power supply?* Most modern motherboards work best with a 225-watt or higher power supply (depending on the type of chip and motherboard chipset used). Know what your power

supply's rating is and make sure the motherboard doesn't require more power.

● *Do you need a new CPU?* If you do, purchase the CPU and motherboard together if possible. This will help ensure that the two are fully compatible. If you're not interested in a new CPU, know the exact CPU you'll be using with the new motherboard. Gather all the information you can by looking at the CPU chip or reading your computer's manual. Be sure to include the manufacturer (Intel, AMD, Cyrix, IBM), the type (386DX, 486DX4, Pentium MMX, Pentium II), the megahertz speed (60 MHz, 266 MHz), and any other model numbers or serial numbers you can find. Take that information (or the CPU itself) with you to the dealer (or the catalog or Web site) so you can verify that the motherboard supports your CPU before you purchase it.

● *Do you need input/output interfaces on the motherboard?* Your old computer setup may have included an interface card that offered serial, parallel, IDE (hard drive), floppy, and other technologies. While you may be happy replacing that card with the interface built onto the newer motherboard, if you decide to use the older card (or a higher-performance card), you may need to disable the interfaces on the motherboard. Make sure disabling them is documented in the literature included with the motherboard. It's also possible that the new motherboard will not include input/output interfaces. If that's the case, make sure you have an I/O expansion card that will work with the new motherboard.

● *What type of system bus do you want? Do you have enough slots?* More than likely, your existing computer has a number of expansion cards already installed. Will you want to use those cards with your new motherboard? If so, you'll want to know the type of bus interface for which the card is designed (PCI, ISA, EISA, VESA) as well as the number of cards you'll need to move to the new motherboard. Make sure the motherboard supports that type of card and offers enough free slots for upgrading. (Most new motherboards will only support PCI, ISA, and

AGP, so you may need to shop for a used or replacement motherboard if you want to use older cards.)

❋ ***Note:*** *The various types of expansion cards are discussed in Chapter 4.*

Walkthrough: Upgrading the Motherboard in Your Computer

Upgrading a motherboard is not for the faint of heart, because it usually takes at least a few hours and offers real dangers in terms of static electricity discharge (which can harm expensive components) and electrical shocks or surges (which can harm both people and equipment). It takes careful planning and focus to upgrade a motherboard successfully. It can also be an inexpensive way to increase the performance of your computer in a pleasing way.

The instructions in this box include cross-references to information that you may want to review in other chapters of this book. Read everything first, including any cross-references; then proceed.

Start out with this checklist, which covers everything you need to begin installing a new motherboard in your computer:

- Budget at least three hours for performing the upgrade.

- Use the answers and criteria earlier in this chapter to purchase a motherboard (and/or CPU) that is designed to fit in your computer's case.

- Have labels or masking tape and a pen ready so you can label wires, cables, and slots, as necessary.

- Have a pad of paper handy for settings, notes, and procedures. It is recommended that you write down everything you do in the order in which you do it, so you can think through every step and review, if necessary, to see where something may have gone wrong.

- Have a Phillips screwdriver and a pair of needlenose pliers on hand.

- You may also want to have some #6-3 and some #4-40 machine screws (hex or Phillips head) on hand whenever you upgrade, because it's always possible to lose some along the way. Buy the screws from a computer store if possible, since they'll have the exact sizes you'll need.

- Wear a grounding strap or make sure you have some other solution for grounding yourself before handling computer components. (Electrically grounding yourself is discussed in Chapter 2.)

- Clear a workspace where you can stand or sit, making sure that you have enough room for the opened case and two motherboards side by side (about 5 feet by 3 feet of space). If possible, the work surface should be clean and unfinished—computer components can be sharp and can scratch surfaces. The surface and surroundings should be clean and dust free.

- Have a can of compressed air handy, available at many art supply, office supply, hardware, and computer stores. Compressed air is a good way to remove dust from computer cases. Don't spray the air directly on the motherboard, however; use a small vacuum instead.

- If possible, lay down static-free mats on your workspace surface. (Consult your computer supply store and Chapter 2.)

- Make sure you have a working video card that is compatible with the new motherboard, along with a monitor, keyboard, and mouse that you can use for testing purposes.

Now you're ready to remove the original motherboard from your computer. It's important to pay attention through every step of this process, because installing the new motherboard will, hopefully, simply be a reversal of the steps it took to uninstall the original. Write down everything you do and label every wire! You can easily forget a setting, switch, or the purpose of a particular wire. If you do, you'll either be struggling with the documentation for your computer or you'll be forced to take it to a service center and hope they can fix it.

To remove the original motherboard, follow these steps:

1. Ground yourself appropriately, discharge any static electricity you may have built up in your body, and unplug your computer. Remove any other cables that are attached to expansion ports on the back of the computer. Remove the outer shell of the computer case.

2. Lay the case flat so that the motherboard is at the bottom of the case. (You will need to turn a mini-tower or tower-style case on its side to achieve this.) Make a visual confirmation that the new

motherboard will fit and that it offers the expansion slots you need for existing cards, and look to make sure that key ports— like the keyboard port—are likely to line up correctly with the computer's case.

3. Unscrew the retaining screws on each expansion card that is currently in the computer. Remove each card by grabbing it at each top corner and pulling up. You may need to rock it slightly from back to front to unseat it from the expansion slot, as shown here. Be sure to rock it as gently as possible, and do not rock it from side to side. (For our purposes, the back of the card is the part that you screw into the case, and the front of the card is toward the middle of the case.)

If your system has a special I/O expansion card that connects to the ports on the back of the machine and/or the storage drives in your computer, leave it installed for the moment.

4. After the cards are out, remove any other components that interfere with your access to the motherboard. In many cases, there is a drive cage, which often blocks the motherboard. Remove the drive cage, if necessary. You'll need to remove the ribbon cables and power connectors for any drives that are part of the drive cage. (Consult Chapter 8 for information on uninstalling

hard drives and floppy drives.) In most cases, you won't need to remove the ribbon cables or power connectors from any of the other drives in your system.

5. With access to the motherboard, you're ready to remove any ribbon cables that may be attached to the motherboard or to a special I/O expansion card. Choose a ribbon cable, then determine what it is attached to. Write down the device or port it connects to the motherboard (or the I/O card) on a piece of tape, and then label the ribbon cable:

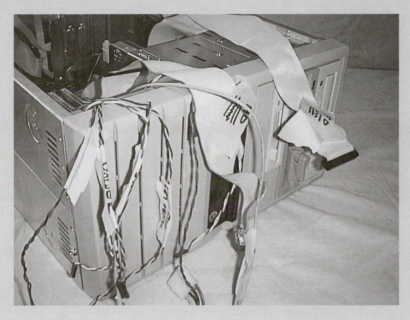

It's best to avoid taping the connector; simply wrap the tape around the cable or wire. Now, remove it from the motherboard (or I/O card) by holding the ribbon cable connector on either end with your fingers and pulling gently away from the motherboard's connector.

If you can, avoid removing the ribbon cables from storage devices or the ports on the back of the computer. It's also a wise precaution to label the direction that the ribbon cable connector should be in when it's connected. (For example, label the "top" of a ribbon cable that's connected to your floppy drive so you know which way to reinstall it.)

6. Repeat the process for each remaining ribbon cable until you have them all labeled and removed. Remove the I/O expansion card, if you have one.

7. Next, you can remove the motherboard's power connectors. Locate the multicolored wires coming from the power supply and going into the motherboard. Remove the first connector and give it a label that tells you which side it's on (closer to the back of the case could be "back," for instance.) Remove the other connector.

8. Now you're ready to begin unplugging all the switch/indicator wires that are currently attached. First, choose a wire. Then, determine what that wire is used for. It can be a bit tricky to figure out, but most of the wires are color-coded—look to see where the wire goes. Is it wired to the key lock? The turbo button? The power switch?

   After you've figured it out, write the wire's function on a piece of tape. Also write down the code next to the jumper terminals where that wire is plugged in and the direction in which that wire comes closest to one of the sides. For instance, you might create a label that says "Reset/Red," which means, "This wire is for the Reset button; and the red wire is closer to the left."

   This is a great time to be jotting notes in your notepad. If you develop a special system for "lefts" and "rights," write down exactly what the system represents. Otherwise, you could be staring at your label 30 minutes from now wondering what the heck you meant.

9. Create labels for each of the switch/indicator wires and remove them from the motherboard (assuming that your case doesn't have labels.) If you have RAM modules you'd like to transfer from this motherboard to the new one, you can remove them now. (See the section, "Upgrading Your System Memory" later in this chapter for hints on how to remove and install RAM.)

10. Now you're ready to remove the motherboard. The motherboard may have one or more screws securing it to the bottom of the case. Remove that screw(s), if you find any. Otherwise, the motherboard will probably slide right out of the case. Grab it by

the corners and slide it toward the back of the case. With some cases you can look at the underside of the case (or the side, if it's a mini-tower) to see how it should slide:

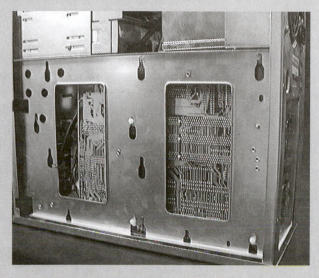

11. Now, place the motherboards side by side and note where the holes for the plastic standoffs fall on the new motherboard. You'll want to take the standoffs for the original motherboard and put them in the exact same spots on the new board, if possible. (If this isn't possible, lay the new board in the case so that the slots and keyboard connector line up, then note which holes in the board correspond to standoff points in the case.)

12. Remove the standoffs from the original motherboard, using needlenose pliers to pinch the top of the standoff together, then slide the standoff out the bottom of the motherboard.

And that completes the removal process. Now, if necessary, remove the CPU from the original motherboard and mount it on the new motherboard. (If your new motherboard came with a CPU, you don't need to do this.) You can find answers to your questions about installing CPUs in the next section.

Now you're ready to install the new motherboard. Follow these steps:

1. Install the plastic standoffs in the new motherboard so that the motherboard will slide into the case and lock into position, with the expansion slots and keyboard connector lined up with their respective holes in the back of the case.

    If your two motherboards aren't an exact match, make sure you place the standoffs on your new motherboard so that the motherboard is securely balanced on them. If you place all the standoffs on one side of the board, for instance, it will dip lower on the other side, making it difficult to securely install expansion cards. It could also electrically short out against the case.

2. Carefully line up the motherboard inside the case so that the standoffs fall through the case into position, then slide it back until it locks into place. If an anchor point for a screw exists, screw the board down to the case. (Note that a special red absorption washer is often necessary between the screw and the motherboard to avoid electrical shorts.)

3. Install any RAM modules or cache memory that you took from the other board. (This assumes the RAM is compatible with the new board. See the section, "Upgrading Your System Memory" later in this chapter.)

4. Begin installing the switch/indicator wires by matching the function of each wire (or set of wires) to its appropriate place on the motherboard. You'll need to consult the documentation that came with the board. (The numbered codes, like J11, may not always be the same across different manufacturers' motherboards.)

5. Install the power connectors from the power supply to the new motherboard, taking care to position the connectors in the right order. (The rule of power: Black wires should meet in the middle.)

6. Install the I/O card(s) (if necessary) and begin plugging your ribbon cables into the appropriate slots for your ports, hard drives, floppy, and CD-ROM.

7. Reinstall any other components you took out of the case, including the drive cage or any drives you disconnected.

8. Once everything looks good, install a video interface card in one of the available slots. Plug a monitor into the monitor port on the outside of the video card.

9. Plug a keyboard into the keyboard connector.

10. Plug the power cord into the power supply on the case, then press the power button on your computer.

Did anything go wrong? You need to check a number of factors to make sure you've installed everything correctly. Here are some questions you'll want to answer in the testing phase:

● *Did anything seem to happen?* If not, check the power connectors on the motherboard and the power supply.

● *Did the power light, digital readout, or any other indicators light up like they should when the machine got power?* If not, check the switch/indicator wiring for any lights that don't seem to be working correctly.

● *Did an image appear on the screen?* The memory check and/or BIOS information should appear onscreen. If nothing happens, check the monitor's power and monitor-to-video interface connection, then check the video card and make sure it's properly seated. Also, check the power connectors on the motherboard to ensure that the motherboard is getting power for the video card. Also, your RAM modules might not be properly seated on the motherboard. Check them again and consult the RAM upgrading answers later in this chapter.

● *Did the hard drive start up?* If you've gotten through everything else but then see an error message related to the hard drive—or the computer can't load DOS—check the ribbon cable for your hard drive and make sure it's installed correctly. Also, make sure it's installed in the correct connector (and not the connector for floppy control, for instance).

● *Is the CD-ROM or floppy drive working oddly or just spinning constantly with the light on?* CD-ROM drives have a tendency to ignite their lights and spin a bit as the computer starts, but if it keeps going and going (or if a floppy drive does the same), it may be plugged into the wrong controller connector or its ribbon cable might be installed backward.

Some motherboard and I/O cards provide a clue to help you line up ribbon cables. Most ribbon cables have a red line running down one side. And most connectors on the motherboard have a notch taken out of the bottom. Once you find the notch in the connector, picture that as the bottom of the connector, then plug the ribbon cable in so that the red line is on the left side of the connector.

● *Do the ports work?* As your computer boots, you'll see a screen that describes your computer to you—it tells you what processor you have, how much RAM, etc. Pay attention to the part where it shows you how many COM and LPT ports you have—if you don't have as many as you plugged in, you may need to check your ribbon cables.

You may have other troubleshooting to do, but if your system passes these test questions, then you've successfully installed your motherboard. For more information on other issues, consult the following:

● Power supply and power connectors (Chapter 2)

● Configuring storage drives (Chapter 8)

● Dealing with I/O ports and cabling (Chapter 4)

● Keyboard and other input issues (Chapter 5)

❓ I'm trying to install a new CPU on my motherboard. How can I tell which bus speed and multiplier to use?

First of all, you may be confused by the terminology. When you install a new CPU in a motherboard, you need to tell the motherboard how to talk to the chip. They run at different speeds, and need a way to communicate. Your motherboard has a specific bus speed, usually 66 or 100 MHz. As a result, you must configure a multiplier to bridge the two different speeds. You do this by moving a jumper on the motherboard. If you don't move the jumper to configure the multiplier properly when installing a CPU in the motherboard, your PC will not work.

Most of the time, your CPU or motherboard will ship with a guide to help you set it up. The rule, though, is that the CPU's speed must be an integer or integer-and-a-half multiple of the motherboard's bus speed.

For example, suppose you had a 400-MHz Pentium II processor. To properly install this CPU, you would need a motherboard that runs at 100 MHz, and you would set the motherboard multiplier to 4. By the same token, a 350-MHz processor would need a multiplier of 3.5 in the same 100 MHz motherboard.

We don't cover very possible combination here, but you can use this chart as a reference to configure your new CPU/ motherboard combination:

CPU Clock Speed	Motherboard Bus Speed	Motherboard Multiplier
233 MHz	66 MHz	3.5
266 MHz	66 MHz	4
300 MHz	66 MHz	4.5
333 MHz	66 MHz	5
350 MHz	100 MHz	3.5
400 MHz	100 MHz	4
450 MHz	100 MHz	4.5
500 MHz	100 MHz	5

THE CPU AND BATTERY

 ### What is the difference between a 486 and a Pentium?

Pentium is the trademark name given to the 586-class of CPU chips created by Intel. Originally, all Intel processors had numeric names, such as 8086 and 80286. Later, Intel attempted to trademark the names *i386* and *i486,* but they had little luck getting consumers to refer to their products by names different from other chips whose manufacturers were also able to refer to their chips as 386 and 486 processors.

So the Pentium is the successor to the 486. It's faster at the same clock speed that the 486 (so a 66-MHz Pentium is faster than a 486DX2 running at 66 MHz). The Pentium also incorporates more modern technology, including increased on-board cache memory, a more advanced integrated floating-point unit (for high-speed decimal math), and additional data pipelines for moving data around more quickly.

? What does DX mean (as in DX2 and DX4)?

The DX appendage for chip names has meant different things through the years. First used with 386-level processors, the DX designation originally meant a processor that communicated with the motherboard along a 32-bit-wide path. (The 286 and 386SX chips used 16-bit-wide data paths.) Later, in 486 chips, the DX was used to refer to 486 chips that didn't have the floating-point unit disabled.

The numbers after 486DX refer to the multiple of clock speed to motherboard system bus speed. For example, a 486DX2/66 is clock-doubled, meaning the processor runs at 66 MHz, but the system bus runs at 33 MHz. Unfortunately, DX4 was used by Intel to represent a clock-tripled processor for marketing reasons. (The logical choice would have been DX3.) Therefore, a 486DX4/75 offers a 75-MHz processor designed to communicate with the motherboard at 25 MHz.

Pentium processors are routinely clock-doubled, clock-tripled, and beyond, but no longer make a point of it in the naming scheme.

? What is MMX? Do I need it?

Originally MMX stood for *MultiMedia eXtentions*—but, in the continuing wisdom of the Intel marketing department, the public was eventually told that MMX meant absolutely nothing. Instead, it refers to the ability of certain Pentium and above processors to reallocate floating-point registers (data storage on the processor chip) from the floating point duties to multimedia-specific purposes. For programs written to take advantage of MMX, this technology allows a 15 to 30 percent increase in the speed of high-end video and graphical processing.

If you're shopping for a Pentium or Pentium Pro processor, you can generally get MMX technology for little or no extra cost—and it's a good idea for gamers, video hobbyists, and professional graphic artists. Even better for those people, though, are Pentium II and beyond processors, which all incorporate MMX.

Help! What are the differences between a Pentium, a Pentium Pro, a Pentium II, a Celeron, and a Pentium III?

Originally, the Pentium was the first logical upgrade to the 486 family of computers, incorporating incremental updates and significant performance increases to make Windows, Windows 95, and similar applications run more quickly. Soon afterward, the Pentium Pro chip was introduced; this was Intel's first 32-bit "clean" processor, requiring 32-bit operating systems and 32-bit applications for optimum performance. (For instance, early versions of the Pentium Pro worked quickly with Windows NT, but could run a tad slower than a same-speed Pentium when both ran Windows 95, which is not a 32-bit clean operating system.) Later, MMX was added to both processors as an interim technology for speeding up multimedia functions.

The Pentium II introduced a number of differences, although it is the clear successor to both the Pentium and Pentium Pro architectures. Most significant is the Pentium II's reliance on a new interface technology, Slot 1, which places the CPU in a special cartridge, offering better heat control as well as decreasing the fear of problems from static electricity discharge (see Figure 3-5).

The Pentium II directly incorporates MMX technology and is higher performing than either the Pentium or Pentium Pro at the same clock speed. The Pentium II has the added advantage of being capable of clock speeds of 300 MHz and beyond.

A Celeron is a lower-cost version of the Pentium II that runs at slightly lower speeds and features less on-board cache RAM. This makes it a little slower than a same-MHz Pentium II, but otherwise it's pretty similar.

The Pentium III processor incorporates the Internet Streaming SIMD instruction set that makes certain types of multimedia display faster—especially memory-intensive applications and special applications over the Internet. The Pentium III is also designed to work at higher MHz speeds (450 MHz and up).

Figure 3-5 The Slot 1 (and Slot 2) architecture places the CPU in a special cartridge.

 ### What does "Xeon" mean?

Xeon means higher-priced. (That's the joke part of the answer.) Actually, Xeon CPUs are most obviously differentiated by the fact that they have more Level 2 cache RAM and they're more capable of being used in multiprocessor machines, allowing four, six, or more Xeon CPUs to work together in a single, high-end machine. Most Xeon CPUs are purchased for server and workstation-type computers.

 ### What is a 586? A 686?

A 586 is usually the rough equivalent of a Pentium processor, but manufactured by AMD, Cyrix, IBM, or another processor company. The 586-level processors are almost always

completely compatible with Pentium processors, and can sometimes outperform them at a lower cost.

The 686 designation is generally used to suggest that an alternative processor competes with either the Pentium Pro or the Pentium II processor. For instance, the AMD-K6 is said by AMD to compete directly with the Pentium II, even going so far as to offer a competitor for MMX technology. Cyrix's 6x86 and M-II CPUs compete with both Pentium and Pentium II processors.

Note: *While the clone processor manufacturers can often rightly claim that their performance equals the Pentium II, direct compatibility with Slot 1 and Slot 2 interfaces may be slow in coming, because Intel owns patents on many aspects of Slot 1 and Slot 2.*

What are the differences between AMD's K6-2, K6-III, and K7 processors?

Advanced Micro Devices, Inc. (AMD) produces CPUs that compete with Intel Corporation, which makes the industry-standard Pentium line of processors. The main difference between all AMD processors and the Pentium II (and higher) line from Intel is the fact that AMD processors support the Socket 7 interface that late-model 486 and earlier Pentium motherboards feature.

K6-2 processors are roughly equivalent to Pentium II and Celeron processors, including support for MMX instructions and some additional speed-up for 3-D graphics. The K6-III is designed to compete with the Pentium III CPU, because of its inclusion of creative cache memory schemes. AMD claims the K6-III is faster than a same-speed Pentium III in real-world tests; magazines and other third-party testers generally find that some tasks are faster, while some tasks are slower on each processor.

The K7 processor is in the latest stages of development at the time of writing. It promises fast clock speeds, 200-MHz system buses, and other exciting advances that may well make it one of the fastest chips on the market.

 ## What are the differences between Cyrix's 6x86, M-II, and MediaGX processors?

Cyrix's processor use Socket 7 technology, allowing them to upgrade older 486-based and original Pentium systems (in some cases).

The 6x86 is a competitor for Intel's original Pentium processor, now discontinued. It's still a decent value if you'd like to get Pentium-like performance out of an older machine, if you can find a used 6x86 CPU (or complete PC).

The M-II is Cyrix's competitor for the Pentium II, offering support for MMX-instructions and higher clock speeds.

The MediaGX processor is a bit more unique. A low-cost processor, the MediaGX is designed to do more than just process—it also handles graphics and sounds for low-cost computers. Popular in sub-$500 and portable PCs, the MediaGX compares to an original Pentium MMX processor in speed.

 ## What is a "P rating"?

The *P rating* is Cyrix's method for measuring how its chips compare to Intel Pentium chips. For instance, a Cyrix chip may only run at 133 MHz, but Cyrix feels that it competes in performance benchmarks with a 166-MHz Pentium. Because the 133-MHz processor sounds slower, even though it's competitive, there's a marketing disadvantage—so Cyrix calls it a 6x86 P166 (or PR166).

Should I buy a Celeron to save some money?

That depends on the Celeron. If someone offers you a good deal on a first-generation Celeron, walk away. Those early Celerons had no on-board cache, and they performed abysmally. Newer Celerons—ones that include a cache—perform pretty well, even when compared to full-bore Pentium IIs of the same clock speed. That means you can get a 350-MHz Celeron at a great price, and it'll run almost as fast as a real 350-MHz Pentium II.

 ### How can I tell if my current motherboard will accept a new CPU?

While there are some manufacturer-specific options for upgrading a CPU in some computers, most upgradable computers offer a few different telltale signs that the CPU can be upgraded. For the most part, you can only upgrade by one family of processor—386 to 486, 486 to Pentium, etc. If you happen to have an old 286-level machine currently working as a doorstop, it can at least be upgraded with special 386 upgrade kits. Of course, those kits would be impossible to find retail— you'll need to shop the classifieds or computer swap meets.

Note: *If you have a 386-level machine, you probably have only one option for upgrading—a replacement 486-level chip from Cyrix or AMD. Both companies made pin-compatible 386-style chips that offered 486-like performance. You can also upgrade some earlier 386SX chips to 386DX/33 or 386DX/40 processors by swapping the CPUs.*

Here are a few hints that suggest CPU upgradability in 486 systems:

- *Your current CPU is socketed.* CPUs are either soldered or socketed on the motherboard—a socketed chip can be removed.

- *Your CPU is in a ZIF socket.* The ZIF (zero-insertion-force) socket was designed to make it easy to mount and remove CPU chips. Figure 3-6 shows a ZIF socket.

- *You have an open 487SX socket.* If your current chip is a 486SX, there's probably an open processor socket that was originally designed for a math coprocessor. This slot can be used instead of an Overdrive or similar upgrade processor.

Figure 3-6 A Pentium-style CPU chip has a little lever to secure it in place.

- *You have a special socket for an Overdrive CPU.* If you have an older 486DX motherboard that doesn't include a ZIF socket, it may still include a special, open socket that will allow you to add an upgrade chip.

If you already have a Pentium, chances are good that your processor is mounted in a ZIF socket, either Socket 5 or Socket 7. If that's the case, you can replace your processor with any Pentium processor for which your motherboard is rated. (Consult your motherboard's manual.) You can also use an AMD or Cyrix processor in these machines if the processor supports your motherboard and system bus speed.

The move from Pentium to Pentium II or Pentium III can't be accomplished with a CPU upgrade. Instead, you'll need to install a new motherboard or buy a new system. The problem is the connection—the Pentium II/III use the Slot 1

and Slot 2 connectors, which aren't compatible with original Pentium and Pentium MMX motherboards.

Tip: *For more information on whether your computer can support an Intel Overdrive chip, visit **http://www.intel.com/ overdrive** on the Web.*

I want to put a new processor in my Pentium-class PC. Can I do it?

While the earliest Pentium motherboards (those designed for 60- and 66-MHz Pentiums) can only be upgraded using an Intel Overdrive processor, many Pentium and higher motherboards are designed to accept more than one speed of processor, within certain limitations. CPU speeds need to be an exact multiple of the system bus speed. For instance, a 75-MHz Pentium motherboard would generally have a 50-MHz system bus, which might allow to upgrade by installing a 100-MHz or 150-MHz Pentium processor. Other motherboards can accept anywhere from 90-MHz to 200-MHz processors because their bus speeds can also be changed.

Caution: *Not all motherboards can simply accept a different Pentium processor. In many cases, you'll need to set specific jumper settings on the motherboard, and you'll need to consult your motherboard's documentation to determine those settings.*

You can also try the following Web sites for information on whether or not your motherboard can accept a new processor:

- **AMD processors** http://www.amd.com/products/products.html

- **Intel and Overdrive processors** http://support.intel.com/motherboards/

- **Cyrix processors** http://www.cyrix.com/process/support/mboard/mx-brds.htm

➕ ***Tip:*** *If you don't have documentation for your motherboard, check the Web site of the your computer's manufacturer; you'll probably have the best luck here if you're using a brand-name machine. If that doesn't help, try the Web site of the manufacturer of your original CPU— probably Intel, AMD, or Cyrix. All three companies often sell both processors and motherboards to PC manufacturers.*

Can I upgrade from a 486 to a Pentium?

In many cases, you can. Early 586-level processors from AMD and Cyrix were designed to directly replace 486-level processors from Intel. You could buy one of these processor upgrades, remove the old 486, and install the new 586-level CPU. You can also often upgrade 486 machines with Pentium Overdrive processors directly from Intel.

Can I upgrade from a 386/286/8086 to a Pentium?

In most cases, you can't. If you have a 386 and you want to upgrade to a faster computer, you might consider some AMD and Cyrix processors that were designed to directly replace a 386-level processor. They're rarely available retail, however, so you'll have to scour for them. Your best bet is to buy a new Pentium II, III, or Celeron (or an equivalent from AMD or Cyrix) computer or upgrade the motherboard in your 386 to a Pentium-level motherboard, assuming you have a standard case size.

Can I upgrade from a Pentium to a Pentium II or Pentium III?

Not with a simple processor upgrade. The Pentium and Pentium II and III use a different interface to connect the CPU to the motherboard (Pentium uses Socket 5 or 7, Pentium II uses Slot 1, and Pentium III uses Slot 2). However, AMD and Cyrix both offer Pentium-compatible chips that claim performance levels similar to or surpassing Intel's Pentium II. Those companies' processors can generally replace original Pentium processors.

What is "overclocking" all about?

You can *overclock* your CPU by running it at a faster speed than it was intended to perform. This is sometimes called *speed margining,* which sounds a bit more technical, but the bottom line remains the same: You simply need to move the multiplier jumper on the motherboard to give your motherboard the impression your CPU is faster than it really is.

Overclocking works because chips aren't designed to run at exactly a specific speed; instead, there's a performance window in which the chip will work. CPUs are rated to perform safely at a certain speed, though, and overclocking voids the warranty and poses risks to your system. An overclocked chip runs hotter than its design specification, is more likely to crash your applications, and could die prematurely. Peripherals may also act erratically.

Is it worth the risk? Some people enjoy wringing every last percentage of performance out of their hardware, and overclocking certainly does make your PC run faster for free. On the other hand, it can be expensive in terms of lost data from more frequent crashes and premature CPU failure. Since the performance gain probably won't be dramatic, it's more of a game for tech hounds than a real-world upgrade you can sink your teeth into.

If you want to overclock your system, take these precautions:

- *Use additional cooling.* Install a second fan or a larger heat sink to keep the CPU as cool as possible. This is absolutely essential to successful overclocking!

- *Start modestly.* Try overclocking your system as little as possible and work your way up to higher multiplier values if you have good luck at more conservative speed margins.

- *Abandon your overclock experiments if you have frequent hardware or software failures.*

How do I overclock my CPU?

If you've read the previous definition of "overclocking" and you're ready to try, remember that we do advise against it unless you're willing to put up with a little frustration and the potential for real hardware failure. In other words, your CPU may burn out early if you run it faster than it's designed for. If you're still here, do this:

1. Install additional cooling by adding a fan or heat sink.

2. Refer to your motherboard manual to find the bus speed and multiplier jumpers.

3. Try bumping the speed up modestly by changing the bus speed from 66 MHz to 100 MHz, for example. Or increase the multiplier by a half integer, such as from 1.5 to 2.

4. If step three doesn't work, restore your original setting, reboot, and make sure your PC still works. Then shut it down and try the opposite. If you tried increasing the multiplier, increase the bus speed instead.

5. Don't try to clock more than 50 percent faster than the rated speed of the CPU or you'll end up frying it.

6. Try to keep the relationship between the bus and CPU in integer or integer-and-a-half multiples, just like you would when installing a CPU normally.

 What should I do to prepare for a CPU upgrade?

You'll need to do a few things before you're ready for your CPU upgrade:

- Purchase an upgrade processor chip or an Intel Overdrive chip.

- Read the specific instructions in your computer manual regarding jumper settings for different CPUs. (This is not as important for Overdrive chips, only for adding a faster Pentium processor to your existing motherboard.)

- Check for BIOS upgrades from your motherboard manufacturer. Call their tech support line to let them know your plans and ask if there's a BIOS upgrade that's necessary for the upgrade. You might also consult their Web site for information on upgrading.

Is it worth my time to upgrade my system's CPU?

You might be better off replacing the entire motherboard. If your motherboard is older, even doubling the CPU speed may have a marginal—perhaps 20 percent—effect on the overall speed of your system, and you can get a new motherboard and CPU for just a bit more than a new CPU by itself.

 ## Can I upgrade the CPU in my notebook computer?

In most cases, you can't. To conserve space, notebook motherboards are built with soldered CPUs and no special upgrade sockets. In rare cases, a notebook may be upgraded by contacting the original notebook manufacturer and installing a special upgrade card or replacing the motherboard. In most cases, it's an upgrade that needs to be performed by a factory technician.

When should I upgrade the BIOS in my computer?

Whether you're planning an upgrade or not, you may want to look into any BIOS upgrades that your computer manufacturer might offer. The basic input/output system (BIOS) is responsible for a number of low-level interactions in your computer—including getting it to boot successfully.

Often, BIOS upgrades are necessary for your motherboard to accept a new CPU. But a BIOS upgrade can also be updated by the manufacturer to fix problems, offer programming improvements, and add features to your motherboard that the manufacturer didn't get the first time around. For instance, a new BIOS upgrade might improve your computer's ability to support plug-and-play upgrading with Windows 95 or Windows 98.

How do you know if you can upgrade your BIOS? Determine the exact model number or name of your computer and contact the manufacturer. Many of the larger manufacturers offer downloadable BIOS upgrades from the Web, so try the following Web sites:

- **Compaq** http://www.compaq.com/support/index.html
- **Gateway 2000** http://www.gateway.com/home/support/hardware/

- **Dell Computer**   http://www.dell.com/filelib/index.htm
- **Acer America**   http://www.acer.com/aac/support/index.htm
- **Hewlett-Packard**   http://www.hp.com/cposupport/eschome.html
- **IBM**   http://www.pc.ibm.com/support/
- **Micron**   http://www.mei.micron.com/support/support.html
- **MidWest Micro**   http://www.mwmicro.com/support/ftp/
- **NEC**   http://support.neccsdeast.com
- **Packard Bell**   http://support.packardbell.com

Note: *For more on BIOS upgrades, flash BIOS, and other related technologies, see Chapter 4.*

Protecting Your CMOS Settings

The settings that your CMOS retains—like the size of your hard drive and amount of memory in your PC—are so important, particularly in older PCs, that it's worth protecting them from battery failure. Many utility packages like Norton Utilities and Helix Nuts and Bolts can save the CMOS settings to disk. You can easily restore those settings if there's ever a power failure. (Newer computers tend to detect all these things automatically, relying on the CMOS battery for date and time only.)

Sometimes, the low-technology solution works the best. Even if you use a program like Norton, we recommend that you enter your BIOS setup program and write down every setting on a piece of paper. Store it with your PC manual so you can restore the values in a disaster. It goes without saying that you shouldn't record the BIOS values in a word processor or spreadsheet document, unless you immediately print them and store them with your manual.

 How do I pull out and replace the CPU chip without doing any damage?

There are generally two ways to remove a CPU from the motherboard. One is used for socketed CPUs installed on motherboards that don't feature a ZIF socket. To remove the CPU, you'll need a chip-pulling tool and delicate hands. Follow these steps to remove a chip:

1. Get a chip puller for the kind of chip you plan to remove—a CPU and a math coprocessor are different kinds of chips and generally require different tools for removal. Computer stores sell generic chip pullers, but the chip's manufacturer may also sell a puller that is designed for the chip in question, designed to catch the chip's edges in just the right way. Some look like overgrown tweezers, while others pry chips out.

2. Remove the cover of your PC in accordance with the instructions in Chapter 2. Also, unplug the PC and ground yourself.

3. Locate the chip you want to remove and look for any edges or ridges for the chip puller to grip. Get a tight fit around the chip and try pulling it up by working one side out of the socket. Don't pull it straight up—that's too hard, and you'll end up stripping the chip puller, coming dangerously close to breaking something in the process. Keep in mind that it'll take a few minutes to work the chip out of the socket and that it probably wasn't really designed to come out in the first place—so be patient. When you get a little leverage on the chip from one side, switch sides and work on popping it out from the other side as well. If you get any one edge out too far, the chip's pins may start to bend or break from the angle. That's a bad thing, best avoided.

 How do I upgrade my ZIF-socketed CPU?

The actual upgrading process depends heavily on the type of upgrade that will work in your system and which CPU upgrade you purchase. If you have an official Intel Overdrive processor, then you'll want to follow the instructions for that processor and install it in an available Overdrive socket, a 487 math coprocessor socket (if available), or in the slot currently occupied by your older processor.

If you're not using an Overdrive chip, most likely you're installing the new processor in either a special Overdrive socket or you're installing it in the current ZIF socket. If you're using a special Overdrive socket, line the processor up with the socket as instructed in your motherboard manual, then lightly press down on the chip. If it's seated correctly, it should begin to slide uniformly into the slot. Press down the rest of the way until it snaps into place.

Caution: *Usually, Pin 1 is marked with a diagonal cut on the edge of the CPU. Make sure you're inserting this diagonal edge in the correct corner of the socket or the chip will cease to live when power is applied.*

For a ZIF-socketed CPU, you'll need to begin by pulling the original CPU. To do that, pull the small ZIF slot lever away from the socket slightly, then pull it up:

Now, grab the top of the processor between your thumb and forefinger and lift it gently out—it should come out with almost no effort. If there's any resistance, make sure the lever is completely up, perpendicular to the motherboard. If there's still resistance, lower the lever and raise it again. If resistance continues, you should have your motherboard professionally serviced—applying any more force to extract the processor could cause damage to the motherboard and/or CPU.

Now, place the new CPU or Overdrive processor in the socket. Using your motherboard manual as a guide, ensure that you've placed the CPU correctly. Often, the chip will have a mark or indent that guides you to install in a certain direction. Look for that. In all likelihood, Pin 1 is marked with a diagonal-cut corner. (In most cases, the socket will only allow the CPU to be oriented in the correct way—otherwise, some pins will not match up with some holes.)

The processor chip should begin to slide into the socket on its own—you may need to tap it ever so slightly or push it very gently to seat it completely in the socket. Then, push the ZIF level back down into its locked position. If the lever doesn't want to go down, don't force it—you may not have the pins aligned properly. Stop, check the chip orientation, and try again.

I've installed an Overdrive CPU (or a new Pentium-class processor). Do I need to do anything else?

If your upgrade processor is a true Intel Overdrive, then you probably don't need to do anything else—most Overdrive chips are designed to replace specific processors and will work correctly in most any system for which they're certified.

If you've replaced an older chip with a new Pentium-class chip or above, though, you may need to set some jumper settings. You'll probably need to set jumpers for the following:

- **Host bus frequency (external CPU speed)** Sets the clock speed in MHz at which the processor will communicate with the system bus, as well as other parts of the system (most often the PCI and ISA buses).

- **Bus multiplier (internal CPU speed)** Tells the motherboard the speed in MHz of the processor by telling it the ratio of host bus frequency to the processor frequency. For instance, if the bus speed is 60 MHz and the multiplier is 2.5, then the processor frequency is 150 MHz.

● **Processor voltage**   The voltage required by processors can vary slightly, so this jumper will set the voltage to VR or VRE (in most cases). Consult your CPU's documentation to determine which is appropriate for your upgrade.

My computer is a few years old, and lately, every time I turn it off it forgets the settings for the hard drive. Is it dying of old age?

You probably just need a new CMOS battery. All PCs have a CMOS (*Complementary Metal-Oxide Semiconductor*), which is responsible for storing basic settings that the computer needs to power on successfully. To keep those settings current, a small battery supplies power to the CMOS so that the settings can be stored.

After a few years (three or four, usually) the CMOS battery can weaken and go dead. The battery is easily replaced, although you'll need to know what model of battery works best in your computer. (Your user's manual, your manufacturer's Web site, or a knowledgeable retailer should be able to tell you.)

Replacing the battery is simply a matter of fishing the old battery out of its socket, replacing it with the new battery, and re-anchoring it to the motherboard. Figure 3-7 shows a CMOS battery being replaced. After the battery is replaced, you'll need to set the PC's clock and restore the BIOS settings that were lost when the battery was removed.

  Note: Some old motherboards have batteries that are actually soldered down. The theory, apparently, was that the battery would work for as long as the computer's useful life, which was a generally bad assumption. If you have such a PC, contact the manufacturer (assuming that the manufacturer is still in business) to determine the best way to replace the battery—or if it's even possible. In most cases these older batteries can be clipped out, and then wires can be soldered to the leads and attached to an AAA battery holder.

Figure 3-7 The CMOS battery usually resembles a large version of the batteries used in watches and automatic cameras.

UPGRADING YOUR SYSTEM MEMORY

 What exactly is "memory"?

Computer memory, or *random access memory* (RAM), is made up of little chips that store computer data while the computer is in use. For instance, everything that's shown on the screen of your computer is currently stored in RAM, which is more active than other means of storage. It's easy to think of RAM as short-term memory—it's the storage area that a computer uses while it's thinking about a particular task, just like you can keep quite a bit of data "up front" while you think about something important. For longer-term storage, the computer will generally write the data to a hard drive or other

removable storage device, just as you might jot down some notes about something you want to remember later.

It's also important to remember that anything that's in RAM—like a report or e-mail you're currently editing—will be lost instantly if the PC is turned off or the power is interrupted. That's why it's recommended that you save often. The process of saving writes data to the hard drive so it can be retrieved even after the computer has been powered off.

 ### What type of RAM does my computer's motherboard require?

Random access memory (RAM) is the "live" memory that your computer uses to store applications and data that are active and open while the computer is in use. While adding RAM to a computer doesn't actually speed up its processing ability, it can allow the computer to deal with data and applications in a more efficient way. RAM is often the first and easiest upgrade that someone should make to an aging computer.

RAM can come in a few different form factors:

- **DRAM (dynamic RAM)** Individual RAM chips are soldered or mounted on the motherboard. This was common in XT, 286, and some early 386-level computers.

- **SIMM (single inline memory module)** A printed circuit board, or module, where RAM chips are mounted, that plugs into a special socket. Very common in 386, 486, and many Pentium machines.

- **DIMM (dual inline memory module)** Similar to a SIMM, a DIMM generally has more pins and allows for wider addressing (64-bit). Where SIMMs are generally limited to communicating with the system bus 32 bits at a time, DIMMs offer twice that, allowing data to flow more efficiently. DIMMs are common in Pentium Pro, Pentium II, and other modern systems.

Aside from the sizes and shapes of RAM, there are also a few different types that you need to consider when

purchasing upgrade RAM for your computer. Consult your documentation to determine which of these types you need:

- **30-pin SIMMs**   Early SIMMs, especially those designed for 386 and 486 motherboards connected to the motherboard using 30 pins. A 30-pin Fast Page mode RAM is available in parity and nonparity versions.

- **72-pin SIMMs**   These are the type of SIMMs used in Pentium machines. Regular (Fast Page) and EDO varieties exist, although you can't get EDO parity RAM.

- **168-pin DIMMs**   These can come in different flavors, but include the newer SDRAM (*synchronous* DRAM) technology that, while requiring a price premium over EDO and Fast Page, is also somewhat faster with modern processors. Pentium Pro and Pentium II machines tend to require DIMMs, but sometimes leave some room for you to choose SDRAM, EDO, or Fast Page.

So determine which your motherboard will support, then you're ready to decide what your budget can tolerate and what sort of RAM you need.

 ## Which type of RAM should I choose?

There's plenty of argument over which memory type and technology you should go with, and what you hear elsewhere may not agree with what we say. But—here goes anyway:

- *There's not much need for parity*. Unless you're fascinated by memory problems that most modern operating systems work around anyway, opt for the less-expensive nonparity RAM. Modern motherboards tend not to support parity, anyway. (An exception is ECC RAM, which is often supported on Pentium Pro motherboards.)

- *Choose EDO over Fast Page*. Although the two technologies are reasonably interchangeable, choose EDO whenever you can (and read your manual to make sure your PC specifically supports EDO). There is a slight performance benefit.

● *Consider the costs of SDRAM before making that leap.*
If you have the kind of motherboard that can use either
SDRAM or EDO, look carefully at the cost difference. You
may be able to add cache memory or some other component
that will make your computer experience more pleasing,
using the extra money you save by skipping SDRAM.
If you're a speed demon, though, you should really get
SDRAM if your motherboard supports it. (Keep in mind
that most motherboards support only one or the other—so
you may not have much a choice.)

Tip: *Whatever you do, shop your local computer store
before taking our advice. It's certainly possible the prices of
SDRAM have come down considerably by the time you're
reading this.*

What's the relationship between DIMMs, SIMMs, EDO, and SDRAM?

Terms like *EDO, Fast Page memory,* and *SDRAM* refer to the
RAM technology—and hence, the overall performance of the
chip. *SIMMs* and *DIMMs* refer to the type of chip layout and
number of pins the memory uses. A DIMM is simply more
advanced than a SIMM, allowing more chips on a similar
module.

What you need to know first is what sort of RAM module
(SIMMs or DIMMs) your motherboard requires. Then, you
need to know what sort of RAM technology your machine
supports—FPM, EDO, or SDRAM. Once you're clear on these
points, you're ready to buy.

What is PC100 RAM? PC133 RAM?

PC100 RAM is high-speed SDRAM specifically designed
to run at 100 MHz, which is the speed of most late-model
Pentium II computers. PC133 is designed to run at 133 MHz,
the speed of the Pentium III's system bus. In fact, all SDRAM
is designed to run at the same speed as the system bus, but
the PC100 and PC133 names help differentiate the newer

types of SDRAM required for Pentium II and Pentium III motherboards.

Can I mix SIMM and DIMM memory on my motherboard?

Even if your motherboard has both SIMM and DIMM sockets for older EDO memory and newer SDRAM, respectively, you generally can't install a little of each. Most motherboards require that you use one or the other, so decide whether you want to use the more expensive and somewhat faster SDRAM before you go shopping.

I need 30-pin memory. Does it matter how many chips are on the memory module?

Yes and no. Most computers don't care how many chips are on the module—they just want to see 30 pins. In that case, you can just buy three-chip memory because it's cheaper. If your PC reports memory problems—they're very rare—you'll need to replace them or trade them in for eight-chip or nine-chip variations.

Should I add more than one RAM module at a time?

What you need to do is fill a memory bank. Most motherboards have at least two memory banks (0 and 1), and each bank can have one or more SIMM sockets. In older (386 and 486) systems, it was generally necessary to add SIMMs either in pairs or, occasionally, in groups of four. In later systems, it became more typically possible to add just one SIMM at a time, but you'd still need to add them in pairs to take advantage of memory interleaving, which speeds things up a bit. DIMMs can always be added one at a time in Pentium and Pentium II systems. PC100 and PC133 RAM can also be added one at a time.

So, in general, you need to

- Fill an entire bank of memory.
- Use the same size SIMM or DIMM (in MB) in each slot of a bank.

How fast does the memory in my system need to be?

Your PC manual should tell you what the minimum speed rating (in nanoseconds) your memory needs to be. If your motherboard requires 70-ns memory, for instance, you can use any memory that's rated for 70 ns or less. You won't improve the performance of your system by purchasing dramatically faster memory, however, because the bottleneck is the motherboard—faster RAM won't accomplish anything except to wait longer for something to do.

With newer SDRAM, though, the nanosecond speed becomes less important than matching up the system bus speeds with the type of SDRAM, PC100 or PC133 modules you need to buy.

Caution: *In most any PC, you need to install the same speed RAM in each memory bank to avoid problems, some of which can be difficult to troubleshoot. Many manufacturers go so far as to recommend the same speed RAM for every memory module in your computer.*

Walkthrough:
Upgrading the RAM in a Computer

Upgrading RAM in your computer is generally one of the easiest upgrades to accomplish. All it takes is a little careful positioning to add a SIMM or DIMM to your computer's motherboard:

1. To begin, make very sure that you're electrically grounded and that you've discharged any static electricity built up in your body. Static electricity can easily ruin RAM modules. Also, ensure that your workspace inside the computer case is free from obstructions and that you can get to the RAM sockets easily.

2. Take one of the RAM modules and—by comparing it to the others already installed, your documentation, or by loosely placing it in the socket—ensure that it's positioned correctly. In most cases, there are notches that force the module to fit in only one orientation.

3. Slide the module into the socket at about a 45-degree angle. It should slide into the socket easily—apply only a small amount of force. A properly inserted module looks like this:

(The 45-degree rule is true for most RAM sockets. Check your motherboard documentation to make sure this is true for your board.)

4. Now, roll the module back by pushing on the top of the module until it reaches about a 90-degree angle. It should lock into place, usually held by clips at the edges of the modules.

That's really all there is to it. To remove a module, you'll often need to spread the plastic or metal locking mechanism a bit with two fingers, then push on the back of the module until it's back to a 45-degree angle, then pull it out of the socket.

How can I tell whether all my memory is installed correctly?

The fastest way to know is to boot your computer and watch the startup memory test. (If your computer doesn't even get that far, then the RAM module is probably not seated correctly in its socket.) If you have an old version of Windows, you can also run MSD.EXE (Microsoft Diagnostics) in the DOS or Windows directory on your computer. (You need to be in DOS for the program to work correctly.) Unfortunately, MSD isn't included in Windows 95, 98, or 2000. In these versions of Windows, right-click My Computer, choose Properties, and click the General tab. You should see a list of all the RAM installed on your machine.

What do I do if some of my installed RAM doesn't appear in the startup test?

If it doesn't seem like you have all the RAM you expect to have, you could have one of four problems.

- *The RAM isn't installed correctly*. Test to make sure it fits exactly right, that it's flush and level in the socket, and that it isn't backward or installed in a bank that requires additional RAM modules. Also, make sure that you've installed identical modules (in terms of size and type of technology) in each bank.

- *A RAM module is bad*. If you've decided a RAM module might be bad, take it to a computer repair shop to have it tested. If a RAM module really is bad (and that's rare) you can sometimes get different results from the startup memory test just by changing the order of memory modules inside the computer!

- *Your BIOS or motherboard doesn't support as much RAM as you're trying to install*. Double-check your motherboard documentation to ensure that your motherboard can accept the amount of memory you're trying to install. Consult your PC manufacturer to see if there's a BIOS upgrade available.

- *Your motherboard doesn't support a mix of chip sizes.*
  The occasional motherboard will come along that will
  only allow you to install modules that are the same size
  in MB. Consult your manual and the manufacturer to
  see if you *must* install modules that are all identical.

How can I troubleshoot my RAM problem?

If you think you have defective memory after installing it in a
PC, there a re a few things to look for. Suppose you install a
128MB SDRAM DIMM. If only 64MB is reported at startup,
the chip was almost certainly mismarked at the store, and
you need to return it. If, on the other hand, you installed two
DIMMs and only half the memory is reported, the first thing
you should do is test the memory by booting your PC with
only one DIMM installed at a time. That should help isolate
which of the DIMMs is, in fact, defective. You can also
install both memory chips and reverse their positions on
the motherboard to see how they behave. You should be able
to figure out which is the defective chip and return that one
to the store.

I've added memory to my PC, but DOS still claims I have only about 550K of memory to run my programs! What's wrong?

Sad, but true. You're confusing the total RAM in your PC
with the way DOS divides the first megabyte of RAM. Only
a maximum of 640K of RAM is ever available in MS-DOS to
run executable programs—the rest is for storing data and
holding parts of programs that are rapidly moved in and out
of that first 640K of RAM as the program runs. Adding 16,
32, and even 64MB of RAM can improve your system
performance—especially in Windows—but it'll never change
the fact that only 640K of RAM is available in DOS to operate
your software. To get the most out of that RAM, try typing
memmaker at the DOS prompt. You might also try
installing a third-party RAM manager, such as QEMM.

 ## How do I know whether my system can use cache RAM?

Cache memory is a small quantity of high-speed RAM that's used to store frequently accessed data and problem bits so the CPU can get to it more quickly than with conventional RAM. Most computers see a reasonable increase in processing speed after adding cache memory. Pentium and higher machines tend to use cache RAM, but you'll need to consult your motherboard's documentation to ensure that the motherboard will accept a cache module. (Some cache memory is hardwired into the motherboard and can't be expanded or removed.)

 ## Aren't there different types of cache memory?

Yes. Cache memory actually comes in two types: Level 1 and Level 2. Level 1 cache is usually built into the processor itself, and is generally very small (sometimes only 4 or 8 kilobytes) and very fast.

Level 2 cache is generally located in a special cache SIMM on the motherboard, and generally ranges from 128K to 1MB or more. On many PC motherboards, the cache RAM is hardwired in, so it can't be added to or changed. Some motherboards feature the cache RAM on a SIMM, however, allowing you to upgrade it.

 Tip: *Ever heard of Level 3 cache? In some cases, a processor is designed with a built-in (Level 1) cache, then given an additional built-in (Level 2) cache—this is actually common on new PowerPC (IBM and Motorola) processor designs. The cache memory on the motherboard, then, becomes the Level 3 cache.*

My PC seems okay, particularly when I work from DOS, but it's recently started running extremely slowly in Windows. What's happening?

It's possible that something has happened to your cache RAM. You can test it by disabling the cache in the BIOS setup and restarting Windows. If Windows runs faster, you'll need to replace the cache—or, if it's not replaceable, get a new motherboard.

Walkthrough:
Adding Cache RAM to a Computer

Adding a cache RAM SIMM is about as easy as adding a regular SIMM. The only major difference is the fact that you'll need a special cache SIMM designed at the speed and specifications required by your motherboard.

After you have an appropriate cache SIMM:

1. Locate the cache SIMM socket on the motherboard.

2. Place the SIMM carefully in the socket, making sure that you have the SIMM facing the correct way. (Often, little notches will show you how the SIMM should eventually fit in the socket.) Place the SIMM in the socket at about a 45-degree angle, as shown here:

(Cache SIMMs sometimes install at a 90-degree angle. Check your manual to be sure.)

3. Slowly tilt the SIMM up until it reaches a 90-degree angle to the motherboard. If all goes well, it should snap into place and be locked in by the SIMM socket's plastic housing.

After everything is installed, start your computer. On the screen that shows your processor type, memory, serial ports, and so on, you'll likely see a report of your cache RAM, usually just above the "Starting Windows" or "Starting DOS" statement.

> **!** ***Caution:***   *Cache RAM, just like regular RAM, should fit easily—don't force it! If you're having trouble getting the RAM to seat in its slot, make sure that you're inserting it completely into the slot and that you have the SIMM facing the correct direction. Consult your motherboard's specification to ensure that you've purchased the correct SIMM.*

Chapter 4

Interface Issues

Interface Issues @ a Glance

You've probably heard the term *plug-and-play* more than a few times, and perhaps you're still wondering exactly what it means. Plug-and-play technology allows your *expansion cards*—the cards you plug into your computer's motherboard to get increased capabilities or performance—to work together more easily with your PC's motherboard. In fact, plug-and-play technology can even work with parallel ports and other PC ports to automate the configuration process. For years, PC users have self-configured their cards using tough-to-reach DIP switches and propeller-head driver software to get things working right. Some of that has changed.

Should you upgrade the BIOS in your computer? In the last few years, new BIOS technologies have begun making it easier to upgrade, and people have been asking this question. If you're adding a hard drive or certain types of upgrade cards, or if you simply want to play with your PC's settings, you'll want to dig a bit deeper into the BIOS.

When you buy a new expansion card, you need to know a bit about your system to get the most out of the card. For example: What system bus is your motherboard using? Do you need a plug-and-play card? What do you do in Windows after the card is installed? We'll also walk through the installation of common cards and cover what you can do if you run into trouble.

Want to simply plug your peripheral into the back of your PC? Well, the newer your machine, the more ports you probably have. You'll want to pick the right one—not just so the cable will fit, but so you'll see the best performance as well.

If you delve deeper into expanding and upgrading your PC, you'll run into an interesting phenomenon—the system *interrupt*. Interrupts, or *interrupt requests* (IRQs), are used by devices to communicate with the CPU. Whenever a device—a modem, for instance—has new data to bring to the attention of the CPU, it signals the CPU, which then checks the priority of the request and, if necessary, interrupts what it's doing to work with the device. The problem is, if something gets configured wrong and two devices use the same IRQ, the CPU can accidentally use data from one device, thinking it's the other device. Best case scenario: One of the devices doesn't work. Worst case: You have a crashed computer and you lose your data.

Finally, you have some new ports to play with on modern PCs— the USB ports. These ports offer unprecedented speed and flexibility, including the ability to support up to 127 devices on a single PC. There are some unique issues associated with them, however, an upgrade to Windows 98 tends to solve the bulk of them.

PLUG-AND-PLAY TECHNOLOGY

 ### What is the system bus, and what does it do?

The *system bus* can be described as the path data takes when it's traveling between peripherals and the processor on your motherboard. The system bus supports the ports, the processor, the RAM, and other parts of the computer. When data is input from a sound card, for example, it travels over the system bus to the RAM, and then to the CPU of your computer for processing.

The type of system bus on which your PC's motherboard is based also dictates the most advanced type of expansion card your computer can accept. A PCI system bus, then, is designed to work with PCI-based expansion cards. (The motherboards can also be backward compatible with older expansion cards, so it might support ISA cards as well.) If your computer has a much older ISA bus, then it can only accept ISA expansion cards.

Finally, the type of bus your system uses and the age of your motherboard dictate the number and type of steps it takes to add expansion cards to your system. If you're lucky, your computer is relatively new and based on a PCI expansion bus featuring plug-and-play technology. If not, you're in for some fun experimentation.

I see "plug-and-play" splashed all over just about every box in the computer store. What does it mean?

It's safe to say that there are two separate meanings for the term *plug-and-play*. For most folks, it refers to a PCI-based PC's relatively newfound ability to configure expansion cards automatically, making it unnecessary to adjust the software drivers and hardware DIP switches manually when installing expansion cards. Often when you hear "plug-and-play," this is what people are referring to. When you buy a PCI card, there's a good chance that it will simply configure itself automatically when you plug it into your motherboard.

PCI and Host Buses

For PCI-based motherboards, the previous description isn't perfectly accurate, because the processor does not sit on the PCI system bus. Instead, the processor and RAM generally sit on a "host" bus, which can run at high speed and usually with a 64-bit or wider data path, allowing instructions and data to flow very quickly between RAM and the processor. Data is then handed off to the PCI bus, which is responsible for redirecting it to any PCI expansion cards or devices. If necessary, the data is then routed to the ISA bus (a third, separate bus) or a controller that's responsible for storage activity, such as an IDE or SCSI bus.

To true gear heads, though, plug-and-play refers to older technologies—such as ISA-based expansion cards and parallel ports—that have this added ability to auto-configure. By definition, any PCI-based expansion card should auto-configure, and, while the result feels like you're plugging and playing, the actual technology and process being used is not referred to as "plug-and-play." In order to bring PCI-like ease of upgrading to older interfaces, Intel and Microsoft developed the plug-and-play standards.

How does plug-and-play work?

The plug-and-play system is more than something physical on the motherboard—to auto-configure ISA cards, the motherboard, BIOS, and Windows (version 95 or later) must work together to configure the cards.

Every expansion card (and similar device or port) needs a digital address that the computer can use for sending and receiving data. Plug-and-play ISA cards begin without a set address. As the computer boots, the BIOS sets up the basics—video, keyboard, and the boot storage device—and gets Windows 95 (or later) up and running.

Then, Windows takes over. The expansion cards are surveyed by the system and asked what their requirements are. The system also checks for any non-plug-and-play cards that might have fixed addresses. Finally, the system passes out addresses for all the plug-and-play cards automatically, making life a bit easier for you.

Do I need special stuff to get plug-and play to work on my system?

Yes. For plug-and-play ISA expansion cards to work, you need the following:

● A PC with a BIOS that recognizes plug-and-play technology

● Windows 95 or a later release (e.g., an operating system that supports plug-and-play technology)

With these installed you'll find it fairly simple to install the card. (See the Walkthrough box, "Installing a PCI Expansion Card," later in this chapter.)

Plug-and-play sounds great, but what if I only want to install PCI expansion cards?

If you have empty PCI expansion slots, then installing a PCI card is a good idea. PCI cards configure themselves automatically (with operating systems that support PCI devices) and tend to be faster than even plug-and-play ISA cards. With that said, remember that you have a limited number of PCI slots; they should be used, when possible, for cards that require a high-speed interface.

Note: *Certain cards, even though they're PCI-based, still require some additional installation steps. Consult the related chapters in this book for more information on specific types of upgrades, such as video (Chapter 6), sound (Chapter 7), networking (Chapter 9), and modems (Chapter 11).*

THE BIOS

What exactly does the BIOS do?

BIOS stands for *basic input/output system.* It's a collection of programs that perform the very low-level operating instructions responsible for getting your computer booted up and started on its way to loading Windows or a similar operating system. It's also responsible for most of the basic input/output functions of the motherboard like reading the keyboard, communicating with the serial and parallel ports and so on. A BIOS chip may also be present on an expansion card to add the card's unique input/output personality to the system BIOS. For instance, many video cards include their own BIOS information that helps them control the video monitor.

The BIOS is a read-only memory (ROM) or flash memory chip. Data for BIOS settings are kept in a very small portion of RAM that requires a battery on the motherboard to ensure long-term storage.

Walkthrough:
Installing a PCI Expansion Card

Installing a PCI expansion card is as simple as card expansion has ever been with Intel-based PCs. In almost every case, you don't have to set any small DIP switches or jumpers; these cards plug right in, and work with Windows and similar operating systems. Here's the drill:

1. Shut down your PC and ground yourself electrically.

2. Open the case on your computer and locate an empty PCI slot.

3. Remove the screw and metal dust plate that covers the hole in the case for that PCI slot.

4. Position the card so that its interface is directly over the PCI slot.

5. Press down lightly and uniformly on the top of the PCI card until it's completely plugged into the slot:

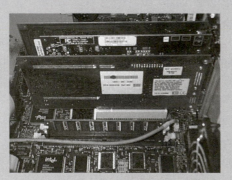

   Be sure that the card is fully seated. If it sticks up a little at either end, some of the leads on the card may not be making proper contact, and the card will fail to work.

6. To test the card, turn on the computer and start Windows. If installation is successful, a screen in Windows 95 or later will tell you that Windows has detected the new device. Follow the onscreen instructions to choose a Windows driver or to install the new software drivers that shipped with the card.

   If all goes well, the card should be installed and working with no trouble. Shut down the computer and reinstall the case as normal.

 ## What's the difference between EPROM and EEPROM?

Erasable programmable read-only memory (EPROM) represents an older style of ROM used to store BIOS settings in 486-and-earlier PCs. EPROM memory can be wiped out and restored, but it's a process generally reserved for qualified computer technicians because erasing it requires exposing the EPROM to a bright UV lamp for a period of time. And to reprogram the EPROM, it is necessary to write the data with pulsed, high-voltage data signals.

Electrically erasable programmable read-only memory (EEPROM) is similar to EPROM, but it can be erased by giving it a simple command. EEPROM is the precursor to flash memory. It can be written to and erased a number of times using high-voltage signals. Flash memory is a highly refined version of the older EEPROMs.

What is flash BIOS?

Flash BIOS is a type of BIOS that features an EEPROM— or flash memory—chip that you can upgrade simply by downloading a data file into your PC, often from the vendor's Web site or BBS. (You then have to install the upgrade, as described in the next question.) A PC equipped with a BIOS that uses flash ROM can be easily upgraded, because the instructions stored in that ROM can be rewritten. Instructions written in an older-style EPROM chip cannot be overwritten easily. (Check your manual to see if your BIOS features EEPROM flash memory.)

How do I upgrade a flash memory BIOS?

If you want to upgrade your BIOS, you should first make sure the motherboard is ready to accept the upgrade. Often, a DIP switch or jumper disables the flash capability until you need it. (This prevents the BIOS from being corrupted by stray data.) Move the switch in accordance with the computer's instruction manual. Remember to disable the flash capability when you're done.

You'll then either reboot using a system floppy and run a flash upgrade utility program, or you'll insert a floppy with the flash upgrade file on it and use a special keystroke sequence to set the update in motion. While different manufacturers may recommend a slightly different process for upgrading a flash ROM BIOS, here's one way it's done:

1. Download the BIOS upgrade file. You'll usually find it on the motherboard or BIOS manufacturer's Web site.

2. Create a bootable floppy diskette from DOS. Typing the command **format a:/s** creates a system diskette.

3. Copy the BIOS upgrade files (you may have both a file and an upgrade utility) to the diskette.

4. Place the upgrade diskette in drive A and reboot the computer.

5. At the A: prompt, begin the upgrade utility, telling it which file to use, as in, **flashprg newbios.bin**. (This command is a fictitious example; your utility will have a different name and a different upgrade BIOS file associated with it.)

6. The program may prompt you to write the old BIOS to a file. This is a good idea. If you have trouble with the upgrade, you can use the same bootable floppy to reinstall the old BIOS.

7. Otherwise, the program will guide you through the update, then it will reset the system (or tell you to) so you can use the new BIOS.

Again, be sure you read your manual and any instructions your motherboard and/or BIOS manufacturer have written on the subject of upgrading a flash memory BIOS. Each can have a slightly different routine.

Can I modify the BIOS settings on my PC?

The BIOS can be modified every time you start your PC. When the computer begins its boot sequence, you'll typically see a message that says something like, "Press F1 for setup." The correct key is often F1, ESC, or DEL. This will take you to

Upgrading an EPROM chip

The easily erased BIOS memory chip (EEPROM) requires only a special software update program that you place on a floppy disk. Boot the PC, and the BIOS is updated (this process is described in the answer to "How do I upgrade a flash memory BIOS?" earlier in this chapter). With older-style EPROM, however, it's tougher.

EPROM can be deleted and reprogrammed, however. First, you remove the EPROM chip. Then, you expose it to intense ultraviolet light through a window in the chip. After everything is erased, a special device is used to reprogram the EPROM.

As you can see, it's a process usually reserved for specially equipped labs. In many cases, upgrading the EPROM in an older machine is a matter of swapping the old chip for a new EPROM chip. This, too, usually takes place in a repair center.

the BIOS setup program, where you can change many settings, including the following:

- The number and size of your hard disks
- The power management settings, such as if or when the hard drive stops spinning to save electricity
- The status of your I/O ports
- Password protection at startup

When it comes to the settings for your drives, for example, or the addresses assigned to your devices, you really shouldn't experiment too much; however, you *can* safely enter your BIOS setup without hurting anything. Simply look for the instructions that tell you how to exit without saving any changes. It's hard to screw up your computer too badly by playing with the On/Off settings in a typical BIOS. And while you're not likely to speed up your computer significantly (especially if it came from a reputable manufacturer who preconfigured the BIOS for optimum performance), you might have a bit of fun trying.

The only real caveat: While the BIOS will likely revert to factory settings on request (see the next answer), you should keep a written record of everything you change, just in case something does improve (or compromise) your system's performance.

A few final points of advice:

- Try to limit yourself to one setting adjustment at a time. This way you can easily observe the exact effects of each change you make. And remember, if you make any accidental changes, you can always exit without saving them and try again later.

- Consider leaving the memory test on at all times.

- Activate password protection only if you think you really need it—and *only* if you are absolutely certain that you won't forget the password.

- Make sure to write down your hard drive settings and keep them in a safe place.

- If you plan on tweaking your BIOS settings heavily or frequently, consider using a system utility, such as Norton Utilities, to save the initial settings to a diskette. This will make it easy to restore them if there's a serious problem.

 ## How do I restore the factory settings for my BIOS?

Restoring factory settings is usually an option on the main screen of your BIOS. After pressing the appropriate key sequence for displaying the BIOS configuration screen, you'll see options such as:

Change Settings

Save Settings and Exit

Don't Save Settings and Exit

Restore Original Settings

The last option, Restore Original Settings (often called Restore Factory Settings), should return your BIOS to its original, manufacturer-determined settings.

 ## Won't I need to change the BIOS settings if I add a hard disk or memory?

Sometimes you will, depending on the age of your system. If your PC is a 486 or higher, the BIOS will probably detect changes to hard disk and memory status by itself. If your PC is much older than that, you may need to enter the BIOS setup screens and make those changes manually. In the case of new memory, you'll often have to start the setup program so it can verify the new total memory. Then save the new settings and restart your PC.

 ## How do I know what kind of BIOS I have?

The easiest way to determine your BIOS is to watch your PC boot. It will display the name and version number of the BIOS after the memory test. You can also check the instruction manual or—if you feel adventurous—open the case and look on the motherboard. Or, of course, you can call the manufacturer and ask.

Tip: *Don't be thrown by other BIOS chips, such as the ones you might find on your video card. Keep your eyes on the motherboard—that's where your system's main BIOS resides!*

 ## My computer keeps beeping at me when I try to boot up. What's it all mean?

The BIOS is designed, among other things, to beep when it encounters unrecoverable errors that prevent the PC from booting. If you count the beeps, you can learn the actual status of your PC. Common error codes are listed in Chapter 13.

EXPANSION CARDS

 ## What's an expansion card?

An *expansion card* is a computer circuit board designed to increase or enhance a computer's ability to deal with input and output. These cards are generally added inside the case of the machine, by plugging them into special slots on the motherboard or on a "riser" card that acts as a go-between for

the motherboard and expansion cards, depending on the way your computer's case is designed.

 ## What do expansion cards do?

Expansion cards tend to run the gamut of input/output tasks in computing. In general, they fall into four major categories:

- **Computer video**   VGA, super VGA, Windows accelerator, 2-D graphics accelerators, and 3-D graphics accelerators are all types of computer video expansion cards.

- **Multimedia**   Popular upgrades include digital video cards (for connecting to video camcorders), TV tuner cards, audio cards, surround sound audio add-ons, and MIDI music interfaces.

- **Interfaces**   These cards are generally designed to interact with other I/O and storage devices, such as SCSI or IDE expansion cards, CD-ROM interface cards, serial/parallel cards, and proprietary scanner cards.

- **Communications**   Cards also exist for getting your PC to communicate with the outside world, including modems, network interface cards, and ISDN adapters.

What type of expansion card should I buy?

By "type" we refer to the different types of expansion buses for which cards can be purchased. If you buy an ISA-based expansion card, for example, then you need an available ISA slot, even if your motherboard is based on PCI technology. So deciding which one to buy depends on several factors:

- What types of cards does your motherboard support? It sounds like an obvious question, but many folks get to the computer store only to discover that their favorite expansion card comes in a couple of different interface types—and uninformed shoppers may not know which cards are best suited for their PCs.

- What slots do you have available on your motherboard? If all your PCI slots are taken, then you'll probably want an ISA card, unless you plan to replace an existing PCI card. Obviously, the reverse might also be true.

- Does the card beg for a high-speed interface? The latest video, accelerator, multimedia, and Ethernet network cards all tend to enjoy being plugged into a higher-end PCI expansion slot. But some cards, such as modems, I/O cards, and scanner interfaces, don't need such a zippy slot. In that case, it's perfectly reasonable to buy and install an ISA-type card.

- If the card comes in both ISA and PCI varieties and you have both slots available, opt for the PCI version. Odds are good that it will install more easily and perform better. (Consider, though, whether you might want that slot for something else later.)

- Is the specific card you're buying compatible with your system? While you're shopping, it's a good idea to visit the manufacturer's Web site and check their customer service pages for any mention of incompatibilities that have been reported about their product. If you already have something in your system that will cause the new card trouble, it's best to steer clear of that particular upgrade. (You might also consult your PC manufacturer's documentation and Web site for similar incompatibility reports.)

Note: *You may have reason to consider buying a VL-bus card for your aging system. Although they're getting tougher to find, the decision to buy a VL-bus card ultimately depends on how long you will be keeping your motherboard. If you upgrade to a new motherboard or new computer, your VL-bus card will most likely be useless. So unless you plan to keep the system for a few more years, stick to ISA or PCI.*

I have a new plug-and-play ISA card. How will installing it be different from installing a PCI card?

The two cards work the same way when it comes to installing with Windows: just fire up the computer and let Windows 95 (or later) recognize the card.

Windows doesn't auto-detect some ISA cards. This doesn't mean that the card won't work; it's just a fact of life for ISA cards. Install the software drivers that came with the card, then you will probably have to reboot the PC. If the card doesn't work properly after that, you can begin to troubleshoot. Often the card's instructions will indicate if it expects Windows to recognize the card at startup.

Windows doesn't recognize the card I just installed. What should I do?

Your card, your BIOS, or both may not be plug-and-play—or another card in your system may not be playing fairly with your new installation. In either case, try these troubleshooting maneuvers:

- Read the card's documentation and follow any instructions for troubleshooting the expansion card.

- Run any driver installation software that came with the card. Insert the diskette or CD in the appropriate drive, and look for a program called setup.exe or install.exe. Run that program. After the appropriate drivers are installed and any self-tests have been successfully initiated, you can reboot your machine to see if Windows recognizes the device.

- If it starts and Windows still doesn't mention the card (in a dialog box, for example), right-click My Computer and choose Properties. Click the Device Manager tab, then click the plus sign next to the type of device you've installed to see if the device and its associated drivers are listed. If there is a problem with your device, the entry will be identified by a yellow warning sign (and you won't have to click on the plus sign, because the category will already be "exploded" to expose the offending device). Select the device and click Properties. You can click on the Resources tab and change settings, such as interrupts, to see if that will fix the card. To change resources, first remove the check mark from Use Automatic Settings; then select alternative settings and restart the system.

Note: *Sometimes a new card won't be recognized at all, even in the Device Manager. In this case, your best bet is to install the appropriate drivers included on the diskettes or CD-ROM that came with your new device.*

- If you're still having trouble, check for new Windows drivers or flash BIOS upgrades on the manufacturer's Web site or contact their customer support line. Many different types of expansion cards have BIOSs, just like computers do, and these can sometimes require bug fixes or improved code to work with certain computers. Also check the manufacturer's Web site or other technical support references for any incompatibilities the card may have with other devices in your system.

- Now, if things still aren't working, try the card in a different slot, especially if it's a PCI card. While any type of interface slot can be nonfunctional, PCI slots can be exceptionally finicky, because some slots can be designated as "bus masters" and some PCI cards can require that they be placed in such slots.

- Next, try physically removing any other cards you have in the system, starting with the oldest cards. (You may not be able to use the computer in this state, but it can potentially give you an indication of whether or not your new card is faulty.) Obviously, some cards will need to be left in place: You'll need an I/O interface for your hard drive and floppies (usually built into the motherboard, but sometimes on an expansion card), and you'll need a video card to boot the computer. Otherwise, modem cards, Ethernet cards, 3-D accelerators, and similar devices can be temporarily removed for testing. If your new card begins to work, try to isolate the older card with which the new card has a conflict. Do that by reinstalling each older card, one at a time, then testing the configuration to ensure that everything is working. If you install an older card, then notice that the new card stops working, you know that particular older card needs to be looked at more closely. There's a good chance it has been told to use certain settings (for example, IRQ or DMA settings) that the new card is also trying to use. Consult the manual for both cards and attempt to change one or the other to resolve the conflict.

+ *Tip:*   *In Windows 95 or later, you can easily find out what resources your PC is using. Windows is immensely helpful when it comes to troubleshooting conflicts with expansion cards. Right-click on My Computer and choose Properties. Then choose the Device Manager tab and double-click on Computer, the top entry. You can view IRQ, DMA, and memory address settings.*

● With all this information gathered, you can call the company's customer support line (or consult their Web site) if you still can't seem to identify the problem on your own. They can at least tell you if your specific problem has been reported in the past and if it seems to be a faulty card, a conflict, or a software problem that can be solved. If worse comes to worst, return the card to the store for an exchange or refund.

PORTS

 ### What are the different ports for?

On the back of most computers, you'll find a number of different ports for hooking up various external peripheral devices. Although the interfaces for these ports don't necessarily have to be on the motherboard itself, in many cases they are. In other cases, they're on expansion cards, even though these ports are standard for nearly every single Intel-based PC. Figure 4-1 shows these ports in detail.

Although some of these ports have specific tasks, others can accept a wide range of devices:

● **Serial ports**   Used for connecting external modems, older-style pointing devices, wireless mice, IRDA ports, PDA docking ports, and some multimedia devices.

● **Parallel ports**   Used to connect printers, external storage devices, digital cameras, and some scanners.

● **Video port**   Used to connect a standard VGA-capable monitor to the computer; can also be used for video-out devices and television converter/encoder boxes (for displaying computer video on a TV screen).

● **Keyboard port**   Used to connect a PS/2-style keyboard.

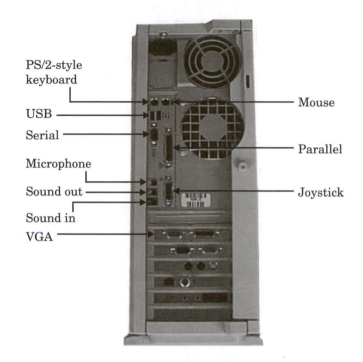

PS/2-style
keyboard

USB

Serial

Microphone

Sound out

Sound in

VGA

Mouse

Parallel

Joystick

Figure 4-1 The most common ports on your PC

❋ ***Note:*** *Older PCs include a large, round, connector with five big pins for an AT-style keyboard.*

- **Joystick port** Used for connecting joysticks, game controllers, and MIDI devices.

- **Mouse port** Used for connecting a PS/2-style mouse.

- **Sound in** Used for connecting line-level audio sources (like an external CD player).

- **Sound out** Used for connecting to an amplifier or some powered PC speakers.

- **Microphone** Used for connecting a recording microphone (or similar device).

- **USB ports** Used for connecting high-speed, next-generation Universal Serial Bus devices.

● **IEEE 1394**   Like USB, used for connecting high-speed, next-generation devices such as DV camcorders. This type of port is also known as *FireWire*. (FireWire and USB devices are not compatible, and FireWire is much faster than USB.)

How do I tell which are the serial ports and which are the parallel ports just by looking at them?

Serial ports come in two sizes: There are 9-pin ports (with 5 pins stacked on top of 4 pins) and 25-pin ports (with 13 pins stacked on top of 12 pins). The 9-pin ports are far more common these days, if only because the 25 pins are unnecessary for most serial devices, while the 9-pin ports are cheaper to make. So if it's 9-pin, it's definitely serial.

Parallel ports are also 25-pin ports, which can make them more difficult to identify. Just remember that parallel ports have female pin slots, meaning there are only holes, not pins sticking out. Serial ports are all male ports, with the pins sticking out of the actual port on the computer (see Figure 4-2).

What do "COM" and "LPT" mean?

COM is short for *communication,* and it's simply another way to refer to a serial port. COM ports and serial ports are one and the same. LPT stands for *line printer.* An LPT port is the same as a parallel port.

In fact, both COM and LPT are naming conventions for their respective ports. So, COM1 refers to one of your serial ports; COM2 is another one. LPT1 refers to your parallel port; if you installed a second parallel port, it would be LPT2.

Note: *Your system can have more than two COM ports; the rest are virtual COM ports that are generally accessed by peripherals in internal expansion slots. It's also possible, but problematic, to install a third or fourth physical COM port.*

What's the difference between a serial port and a parallel port?

Aside from the obvious visual differences, serial ports transfer data one *bit* at a time, while parallel ports transfer

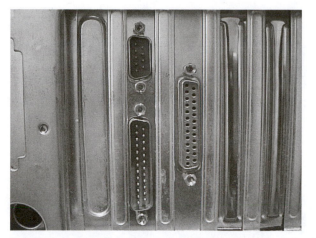

Figure 4-2   Parallel and serial ports are similar, but easy to differentiate.

entire *words* at a time. Also, some parallel ports are bidirectional, allowing information to flow in two directions at once between the computer and the peripheral device. Serial ports are therefore slower. If you have a choice—such as with a printer or a Direct Cable Connection for Windows networking—choose the parallel option. You'll get significantly better performance.

 What in the world are"EPP" and "ECP"?

EPP and ECP are both aspects of the newer IEEE 1284 standard for parallel ports. This standard was created to improve the speed of parallel ports (which are a popular option for hooking up a variety of external peripherals) while increasing the plug-and-play capabilities of the parallel port. These parallel ports all feature new technology that makes them faster and bidirectional, allowing devices to communicate error codes and other information back to the PC. Bidirectional capabilities also make it possible to hook up external, removable drives (like Jaz and Zip drives) using the parallel port.

Enhanced parallel port (EPP) technology is generally used for non-printer peripherals such as CD-ROM drives and removable media drives, allowing them to communicate with the computer at around ten times the speed of a traditional port.

Walkthrough: Connecting a Peripheral Device to an Expansion Port

External peripherals are usually incredibly easy to connect, which is one reason they're popular. Generally, they require few tools and there's no need to open your PC's case. For example, you follow these steps to install an external modem:

- Shut down your operating system, and turn the computer off.
- Locate an empty serial port.
- Using the serial cable that's connected to the modem, align and orient the connector on the cable with the available serial port. Plug the cable's connector into the port.
- Locate the thumbscrews on either side of the cable's connector:

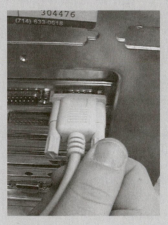

Screw these in a clockwise direction to tighten and secure the connector. It isn't necessary for these screws to be terribly tight, but the connection between the cable and the port should be secure and complete.

The procedure is basically the same for connecting a parallel device. The only minor difference is that many parallel cables use special tensioners to connect to the printer. (You still use thumbscrews for the parallel port itself.) To secure these tensioners, squeeze them toward the connector, then release them after they've cleared the metal guards on either side of the printer's interface port.

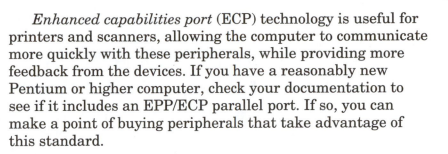

Enhanced capabilities port (ECP) technology is useful for printers and scanners, allowing the computer to communicate more quickly with these peripherals, while providing more feedback from the devices. If you have a reasonably new Pentium or higher computer, check your documentation to see if it includes an EPP/ECP parallel port. If so, you can make a point of buying peripherals that take advantage of this standard.

Can I safely assume that all serial cables are interchangeable?

Most are. In the old days, there was no rigid standard, and you might have a different serial cable for every device attached to your PC. These days, however, all serial cables are the same except for *null modem* cables (also called LapLink cables), which swap pin positions, enabling you to directly connect two PCs for data sharing.

What's the longest serial cable I can buy?

Serial cables can be as long as 200 feet, making them a good choice for temporarily connecting two computers in different rooms, for instance.

What's the longest parallel cable I can buy?

The parallel port operates much faster than the serial port, but unfortunately it doesn't work when the cable connecting it to its destination is more than 25 feet long. (Some peripherals are rated for no more than 15 feet, so consider the length of your parallel cable if you're having trouble with a peripheral.) And shorter is always better—use the shortest parallel cable that will work for your needs.

Yikes! I've got a serial cable that won't fit my only available serial port. What to do?

Get an adapter. Because serial ports only have 9 active pins, the 25-pin variety can be easily adapted to the 9-pin variety (and, vice versa, although it's more rare). Drop into your local computer store and get a 25-pin-to-9-pin adapter. They tend

to be inexpensive. You might even already have an adapter from another product you've bought, like a modem or mouse. They're 100 percent interchangeable.

How do I set the COM and LPT numbers?

Sometimes an I/O expansion card or motherboard offers jumpers that allow you to determine which serial port will be COM1 and which will be COM2; other times, it simply depends on the socket into which you plug that particular serial port's ribbon cable. Check the documentation for your motherboard or your I/O card.

Here's your rule of thumb for most modern PCs: The small serial port is pre-wired as COM1 and the larger port is COM2.

I want to add more goodies...can I install additional ports?

Often you can, although you'll have more luck installing a second parallel port than you will have installing more serial ports. While it is possible to install more than two serial ports, they will, by design, conflict with one another (and may conflict with internal devices, too). The conflict isn't always bad, but can sometimes account for erratic behavior.

To install additional ports, simply add another I/O card that includes the ports you want installed. Be ready for a few caveats:

- You're limited to four serial and two parallel ports. (You can have more "virtual" COM ports, if you need them for things like internal modems and other devices.)

- If you have an internal serial device (like a modem), be aware that it's using an assigned COM port, so you can only install one additional serial port. This is because the four available COM ports are designed to share interrupts. (See the answer to "What's an interrupt?" later in this chapter.)

- You'll need to set the ports to respond to the available COM and LPT numbers. If you have a typical setup, then a new parallel port should be called LPT2 and new serial ports should be called COM3 and COM4.

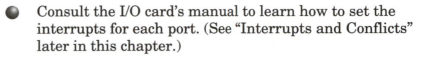
● Consult the I/O card's manual to learn how to set the interrupts for each port. (See "Interrupts and Conflicts" later in this chapter.)

● You may need to change settings in your computer's BIOS to recognize the new ports. Use your BIOS activating keystroke sequence after the boot memory test, then check for BIOS entries that allow you to add COM3, COM4, and LPT2 settings.

● To check whether they installed correctly, wait until your computer boots; it should give you a system status table along with the "Starting DOS" or "Starting Windows" message. Look in that table and make sure you see as many entries for COM and LPT ports as you should have, depending on how many you had initially and how many you've added.

 ## My serial port isn't working correctly. How do I get it to cooperate?

Assuming the device you're trying to attach does work and that the serial port is functional and properly installed, the most common reason for a serial port to work incorrectly is called an *interrupt conflict*. This happens most often when another serial device—like an internal modem—is installed in an expansion slot inside your PC. This card is assigned a COM number, usually by setting DIP switches on the card itself or by using its installation software. (By default, most internal modems are COM2.) This creates a conflict if you forget to uninstall the physical, external COM2 and you have a device connected to it. Other cards and devices can also interfere if they are assigned the same interrupt as the serial port in question.

How do I deactivate an external COM port?

You can generally do this one of three ways. The first way is to set the appropriate jumpers on your motherboard to disable the COM port in question; consult your manual for specifics. Your BIOS setup screens may also allow you to disable a port; use the special keystroke sequence for your computer when it boots, and check for this ability in your BIOS. The final way is to simply open the case, properly ground yourself, and pull the offending COM port's ribbon cable from the motherboard. In many instances, this will at least keep you from trying to use the COM port.

 ### I've just installed a new component, and the setup program wants to know what COM port it's using. How do I determine which port is correct?

This one is easier than it sounds. As we've said earlier, there are some rules of thumb you can use for determining which COM port is which, and they are listed here:

If you plugged the component into this...	It's probably using this COM port
The small serial port in back of the PC	COM1
The only serial port in back of the PC, regardless of size	COM1
The big serial port in back of the PC	COM2
An internal expansion card, and COM1 is already in use	COM4
An internal expansion card, and COM2 is already in use	COM3

If all else fails, you'll need to experiment and see what works!

Tip: *Write down in your PC manual (or on the Instant Answers! card included at the front of this book) what each of your COM ports is doing. That makes it easier to install new serial hardware later.*

 ### Can I attach more than one parallel port device to a single port?

Yes, you can. You'll find that many popular devices such as scanners, digital video cameras, and external storage devices require parallel ports—yet, for historical reasons, PCs generally only have one parallel port. In this case, there are two alternatives:

● Some devices allow you to "daisy chain" parallel devices by plugging the second cable into a port on the first device.

● Get a switch box—either a manual switch or an electronic one. These boxes allow you to connect two or more devices to a single box, which then connects to the parallel port. To use a particular device, you simply throw the switch. (Or, in the case of an electronic switch box, the particular device's driver is sensed and that device is activated automatically.) Check your manual, though. Switch boxes don't work well with some printers. See Chapter 12 for details.

I've installed a switch box, but now my printer doesn't work! What do I do?

So much for the advice we gave in the preceding answer. Many modern printers make use of a bidirectional parallel port. That means that instead of simply sending information to the printer, the computer also receives data from the printer. A switch box can interfere with that ability, even when it is switched to the printer. Hewlett-Packard printers are particularly notorious for this behavior.

If your printer doesn't get along with a switch box, stop using it. There are always those special active switches that cost a lot—more than $50, typically—but they don't interfere with the bidirectional port.

Caution: *Using a switch box of any kind can occasionally void the warranty of some printers and other devices. Check your device's documentation before installing one.*

I removed my old printer from Windows, or so I thought—but now when I start my PC, it always stops on a blue screen and reports something about bi-di.386 not being found. How do I make it go away?

You need to remove the references to bi-di.386 from the system.ini file. Do this:

1. Choose Start | Run.

2. Type **SYSEDIT** in the Run dialog box and press ENTER.

3. SYSEDIT, a central editor for startup files, opens. Choose Windows | system.ini.

4. Put a semicolon in front of every line that says device=bi-di.386. There should be two such lines.

5. Save the system.ini and close SYSEDIT. When you reboot, the problem will be gone.

Caution: *Be sure to back up any system file, such as system.ini, before you edit the file. You can simply copy the file to a different directory on your hard drive, and then restore the old version if you make an error while editing.*

 ## Sometimes when I move my mouse, it locks up my whole system and I have to reboot. How do I fix this?

Your mouse is sharing a COM port with another device—perhaps a docking cradle for a PDA, a modem, or some other device that is only used intermittently. In any case, you can't share COM ports with a mouse, since it needs exclusive access to its IRQ. (See the "Interrupts and Conflicts" section later in this chapter.) Track down the offending device and remove it or change its IRQ to another number that is still available in your system. (See the questions regarding IRQ settings later in this chapter.)

Can I change the parallel port settings in the BIOS for better performance?

It doesn't hurt to try, as long as you remember what you did if it doesn't work. Many BIOSs have a setting for the parallel port where you can select Standard, EPP, or ECP. The standard parallel port could traditionally transfer data at about 300 Kbps, but ECP (Enhanced Capabilities Port) can move bits at 2 Mbps. Because that's so much faster, be sure your BIOS is set up for ECP. EPP is a variation on ECP that you can probably ignore unless your printer calls for it.

Generally, speeding up the ports will only result in a significant change if your parallel port peripherals support ECP/EPP technology. You may also need to set the parallel port's driver software in Windows for increased performance. (See the next question.)

Tip: *Keep a written log of any changes you make to the BIOS. Also, don't change more than one thing at a time; then you can judge the performance difference, if any, before changing another setting.*

 ## How can I be sure I'm getting the most from my ECP/EPP port?

If you have a high-speed ECP/EPP port, and you have peripherals that support the high-speed parallel connection, you may need to change some Windows settings. Here's how to check for the correct driver:

1. Right-click on My Computer and choose Properties.
2. Click the Device Manager tab.
3. Click the plus sign next to Ports (COM and LPT).
4. Double-click the LPT port.
5. In the Printer Port Properties dialog box, click the Change Driver button.
6. In the Select Device dialog box, choose ECP Printer Port and click OK.

You may also need to change or update the driver for your ECP-compatible printer or device. Check the device manual for details.

INTERRUPTS AND CONFLICTS

What's an interrupt?

Aside from being the bane of many an upgrader's existence, *interrupt* refers to the way in which a peripheral device gets the attention of the CPU. The CPU, generally content just to compute, needs to be told by external devices when they have something it needs to see—such as a keystroke or a bit of modem data, for instance. To tell the CPU about this data, the peripheral uses its assigned interrupt to make an interrupt request, or IRQ.

A typical PC has 16 interrupts, many of which are preassigned, and some of which are available to peripherals. Interrupts are numbered from 0 to 15, and many have specific functions, which are listed in Table 4-1.

 ## Windows is reporting an interrupt conflict between two devices. How can I resolve this?

Thanks to plug-and-play, interrupt conflicts have become almost an endangered species. And that's great. Sometimes they'll still happen, though, and they're much easier to solve than in the old days. If you install a new device and it doesn't work, first check for a conflict. Try this:

1. Right-click My Computer and choose Properties from the drop-down menu. The System Properties dialog box will appear.

Interrupt/IRQ #	Available?	What It's Used For
0	No	Computer's internal timer
1	No	The keyboard
2	Rarely	Most modern video interfaces
3	No	Serial ports: COM2 and COM4
4	No	Serial ports: COM1 and COM3
5	Yes	Second LPT port, sound cards, multimedia cards
6	No	Floppy-disk drives
7	Sometimes	LPT1, but can be shared
8	No	Computer's clock
9	Rarely	Network cards, other internal uses; can be video
10	Yes	Free
11	Yes	Free
12	Sometimes	PS/2-style mouse
13	No	CPU/math coprocessor
14	No	Hard drives
15	Yes	Free, but rarely used. (On Pentium-class machines, used for EIDE interface in conjunction with IRQ 14.)

Table 4-1　IRQ settings and availability in typical PCs

2. Look in the list of devices in the Device Manager tab. You should see at least one device with the yellow exclamation point, indicating a problem.

Now that you know where to look, you need to resolve the conflict. Follow these steps:

1. Double-click the device that's experiencing a problem. The general tab should explain the conflict.

2. Click the Resources tab. Here you will select a different IRQ.

3. Click the Use automatic settings button to disable automatic resource selection.

4. Select a different option from the Setting Based On list menu. Choose a selection that features a different IRQ; some experimentation may be necessary.

If the problem persists after rebooting your PC and you try all the options without solving the problem, there's still hope. The IRQ that your PC assigns to each device is determined by its relative position in the PCI bus. That means you can rearrange the expansion cards and effectively change the IRQs that each device uses. Open your PC, find the cards causing problems, and move them to other locations. In most cases, this will solve your problem.

 Why would I be having interrupt conflicts in the first place?

A conflict occurs when more than one device tries to use the same interrupt at the same time. Suddenly your computer can't tell whether it's being told something by a modem or a mouse, for example. Note that this happens often with COM ports, because they share two IRQs between the four possible ports.

Serial ports are particularly susceptible to conflicts. The problem is, while you can have up to four serial ports in any given computer, there are only two interrupts available to all four serial ports: COM1 and COM3 share interrupt 4, and

COM2 and COM4 share interrupt 3. This can be the source of a lot of headaches, especially during modem installations.

Tip: *See Chapter 11 for details on troubleshooting your modem.*

How do I set the interrupts correctly for my system?

Each device or expansion card will probably have a slightly different way of setting interrupts. In Windows 95, with PCI and/or plug-and-play devices, it isn't necessary. But even plug-and-play may not work if you dual-boot into DOS to play a game, for example. In that case, you'll need to consult the device's manual and set the interrupt manually.

There are generally three different ways you can set a card's interrupt—manually using DIP switches, through a software configuration program, or by the specific order of cards in the PC's expansion slots. Figure 4-3 shows an example of IRQ-related DIP switches.

My devices don't work so well when I dual-boot into DOS. How can I troubleshoot this problem?

If you play a lot of games or multimedia *edutainment* (education and entertainment) titles, you probably still spend some time in DOS—even as a Windows user. So you may be familiar with shutting down Windows 95 and choosing the "Restart the computer in MS-DOS mode" option. But this can sometimes cause devices that work under Windows to mysteriously become unavailable.

The solution? Boot into DOS as we just described. Then, when you're in DOS, run any DOS-based configuration programs that shipped with your devices. This is especially true of sound cards, and sometimes is helpful for modems. You may have already run a configuration program in Windows—that's okay. By running the configuration program again in DOS, you can make sure that the DOS-specific configuration files (specifically DOSSTART.BAT) are fed the correct configuration info for the device. Now, when you use DOS in the future, your settings will be correct.

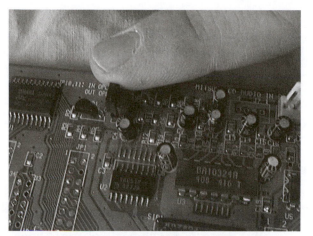

Figure 4-3 If you need to set an IRQ using DIP switches, consult the manual that came with your device.

 I've tried all that and it still doesn't work. Is there anything else I can do?

Some devices, like sound cards, use specific DMA channels. DMA stands for Direct Memory Address and it's a way for a device to get fast, direct access to memory by bypassing the CPU. It's possible that your new device is trying to use the same DMA as another device already in the system. Check the manual for instructions on changing the DMA (usually with a jumper or DIP switch). Thankfully, PCI cards don't have this problem, but some ISA cards might.

USB PORTS

 What is "USB"?

The *Universal Serial Bus,* or USB, allows you to attach USB devices in much the same way that you attach serial devices, except that USB technology offers higher-speed connections and support for many more peripherals. USB offers connections of 1.5 Mbps and 12 Mbps, depending on the peripheral and the cabling. It also, theoretically, allows up to 127 devices to be connected to the bus at once, although your desk space probably limits you to fewer than that.

USB is a fully plug-and-play feature. In fact, it's "hot-pluggable," meaning that you can connect and reconnect devices while your machine continues to run. The bus is also powered, meaning that certain low-power devices don't require their own power supply.

 ### How can I get USB to work for me?

To begin with, you need USB ports. Many Pentium-class and higher machines offer USB ports right along with the other ports on the back of your PC. If you see them (look again at Figure 4.1), you're capable of adding USB peripherals.

In order for USB to work properly, an upgrade to Windows 98 is the best solution, because Microsoft no longer supports full USB compatibility with Windows 95 and there's no guarantee it'll work.

If your PC shipped with Windows 95 and USB ports, then you likely have Windows 95 OSR 2.1 or 2.5. (OSR stands for *OEM Service Release*, and it refers to versions of Windows that are updated from the original and included with new PCs.) You may need to install the USB Supplement selectively from your Windows 95 with USB Support CD-ROM. (See Chapter 14 for more on updating Windows.)

 ### What sorts of devices work with USB?

Tons of them. You can get USB keyboards, mice, joysticks, printers, scanners, digital cameras, videoconferencing cameras, point-of-sale devices, modems, CD-R drives—pretty much anything. The only limitation is the speed of the USB bus, which is slower than the connections used for internal hard drives, for instance. Most any external device can be found these days with a USB interface or option.

How do I add a USB device to my system?

Just plug it in and insert the driver disk when asked to. The ports will only accept the flat USB connector in one direction and it plugs in rather easily—if you have to force it, try turning the connector over. If you have a version of Windows that supports USB, the devices should be recognized immediately—you'll see a Wizard dialog box (as shown in Figure 4-4).

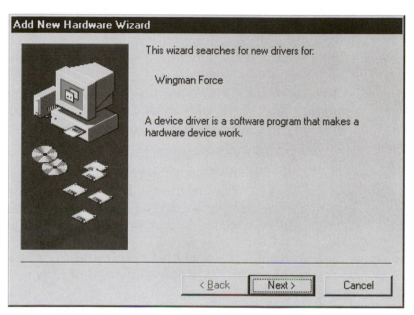

Figure 4-4 USB devices are always plug-and-play. Windows should recognize them as soon as you plug them in.

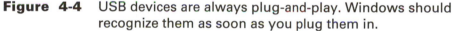 Is it safe for me to unplug a USB device when my PC is turned on?

Yes. You can also plug it back in with the PC turned on.

Two ports don't equal 127 devices. How do I add more than two USB peripherals?

USB won't allow you to daisy chain devices like you can some parallel port peripherals. Instead, you'll need to purchase a USB hub. This device plugs into one of your USB ports and allows you to connect between four and eight additional devices. You can daisy chain your USB hubs, but not actual devices. Because the bus is powered, USB hubs use a power supply to offer power to additional low-power USB devices.

Sometimes when one of my larger USB peripherals kicks in, it affects the how the others perform. What can I do?

The best advice is to move things around a bit. If you have a scanner, removable drive, or other device that interferes with other USB devices when it's activated, you can try isolating

that device on its own USB port, while connecting other devices through the second port or via a hub that's connected to that second port.

 I've added a new USB device and it doesn't seem to work right. The other USB devices on my PC still work fine…what's the problem here?

The most likely problem is that you've run out of USB bandwidth or electrical juice. USB isn't real smart about allocating either of those, and if the port you're using doesn't have enough power, it'll just terminate the last device in the USB chain without an error message. You have two solutions:

1. Add a powered hub. Some hubs are unpowered, and if you're using one of those, that may account for the device failure.

2. Move one or more devices to another USB port. Most PCs come with two ports. This is the best solution if you're using hardware that requires a lot of bandwidth—like a video teleconferencing device.

 I've added USB speakers to my PC, and now the sound frequently breaks up. What's going on?

It's not the fault of the USB port—exactly. The problem is that your CPU—instead of a sound card—is now responsible for generating sound. Many people have found that these newfangled sound systems put too much load on the CPU and sound breaks up badly when the processor is busy doing something aside from concentrating 100 percent of its energy on making sound. We recommend that you shop carefully before committing to a USB sound system.

 I don't see any USB ports at all on my machine. Can I add them?

Yes you can—a number of vendors offer PCI adapter cards that provide USB ports. Usually, you just plug in the card and it's automatically detected if you have Windows 95.

You should be aware, though, that some Pentium-class machines shipped with USB capability on the motherboard

but not the connectors themselves. USB ports can actually be purchased from suppliers like Belkin Components. To discover if you have USB capability, download a freeware evaluation utility from the USB Organization at **http://www.usb.org/usbready.exe**. It will examine your PC's hardware and software, then let you know if your PC is USB-ready.

If USB is detected, you can buy the ports and ribbon-cable connectors, then add them by plugging them into the USB connectors on the motherboard. Your motherboard's documentation should show you where they are.

You may also need to change BIOS settings. This varies according to your BIOS manufacturer—look for a USB Interface field that can be enabled. It will often appear under Peripheral Configuration, Advanced Setup, or PCI Control.

 ### How come some of the PCs in the store have USB ports in the front of the case?

Many manufacturers have started building USB ports into the front of the PC's case to make them more accessible. If you have a USB camera, for example, wouldn't it be handy to plug it into the front of the system instead of reaching all the way around back? If you like the sound of that, keep an eye out for PCs with USB in front *and* behind. After all, you probably don't want everyday components like your mouse plugged into the front, too.

I've bought a PCI USB card, and now there's some sort of conflict. Any thoughts?

It's possible that you have USB built into the motherboard and that driver is conflicting with your PCI card. The built-in USB support may have caused the USB host controller to install itself, which is conflicting with your new USB controller. This is often fixed by upgrading to Windows 98. You can also solve it this way:

1. Open the Device Manager by right-clicking My Computer and selecting Device Manager from the menu.

2. Double-click Computer at the top of the Device Manager.

3. Select the Reserve Resources tab.

4. Click the Add button.

5. Enter the IRQ # that the USB host controller is currently using, then click OK three times to finish.

6. Go back to the Device Manager main screen and select the USB host controller device. Click the Remove button.

7. Restart the system. Now, the USB host controller should be re-detected by Windows and assigned an IRQ other than the one that was being used.

8. After successfully moving the host controller to a new IRQ, repeat the process in the Device Manager, this time removing the original, now reserved, IRQ so that the conflicting device works properly.

Chapter 5

Input Devices

Answer Topics!

Input Devices @ a Glance

The keyboards are perhaps the simplest part of a PC. A clean keyboard is a happy keyboard—whether you're rescuing a drenched keyboard or simply performing routine cleaning. Learning the right steps to take can save your keyboard to type another day. This chapter contains an abundance of other useful keyboard information as well, such as the various types of keyboards available, the difference between keyboard connectors, and how to install a keyboard.

You can easily install a new mouse or replace a broken one—you simply need to understand the differences between bus, serial, and PS/2 mice and choose the appropriate one for your PC. This chapter will also help you solve a host of other problems that can occur with mice.

 If you want to unwind with your computer after a long day at work, nothing beats a game. For most games, you'll need a joystick, and they're easy to install. However, you might need some help getting your joystick registered and calibrated; this chapter can help.

Don't like using a regular mouse? There are other options, most notably a touch pad. Learn what touch pads are and if you want to add one to your system.

THE KEYBOARD

 ### What are the different types of keyboards?

In general, most keyboards for the PC are interchangeable. The keyboard is one of the few items for your PC that is unlikely to ever experience a conflict with something else. There are important variations on the basic keyboard design, though. Here they are in a nutshell:

● **XT keyboard** The XT is the oldest kind of keyboard you can find for a PC. You might have one if you have an old 8088-based PC sitting in a closet somewhere. The biggest drawback with this keyboard, if it works with your PC at all, is the lack of a numeric keypad, making this keyboard work like a notebook computer. It doesn't have any lights for the CAPS LOCK or NUM LOCK, either. Total keys: 83

✳ *Note: XT keyboards are a relic of history, like disco and "The Partridge Family." Their internal circuitry is different than that of AT keyboards, and they aren't compatible. Some keyboards have an XT/AT selector on the back so you can specify what kind of PC you're using.*

● **AT keyboard** This keyboard includes status lights and a numeric keypad, making it more useful. It caused XT-style keyboards to disappear essentially overnight. Total keys: 84

 AT-enhanced keyboard This keyboard adds a few new function keys, as well as separate cursor controls between the main keys and the keypad. The AT-enhanced (or just "enhanced") keyboard is virtually the only style you'll encounter today if you purchase one new. Total keys: 101

 Windows keyboard This variation on the AT standard is very popular, with the addition of Windows-specific keys, including two Start menu keys and another menu key that is equivalent to pressing the right mouse button. The disadvantage of this keyboard—primarily for gamers—is that accidentally striking the Windows key while playing in a DOS session brings Windows to the front, often crashing the original DOS session. Total keys: 104

Can't I set my NUM LOCK key so that it stays on—or off—automatically?

Some people like the NUM LOCK key to be on as soon as the PC starts; others prefer that the numeric keypad just be a block of cursor control keys. It's easy to configure either preference by entering your BIOS setup. (See Chapter 3 for details on the BIOS.) When you start your PC, press the key that enters your setup program (it's usually F1, DEL, or ESC) and look for a Num Lock option. Use the DOWN ARROW key to move the cursor over the option and set it to On or Off, as desired. Choose the option to Save Changes and Exit.

Walkthrough: Installing a Keyboard

Installing a new keyboard is one of the easiest upgrades you can perform. Here's what you need to do:

1. Shut down your PC.

2. Remove the old keyboard. Grasp the connector, not the wire itself, and pull it straight out without twisting.

3. Insert the new keyboard cable. Look for a ridge or bump to line up the cable, or look into the port and see the orientation of the pins themselves if you need help aligning them:

4. Start your PC. The keyboard should work just fine.

5. Some keyboards come with an installation disk, especially if they use nonstandard features to enhance the typing experience. If you want the extra features, install the disk and run the setup or install program. That's entirely optional, however, because the keyboard will work fine without the software.

 ## When my PC starts, it says, "Keyboard not found." What do I do?

There are three possibilities:

- *The keyboard cable has come loose from the PC.* If you're using an extension cable, check all the connectors. This is almost always the cause. To fix the problem, power off the PC and reseat the keyboard connector. When you turn the PC back on, the PC should recognize the keyboard.

- *The keyboard's internal electronics have died.* This is very unlikely, and there is little you can do about it other than replacing the keyboard.

- *The keyboard port has blown out.* This is also very unlikely, but it can happen if you repeatedly insert and remove the keyboard while the PC is powered on. The port is on the motherboard of the PC, not the keyboard, and, again, there is little you can do about it (except replace the motherboard).

Note: Don't just push the keyboard connector in while the PC is powered on. The BIOS only looks for the keyboard once at startup, so plugging it in after the fact won't accomplish anything.

I've installed an old keyboard I found in the garage, but it doesn't work with my machine. Should I just throw it away?

Look for a switch on the bottom of the keyboard that lets you choose between XT and AT mode. Because XT keyboards are wired differently than AT keyboards, some keyboards allow you to choose between these two modes. Change the switch position and see if that fixes the problem. If not, the keyboard doesn't work and you need to replace it.

I bought a new keyboard, and without thinking, I installed it with the PC turned on. Nothing bad happened, but isn't this dangerous?

You can replace your keyboard with the power on, but we don't recommend it if your keyboard uses a standard keyboard connector (the round port). There are several ports on the back of your PC that are prone to damage if you swap cables while the ports are "hot," or powered-on (meaning they have electric current going through them). The keyboard port is one such port. While we've never known anyone who has lost a keyboard port through this kind of negligence, the possibility exists, so always power off your computer before swapping keyboards, reseating a loose connector, or installing a pass-through device between the PC and the keyboard.

USB keyboards and other controllers can be "hot-plugged" with no undo consequences; in fact, they're designed to work that way.

Oops! How do I clean spilled liquid out of my keyboard?

If you've spilled something in your keyboard, you might want to just discard it and purchase a replacement. Keyboards can be difficult to clean, and a new one can be had for as little as $30 and often lower if you don't mind a slightly cheaper feel.

However, if you're one of those users who frequently eats or drinks while working, here are a few steps you can take to rejuvenate a keyboard that suffered the Pepsi Syndrome:

1. Power off the PC and unplug the keyboard.

Caution: *Avoid using the keyboard until it is dry.*

---

2. Dry all the external surfaces with a sponge or dry cloth. If you spilled a sticky liquid like a soft drink, be sure to use a damp rag to clean all the residue on every exposed surface.

3. Turn your keyboard upside down and use compressed air to blow out as much liquid from the crevices between the keys as possible.

4. Use a cool setting on a hair dryer to dry the inside of the keyboard. Be careful that you don't get too close or melt anything.

5. Let the keyboard dry for at least another 6 to 24 hours. Then plug it in and test it.

You'll probably want to perform more detailed surgery, particularly if you've spilled a sticky soft drink on the keyboard. The soda will dry, leaving a sticky residue that collects dirt and makes the keys stick. You might want to get a keycap removal tool from a specialty PC store and carefully lift each keycap off the keyboard. (Don't try to remove the spacebar, though, because there are a wide variety of hard-to-replace springs under it.)

If you can't remove the keys, you might want to run the disconnected keyboard under a strong stream of running water to wash away the contaminating liquid. Then dry it thoroughly with a hair dryer on the "air dry" cycle and wait the requisite 6 to 24 hours before use.

I haven't spilled anything in my keyboard, but it's looking a little gross. What's the best way to clean it up?

At least once a year, you should turn the keyboard over and blow compressed air between the keys to exhume the dust, dirt, and pet hair that has accumulated between the keys. Don't, however, remove the keycaps for this sort of routine maintenance—save that for catastrophic events like 7-Up spills.

I need a new keyboard, but I'm confused by the different models. Why do some have more keys than others?

The enhanced keyboard, the most commonly used style today, has 101 keys. That includes 12 function keys, a numeric keypad, separate arrow keys, and a PAGE UP/PAGE DOWN, INSERT/DELETE, and HOME/END block of keys.

The Microsoft Natural keyboard has three additional keys, bringing the total up to 104. This keyboard gives you

two Windows Start menu keys, and a key that is equivalent to pressing the right mouse button.

If you're shopping for a keyboard, make sure it has the essential 101 keys. Some keyboards, especially wireless or space-saving models, skimp and omit essential keys.

? Uh-oh! My new keyboard has a different kind of connector than my old one. Do I need to exchange it?

Old keyboards come with a large, round connector, while new keyboards use IBM's smaller PS/2 connector (see Figure 5-1). It takes up less space, but be warned: It looks exactly the same as the PS/2 mouse port, inviting confusion. Most new PCs color-code the connector or put a handy picture next to the port.

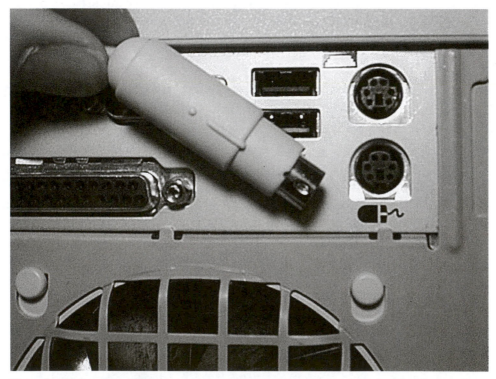

Figure 5-1   The PS/2 connector is now the standard for both mice and keyboards.

The newest keyboards use USB for the connector. There isn't much of an advantage to this, except that the keyboard is hot-pluggable. (In other words, you can plug it in without turning off your machine.) Some USB keyboards also act as USB hubs, allowing you to connect additional USB devices to your PC.

If you purchase a new keyboard for an older PC, odds are good that the computer will have a large port, but your keyboard will have a small PS/2 connector. Simply choose one of the following options:

● Buy a keyboard that includes an adapter in the box; many do.

● Purchase an adapter at the computer store before you go home.

Don't worry—the only thing that changed is the size of the connector. The keyboard itself is still 100 percent compatible, as long as it's not USB. USB keyboards aren't designed to be adapted to the older connectors, so read the labels carefully.

Friends rave about their Dvorak keyboards, but they just look strange to me. What's the attraction?

The Dvorak keyboard is unique in that it doesn't use the standard QWERTY key layout found in traditional keyboards. You're probably aware that QWERTY keyboards were designed to slow down fast typists when typewriters were in their

infancy, much like rotary dial phones kept people from entering numbers faster than the phone's mechanics could keep up. That has hobbled typists ever since, but there is an alternative. The Dvorak keyboard is designed to place keys in logical groupings for faster typing (see Figure 5-2). It takes some getting used to, particularly if you're an efficient QWERTY typist, but many people report that it's worth the effort.

There's a downside to Dvorak keyboards, though. Even after you go through the effort of learning the new Dvorak layout, you'll still have to use the old QWERTY layout on your notebook PC, typewriter, at work, and at other people's houses. In other words, you'll need to remember two completely different layouts, as if you drove American and British cars on alternating days.

You can read more about Dvorak keyboards on the Web at this excellent site: **http://www.ccsi.com/~mbrooks/dvorak**. Dvorak keyboards aren't always easy to come by; not a lot of stores keep them in stock. One source for these keyboards is Fentak Industries, which you can find on the Web at **http://www.fentek-ind.com/dvorak.htm** or by phone at (800) 639-0710.

If you do decide to take the plunge, you don't necessarily have to buy a new keyboard. You can also rearrange the keycaps on many keyboard or you can buy little stickers for the keycaps. In fact, you can even change notebook computers

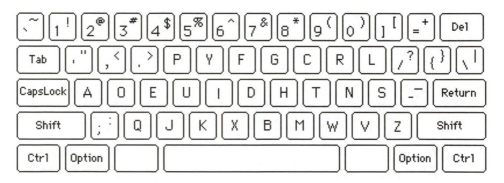

Figure 5-2 The Dvorak layout is much more efficient, but you'll have to memorize a new keyboard layout.

in this way if you like (although we wouldn't recommend putting sticker letters on a friend's notebook).

How do I tell Windows that I've switched to a Dvorak keyboard?

If you install a Dvorak keyboard, you'll need to let Windows know that the keys are all in different locations. Here's what to do:

1. Choose Start | Settings | Control Panel.
2. Open the Keyboard icon and click on the Language tab.
3. You should already see English (United States) selected. Click on the Properties button.
4. Choose the Dvorak option from the drop-down menu:

5. Click OK to save the change.

What's an ergonomic keyboard? Why use one?

Some keyboards on the market are designed with your health and comfort in mind. While they can be difficult to get used

to, they offer the potential of reduced muscle strain and more efficient typing. Ergonomic keyboards tend to do at least two things:

● Elevate the wrist pad so your hand points down at the keys.

● Split the keyboard at the T-Y point to offer better wrist motion and less strain.

Some keyboards offer a user-definable split angle, while most mold the split at what the manufacturer considers the ideal angle.

The Microsoft Natural Keyboard is the most common example of an ergonomic keyboard, and it attempts to reduce strain through a carefully sculptured design (see Figure 5-3). The Natural Keyboard is a bit more expensive than non-ergonomic keyboards, so decide for yourself if you think there's merit in the design. If you don't do a lot of typing, or if you're not a fast touch typist, it probably won't make much difference to you anyway.

The Natural Keyboard also includes the three Windows keys described earlier (two Start menu keys and a key equivalent to pressing the right mouse button) that make it

Figure 5-3 The Microsoft Natural Keyboard is the flagship ergonomic keyboard design.

easier for those with mouse aversions to control the Windows interface. Keep in mind that many keyboards now have those extra Windows keys, so you don't have to pay a premium for a Microsoft keyboard to get them.

Can I use a full-sized keyboard with my notebook?

Yup. You can connect an ordinary keyboard to the PS/2 port and still have the serial port available to connect a real mouse. The best solution we've found is the Darwin NoteBoard, available from Darwin Keyboards on the Web at **http://www.darwinkeyboards.com** or by phone at (888) 4-DARWIN. This clever keyboard has legs that allow it to stand over the notebook's own keyboard. Hence, you get the freedom of a full-sized keyboard without taking up any extra desk space (see Figure 5-4).

Figure 5-4 The Darwin NoteBoard is a neat external keyboard and mouse that you can add to your notebook PC.

THE MOUSE

I need a new mouse, and there are so many choices! Any advice on what I should buy?

In general, all mice work the same basic way: They sense movement, which they accurately reflect in the position of the pointer on the computer monitor. There are three major kinds of mouse mechanisms in the world:

- **Mechanical** A mechanical mouse uses a hard rubber ball and a set of rollers. The mouse's movement is sensed by differences in electrical charge generated by copper brushes and a conductor. Mechanical mice aren't particularly common.

- **Opto-mechanical** Like a mechanical mouse, the opto-mechanical version uses the rubber ball and rollers. Instead of measuring electrical charge using brushes, however, this one has a slotted wheel that allows light to pass through in carefully calibrated pulses. A light-emitting diode (LED) shines through these slots, and distance is measured by counting pulses.

- **Optical** The least common variation, an optical mouse, has no moving parts. Instead, you must use a special reflective mouse pad. (Some new optical models don't require a special pad, although most in the past have.) An LED in the mouse shines on the pad and is reflected back into the mouse's optics, which measure the mouse's position. Optical mice feel different—they glide instead of roll—and are used in specialized applications such as CAD/CAM and graphic design where accurate mouse movement is critical.

The typical mouse that you'll find in a computer store or that ships with a new PC is the opto-mechanical variety. It is dependable, robust, and usually more accurate than the purely mechanical variety. When you're mouse shopping, the more important consideration is usually what kind of interface the mouse uses.

❓ What's the difference between a bus mouse and a PS/2 mouse?

The older, PC/AT bus mouse is sometimes mistaken for a PS/2 mouse because the kind of port it connects to looks similar to IBM's PS/2 connector. The bus mouse actually has a larger, 9-pin plug that will not fit into the smaller, 6-pin PS/2 port. To be more specific, a bus mouse usually ships with its own ISA expansion card—an I/O card to which you connect the mouse. A PS/2 mouse plugs directly into the motherboard.

❓ What's the difference between a serial mouse and a PS/2 mouse?

Not all mice are born equal—not even mice that use the same mechanism for sensing movement. Most new PCs being sold these days use one of two kinds of input interfaces for mice: serial and PS/2. This is a very important distinction, and one that should be considered before purchasing a new PC. For us, the difference has "killed the deal" when we've been considering purchasing new computers. In a nutshell, here's the difference:

● **Serial mouse**   A serial mouse connects to a serial port on the back of the PC. It uses a COM port (just like a modem), and is generally a headache to use if you plan to upgrade your PC.

● **PS/2 mouse**   A PS/2 mouse uses an IBM PS/2-style connector and plugs not into the serial port, but into a port directly on the motherboard. A PS/2 mouse is a simpler mechanism that allows the computer to do more of the work; often this results in a cost savings. Most importantly, though, a PS/2 mouse won't take up a valuable COM port.

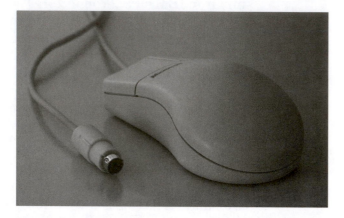

 ## Which is better: a serial mouse or a PS/2 mouse?

In our opinion, the PS/2 mouse is superior. Here are the consequences of installing a serial mouse:

● One of your serial ports will be dedicated to the mouse, which means you won't be able to install a modem or some other serial device like a docking station for a PDA (personal digital assistant) in that port.

● One of your COM ports will be taken. As discussed in Chapter 4, COM1 and COM3 share a common IRQ, as do COM2 and COM4. Because a mouse needs the COM port full time, you're starting out with just one available COM port IRQ for all your other devices.

A PS/2 mouse steals no resources from other expansion products. If your motherboard doesn't have a mouse port (as is the case with many older PCs), then you can either use a serial mouse or add a bus mouse on a card. The disadvantage to the latter method is that you're forced to dedicate an ISA expansion slot to a mouse. Depending on your needs, that may be better or worse than using a serial mouse.

Walkthrough: Installing a New Mouse in a Desktop PC

1. Shut down your PC.

2. Determine the kind of mouse you have and plug it into the appropriate port. You can plug a serial mouse into an existing serial port or a PS/2 mouse into the PS/2 port. If you have a convertible PS/2 mouse, you can add an adapter and plug it into a serial port. If you have no available ports, you'll need to install a bus mouse expansion card (called an I/O card). If you're installing a bus card, follow these steps. Otherwise, skip to step 9.

3. Open the cover of your PC in accordance with Chapter 2.

4. Locate an empty ISA slot (they are the long, usually black slots, as opposed to the shorter, white PCI slots) and unscrew its back plate. Remove the back plate and keep the screw handy.

5. Carefully insert the I/O card and slide it into the ISA slot. It might help to rock the card into place, but never push or force it.

6. Screw the card into place with the screw you had left over from removing the back plate.

7. Replace the cover on the PC.

8. Plug the mouse into the port on the back of the I/O card.

9. Start Windows. If Windows asks for an installation disk, insert it. If not, Windows will likely recognize the mouse just fine, and you can begin working with it right away. If your mouse has special features, you may need to run a separate setup program to take full advantage of them.

 Can I use a PS/2 mouse in my serial port?

Possibly; it depends on which mouse you buy. Some PS/2 mice come with adapters that let them connect and communicate with serial ports. However, there is no adapter available for converting a serial mouse into a PS/2 mouse.

❓ Just bought a USB keyboard...should I get a USB mouse?

USB is used as a connection technology for mice and other pointing devices. If you have a USB keyboard, then a USB mouse is probably a wise purchase—it can connect to the USB port on the keyboard. It's not mandatory, though—some USB keyboards include PS/2 connectors for mice, and you can always plug the mouse into the PS/2 connector on the back of your computer, if the cord will reach.

The main advantage of a USB mouse is that it doesn't require an IRQ. It's also hot-pluggable, which may appeal to some users.

❓ What kind of interface should my replacement mouse have?

First, the flippant answer: Replace your old mouse with a new one of the same interface.

Look at the end of the mouse connector. If you see a small round connector with 9 pins, it's a bus mouse. If the connector is very small with only 6 pins, you've got a PS/2 mouse. If the interface is rectangular (or sort of D-shaped), however, then it's a serial mouse.

Of course, you can install a different kind of mouse if you prefer. You may, for example, want to free up the serial port that your current mouse is using—but if you already have a serial mouse, it's a fair bet (although not 100 percent) that the PC doesn't have a PS/2 port on the motherboard. If not, you'll have to buy a bus mouse that comes with its own controller card, and you'll need to install it in a free ISA slot.

If your PC has USB, you can get a USB mouse. Again, there's not a great reason to choose it, but it's an option.

❓ Do I need a mouse with that wheel between the buttons?

A great innovation in mousedom is a wheel or dial that resides between the left and right mouse buttons. This is a handy tool that puts the ability to scroll, like around a Web

page or in a word processing document, on the mouse instead of on the screen. It might sound like a silly or trite gimmick, but the reality is that the wheel is a very handy control, one that quickly grows indispensable. You might not want to run out and buy one right now, but if you replace your mouse in the near future, look for one with the scroll wheel:

 Why doesn't the wheel on my mouse work with my Packard Bell computer?

If you have a Fast Media system, it may be interfering with the mouse. You need to disable Fast Media by following these steps:

- Choose Start | Run.
- In the dialog box, type **SYSEDIT** and press ENTER.
- SYSEDIT opens a program called the System Configuration Editor that opens all your PC's critical startup and configuration files in one place. Choose the Window menu and select win.ini (see Figure 5-5).
- Delete any reference to fmedia.exe on the "LOAD=" or "RUN=" lines.
- Choose File | Save and close the System Configuration Editor.
- If Fast Media is in the Startup folder in the Start menu, delete it from there as well.
- Restart your PC, and the wheel should work just fine.

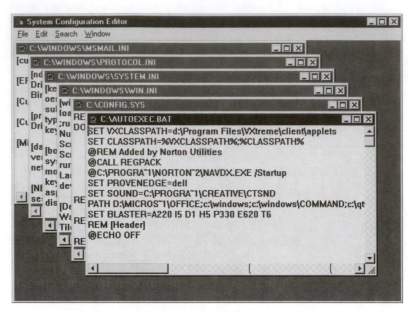

Figure 5-5 The System Configuration Editor loads all the common configuration files at once.

? My mouse is jerking all over the screen! What's going on?

Your mouse lets you know when it needs to be cleaned. If you experience jerky motion and the pointer either jumps erratically or doesn't move smoothly when you move the mouse, it's time for a cleaning.

Cleaning a mouse is easy. You don't even need to shut down your PC or unplug the mouse. It's hard to write cleaning instructions for a mouse ball without inviting all sorts of sophomoric humor, so please bear with us. Just follow these steps:

1. Turn the mouse over. You should see the ball peeking through a small hole.

2. Turn the dial on the surrounding plate to remove the ball. There should be an arrow indicating which way to turn it.

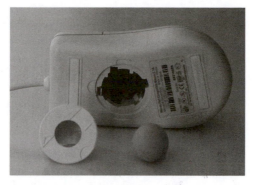

3. Let the mouse ball drop into your hand. Rinse the ball with soap and water to remove the outer layer of grime.

4. Using a Q-tip and some rubbing alcohol, swab the rollers to remove the dirt, which will seem baked-on.

5. Look for any other obvious collections of dirt in the ball cavity and clean it as appropriate. You can use a few squirts of compressed air to blow out debris.

6. Using a toothpick, very gently scrape and remove all the crud from the rollers inside the mouse cavity. In fact, this is where you're most likely to find problem-causing dirt.

7. Drop the ball back in place and twist the plate until it locks.

 Caution: *Don't squirt water into the mouse cavity and make sure the ball is dry before you put everything back together.*

If that doesn't fix the problem, it doesn't mean the mouse is broken. It might be your mouse pad! That's right—a mouse pad can get so dirty and matted down that it makes the mouse behave as if it were dirty. Try the mouse on a plain tabletop or on the surface of a book or magazine—if it works, throw the mouse pad away and get another one.

 I caught my teenager installing our new mouse with the PC still turned on! Isn't this dangerous?

Yes and no. The risk of damage to your PC is very low if you remove or replace a serial mouse with the power on (though you might want to avoid doing it). However, you can blow your PS/2 port very easily if you jack a mouse in and out of it when the power is on. Always turn your PC off before messing with the PS/2 port.

 I want to get a wireless mouse. What kind should I buy?

There are two kinds of wireless mice in the world: infrared (IR) and radio frequency (RF). IR is the name for the oldest kind of wireless devices. An IR device fires an invisible beam of infrared light between the mouse and the base station (which is connected to the mouse port via a normal cable). The mouse needs to be in direct line of sight with the base station at all times for communication to occur. Typically, IR mice have a fairly wide operational angle, like 60 degrees, so you can work off to the side of the base station's emitter and still get the job done. Because IR energy dissipates quickly, however, you're limited to about a five- or six-foot distance between the base station and mouse. That means you can't use it as a pointer in a conference room, or to Web surf from the couch on the other side of the room. And because an IR mouse is like a flashlight that transmits light you can't see, its battery life is usually fairly short—a few dozen hours at best.

RF mice are increasingly popular because they're significantly more flexible. An RF base station plugs into the mouse port. Because it uses radio energy, it doesn't need to be kept on the desktop; no line of sight is required. You can put the base on the floor and the mouse will work just fine. The mouse also works much farther away—15 feet or more—and battery life is better as well. The downside is that RF mice are a bit more expensive than IR mice.

 Why is my wireless mouse acting erratically?

Some multimedia PCs (like the IBM Aptiva) come with wireless mice. Is your wireless mouse giving you trouble? There are a few obvious things to check:

- Replace the batteries in the mouse.

- Make sure you're operating the mouse close enough to be properly received by the base unit.

- Ensure that the base unit is pointed roughly at the mouse. Your base unit has some acceptable range of viewing angles, but it might take some experimentation to determine exactly what that range is.

- If your mouse is connected to the serial port, make sure that you don't have another device trying to use the same COM port. An example would be a modem or a docking station for a personal digital assistant like a PalmPilot. If necessary, disable all the other devices to see if something is interfering.

- Some cordless mice (like the VersaPoint) use a special program, in addition to the mouse driver, that has to be running in Windows. Check the mouse's documentation to be sure, and if a program such as this is necessary, make sure it is running.

 Don't all mice use the same driver, like keyboards do?

No, not by a long shot. There are two common mouse driver standards—the Microsoft mouse and the Logitech mouse—so odds are fairly good that if you have a mouse, it'll respond to one of those. For best results, though, you need to install the driver that came with the mouse. If you have Windows 95/98, simply install the mouse and it will likely be auto-detected.

 Which COM port is my mouse using?

If you're using a PS/2 or bus mouse, then it doesn't use a COM port at all.

If you have a serial mouse, on the other hand, it uses one of your COM ports. To find out which one, choose Start | Settings | Control Panel and start Modems. Click on the Diagnostics tab. You should see an entry for the mouse, and it will report which COM port is in use.

You can probably inspect things physically as well. If you have two serial ports on your PC, the smaller one is usually COM1 and the larger one COM2. If you only have one serial port, it's COM1.

 ### I'm left-handed. How do I get my mouse to work for me?

Left-handed users can easily switch the functions of the mouse buttons. Simply choose Start | Settings | Control Panel and open the Mouse icon. On the Buttons tab, click the Left-handed button and click OK.

I'm tired of looking at that arrow. Can I change the mouse pointer?

Yes. Windows includes a variety of pointers you can choose from. To experiment, choose Start | Settings | Control Panel and open the Mouse icon. Click on the Pointers tab and edit the pointer to suit your taste.

 Tip: *You can click on Apply to see what the effect will be without closing the dialog box.*

My notebook computer has a mouse trails feature...why would I want to use it?

The mouse trails feature makes it easier to see the mouse in low-contrast display situations, such as you're likely to encounter with a notebook PC in low-power mode or in direct sunlight. To enable the trails, choose Start | Settings | Control Panel and open the Mouse icon. Click on the Motion tab and in the Pointer trail section, click on Show pointer trails. You can set their length and test this feature with the Apply button.

Why isn't my mouse responding?

Your mouse might be conflicting with another device that is trying to use the same IRQ. If you have a serial mouse, try moving it to the other serial port. If that doesn't solve the problem, try removing devices, such as scanner cards and modems, that could be causing a conflict. If all else fails, try replacing the mouse to see if the problem is with the mouse itself.

If it's a PS/2 mouse, the most likely problem is that the BIOS is set up to ignore the PS/2 port. Read the upcoming box, Walkthrough: "Installing a New Mouse in a Notebook PC," to learn how to solve your problem.

Help! My USB mouse isn't responding at all. What should I do?

A USB mouse will sometimes not respond because it's conflicted with another hardware device, or it's been misidentified (or not identified) by the USB controller software. Usually, this can be fixed by unplugging the mouse, and plugging it in again. Other times, it may require a restart.

With USB devices you may also need to update the IntelliPoint software included in Windows 98. Version 2.2 is recommended for dealing with USB pointing devices, even if they aren't Microsoft branded. The software can be downloaded from **http: //www.microsoft.com/products/ hardware/mouse/default.htm**.

My USB device seems to stutter or hang when the hard drive (or other drive) is accessed. What can I do?

Sometimes drive access can take quite a few system resources. Microsoft recommends that you attempt to assign a DMA channel to the drive. Here's how:

1. Open the Control Panel.
2. Double-click the System icon.
3. Select the Device Manager tab.

4. Double-click CD-ROM or Disk Drives, depending on which is causing the device trouble.

5. Double-click the drive that is interfering with the USB device.

6. Select the Settings tab, then select the DMA check box.

Click OK, then follow the instructions offered by Windows. If it tells you that you need to restart the computer, go ahead and do so.

I've added an external mouse to my notebook computer, and it's acting weird. How can I fix it?

If you've added a mouse to your notebook and it behaves erratically or you get Windows error messages, it may be that the internal pointing device, such as a touch pad, needs to be disabled because it is interfering with the new mouse. Enter the BIOS setup and disable it, as discussed in the following Walkthrough box

Walkthrough: Installing a New Mouse in a Notebook PC

If you have a Microsoft-compatible mouse, installing it on a notebook PC is pretty simple. Power the notebook off and insert the mouse in either the PS/2 port or serial port, depending on which kind of connector you have. In most cases, the PC will recognize the new mouse when Windows loads and allow you to use it immediately instead of the built-in input device.

In some cases, the BIOS controls whether the mouse port or built-in device is active. If you plug in a mouse and nothing happens, restart your PC and enter the BIOS setup program. (See Chapter 3 for details on the BIOS.) When you start your PC, press the key that enters your setup program (it's usually F1, DEL, or ESC). Look for an option to choose between the mouse port and the touch pad (or whatever control device your notebook has). Make the change and save the new BIOS setup.

 I have a Packard Bell computer and a Logitech mouse, but they don't seem to get along. I just want to get back to work...what can I do?

There are a variety of problems that can arise from using a Logitech mouse with a Packard Bell computer, particularly a Packard Bell that includes the Media Select or Fast Media system. Two problems can occur:

● The Fast Media component fails to work because it works properly only with a Microsoft mouse driver. In other words, you can't use a Logitech mouse with a Fast Media system.

● Windows incorrectly identifies the mouse when using Media Select because Media Select uses a nonstandard PS/2 pass-through that interferes with the detection of the mouse. There's a workaround for this, but it's detailed. Visit Logitech's Web site at **http://www.logitech.com** for the entire procedure.

 My mouse works in Windows but not in DOS. How do I fix that?

Windows 95 doesn't load the mouse driver for DOS unless you tell it to. So if you load a DOS session or restart your PC in DOS mode, you won't have a mouse available. Here's how to temporarily enable the mouse in DOS:

● From the DOS prompt, type **C:**. That should start the DOS mouse driver that Windows puts by default in the C drive's Mouse folder.

To make the mouse available permanently in DOS, you need to edit the autoexec.bat file. That's not all that hard to do either. From Windows, do this:

1. Choose Start | Run.

2. In the dialog box, enter **SYSEDIT** and press ENTER.

3. SYSEDIT opens a program called the System Configuration Editor that opens all your PC's critical startup and configuration files in one place. The top

window should be autoexec.bat. If it isn't, choose the Window menu and select autoexec.bat.

4. After the last line in the file, type **C:**.

5. Choose File | Save and close the System Configuration Editor.

Tip: *Make sure that your C drive really has a Mouse folder, and that there's a program called mouse.exe in it. If not, you need to locate a copy of mouse.exe and copy it to a Mouse folder on your hard drive.*

JOYSTICKS

How do I calibrate a joystick in Windows?

Thankfully, more and more games are running within Windows. Instead of using a DOS game's proprietary calibration routine, you can install and calibrate a joystick just once for all your Windows games.

Follow these steps to calibrate your joystick:

1. Choose Start | Settings | Control Panel.

2. Open the Game Controller icon and select the General tab.

3. Click on the joystick and select Properties.

4. Click on the Calibrate button and follow the Calibration wizard:

Controller 1 Calibration   ⊠

┌─ Calibration Information ─────────────────────────┐

To set your controller's center position, leave its handle centered, and then press a button on the controller.

┌───────┐   ✥
│   │
│   +   │   Point of view
│   │   hat
└───────┘

Axes 1 (X) and 2 (Y)

<Back   Next>   Cancel

? Can I connect more than one joystick to my PC?

Yes, you can. It turns out that the standard joystick port is designed to handle two game devices simultaneously. Just purchase a Y-connector cable from your computer store and jack the two joysticks into it.

On the other hand, keep in mind that some joysticks, particularly sophisticated ones such as the Logitech Wingman, use both joystick data lines to get all the controls and features on one platform. For this type of system, splitting the Y-cable will mean you have to stick to two simple joysticks.

Because your PC can handle up to 127 USB devices, it's possible to attach as many joysticks as you have USB ports available. For more ports, add a USB hub as detailed in Chapter 4.

? I have an old PC without a joystick port. How do I add a joystick?

If you have a particularly old PC, you might not have a joystick port. That's because many old systems don't have sound cards, and the joystick port is almost always found there. The answer, then, is to add a sound card to your PC. There's little reason to have a joystick without sound anyway, and for about $100 you can get both.

Although they're increasingly difficult to find, another option is to get an I/O card designed just to provide a joystick port.

? I've been shopping around, and I'm confused. What is a force-feedback joystick?

A new class of joystick is the force-feedback joystick. Used in the military for highly realistic training for years, it is just now emerging into the world of personal computers. A typical force-feedback joystick includes a microprocessor, motors, sensors, and perhaps even gyroscopes to convey physically what is seen on the computer display. When flying an aircraft in a flight simulator, for example, force feedback can accurately model the shudder of stall conditions or the tension of pulling the elevator up in a dive.

Microsoft's Sidewinder (see Figure 5-6) is one such joystick, and it has the power of Microsoft behind it. A wide variety of games and applications are beginning to appear that use Microsoft's advanced development tools with pre-designed effects.

My favorite game doesn't detect my USB joystick! What can I do?

For some games you may need to set the USB game controller to "Controller ID 1" before games will recognize it. Here's how:

1. If the game is open, quit it.

2. Open the Game Controllers control panel (Start | Settings | Control Panels and double-click Game Controllers).

3. Click the Advanced tab.

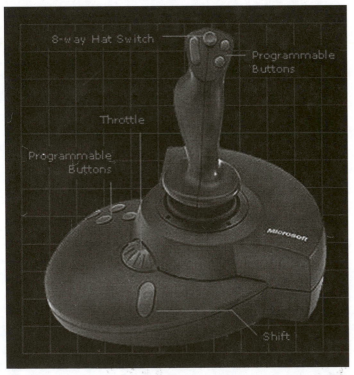

Figure 5-6 The Sidewinder joystick makes a lot of noise and requires a power outlet, but it dramatically improves game play.

Walkthrough: Installing a Joystick

To install a joystick, follow these simple steps:

1. Power off your PC.

2. Locate the joystick port. It is almost certainly on the sound card, just above or below the audio connections.

3. Plug the joystick into the port.

4. Start Windows and choose Start | Settings | Control Panel.

5. Open the Game Controller icon and select the General tab.

6. Click on the Add button and choose your joystick from the list. It might appear by name, or you might need to select the kind of joystick that it is, such as two-button, four-button, or flight yoke.

7. Click OK.

4. Under Controller ID Assignment, you'll see a game controller listed next to Controller ID 1. Select that control and then select Change.

5. In the Game Controllers dialog box, select the name of the USB game controller you want to use in the game and select OK.

If the USB game controller you changed to use Controller ID 1 was previously using another ID number, you'll need to reset that Controller ID number so that no device is using it. Click the Controller ID, select Change, then select None. Now select OK to finish up.

OTHER INPUT DEVICES

 What is a touch pad? Why might I need one?

A *touch pad* is an increasingly common alternative to a mouse on the desktop or on a portable PC. It allows you to drag your finger on a small, rectangular pad to guide the pointer onscreen. You can tap the pad for mouse clicks or press a pair of nearby buttons for the same effect.

Many people prefer touch pads because they're often easier to use. Moving your finger around the pad translates directly into cursor movement, and tapping on the pad is equivalent to clicking the mouse button. Touch pads are especially popular on portable PCs.

Some touch pads feature additional tools as well. Interlink's VersaPad, for example, offers the ability to digitize your signature:

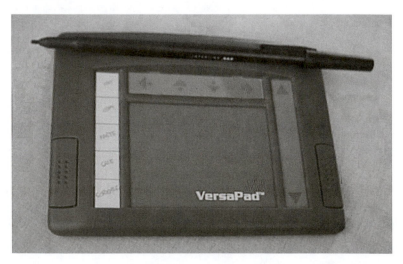

I got my touch pad wet and now it doesn't work. Is it ruined?

Not necessarily, but it won't work until it's completely dry. Most touch pads rely on a capacitance field to determine where your finger is, in which the moisture on your finger flags your position and the distance from the center of the touch pad is calculated. That's what determines where the cursor shows up onscreen. That also explains why most touch pads don't respond to contact with pens, pencils, or other inanimate objects.

To solve this problem, blot up the liquid as quickly as you can so it doesn't seep through the border of the mechanism and get the underlying electronics wet. Once it's dry, it will respond to your finger again.

Not all touch pads use a capacitance field. Interlink's VersaPad, for instance, is truly touch sensitive. Not only can you use your finger, you can use a hard, dry object such as a pen to control the device.

Chapter 6

Computer Video

Answer Topics!

Computer Video @ a Glance

Before you get a new monitor or swap video cards, it helps to have a solid understanding of video fundamentals. For example, what is color depth? How about video RAM? Read this chapter for an explanation of the basics.

Your monitor is the biggest PC purchase you're ever likely to make. The monitor might even outlast the PC itself. It makes sense to invest wisely in a monitor that does what you need, not just now, but for years into the future.

Video cards control the size of the images, number of colors, and overall speed of your display. They're one of the last sources of black magic left in your PC.

Want to play the newest games? Many of them feature standup-arcade-quality graphics, which only shine through with extra hardware. If you're a gamer, you absolutely must have a 3-D accelerator card. It's not an option. These cards can replace your existing video card or complement it, depending on which you choose.

These days, computers just aren't complete without some sort of video capability. You can capture video and store it on your PC, or use a TV card to watch CNN while you work. If your card isn't behaving the way you think it should, look here for some troubleshooting tips.

THE ESSENTIALS OF PC VIDEO

 I'm shopping for a monitor. What is "resolution"?

The *resolution* of a video display indicates the number of *pixels* that are used to form the display. (A pixel is a "picture element" or the smallest individual dot shown on your computer screen.)

Resolution in computer lingo is *relative resolution*; this is different than dots per square inch (dpi) used in print media, which is an absolute measure of resolution. What does that mean? Well, for starters, a pixel isn't always the same size. It depends on the size of the monitor it's being displayed on. So if you have a display that is composed of 307,200 pixels (480 horizontal lines at 640 pixels per line, or 640×480), projecting those pixels on a tiny 5-inch monitor will make an incredibly sharp, but minuscule, display. Send the same 307,200 pixels to a drive-in theater screen, and the pixels will be so large that you might not even be able to determine what the image is supposed to be (see Figure 6-1).

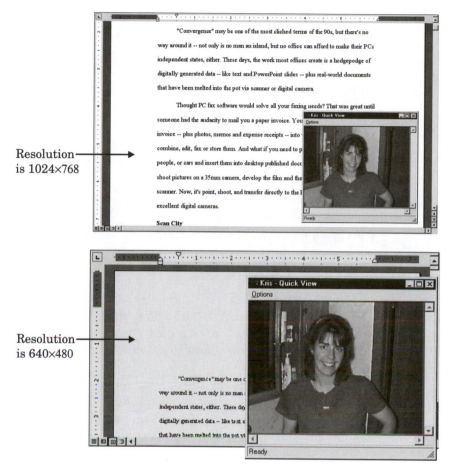

Resolution
is 1024×768

Resolution
is 640×480

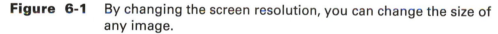

Figure 6-1 By changing the screen resolution, you can change the size of any image.

The bottom line is that resolution means how many pixels are used to create the computer display, described as *horizontal×vertical*. Pixels vary in size, so visual quality onscreen depends on which size monitor you're using. There is no direct correlation between screen resolution and print resolution.

As a rule of thumb, however, you can assume that a standard 640×480 display is about 100 dpi on a 15-inch monitor—only about a tenth of the lowest desktop printer resolution. Professional magazines are printed over 20 times sharper than a common computer visual display.

Note: *On a single monitor changing the resolution to something higher—from 640×480 to 800×600, for instance—has the practical effect of making everything on the screen smaller and allowing more to fit on the Windows desktop. Why? Because fitting more pixels on the same size screen means that the pixels must be smaller. Sometimes it's easiest to think of resolution as the size of the picture it displays on your monitor.*

What is "color depth"?

When we talk about *depth,* or *color depth,* we're talking about the other half of the video card and monitor's capability. While resolution is a measure of how many pixels are being drawn on the screen, color depth refers to how many colors the display can draw.

Color depth is usually measured in bits per pixel, as in a 24-bit display. A 1-bit display is capable of displaying two colors; the pixel can essentially be turned on or off. The original Macintosh is an example of a 1-bit system; rather than displaying true grayscale, each pixel could be either black or white, and the impression of gray could only be achieved by *dithering* a lot of pixels in a varying black-and-white pattern.

Actually 2-bit color is four colors (in this mode, each pixel can have one of four states), and 24-bit color is the threshold of human color perception, with 16.7 million possible colors. Common color depths used on PCs are listed here:

Bits per Pixel	Colors	Application
1	2	Original Macs; line art mode for faxes
4	16	Simple grayscale
8	256	True color grayscale or simple color
16	65,536	High color mode looks almost as good as true color

Bits per Pixel	Colors	Application
24	16,777,216	True color is generally considered the threshold of human perception
32	4,294,967,296	Beyond human perception; good for computer analysis

It's an important distinction that a 24-bit display can't possibly show all 16 million colors—there aren't enough pixels on the screen to do so. Instead, when we talk about color depth what we're saying is that each pixel has the *opportunity* to display any one of the 16 million colors visible to humans, and that's what makes the display photorealistic. In reality, a photorealistic scene might only have a few thousand colors on the screen at any one time.

 ### What has more impact on resolution and color depth—my PC or my monitor?

The video card or video circuitry built into your computer determines resolution and bit depth. The monitor displays whatever signal is sent from the video adapter (within its design limitations), but it's the video card itself that determines what your display looks like. Of course, your monitor may have a limit on the upper end of what it can display, especially if it's an older model.

Why can't I seem to go above a certain resolution and/or number of colors?

It's the amount of RAM on your video card that determines the combination of resolution and number of colors that you can display on your monitor. Some video cards feature upgradable RAM slots—they're almost always manufacturer-specific, so check your documentation. A video card with 1MB of RAM can display between 640×480 and thousands of colors, all the way up to 1024×768 with 16 colors. Beyond that, you'll need 2MB or more. Video cards tend to come with the following amounts of RAM: 256K, 512K, 1MB, 2MB, 4MB, 6MB, and 8MB.

You may also have trouble going above a certain resolution because of limitations in your monitor. If you notice that, at certain higher resolutions, your screen begins to "roll" like a TV that's out of vertical hold (or if the screen simply goes blank or is full of snow), then you may have reached the monitor's upper limit. In that case, you usually simply wait a few seconds without touching the mouse or any keys and Windows will readjust itself to its previous resolution.

So, how much video RAM do I need?

It depends on the maximum resolution and color depth at which you'd like to run your display. Fortunately, you can easily calculate the amount of RAM that you need. Just use this formula:

Width × Height × Pixel depth ÷ 8 = RAM needed

That's simply the resolution times the pixel depth divided by eight. So, consider the example of basic SVGA—a level that's probably a bit below the standard for day-to-day use:

640 × 480 × 8-bit ÷ 8 = 307,200 bytes

For basic 256 colors at 640×480, you don't need more than about 300K, which in practical terms, would be 512K of video RAM. For higher resolution, more typical of the Windows 95 office or home user (good for a 15-inch monitor), use this formula:

800 × 600 × 16-bit ÷ 8 = 960,000 bytes

You'd need a full megabyte of video RAM to support this resolution. If you want resolution and color depth more fitting a graphic designer (good for a 17-inch monitor), then use this formula:

1028 × 764 × 24-bit ÷ 8 = 2,359,296 bytes

That's over 2MB, which means you'd need at least a typical 4MB card to get the higher resolution.

 ## What resolution should I use to get the most out of Windows?

Your resolution is really determined mostly by the size of your monitor. The default Windows resolution is 640×480 pixels with 8-bit color (256 colors). We think that this mode is a bit too restrictive for useful Windows work—we prefer either 800×600 or 1024×768.

Try the various resolutions for yourself and decide which one is ideal for you; it'll always be a trade-off between fitting more onscreen and having the individual objects too small to read or use.

You might also be limited by the monitor you use. Early monitors were not all "multisync" capable, allowing them to display (sync to) different resolutions. If this is the case for you, you might need a new monitor.

Also, many applications look better if you set your display to 16-bit mode (sometimes called *high color*). There's generally no advantage to using 24-bit (called *true color*) mode unless you're a graphic artist using a graphic-editing program like Adobe Photoshop. Your system runs significantly slower in 24-bit mode and it rarely looks any better than 16-bit mode.

What's the difference between VGA and SVGA?

Video Graphics Array (VGA) is the original high-resolution display mode that brought the PC into the 20th century. Previously, PC compatibles were stuck in text-only mode unless you added a CGA or an EGA adapter, both of which provided low resolution and few colors. VGA, on the other hand, offered 640×480 resolution with 16 colors. VGA is still considered a lowest common denominator among video cards, and selecting the basic VGA display mode in Windows will give you exactly that resolution.

Super Video Graphics Array (SVGA) is the standard for Windows today. SVGA picks up where VGA left off, offering a wide and flexible number of resolution modes and color depths. Most software that requires SVGA is implicitly requesting a video card capable of supporting at least

640×480 with 256 colors, though SVGA can support much higher resolutions, depending on how much memory is on the video card.

Video Adapter	Typical Resolution	Number of Colors	Year Introduced
CGA (Color Graphics Adapter)	640×200	2	1981
	320×200	4	
	160×200	16	
EGA (Enhanced Graphics Adapter)	640×350	16	1984
VGA (Video Graphics Array)	640×480	16	1987
	320×200	256	
SVGA (Super Video Graphics Array)	640×480	16.7 million	1989
	800×600	16.7 million	
	1024×768	16.7 million	
	1280×1024	16.7 million	

These days, it's virtually impossible to find a "plain-vanilla" VGA card with just 256K of RAM; a simple SVGA card is the most inexpensive one in most stores. In addition, video is such a critical bottleneck in the overall speed of your PC, so it makes sense to buy a good video card to begin with.

What's VESA? Do I need it?

VESA can mean either of two things, depending on whether you mean hardware or software. In days of old—several years ago—the VESA architecture was one of the competitors hoping to gain dominance in the world of high-speed video slots. IBM's PCI standard eventually won. If you have a VESA system (also called VL-bus), you can get better performance by replacing your motherboard with a new PCI-based system.

On the other hand, VESA is also the name of a universal DOS software driver for enabling high-resolution, VGA displays in DOS applications, particularly games.

Is there a way to change the resolution in Windows without restarting my machine?

Yes, but unfortunately many systems (especially Windows 95) come with this indispensable feature disabled. Follow these steps to enable the capability:

1. Choose Start | Settings | Control Panel and start the Display applet.
2. Click the Settings tab and click Advanced.
3. Place a check mark in the box at the bottom that says "Show settings icon on task bar."

4. Click OK to exit the Display properties.

Now that you've set it up, here's how to change resolution without restarting Windows:

1. Right-click the monitor icon in the System Tray (the small part of the Taskbar on the right side of the screen that contains the clock and icons for other applications that run in the background). This will bring up the list box shown here:

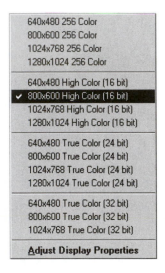

2. Choose the desired resolution and color depth from the context menu.

3. If this is your first time changing the resolution, you'll see a dialog box that asks if you want to change the resolution without restarting. Choose the option to hide the dialog box in the future, and click OK.

 Note: *If you don't have the option of hiding the dialog box in the future, you likely have an early version of Windows 95. But fret not, because you can download the PowerToys add-on from Microsoft's Web site at **http://www.microsoft.com** to add the ability to change resolutions without rebooting.*

 Can I get Windows to start up in different resolutions for the different people who share my machine?

If you have visited the Password Properties or User Properties in the Control Panel, you've no doubt noticed that you can customize Windows for each user in your home or office. But while you can make the Start menu, background image, and other features unique for each user, there's no way for one user to get a 640×480 display automatically and another user to get 1280×1024 in Windows 95 (it does work in Windows 98, though). Sorry! On the other hand, you can change the resolution and color depth instantly without restarting Windows (see the answer to "Is there a way to change the resolution in Windows without restarting my machine?" earlier in this chapter).

 I want to hook up a larger monitor to my laptop. Do I need a video card?

No, you don't need to do anything special in most cases. Look on the back of your notebook and you should see a standard VGA port just like the one on the back of a desktop PC (see Figure 6-2). With the notebook and monitor turned off, plug a monitor into that port. When you turn the notebook on, it'll display on the monitor. If you have a fairly modern notebook (486 or better) that doesn't feature a VGA port, consult the manufacturer; it may be an add-on you need to purchase.

✳ *Note:* *Depending on the notebook, the normal LCD display may or may not function while a monitor is plugged in.*

MONITORS

Why isn't my 17-inch monitor actually 17 inches?

Welcome to the great PC debate (and hardware lawsuit) of the 90s. For years, PC monitors were sold using the common

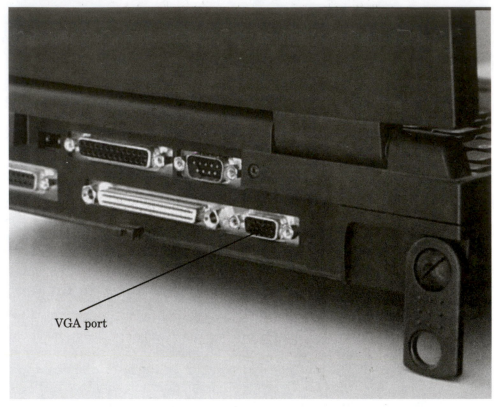

VGA port

Figure 6-2 A VGA port on the back of a typical notebook computer

designations of 14-inch, 15-inch, 17-inch, and 21-inch. The actual dimension in question is a diagonal of the entire picture tube, from corner to corner (which is also the way televisions are measured). That measurement includes part of the tube that isn't actually visible because it is hidden behind the outer casing and frame of the monitor chassis. Every manufacturer builds their monitors a bit differently, so a 17-inch monitor at one company might have 16 inches visible while a similar 17-inch monitor elsewhere might reveal only 15.8 inches.

Is this a big deal? Perhaps; it depends on whom you ask. These days, a new monitor is required to advertise the actual viewable tube dimension, even if it claims to be, for instance, a 17-inch monitor. This makes it easier to compare monitors of similar price, quality, and features. Also keep in mind that

the usable display area will be even less than the new "truth in advertising" dimensions. While televisions use a technique called *overscan* to display the video image from edge to edge of the screen, PC monitors don't do that—they *underscan*, so that the edges of the tube (where distortion is greatest) aren't used (see Figure 6-3). A typical 17-inch monitor might have 16.8 inches of viewable tube, but the display will only cover 16 inches total. Remember to compare apples to apples—that is, the viewable diagonal. Best advice: Eyeball monitors in a computer or electronics store (even if you end up buying online) when you do comparison shopping, and see which seems to give you more viewing area.

Figure 6-3 A typical computer monitor actually underscans an image to prevent distortion at the outer edges.

How big a monitor should I buy?

Some new PCs, especially the sub-$1000 variety, are bundled with 15-inch monitors. That doesn't mean you *have* to buy them that way. The price of 17-inch monitors has dropped so low that we recommend everyone looking for a new PC or monitor get that size. A 17-inch monitor has considerably more viewing area than a 15-inch model, and that means less eyestrain, more surface area to work with, and an overall better computing experience.

Another alternative is the new 19-inch monitor class. Only slightly bulkier and more expensive than 17-inch models, the 19-inch monitor has significantly more screen area and is a good compromise for people who want more room to work, but don't want to invest in the much more expensive 21-inch monitors.

A third alternative is to use two monitors at once. That may sound decadent, but by using two 17-inch monitors, you can work much more efficiently than by switching to one large and expensive 21-inch display. See the answer to "Can I hook up two monitors to my PC?" later in this chapter for more information.

What is "dot pitch"?

The *dot pitch* of your monitor is a measure of the distance between individual dots that are drawn onscreen. The smaller the dot pitch the better, and most monitors today have a reasonable .28 dot pitch. Older and very cheap monitors have a dot pitch as high as .46 or .51, and they're visibly blurry. Monitors with a dot pitch higher than .28 are a headache waiting to happen.

Also keep in mind that the higher your resolution becomes with a given monitor, the more important dot pitch becomes, because you need to more accurately draw pixels that are closer together. If you want to display 640×480 on a 21-inch monitor (not a sight we'd want to see), the dot pitch can safely be as high as .60 and still have an acceptable display. Increase the resolution to 1280×1024 on that same monitor, however, and you'll need a dot pitch of .30 to draw the screen.

 ## What's the "refresh rate"?

Refresh rate is a term that describes how often the image on your screen is refreshed. It is measured in *hertz,* or cycles per second. A 72-Hz monitor can redraw the screen 72 times each second, reducing eyestrain and making the screen look more stable. Lower refresh rates are okay, but below about 60 Hz, your monitor starts to flicker noticeably. Higher than 72 Hz, and you'll feel like your display is rock-solid. Again, when you're shopping for a monitor, think about the long-term health and happiness benefits of a high refresh rate.

Do I need a multisync monitor?

Yup. Before multisyncs were common, you'd get a monitor that was locked into a single frequency, such as 31 MHz, designed for VGA. But VGA was all you could display, even if your video card supported SVGA graphics. That's because each graphics display mode uses its own frequency.

Multisync monitors can automatically lock onto whichever frequency the video card puts out, allowing it to switch on the fly among many display modes. If you have an old monitor, you might need to replace it before you can take advantage of the benefits of a new video card.

I have a "digital" monitor. Aren't all computer components digital?

You might think so, but...

Actually, VGA monitors (the only kind you can find in PC stores these days) aren't digital—they're analog. Old displays like CGA and EGA cards sent graphic information to the monitor digitally, as in 0s and 1s.

VGA and SVGA cards send analog voltage information to the monitor. Each pixel needs a red, green, and blue color value from 0 (black) to 255 (white). The higher the voltage, the higher the color information.

Thus, in an ironic twist on technology, digital monitors are obsolete and only work with old CGA and EGA cards. Analog monitors are designed for VGA and SVGA cards, and they aren't cross-compatible.

Digital is making a comeback, though. Currently new digital video cards are required for some LCD (Liquid Crystal Display) monitors, more often called flat-panel monitors. Certain LCD monitors require digital video information—from a digital video card—to display the computer screen.

Is there a correlation between Windows' screen resolution and the size my monitor should be?

Yes, there is. Higher resolutions, such as 1024×768 and 1280×1024, make the display too difficult to read or use on a small monitor. These resolutions can also be used to make your display close to WYSIWYG (What You See Is What You Get) output. Use this chart to decide which resolution works best for a given screen size. Conversely, if you want to use a high-resolution mode, use this chart to choose a matching monitor:

Resolution	Monitor Size
640×480	14 or 15 inches
800×600	15 or 17 inches
1024×768	17 or 19 inches
1280×1024	19 to 21 inches

Can I hook up two monitors to my PC?

You sure can. With two monitors connected to your PC, the Windows desktop stretches across both displays, effectively giving you a 2048×768-pixel display if both monitors are configured for 1024×768-pixel resolution. That means you can run different applications in each monitor and easily drag and drop between the two. It's an efficient way to work, especially if you spend a lot of time working with two or more applications at the same time. There are two ways to do this:

- Equipped with Windows 98, you can easily connect two monitors to your PC. You'll need to add a second video card to your PC and connect one monitor to each card. Windows 98 has automatic and built-in support for multiple monitors.

● If you're using Windows 95, you can still get multiple monitor action, though you need specialized video hardware. The most popular option is the Appian family of graphics cards, which you can learn about at **http://www.appiangraphics.com**.

 ### I have a video card in the AGP slot. Can I add a second card to the PCI bus for multiple monitors?

Yes, that'll work just fine. Windows 98 recognizes video cards in both AGP and PCI slots, even simultaneously. That may be surprising to someone who has had bad luck with video cards and older versions of Windows, but Windows 98 is pretty smart. Just insert the new card in your PCI slot, connect a monitor, and start the PC. You'll probably have to install the video card's driver, and then you can enable multi-monitor support by opening the Display properties dialog box in the Control Panel.

I'm using two monitors. How can I change the resolution of the second one?

With two monitors installed and running, you can change the resolution of the primary display—the one that appears on the left—in the traditional way by right-clicking the display icon in the System tray and selecting a new view mode. But to affect the monitor on the right, you need to open the Display properties dialog box and click the Settings tab. Click on the monitor marked "2," then change the resolution or color mode from the controls on this tab.

 ### I have a game that crashes when I try to run it on my new dual monitor system. What can I do?

You can easily disable the second monitor for a short time when using finicky software then turn it back on later. To do that, open the Display Properties dialog box in the Control Panel and click the Settings tab. Right-click on the second monitor and de-select the Enabled option from the menu. Click OK to close the properties sheet and reset your display.

Do I need to use a screen saver to preserve the life of my monitor?

Not anymore. Very old digital monitors had a tendency to "burn in" repeated shapes. (You can sometimes see the effect on older ATM machines.) New monitors—and by that we mean any monitor sold since 1993—don't suffer burn-in problems like their older siblings.

Nonetheless, there's a thriving screen-saver market. The bottom line is that you don't need screen savers to protect the monitor, but there are other reasons to use a screen saver:

- **Aesthetics**   There's nothing wrong with using a screen saver that sends little fish or toasters flying across the screen when you're not working.

- **Hiding sensitive information**   If you're not at your PC, you might use a screen saver to obscure what you're working on.

- **Security**   Many screen savers offer password protection, keeping co-workers from accessing your PC when you step away.

To activate a screen saver, choose Start | Settings | Control Panel, and then select the Display applet. Select a screen saver from the aptly named Screen Saver tab and click OK:

I'm monitor shopping. What features are most important?

A monitor is a big investment. Aside from a new CPU purchase or upgrade, the monitor is usually the most expensive part of the system and will probably last the longest, perhaps even surviving its original PC to have a second life with a new system. With that in mind, you should buy your monitor expecting it to last three to five years. Consider these points:

- **Warranty**   The picture tube is the least reliable component of any monitor. Make sure your warranty is written to protect you for as long as possible. Also consider who pays for shipping in case of repair work and how quickly they pledge to turn a monitor around if there's a problem.

- **Energy Star rating**   Energy Star is the power-saving feature built into many PC components. If a monitor is Energy Star-compliant, you can set your PC to shut the monitor off after a certain period of inactivity to save energy and prolong the life of the picture tube. Likewise, Energy Star-compliant monitors draw less power when they're running.

- **Low radiation**   The jury is still out on the long-term health hazards of exposure to PC monitors. Some studies suggest that sitting inches away from a high-powered electron gun for hours at a time might not be really good for you, so many vendors sell monitors that have low radiation ratings to offer some protection. (LCD monitors, by contrast, generate virtually no EMI radiation.)

- **Convenient controls**   Experiment with a monitor's front panel controls before buying it. These controls let you adjust brightness and contrast, as well as fine-tune the position of the display in various modes. If the controls are hard to use now, they'll be annoying for the next five years. You can also check controls for the range of settings they allow. If there isn't a dramatic difference between the highest brightness setting and the lowest brightness setting for a given monitor, you might want to consider a different model.

- **Specifications**　Look for low dot pitch (.28 or less), high maximum resolution, and high scanning frequency—also called refresh rate.

- **Quality**　Compare your favorites side by side in the store (make the store staff move the monitors—you're paying hundreds or thousands of dollars) and look very closely for a clear, crisp, uniform, and bright picture. You'll use this monitor a lot, for a long time, with your own eyes, so invest carefully.

Should I get a flat-panel display?

Flat-panel displays do offer some advantages, the major one being the complete lack of flicker on the screen. That's because the image isn't drawn of phosphors with an electron gun, like it is on a typical CRT monitor or a television set. Instead, individual liquid crystal pixels are turned on and off (or given a color) as needed.

This lack of an electron gun also means the monitor emits less radiation, which may or may not be a long-term health consideration. Some users certainly feel that an LCD monitor offers a more comfortable picture to view, especially since the monitor tends never to lose convergence. (Loss of convergence can result in hot spots on the screen, or a general fuzziness.)

LCD monitors are also less bulky and lighter (usually 5-10 pounds vs. 40-50 pounds for CRTs), so they fit more easily on desks and in notebook computers (see Figure 6-4). And, they tend to offer very solid, color images, although LCDs, in general, are usually—but not always—less bright than CRTs. Also, LCDs don't have the same "viewable image" issues that CRTs do; because there's no loss of quality at the edges due to convergence issues, LCD displays take the image to their full size. That makes a 15-inch LCD comparable to a 17-inch CRT, because the CRT will likely offer a viewable image of 15.8 inches, plus another .4-inch border or so.

There are three major disadvantages. First, LCDs are considerably more expensive, with 15-inch LCD displays often twice as expensive as comparable 17-inch CRT displays. The best LCD displays use digital screen-image information

Figure 6-4 An LCD monitor is slimmer, and takes up much less desk space, than a CRT monitor.

instead of an analog data feed, so that also requires the added expense of a special digital video card.

Second, LCDs generally offer poor image quality if not set to a particular "optimum" resolution. While most LCD displays are able to sync to different resolutions, there's usually one resolution that looks better than the others. An LCD has a fixed pixel size, so non-optimum resolutions have to anti-alias the image (cheat a bit by blurring the edges of images on the screen) in order to achieve, say, a 640×480 image on an LCD that's optimum at 800×600.

Finally, LCDs are often difficult to view from odd angles— you need to be looking directly at the screen. This can be a problem if you often share the screen or use it for presentation.

All that said, the prices are coming down consistently and it looks like many more of us will have LCD displays on our desks over the next few years.

❓ What are the differences between passive, dual-scan, and active matrix displays?

Passive and *dual-scan* displays use less expensive technologies to draw images on the LCD display. They are limited by resolution (they can't display 24-bit color, for example) and they're more difficult to read from an angle. *Active matrix*, also called TFT, is a brighter display that is easy to read from a wide range of angles. It also has more resolution mode options. The disadvantage, of course, is that active matrix displays are more expensive (by about $200) compared to their dual-scan equivalents.

Why the difference? With a passive matrix screen, individual pixels on the display are activated by turning on a transistor in the row and column you want. The display starts at one end of the screen, scans all of the rows and columns, and lights up the needed pixels as it goes. So the image is never all on at once—that's why passive displays are less bright than active displays.

By contrast, active matrix displays also use rows and columns to select the pixels, but they have transistor latches at each pixel that turn them on or off individually. So, each active matrix pixel is on or off until it needs to be changed.

Nearly all desktop LCD displays are active matrix; you'll generally only find passive matrix LCDs in notebook computers.

❓ Can I unplug a monitor from the video port while the PC is powered on?

Nope, don't do that. The video port is one of those "hot" ports on a PC into which you should never try to swap components while the PC is powered on. You can seriously damage the PC.

❓ Why do the corners of my monitor have weird, multicolored distortion?

You have a magnetic source, like unshielded speakers or a telephone, too close to the monitor. Move them further away or get shielded equipment. Prolonged exposure to a magnetic field can damage your monitor.

Walkthrough: Installing a Monitor

Installing a new monitor is a piece of cake—certainly easier than installing a video card. Simply follow these steps:

1. Shut down the PC and the old monitor, if there's one connected.

2. Disconnect the old monitor from the PC's VGA port, and unplug the monitor from the power outlet. (Since almost all monitors use the same kind of power cord, you can simply pull the plug out of the old monitor and leave it handy to plug into the new monitor.)

3. Place the new monitor in position and plug the VGA cable into the PC.

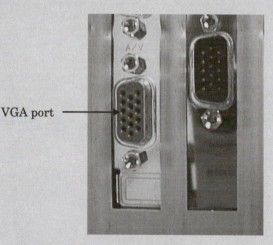

VGA port

4. Plug the power cord into the back of the monitor.

5. Start the PC and the monitor.

If you see the normal BIOS startup screen, then the monitor works and you're probably done. If you have a plug-and-play monitor, Windows should recognize it and install the appropriate driver for you. If not, follow these steps:

1. Choose Start | Settings | Control Panel and start the Display applet.

2. Click the Settings tab:

3. Click the Advanced Properties button.

4. Click the Monitor tab:

5. Click the Change button.

6. Click "Show all devices" and choose your monitor—or its nearest equivalent—from the list:

Select Device

Click the Monitor that matches your hardware, and then click OK. If you don't know which model you have, click OK. If you have an installation disk for this device, click Have Disk.

Manufacturers:
- Compaq USA/Focus Te
- Conrac Display Product
- Cordata Technologies, I
- CTX - Chuntex Electron
- Daewoo

Models:
- CTX 1565GM
- CTX 1765
- CTX 1765GM
- CTX 1785
- CTX 1785GM
- CTX 2085

○ Show compatible devices
● Show all devices

Have Disk...

OK   Cancel

7. Click OK.

8. If your monitor is Energy Star-compliant, make sure you check the appropriate box.

9. Click OK to finish installing the monitor.

 Is it better to leave the monitor on all day or shut it off every time I'm done with it?

Because the picture tube is the element most susceptible to premature damage, we recommend powering off the monitor when it's not in use. If your PC is Energy Star-compliant, however, you don't have to do that manually—let the PC do it for you. Follow these steps to enable the power-saving mode:

● Choose Start | Settings | Control Panel and start the Display applet.

● Click the Screen Saver tab in the Display Properties dialog box.

● Place check marks in the boxes that say "Low-power standby" and "Shut off monitor."

Display Properties dialog box showing the Screen Saver tab:

MGA Settings | MGA Monitor | Color | Web | Settings
Background | Screen Saver | Appearance

Screen Saver
Mystify Your Mind ▼   Settings...   Preview
☐ Password protected   Change...   Wait: 20 minutes

Energy saving features of monitor
☑ Low-power standby   20 minutes
☑ Shut off monitor   20 minutes

OK   Cancel   Apply

● Enter a time in each box that reflects when you want the PC to power down the monitor.

● Click OK to exit.

Keep in mind that you want to specify enough time that the monitor won't go off just because you walked away to get a cup of coffee. Repeatedly cycling the monitor on and off isn't any better for it than leaving it on constantly—but not so long that it's on for a long period for no reason. We suggest 20 minutes as a good starting point.

Why does my monitor's display appear to be degrading over time?

The picture tube can be magnetized over time, and that can affect the picture quality. Most monitors *degauss* the display, which simply means that they remove magnetization every time they're started. However, you may have a stronger tool available: There may be a manual degauss button below the front panel of the monitor. You can use this button occasionally to clear the unwanted magnetic field. You can also take your monitor to a service center to have a full degauss performed (along with other general monitor tweaking and maintenance).

> **Caution:** *Use the degauss button just once each time you need it. Don't press it repeatedly, or you may damage your monitor.*

Is it okay to clean my monitor screen?

Of course—but only when the monitor is turned off. Use isopropyl alcohol, but spray it on the rag and then dust the screen with the damp rag.

> **Caution:** *Never spray liquid directly on your screen. It can run between the seams in the casing and damage the inside of the monitor.*

My monitor suddenly looks all reddish (or bluish). What's wrong?

If your monitor cable is connected properly and it isn't frayed, then it's likely that one of the guns in your monitor has died. This is especially true if you've tested the monitor by connecting it to another computer that you know is displaying screens correctly.

A monitor broken in this way can happen as a result of shipping, age, or poor construction. Whatever the reason, there's nothing you can do to fix it. Send the monitor back for repair and hope it's covered under warranty.

My monitor clicks occasionally. Is this a big problem?

It's no problem if your monitor clicks when you turn it on or when switching between Windows and DOS. It's just synching to a new frequency. If it clicks continuously or buzzes, however, shut it down right away. Some software is trying to make it lock to a mode that's outside its frequency range, and that's fatal to the monitor.

Your monitor might also be dropping out of sync if you use an unconditioned power supply (like a wall outlet) and you suffer frequent undervoltage. This can eventually damage your monitor (not to mention your PC) so you should invest in an uninterruptible power supply (UPS). For more information on the need for a UPS and its uses, see Chapter 2.

❓ Anything I can do about my buzzing, squealing monitor?

It's possible the monitor is being driven at the wrong refresh rate or that the monitor driver software is otherwise doing something inappropriate. Check with the manufacturer of your video card and/or monitor to see if they have procedures, suggestions, or new Windows software drivers to alleviate the problem.

❓ No matter how much I tweak the controls, I can't get the image perfectly square. Is my monitor defective?

Probably not, depending on how bad the error actually is. If you have a sophisticated enough monitor you may be able to use its controls to change the geometry of the picture image. Play with the controls and see if you can make the image worse. (We subscribe to a rule called Murphy's Law of Vertical Hold, which dictates that messing with the picture image of a television or monitor invariably makes it much worse than when you started.)

One odd solution: You might try changing the direction the monitor faces because the earth's magnetic field can actually influence your monitor and affect its display. Turning the monitor to face east can arguably reduce the distortion the most.

Tip: *Many monitors have a "factory default" control or button that allows you to immediately set the monitor to its originally factory-programmed settings. These settings may not be optimal, but in times of visual crisis they may be better than what you and Murphy have managed together.*

❓ My display is usually fine, but it's way too dark when I play DOS (or 3-D accelerated) games.

You'll need to adjust the brightness of the display. You have two choices:

 Adjust the brightness and contrast with the controls on the front of the monitor. (They'll usually look like the sun and the moon, respectively.)

● Use the gamma control built into your game. A gamma correction is like a brightness control except that instead of a diagonal line from brightest to darkest, a gamma correction uses a smart "curve" to brighten the dark parts of an image while protecting the brightest parts from oversaturation. But that's not all that important—just know that you can usually find a gamma control in most DOS games to brighten the display while you're playing that game. That way the screen is still the way you like it when you return to Windows.

VIDEO CARDS

 ### What exactly does a video driver do?

The *video driver* is the software component that allows Windows to use the video card in your PC as a display device. Every video card requires a video driver, but some generic drivers ship with Windows. If all else fails, you can always use those while you get the right driver from the video card vendor. If you use generic drivers, though, you'll miss out on the special features and faster performance offered by your card.

 ### How do I change the resolution (or colors) used on my display?

You can change the display characteristics of your PC using the Display Properties found in Windows. If it's enabled, just right-click the monitor icon in the System Tray and choose the desired video mode from the context menu:

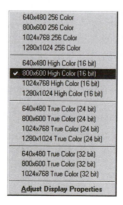

> ✚　***Tip:***　*If you don't see the monitor icon in the System Tray, instructions for displaying it are provided in the answer to "Is there a way to change the resolution in Windows without restarting my machine?" earlier in this chapter. Or you can invoke the Display Properties directly by right-clicking on the Windows desktop and choosing Properties from the menu. Then click the Settings tab and choose the desired mode.*

What's a graphics accelerator?

A *graphics accelerator* is the generic name for a video card that has additional hardware on board for accelerating Windows and other graphics activities. A graphics accelerator isn't an additional piece of hardware—it's built into an ordinary video adapter. These days, almost any video card you buy will have some acceleration features built in.

What is an accelerated graphics port? How do I get one?

The *accelerated graphics port* (AGP) is a fairly recent innovation that's been added to Pentium II and Pentium III motherboards. AGP is a very fast port designed to move video more quickly (even faster than the PCI bus) and handle some 3-D functions on the primary bus. Using AGP, for example, ordinary system RAM can hold textures that would otherwise have to be stored in the limited RAM on 3-D accelerator cards. This means that very high-resolution, detailed textures can be mapped onto surfaces. Some examples include moving morphing textures and video, such as the ability to map a drive-in movie theater screen with actual video, visible from a flight simulator aircraft flying by overhead.

To get an AGP port, you need a Pentium II or III motherboard.

What kind of interface should my video card have?

In the old days—a few years ago—most video cards came in the ISA format because almost all computers used the old

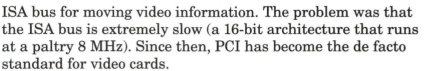

ISA bus for moving video information. The problem was that the ISA bus is extremely slow (a 16-bit architecture that runs at a paltry 8 MHz). Since then, PCI has become the de facto standard for video cards.

If your motherboard doesn't have a few PCI slots, you need to upgrade your motherboard. See Chapter 3 to identify PCI slots. An ISA video card is, quite simply, such a bottleneck that your system can't run at speeds fast enough to support modern multimedia software. If your motherboard offers a VESA local bus slot and you've determined that a motherboard upgrade isn't currently in the cards, you can get reasonable performance by upgrading to a VESA-based, Windows-accelerated video card.

An even better solution: If you have a Pentium II/III-style motherboard, you should definitely use the AGP port for your video. AGP cards aren't identical to PCI cards, so you can't slip your old PCI video system into the AGP slot; you'll need to spend about $100 on a new AGP card. But it's definitely worth it in added performance.

 ## How can I tell if it's time to upgrade my video card?

As in all things, it's time to upgrade your video card either when you notice a performance problem or when an elephant sits on it. If your card is more than two years old or it hasn't enough memory to run at screen resolutions you want to use, it's a good candidate for replacement. Consider these possible reasons for upgrade:

- New software doesn't run properly and there are no updated drivers for a video card as old as yours.
- Your video card is ISA based.
- You can't display high-color modes when running multimedia titles.
- You want to capture video for home movies or watch television with your PC and would like to have an all-in-one video card.
- You want to play new 3-D accelerated games.

Walkthrough: Installing a New Video Card

Installing a new video card takes a little planning and a small amount of confidence. Follow these steps and you shouldn't have a problem. If your system is on the older side, check the manual for any DIP switches, jumpers, or BIOS settings you need to change. Those with newer PCs don't have to worry about any of these things.

1. Before you get started, change the Display Properties to a plain-vanilla, 16-color VGA display. In the Advanced Properties dialog box, choose the Adapter tab and select (Standard display types) on the left and VGA on the right. If plug-and-play fails you, at least now your PC will start in basic VGA mode.

   Select Device

   Click the Display adapters that matches your hardware, and then click OK. If you don't know which model you have, click OK. If you have an installation disk for this device, click Have Disk.

   Manufacturers:
   - (Standard display types)
   - Actix Systems
   - ATI Technologies
   - Boca Research
   - Cardinal Technologies

   Models:
   - Standard Display Adapter (VGA)
   - Standard PCI Graphics Adapter
   - Standard PCI Graphics Adapter (VGA)
   - Standard PCI Graphics Adapter (XGA)
   - Super VGA

   ○ Show compatible devices
   ● Show all devices

   Have Disk...

   OK   Cancel

2. Shut down your PC and remove the cover.

3. Find the old video adapter (it's what the monitor was plugged into) and remove it carefully.

4. Take the new video adapter out of the anti-static bag and install it into the same slot that the old adapter came from, unless the card requires a different slot. (If the new card requires a different slot, such as VESA or PCI, remove the screw and metal slot

protector for the new slot, then screw the slot protector over the old slot's opening.)

5. Screw the video card in place securely.

6. Attach the monitor cable and start the PC to test the new card. Don't worry about the cover yet—make sure the video works first.

7. If Windows starts successfully, follow the plug-and-play instructions to add the new drivers. If Windows starts but doesn't detect the new card, open the Display Properties and add the card manually.

8. Once everything seems to be running properly, shut down the PC and put the cover back on. You're done!

If you've followed these steps, however, and your video card doesn't seem to work, check the following:

● Make sure the video card is securely seated and not sticking up at either end of the slot.

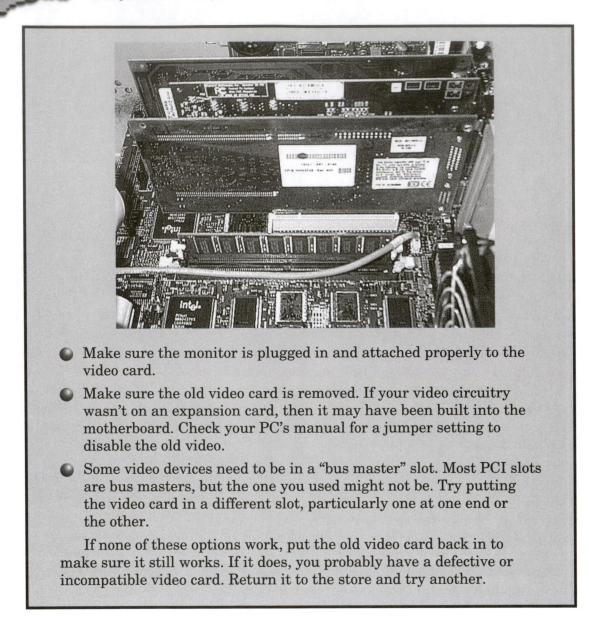

● Make sure the monitor is plugged in and attached properly to the video card.

● Make sure the old video card is removed. If your video circuitry wasn't on an expansion card, then it may have been built into the motherboard. Check your PC's manual for a jumper setting to disable the old video.

● Some video devices need to be in a "bus master" slot. Most PCI slots are bus masters, but the one you used might not be. Try putting the video card in a different slot, particularly one at one end or the other.

If none of these options work, put the old video card back in to make sure it still works. If it does, you probably have a defective or incompatible video card. Return it to the store and try another.

 Caution: *If your monitor doesn't display anything when you first turn the system on, turn it off right away.*

I have two video cards in my PC, but neither seems to work. What's the problem?

With Windows 3.1 or Windows 95, you should only have one video card in your PC at a time. If you have video circuitry on the motherboard, look in your manual to find the jumper that disables it. If neither card seems to work, remove one of them and the remaining card should function properly. Of course, if you're using Windows 98 to display the screen image on two different monitors, it's okay to have two video cards installed at once. If neither work, however, the same suggestions apply—get one of them working before you try to use both at once.

When I installed my new card, I couldn't find an old video card to remove! What's up?

It's entirely possible—particularly if you own a Packard Bell or an older 486-based PC—that the video circuitry is embedded in the motherboard. This was often done to save a card slot for other applications and to speed up the video by avoiding the slow ISA bus. That practice is making a comeback; some new PCs ship with video on the motherboard as well. These newer value-priced systems generally come with good video, but it's soldered directly onto the motherboard, just like in the old days.

If your video is built into the motherboard, check the user's manual or call the system vendor to find out if you need to disable the old video circuitry. Sometimes the motherboard can automatically detect a video card and disable the old stuff on its own. Other motherboards have a jumper you need to set that tells the system to bypass the old video circuits.

I've installed a new video card, but now Windows won't display anything but gibberish. How do I fix this?

For starters, you'll need to boot your system in Windows' Safe Mode. When the PC starts, wait till it says "Starting Windows" and hold down F8. You'll see a menu of startup options; choose Safe Mode. Windows will use a plain-vanilla VGA driver and

start the PC in a no-frills video mode. You can use Safe Mode until you get things working.

Next, contact your video card vendor and get an updated driver. Install the driver and restart the PC normally. Everything should then work.

Even though I have a fancy new video card, I can't select resolutions above 640×480. Why?

Windows doesn't know what kind of monitor you have, so it's staying on the safe side and only letting you select a plain-vanilla VGA display mode. You can fix that by selecting the monitor you own in the Display Properties:

1. Choose Start | Settings | Control Panel and start the Display applet.
2. Click the Settings tab.
3. Click the Advanced Properties button.
4. Click the Monitor tab.
5. Click the Change button.
6. Click "Show all devices" and choose your monitor—or its nearest equivalent—from the list.
7. Click OK.

Still having trouble? You should see if your video card and/or your monitor came with a diskette or CD that includes Windows driver software.

I installed some new software, and now my PC just displays gibberish or a black screen. How can I fix it?

The software probably installed custom drivers for your video card that didn't work the way the software engineers planned. Start Windows in Safe Mode (press F8 at startup) and reinstall the video card's original drivers when Windows is loaded. Then contact the software vendor for a patch that will let you run their program.

 Ever since I installed the new video card, my PC has been crashing frequently. What's going on, and how do I make it stop?

You might need to remove previous driver information from the Windows Registry. Windows doesn't like to keep track of more than one video device at a time. Call the vendor for the old card and find out exactly how to replace every trace of the old card.

One solution that can give you reliable video performance—at least until you get an improved driver—is to reduce the Hardware Acceleration setting in the System Properties. Simply right-click My Computer and choose Properties from the drop-down menu. Then click the Performance tab and click the Graphics button. Move the slider to the left; try it at the halfway point. If all is well, leave it there. Otherwise, keep moving it toward None until your video card works properly.

Another alternative is to use a utility program like Norton Utilities or Helix Nuts and Bolts. Both of these programs optimize the Windows Registry by eliminating references to removed and obsolete hardware.

How can I get new drivers for my video card?

The best way to get software updates is over the Internet; it's fast and free, and most vendors now keep a technical support Web page where customers can get updates, patches, and bug fixes to use with their products. Here are the most common places to look for video drivers:

ATI	http://www.atitech.com
Diamond	http://www.diamondmm.com
Hercules	http://www.hercules.com
Matrox	http://www.matrox.com
Number Nine	http://www.nine.com
S3	http://www.s3.com
STB	http://www.stb.com

 ### What is "DirectX"?

DirectX is a set of drivers developed by Microsoft that allows games and other multimedia software to access hardware-level functions in your PC's sound and video subsystems more quickly. That's a mouthful—but the simple answer is that DirectX is a slew of development tools that finally make it possible for Windows to play games as fast and efficiently as old-style DOS games. DirectX is a required component for the majority of new games to work properly on your PC. Don't worry: DirectX comes on the CD with every game that requires it.

 ### My new game wants to install DirectX. I'm pretty sure I already have it installed—should I let the game install DirectX again?

It's okay; let the game try. DirectX actually inspects your PC for the presence of an older or current version. If you're up to date, DirectX will not try to overwrite the existing files.

 ### Now that I've installed a video game that uses DirectX, the extra features that my video card provided are gone. Why?

The DirectX game thought your video card needed new DirectX drivers and replaced them—probably DirectX 5 or DirectX 6—with your original drivers. Contact your video card vendor for new drivers that are DirectX certified. That way you can play DirectX games and have the extra features in your video card at the same time.

3-D ACCELERATORS

 ### What is a 3-D accelerator?

A 3-D accelerator is a special kind of video card that uses hardware components to speed up the display and manipulation of 3-D data, particularly games. Here are a few of its features:

- **Texture mapping**   Texture mapping is arguably the most impressive feature of 3-D acceleration. Using special memory on the video card, photorealistic textures like walls and terrain can be "mapped" onto computer-generated surfaces with amazingly realistic results. The more memory available, the more detailed the textures can be.

- **Perspective correction** Using the appropriate hardware, 3-D scenes like a long corridor can be rendered with correct perspectives afforded to all the room's elements with little input from the computer's CPU, improving performance.

- **Anti-aliasing** Hardware reduces jagged edges and smoothes the overall image.

- **Smoke, fog, and semi-transparent effects** 3-D hardware makes a wide variety of special effects possible, including realistic fog effects, multicolored lighting, and semi-transparent glass.

Should I get a 3-D accelerator?

If you play games, yes. Few games are released that don't include support for hardware 3-D acceleration, and, in fact, most games require it. The stage has already been set; several 3-D-only games are on store shelves, and many others are best appreciated with a 3-D card.

Which 3-D accelerator do you recommend?

We recommend the Voodoo or Riva chipsets. There are a number of competing video cards on the market, but Riva and Voodoo appear to be the best choices. They're fast, support all the 3-D effects, and are favorites among game developers. Several vendors make a 3-D video card based on the Voodoo chip and they all use the easily recognized 3Dfx banner (see Figure 6-5).

Do I need to replace my current video card to get 3-D acceleration?

Not necessarily. Many 3-D video cards are all-in-one solutions that replace your existing video card and provide both 2-D and 3-D capabilities from a single PCI slot.

Figure 6-5 A Voodoo card

The 3Dfx Voodoo card, on the other hand, is a separate card that occupies a second PCI slot (see Figure 6-6). There are pros and cons to this approach.

You can continue using your existing video card for 2-D Windows acceleration. This is a reasonable solution if you already have a good video card (such as the Matrox Millennium or ATI Mach64) and would sacrifice Windows performance by moving to another video card.

Your video subsystem now consumes two precious PCI slots, which limits what else you can put in your PC. For that reason, these days we recommend you go ahead and move to a new card that does both 2-D and 3-D video. That way you have the slot free, or you can leave the second card in, upgrade to Windows 98, and run two monitors.

 ### What is "scan line interleaving"?

Scan line interleaving (SLI) is a variation on traditional 3-D accelerator technology that allows you to combine two 3-D video cards for twice the performance—each card displays

Figure 6-6   You may be able to add a Voodoo card to your system in addition to your existing video card.

alternating lines of video, for extremely powerful 3-D display capabilities. Do you need an SLI-compatible card like the Voodoo 2? Probably not—at least not right now. One Voodoo 2 card all by itself cranks out enough polygons on a Pentium II PC to deliver fluid game play. A second Voodoo 2 card isn't the smartest way to spend your money right now.

What happens if the 3-D accelerator's frame rate exceeds my monitor's refresh rate?

Some new 3-D video cards promise frame rates in excess of 100 frames per second—but most monitors only provide 72 Hz. What happens to the other frames? Nothing, really. The video will be extremely smooth, because there are more frames being rendered in memory than can be drawn on the screen. The result is video that runs as smooth as silk.

Online Help for Computer Gamers

If you're ever having trouble with a computer game, try visiting the manufacturer's Web site. Here's a short list of games whose publishers use 3-D acceleration:

- **Quake**   http://www.3dfx.com/game_dev/quake_faq.html
- **Tomb Raider**   http://www.eidosinteractive.com
- **Descent II**   http://www.crunge.com/descent_ii/ or http://www.pxsoftware.com
- **G Police** or **Formula 1 Nascar II**   http://www.psygnosis.com
- **Half Life**   http://www.sierrastudios.com/games/half-life/
- **Wing Commander**   http://www.origin.ea.com
- **Forsaken**   http://www.acclaimnation.com

VIDEO OUTPUT

How do I display my PC screen on my TV?

You'll need a VGA-to-NTSC encoder. They're commonly available for a wide range of prices from about $100 to $5000, depending on quality and features. You can inexpensively project your PC's video to a television with one of the low-end devices.

Some PCs ship with the encoder hardware already installed. You can find multimedia PCs and some notebook computers with a video out or NTSC out port.

What's NTSC? PAL? SECAM?

NTSC is the video standard used in North America for broadcasting video. PAL is the equivalent used in Europe, and SECAM is used in Australia. The primary difference among these standards is timing and frequency. The bottom line is that if you travel often—such as to Europe—your encoder needs to be able to support the video used in that country. An NTSC device won't properly display video to a TV in a PAL country, for instance.

I want to display a PowerPoint presentation on a TV set. Anything special I need to know?

TV video is a very different medium than computer graphics. If you want to project your data on a TV set, follow these general guidelines and experiment a lot:

- Most encoders only work in 256 color, 640×480 resolution mode. Get used to developing video content in that format.

- NTSC video doesn't have the bandwidth to display all colors accurately. (In fact, NTSC can only show about 4 million colors in total!) Don't use highly saturated colors—especially reds—in video, or they'll bleed all over the screen.

- Computer resolution and TV video resolution are hard to compare, because they use such fundamentally different technologies, but you can safely say that TV video is something slightly less than 640×480. One thing is for certain, however—single pixels of anything (especially horizontal single pixel lines) disappear into video noise. Use lines that are thicker in TV video than you'd use on a computer screen. And avoid single-pixel-wide fonts.

- Make fonts on the large side so they'll be readable on the TV screen. Don't use anything less than about 24 points for body text, and headlines should be at least 32, preferably larger.

I've just installed my TV tuner (or video capture card), but it doesn't work. What can I do?

Many specialty cards—like video capture, TV tuner, and video encoder cards—insist on being installed in a bus master slot. It's rarely apparent which of your PCI slots are bus masters, so if at first you don't succeed, try again in a different location. If necessary, move existing PCI cards into different slots until you find a combination that works.

 I have my PC's video encoder output plugged into the TV, but there's no display at all. How do I fix this?

Make sure that everything is plugged in, turned on, and set to the appropriate channel. If you're inputting directly into a VCR, for instance, make sure you have the device set to AUX or whatever setting is the correct position for the additional input.

Another problem might be related to S-VHS, if your system is so equipped. In many systems, the S-VHS input takes precedence over any VGA input. If you have a PC-to-NTSC encoder feeding into a standard video connector, unplug any S-VHS sources also connected to the device.

I want to make home videos on my PC and save them to videotape. What kind of equipment will I need?

You can purchase an all-in-one video card/capture device or get an additional capture card and add it to an empty PCI slot on your system. The Matrox Rainbow Runner is an example of an all-in-one solution, while Miro's DC-10 or DC-20 are excellent stand-alone capture cards.

Recently, a whole new class of capture devices has arrived: DV. DV stands for Digital Video, and it is the state-of-the-art in transferring video to a PC. DV camcorders record movies in pure, error-free digital format. You use a FireWire (also called IEEE 1394) card to move video to the PC, where you can edit it and then copy it back to DV or traditional VHS videotape. For more information on DV, see Chapter 10.

In addition to the capture card itself, you'll need the following:

●   **Lots of hard disk space**   You should consider getting a fast UltraDMA or SCSI hard disk for professional results. You'll also need a large hard disk, at least 10GB, to do real video work, since each and every minute of video eats up about 200MB.

● **A nonlinear editor**   Nonlinear editing (NLE) is a breed of software that lets you cut and paste video digitally as if you were manipulating text in a word processor. Good examples are Adobe Premiere, IMSI Lumiere, and Ulead MediaStudio.

Chapter 7

Sound

Answer Topics!

Sound @ a Glance

If you don't yet have sound for your PC, it may be time to join the multimedia age. Whether you're a hobbyist, musician, educator, or business person, you should know the basics of sound. Computer sound comes in two major types: digital audio and MIDI music. Your computer can either record audio directly to the hard drive, or it can create music "instructions" in a special language called MIDI. Tradeoffs exist for both, but your sound card should be capable of handling anything thrown at it.

Are you ready to buy, install, and troubleshoot a new sound card? Sound cards don't have to be pricey to be good. In fact, you should save a few dollars and buy good speakers instead. You don't need a sound card to use a CD-ROM drive, but it can help—and many sound cards can also function as the interface for your CD-ROM drive, hard drive, and other peripherals.

If you're serious about music, you can even hook up a keyboard synthesizer (or similar device) to your computer, and start making music using the MIDI language. Your computer can be taught to pay attention to what you're playing, to write your song in musical notation, or to take control of the keyboard itself and play the song back to you.

It's obvious the Internet is really starting to mature—you can now get great-sounding, CD-quality music from the Web. With the right tools, you can collect and listen to music right from your computer.

THE ESSENTIALS OF COMPUTERIZED SOUND

 Why do I need PC sound capabilities?

Sound is useful for a number of modern computing purposes, including these:

● **Games** This may be the most obvious and prevalent use. It's nice to hear something when you're playing a simulation, role-playing, or shoot-'em-up game.

● **Education titles** Sure, Reader Rabbit and friends should be able to make plenty of noise to keep your kids' attention. But don't forget other educational products, such as encyclopedias, history CD-ROMs, and even foreign language programs, that can all enhance your learning experience with sound.

● **Interface enhancement** Adding sound features to Windows 95 or 98, for example, allows the computer to communicate issues that relate to the interface by making noise—such as error beeps and "You have Mail" audio indicators.

What does sound have to do with computing?

In this age of "multimedia" PCs, having a PC that can play digital sounds and digital music is becoming more and more important. While the typical office machine may have less reason to incorporate sound, nearly all new consumer and home/office machines ship with either an expansion card or special circuitry designed to get sound from your PC to a set of speakers or headphones, or to a stereo receiver.

Does PC audio refer to playing audio CDs in a CD-ROM drive?

No. There are three different types of audio that a computer can deal with. Two of those are audio formats generated by the computer; the other doesn't really involve the computer except as a means of playing the sound:

- **Digital audio**   Ultimately, *digital audio* means that you're using your computer as a recording and/or playback device, almost as if it were a cassette recorder. Many games and multimedia titles use digital audio to store the sounds they play. For example, a speech by Martin Luther King, Jr., in an encyclopedia program would be stored in digital audio. A PC needs a sound card or sound-enabled motherboard to record and/or play digital audio.

- **Digital music**   A computer can also play music using the MIDI (*Musical Instrument Digital Interface*) standard to store instructions for playback. Instead of recording the music (like for a game or a presentation), the music is written on the computer in a special language that the computer can use to control a MIDI device. Like an old-time player piano, the commands in a digital music document are played by software on the computer. This is the way a lot of music for games and presentations is generated. It's also how many music professionals work with computers.

- **Pass-through audio**   The last type of music doesn't really require much interaction from the computer. It's pass-through audio, which is the technology that allows you to play audio CDs using a CD-ROM drive. A small audio cable connects the CD-ROM drive to your computer's sound interface. When you play an audio CD, that audio is sent down the audio cable to the sound card, which then passes the audio signal directly to the audio amplifier that boosts the sound for the speakers connected to the audio card. More than anything, it's just a convenient way to allow the CD-ROM drive to use the speakers that are hooked up to your sound card.

 ### Can I get good sound from a special driver for the PC internal speaker and not use a sound card at all?

No, absolutely not. Yes, there is a driver that allows your internal speaker to play audio intended for sound cards, but it performs poorly. It was meant for PCs years ago, when

sound cards cost hundreds of dollars. And there are many situations in which it doesn't work properly; for example, it won't play long sound samples that take a lot of memory.

If you really want to try it out (or to install it at work, where you can't get a real sound card), you can find the driver at Microsoft's Web site (**http://www.microsoft.com**).

 ## Do I need a new sound card?

If your computer isn't equipped for sound, then you should definitely look into a new sound card. You might also want to buy a sound card if your computer is equipped with a very old sound card—one that relies exclusively on lower-end technologies like FM synthesis and 8-bit sound generation.

A sound card can be useful in business settings, too, especially if you're interested in using text-to-speech (where your computer reads to you) or voice recognition technology. It's usually necessary to have a good sound card if you plan to use your computer for videoconferencing or playing voice mail messages recorded via your modem.

Tip: *Stop by a computer store and check out the sound on the latest PCs. If you don't feel like your PC matches up, you might want to look into a new sound card.*

 ## What should I look for when I buy a sound card?

Our basic advice is this: Pay for exactly what you want in a sound card. Often you'll see all-in-one cards or sound cards that offer many whiz-bang features you'll never use. You'll also find high-quality cards at reasonable prices that do include many elements that will be important to you.

Here are a few tips for buying a sound card:

● *Get a wavetable-based card.* Wavetable-based cards tend to generate much higher-quality digital music and sound effects than other styles of cards. Specifically, cards that are only capable of FM synthesis are based on older technology that doesn't sound nearly as rich or complete.

- *Get a PCI-based sound card.* Old ISA cards are quickly becoming antiques. New PCI-based sound cards produce higher-quality sound without relying as much on the CPU, which means your PC performs better when playing sound files. That's good news for games and multimedia applications.

- *Consider surround sound.* New sound cards like the Diamond MX-300 have outputs for four or more speakers. Using these cards you can create a real Dolby Digital surround soundstage for games and DVD movies.

- *Shop the compatibility of the card.* Ask friends, read magazine articles, and check the Web for any information you can find about the compatibility of a particular sound card. Once you decide on a particular card, stop by that manufacturer's Web site to ensure that they're keeping up with driver updates and technical support answers. Also check your PC and motherboard manufacturer's Web site and customer support to make sure problems haven't been identified with a particular sound card.

- *Keep up with the standards.* Of all sound standards, having a SoundBlaster Pro-compatible card is probably the most important. Some cards will mention compatibility with the Windows Sound System and/or original SoundBlaster, which is less than ideal. If you're shopping swap meets for older cards, avoid Adlib-only sound cards, too.

- *Get at least a 16-bit card.* Sound card manufacturers' marketing departments come up with every conceivable method for adding impressive looking numbers to their cards. Don't let the 64, 96, and 128 numbers fool you. You're looking for a card that can handle 16-bit audio samples.

- *Get plug-and-play hardware.* Although plug-and-play can sometimes cause trouble if you boot into old DOS games, that problem is quickly becoming a thing of the past.

Sound Advice

What do all those sound card terms actually mean? Here's a quick reference you'll find helful when shopping:

- **8-bit and 16-bit sound**   These measurements refer to the *width* of the sound sample. The more information that a sample has, the more detail you can hear and the more realistic it sounds. The threshold of human perception is about 16 bits of sound, so there's little value in extending past that amount of sound data.

- **Direct Memory Access (DMA)**   The DMA is the part of a sound card that directly accesses the memory on your PC without bothering the CPU. A 16-bit DMA is preferable to an 8-bit DMA because it does more work on its own, without bogging the CPU down for mundane tasks.

- **Wavetable**   *Wavetable lookup* refers to a method used by modern sound cards to store samples of musical instruments on the card. This is far, far more accurate than using FM synthesis to manufacture the sound using an FM crystal.

 ### Should I get a sound card with a CD-ROM interface?

This question doesn't really apply to modern PCs. If your PC was made in the last few years, it probably has two IDE interfaces that together support a total of four IDE or EIDE storage devices, including the CD-ROM drive. Your CD-ROM plugs directly into one of these IDE ports. Only older systems, sound-card/CD-ROM combinations would work together.

Should I add RAM to my audio card?

Only if you're a MIDI musician who is interested in adding more voices than the standard 128 sounds you have. In general, this is the main reason to expand a sound card with more RAM. Some cards boast additional sounds and instruments stored in nonvolatile ROM, allowing them to call

the card a "4MB wavetable" card or something similar. In general, though, this amount doesn't need to be expanded.

 ## What is 3-D sound?

3-D audio imaging is a process that adds an element of front and back to the typical left and right stereo elements that you generally hear in a two-speaker system. While this process usually requires a combination of hardware and software (for example, both your speakers and your game software should be 3-D equipped), it is a popular way to enhance the computer audio experience. Using two speakers, a 3-D sound system can generate effects that sound similar to a full surround sound system.

 ## What is the difference between FM and wavetable synthesis?

There are two ways that sound cards generate digital music. Using a process called FM synthesis, the PC does its best to make a sound that resembles the one being asked for. A piano sound, for example, is synthesized in a way that produces sounds somewhat like those of a piano. It doesn't sound exactly like a piano, though. This effect can be noted in lower-cost, lower-quality keyboard synthesizers sold in department stores and discount electronics stores.

Wavetable synthesis, on the other hand, uses an actual digital *sample* of a sound (such as a piano) on which the resulting sound is based—after it has been manipulated to hit the right note for the right duration. This can take quite a bit more processing power (and RAM or ROM memory for storing the sounds), but it results in much higher-quality music and effects.

 ## What is a satellite speaker?

These days, the state of the art for speakers (both for the PC and in-home entertainment systems) includes not just two front speakers but also a subwoofer. If you get one of these three-piece speaker systems, the front (main) speakers are

Walkthrough: Installing a Non-Plug-and-Play Sound Card

Most modern sound cards, even if they aren't Plug and Play, can be configured using their software drivers. While sound cards can be rather finicky, most manage to get configured and working fairly quickly—at least for Windows-based applications.

Here's how to install a sound card:

1. Shut down your PC and electrically ground yourself. Open the case on your computer and locate an empty slot.

2. Remove the screw and metal dust plate that covers the hole in the case for that slot.

3. Position the card so that the card's interface connector is directly over the slot. Press down lightly and uniformly on the top of the ISA card until it's completely plugged into the slot.

4. If you have a CD-ROM drive, connect the audio cable from the CD-ROM drive to the sound card's CD audio-in interface. The appearance of the audio cable may vary somewhat from that shown here, but it's probably similar:

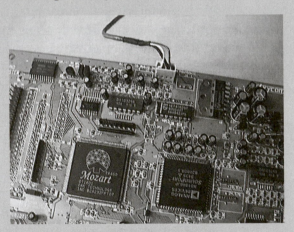

5. Plug in any speakers you have or any that came with the card. (See the following answer for more details.)

6. If you use Windows, run the Windows-based installation program that came with the sound card. (If you also dual-boot into

DOS—especially to play games—you should dual boot into DOS now and run the DOS-based installation program.)

7. Test the card by running a compatible program, multimedia CD-ROM, or game.

If all goes well, you should be hearing complete music and effects in the programs you run. If not, check the other answers in this section for troubleshooting advice.

known as *satellites*. The subwoofer, on the other hand, puts out a nonlocalized bass sound (the human ear generally can't establish the source of very low bass sounds) so you can put it almost anywhere.

Should I buy special speakers?

If you really want to enjoy the sound, yes. The speakers that come with most multimedia and sound card kits can be woefully inadequate. In fact, you're lucky if you find a sound card that doesn't include speakers, because paying anything for those speakers is usually a waste of money. Instead, shop for speakers like you might shop for a monitor—test them out in the store and see which are good enough for your needs. They don't have to cost more than about $100 a pair to be decent for computing, although the more you spend, the better quality sound you're likely to get.

How do I judge speakers?

One of the most important criteria when shopping for speakers is their power rating. While power certainly doesn't tell you everything, underpowered speakers tend to produce noise and distortion. Look for speakers that generate at least 4 watts each for the main or satellite speakers, and no less than 10 watts for the subwoofer, if you get a set that includes one. A 20-watt subwoofer is much better, especially for playing music.

Avoid buying speakers on specifications alone, however. Try to test them in a store, where you can hear what they really sound like. PC speakers are just like speakers for a

228

home entertainment system; they all sound different and they can make or break a multimedia experience.

What are some companies that make speakers for the PC?

Here is a short list of some popular speaker manufacturers:

Manufacturer	Web Site
Altec Lansing	http://www.altecmm.com
Labtec	http://www.labtec.com
Yamaha	http://www.yamaha.com
Koss	http://www.koss.com

Do I have to connect special "PC speakers" to my sound card? I have some decent speakers in my garage that I want to use.

You can use your old speakers with your computer, but remember that if you mount them near your PC, they need to be *shielded*. Speakers—particularly high-powered ones—produce strong magnetic fields that can erase floppy diskettes, scramble other storage media, and produce distortion on your monitor. If they're not shielded, you need to move them further away from your PC.

Also, don't hook up any old stereo speakers to a computer. Very few sound cards offer a signal that's compatible with home speakers. Instead, use the Line Out jack to connect your card to an amplifier (like a stereo receiver or PA system) and run the speakers from that amplifier.

Note: *The only speakers that will hook directly to your sound card's speaker jack are computer-specific speakers or, in some cases, speakers that can be hooked up to the headphone jack on a portable stereo.*

How far away do I need to mount unshielded speakers?

You can determine this by eye. If you don't see any distortion on your monitor, they're far enough away. There are no

invisible effects that you need to worry about unless you store floppy disks nearby.

Can I connect my sound card to my home stereo?

Yes, and you'll get better results than with any set of PC speakers—assuming you have a decent home stereo, that is. You may need some long cables, but you can get them at almost any stereo or electronics store.

What's the best way to mount speakers?

It's all about symmetry. You want the speakers an equal distance from the centerline of your monitor and an equal distance from your ears. For starters, mount both speakers about 12 inches on either side of the center of the monitor and point them straightforward—not angled toward you.

If you have a subwoofer, position it about six inches away from a wall or the inside of a desk. The bass needs to be reflected off of a hard surface for best results.

After you've established this as your baseline position, experiment by moving the speakers around a little. Also, remember not to crank speakers past about 80 percent of their maximum volume, or you'll introduce distortion. By the same token, don't turn them down below their lowest 20 percent position, or you'll have the same problem. Turn the speakers up to a medium position and adjust the final volume settings in Windows.

Should I get USB speakers?

If your computer offers USB support, you can get special speakers designed to connect to your computer via USB. The main advantage of this is that USB speakers don't require a sound card or sound circuitry on the motherboard; everything is built into the speakers. Not only do you cut down on the cost of a card (although the speakers tend to be a bit pricey), the theory is that the digital connection cuts down on interference. Data is sent out to the speakers and is translated directly into sound instead of an analog signal being directed through speaker wire to external speakers.

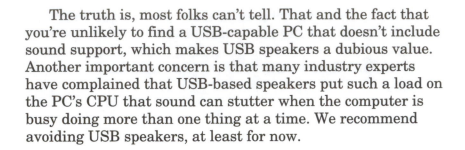

The truth is, most folks can't tell. That and the fact that you're unlikely to find a USB-capable PC that doesn't include sound support, which makes USB speakers a dubious value. Another important concern is that many industry experts have complained that USB-based speakers put such a load on the PC's CPU that sound can stutter when the computer is busy doing more than one thing at a time. We recommend avoiding USB speakers, at least for now.

EQUIPMENT YOU'LL NEED

 ### Do I need to disable something for a sound card to work?

You may need to, depending on your PC's motherboard. If you have an older PC without sound capabilities, you probably don't need to disable anything in particular. Only computers that have sound circuitry built into the motherboard need to have it disabled before installing a new sound card. To do that, consult your motherboard manual or your PC manufacturer's technical support options. It will probably involve setting some specific jumpers on the motherboard.

 ### How do I plug in the speakers?

Actually, this can be important. Most sound cards feature ports on the back of the card that should be labeled as to their function. In most cases, the card requires $\frac{1}{8}$-inch phonograph plug connectors for all the ports. Notice, though, that speakers need to be plugged into a jack specifically designed for a speaker. (Headphones will often work in these same jacks.) Don't plug speakers into a jack labeled Line Out unless you're instructed to do so by the sound card's documentation.

 ### What are the Line In and Line Out ports for?

Some of the ports on the back of your card may be labeled Line In and Line Out—these are not for headphones, speakers, or microphones. *Line In* is designed to accept a

line-level audio source—such as an external CD player, mixing board, or cassette deck. *Line Out* is designed to plug your computer's sound output into a receiver, amplifier, or mixing board.

Line-level devices usually don't support microphones and speakers directly, because those devices lack amplifiers. Instead, your sound card will probably have other ports, called something like Microphone and Speaker that are designed for non-line-level devices.

I'm not hearing anything. What do I do?

First, check the hardware. Do you have speakers plugged into your sound card's speaker outputs? Are the speakers turned on? If the speakers are a powered variety, do they have fresh batteries or a wall power plug attached? Also, check the standard issues associated with expansion cards—make sure the card is correctly installed in the system and that it shows up in System Properties dialog box.

Next, run the software installation/configuration program that came with the sound card. Often the installation program includes a test that will try to determine why your sound card isn't working—or it may help you determine that the card is working fine and something else is wrong. Check the Windows settings and make sure they're all set properly and that the appropriate driver is activated.

If you've still have no success with the sound card, you may be facing an IRQ conflict. Refer to Chapter 4 for more info on troubleshooting IRQ conflicts.

Are there standard settings for sound card IRQs and DMAs?

There aren't official standards, but the industry does seem to stick to a few basic settings. For IRQs, the most common settings for sound cards are 5 and 7. The card will likely be set to a default of 5. Interrupts 2 and 10 might also be available, depending on the devices in your system. An 8-bit sound card will usually use DMA 0 or 1; a 16-bit card will often use DMA 5 or 6. Finally, you might be asked for an I/O address; the most likely settings are 220 and 240.

? How do I get a speaker icon to display in my System Tray?

Sometimes this feature may not be enabled on your system. If you can't see a speaker icon in the System Tray, follow these steps:

- Choose Start | Settings | Control Panel and open the Multimedia applet.

- On the Audio tab, make sure that the box is checked for Show Volume Control on the Taskbar.

- A small speaker-like icon should appear in the System Tray. From now on you can use this to change the volume of your system.

? How do I change settings (like volume) in Windows?

While you can directly change the volume of your sound using the volume control on your speakers, there's a better way: Use the controls in Windows.

To change the volume settings, you can click once or you can double-click the speaker located in the System Tray of Windows. Here's the difference between the two methods:

- *Click the speaker icon.* You'll get a pop-up master volume control that you can use to change the overall volume of the system or temporarily mute the sound.

- *Double-click the speaker icon.* You'll get a dialog box that enables you to modify the volume of each sound component individually. You can make the wave (sampled) sound louder than CD-audio and the line in sound, for instance.

The double-click method comes in handy when you need to radically change the levels of one element—like the Line In, which might be a feed from your television—while keeping the wave sound low.

My sound card often works in Windows, but not in DOS. What's up?

If you're dual booting to DOS, make sure that the DOS installation program has been run from the DOS prompt and that the appropriate DOS drivers have been loaded. DOS probably won't autoconfigure the sound card, so you may need to dig deep in the manual to see what settings are appropriate for it.

✚ ***Tip:*** *Let's face it, most folks are dual booting into DOS to play games. If that's the case, make sure you read the game's manual for any specific instructions on setting up the sound card.*

My sound card works in DOS but not Windows. What gives?

Many sound cards require new drivers when you update to Windows 95 (or higher). In that case, you'll need to consult your sound card manufacturer's Web site or technical support. Here are some typical sites:

Manufacturer	Web Site
Creative Labs (SoundBlaster)	http://www.creativelabs.com
Turtle Beach	http://www.tbeach.com
Orchid	http://www.orchid.com
Diamond Multimedia	http://www.diamondmm.com
Options by IBM	http://www.pc.ibm.com/options/
Acer Open Components	http://www.acerperipherals.com

I get decent sound, but every once in a while I get crackling—especially during games. How do I stop it?

Your sound card and video card may be incompatible on some level. A particular range of Cirrus Logic video cards has been found, in the past, to work poorly with popular sound cards.

Check the manufacturers of both your sound and video cards for new driver software or other fixes.

Sometimes loading a basic VESA driver in DOS for the video card can be the problem. Use your video card's DOS installation program to switch your video card into a basic VESA mode.

I installed a new game but my sound card isn't listed in the installation menu. What do I do?

Most of the time, your sound card is compatible with other cards. Try those. Start with the entry for a plain old SoundBlaster. If that works, write it down so you can always come back to it, but then experiment with other, better drivers. In particular, see if your card will function as a SoundBlaster AWE32 or SoundBlaster Pro.

Can I get sound for my notebook computer?

Yes, you can. In many multimedia notebooks these days, sound is built in for use in presentations or for multimedia titles. In fact, if your notebook computer is fairly new and offers a CD-ROM drive, you probably have sound built in.

If you have an older notebook, you can still add sound capabilities using a PC Card (also called a PCMCIA expansion card). The PC Card slots on many notebooks are used for extra hard drive space or for modems, but a few manufacturers make PC Card sound cards. Turtle Beach (**http://www.tbeach.com**), for example, offers a PC Card for sound. Also consult your notebook manufacturer to see if they have a proprietary solution.

Why does my sound card hiss when it plays certain files?

You may need to clean the needle. (Just a little turntable-era humor.)

The sound files are probably 16-bit sound samples. If you have an older 8-bit card, it can't play these 16-bit files. We suggest you upgrade to a 16-bit card. Slight hissing may also be the result of poor connections, frayed cables, or simply a poorly recorded sample.

Why is it called "sampling"?

Digital recording is called *sampling* because the entire analog source—whether it's a voice or music—is not recorded directly to the computer, like sound is recorded directly to tape. Instead, quick samples of the signal are taken and pieced together to reproduce the original. The samples are taken many, many times a second, so the resulting sound is impossible to distinguish from any other sort of recording.

What frequency should I use to sample voice and music?

The frequency, usually expressed in kilohertz (kHz), is a measurement of the complexity of sample you're trying to take. The lower the frequency, the less distinct and faithful the reproduction of the sound. For example, 4 kHz is the frequency for a telephone call, and while you can easily understand what is being said, the fidelity of a telephone call is rather awful—as you may know if anyone has ever tried to play a CD to you over the phone. In digital sampling, you double the frequency of an analog device, so 8 kHz would result in telephone-quality sound.

On the other hand, CD quality is generally considered to be 44.1 kHz, which allows the signal to include harmonics and sound levels that are slightly out of the range of human hearing, but important for completing the formation of a sound wave.

There's another factor to consider when recording digital audio: The frequency used can increase significantly the amount of disk space required to store the digital sample. Table 7-1 shows the relationships among different types of samples and the disk space they consume.

Notice that one hour of CD-quality audio can take more than a gigabyte of space; half an hour of cassette quality would consume around 150MB.

Sample Rate	Quality Level	Space Required per Second (16-bit)	Good for...
8 kHz	Telephone	32 kilobytes	Recording audio notes for self or for e-mail annotation
11 kHz	PA system	44 kilobytes	Low-quality Web transmission, AM-quality talk
22 kHz	Cassette recording	88 kilobytes	High-quality Web talk shows, music transmissions
44 kHz	CD audio	176 kilobytes	High-quality music recording, professional audio

Table 7-1 Digital audio sample rates

Generally, you'll record with some sort of compression scheme working, too, so your recordings will occupy less space than the table shows. For some computers and programs, though, you may need to compress the audio after recording it—meaning your digital sample may require more space than the table shows, at least while the compression process is taking place.

 How do I get rid of that annoying startup sound (and other event sounds) Windows always makes?

Event sounds are those that are played when something happens in Windows, such as when Windows starts, when you open certain windows, or when an error occurs. Changing event sounds is easy; simply follow these steps:

● Choose Start | Settings | Control Panel and open the Sounds applet.

● Scroll down the list of Windows events until you find the one you want (such as Start Windows).

● In the sound name drop-down menu, select another sound or [None]. Click OK to close the dialog box.

❓ Can I hook up a microphone to my sound card?

Generally, you can hook up just about any microphone to the Mic or Microphone port on your sound card; it doesn't have to be specially designed for computers. Any karaoke, recording, or professional microphone from a store like Radio Shack should work just fine. With that said, you should still check your documentation. Some speakers and microphones don't get along well when used with the same PC.

If your sound card doesn't offer a special microphone j ack, you may need to buy a special line-level compatible microphone. In this case, you can connect the microphone to some other device, like a mixing board or receiver, then plug that device into the Line In jack on the sound card.

Finally, some manufacturers have proprietary solutions for microphones—especially for their multimedia PCs designed for videoconferencing or speech recognition—so check your documentation.

Voice Recognition and Voice Dictation

An increasingly popular application for your sound card is voice recognition. Using special software, you can speak commands into your PC and the computer translates them into immediate action. You can say, "Open file," and the PC will open the file requester dialog box.

Voice dictation is also a fast-growing market. Various programs use dictionaries that range anywhere from 10,000 to 100,000 words and transcribe your real-time speech into text and place it in your word processor. IBM, Dragon Systems, and Lernout & Hauspie are some of the front-runners in this business.

While voice dictation is an exciting field, keep in mind that it doesn't offer 100 percent recognition accuracy and may therefore be unsuitable for some users. If you're in a unique industry or business application (such as one that requires you to enter data while your hands are occupied with some kind of equipment), however, voice recognition and dictation may work well for you. Voice dictation is also a serious boon for computer users who can't type well or at all.

ALL ABOUT MIDI

 ### What is MIDI?

MIDI stands for the Musical Instrument Digital Interface, and it's the language computers use to communicate musical notes and other music characteristics to different devices. For example, a MIDI-enabled sound application can be used to store the required notes—even to create sheet music—based on the keys played into a MIDI-capable electric-piano keyboard.

When an electric piano stands on its own, it's often called a "synthesizer" because it's used to create sounds that seem like a variety of instruments you might find in an orchestra. Using MIDI, it's also possible for your computer to become a synthesizer. Instead of requiring a keyboard synthesizer for playback, the computer itself can translate the MIDI codes and create music, with the help of a sound card.

In fact, this whole MIDI thing is part of the reason that it's important to buy a wavetable-based sound card. Wavetable sound cards are much better at reproducing the instrument sounds required for high-end MIDI playback, which is what makes the music more enjoyable.

What is the difference between digital audio and MIDI music?

Remember that digital audio is an actual recording of something—music, voices talking, and so on—that could easily have been recorded to tape, but was instead recorded to computer. Making such a "digital" recording takes up quite a bit of hard drive space because the hard drive is, in a way, being treated like a cassette tape for digital information.

In MIDI music, only the commands for playing the notes are stored—not a digital recording of those notes. The difference is similar to the difference between sheet music and a cassette. The cassette is an actual recording, while the sheet music is just instructions for making music.

MIDI, then, offers two advantages. First, its files are much smaller than digital audio files. Second, a MIDI file can be played on many different systems and instruments. The

same file that plays on a PC can be downloaded to a MIDI-capable synthesizer and played there.

The disadvantage is that only the sorts of sounds and music you could make with a keyboard synthesizer are possible using MIDI. You can't record talking, singing, live events, or even a live, acoustic guitar. You can only create MIDI instructions that will then be interpreted by the computer or another device.

I want to start creating MIDI music. What equipment do I need?

The least you need is a MIDI-capable sound card and some software that can be used to generate MIDI music. With some software programs, you can use the computer keyboard to mimic a piano's keyboard, and write the music that way. You can also use the mouse to draw notes directly on a music staff, then play them back using the PC's sound card.

But there are plenty of other things you can hook up. Keyboards, drum machines, synthesizer racks, and many other electronic instruments can be hooked together via a MIDI interface.

Can I listen to MIDI on my PC without a keyboard or other special device?

Yes, you can. Any shareware or commercial program designed to play MIDI songs should be able to play them using your MIDI-capable sound card. In fact, if you've played games successfully (or if you've ever heard a song playing in the background while you visited a Web site), you've probably already played MIDI songs through your computer.

Sound cards will often boast about their MIDI capabilities by telling you how many instruments the card has stored. Most cards feature the 128 MIDI instruments, but some even go further than that. Still others offer RAM upgrades that can be used to create and store your own instrument sounds.

What do I need for a MIDI connection?

Most likely you'll need a special adapter and cable to connect a MIDI device—like a keyboard synthesizer—to your sound

card. The MIDI interface will often double for the joystick
port on the sound card, so you'll need to get an adapter that
can translate the port on your synthesizer to the
joystick-style port on the sound card. One may have come
with your card; otherwise, they're fairly standard and should
be available at local computer or musical instrument stores.

 Note: *You may need to set a special MIDI mode on your
keyboard or other MIDI device to make it work correctly with
your PC. Check the synthesizer's manual for more details.*

Do I need special software for MIDI?

Usually, you do. It doesn't have to be very special; shareware
programs and Web browsers are often designed to play MIDI
music. But you will need something a bit more elaborate if
you plan to create MIDI music. Software for doing so ranges
from music lesson software—programs that teach you
music—to professional MIDI studio programs that allow

Walkthrough: Hooking Up
a MIDI Device to Your Computer

Hooking up a MIDI device isn't even minor surgery; it's usually easier
than hooking up a printer. Here are the basics:

1. Turn off your computer and ground yourself.

2. Locate the joystick/MIDI port on your sound card or on front of
   your PC.

3. Using a cable and adapter, hook up the MIDI cable to the MIDI
   port on the sound card.

4. Hook the other end into the keyboard synthesizer's MIDI In port.

5. Fire up the computer and run your MIDI software to test the
   connection.

you to lay many different instrument melodies over harmonies, percussion, and other sounds.

You may also need to load special drivers for your MIDI card—or, at least, activate them. Check the sound card's manual for information about its MIDI drivers. You can also try reinstalling your driver software if you believe the MIDI drivers have not been installed correctly in the past.

MP3 AND STREAMING AUDIO

 ### What is MP3?

You may have heard about MP3 files on the Internet. MP3 is an audio version of the popular MPEG file format for graphics. MP3 sound files are highly compressed audio that generally sound about as good as CD-audio and FM radio, yet they're very small compared to their uncompressed size. A typical three-minute song in MP3 format is generally about 3 or 4 MB in size.

 ### What can I do with MP3?

Many people have found that downloading MP3 audio from the Internet is a fun way to expand their music collections. MP3 files are available for a small charge (less than $1 per song, typically) or even for free. You can store MP3 audio on your hard drive, turn them into audio CDs using a CD-R drive, or copy them to memory cards and listen to them in Walkman-like MP3 players. One popular MP3 player is the Diamond Rio (**http://www.diamondmm.com**).

I want to listen to MP3 files. What software do I need?

Luckily, Windows 98 comes with a media player that automatically recognizes MP3 files. There are also many specialized MP3 players available on the Internet for download. If you're not happy with the Windows Media Player, you can visit a Web site like **http://download.com** and choose from many alternatives.

Where can I find MP3 audio?

MP3 files are all over the Internet. Here is a short list of some Web sites that offer MP3 files for downloading:

- http://www.mp3.com
- http://content.ubl.com/cca/rio
- http://www.rioport.com
- http://www.atomicpop.com/mp3
- http://www.audiodiner.com
- http://www.rollingstone.com

Can I listen to music without downloading MP3 songs?

Absolutely. Many streaming audio radio stations have sprung up across the Internet, and they offer continuous music with minimal commercial interruption. You can listen to music at site like **http://www.real.com** using Real Network's RealPlayer. Microsoft's Internet Explorer 5 also has streaming audio radio station access built in. To try it, open Internet Explorer and choose the Radio option from the Toolbars submenu under the View menu.

Another solution awaits you if you have fast Internet access (such as ISDN, DSL, or a cable modem). Visit **http://www.radiomoi.com**. This site, along with a few other pioneers, offers CD-quality music in numerous categories by streaming MP3 files to your PC. It sounds as good as FM radio, but there are fewer commercials and more listening options.

Chapter 8

Data Storage

Answer Topics!

Data Storage @ a Glance

There are two basic kinds of storage on any computer: the memory in which programs run, and the hard disk platters on which programs and data files are stored. In that second category there are also CDs, Zip drives, and a host of other media that make the PC a jungle of storage options.

Hard disks are designed to last for a long time—five years or more, depending on how you use (or abuse) them. Don't be lulled into a false sense of security, however—there's nothing quite so catastrophic as when a hard disk fails. After all, that's the only part of your PC that can irrevocably destroy years' worth of your work in the blink of an eye. The solution? *Back up your data.*

Want to install a CD? A removable drive? It isn't hard, and upgrades like these can extend your PC's useful life and value faster than just about any other improvement.

THE BASICS OF DATA STORAGE

 ### What's the difference between the megabytes on my hard disk and the megabytes of RAM?

A *megabyte* is simply a unit of measurement in computing that means, roughly, "a millions bytes." (The number is actually 1,048,576, thanks to the computer's reliance on the binary numbering system.) *Random access memory* (RAM) is the temporary storage bin in which applications run and keep data while the PC is on and in use. A hard disk is the master storage container that holds all your programs and data, even when the computer is turned off. While your computer may only need 32, 64, or 128MB of RAM in order to run, the hard drive needs as much as 2, 3, or 6GB (in other words, hundreds of times as much room) to adequately store your files.

 ### I want to increase the storage on my PC. What kind of drive should I buy?

With so many choices available today, it's a hard decision. Consider the options:

- **A new IDE/ATA drive**   IDE (*Integrated Drive Electronics*) drives come in sizes of over 30GB, and they're the cheapest kind of mass storage device available. They're also easy to install—it involves little more than connecting a cable, adjusting some jumpers, and you're done. (Unless you have an aging system, in which case you may also need to dig into the BIOS and change the settings on other drives in your system. See Chapter 4 for details.)

- **A SCSI drive**   SCSI (*Small Computer System Interface*) is a fast alternative to IDE—great if you're interested in storing full-motion video and sound on a drive for desktop video editing. SCSI is tricky to set up, however, and isn't as commonly found in the PC

industry as in the Mac world. If it's time to gut your PC, though, SCSI isn't an awful idea, especially because adding a SCSI card to your PC allows you easy access to other upgrades, including high-end scanners and many removable drives. The truth of the matter, though, is that SCSI is typically more trouble than it's worth unless you need super-fast hard drives for audio/video work. Plus, the latest IDE technologies rival the speed of high-end SCSI.

 Removable drives   Drives such as Zip and Jaz from Iomega, plus the Orb from Castlewood Systems, are good because they're fairly common removable storage formats. In fact, Iomega's Zip has become something of a de facto standard, especially in business, multimedia, and the graphic arts. That means you can share a 100MB file with a co-worker or friend because many, many people have these drives. You can extend the storage of your PC infinitely, because you can keep adding more Zip cartridges like floppies.

How do you pick? Decide what your goals are. If you never share data, a new IDE drive is a good solution that will allow you to store many more programs and documents. If you want to take data on the road with a notebook PC or you want to exchange huge files with friends, get a Zip or one of its cousins. And if you are adventurous and want fast transfer rates, get a SCSI drive. Keep in mind, however, that SCSI drives don't plug into the PC motherboard like IDE—you'll need to purchase a SCSI adapter and install it in a PCI or ISA adapter slot. And, for a removable drive, you'll also either need a SCSI connection, a free parallel port (or a pass-through connector), or a proprietary expansion card.

What's the difference between IDE and EIDE?

This is actually a somewhat complicated question that requires a three-part answer. The easy response is that EIDE (*Enhanced Integrated Drive Electronics*) is an extension of the IDE interface for getting PCs and hard drives to talk to one another. The original IDE specification wouldn't allow for more than two IDE drives at a time, and limited each drive

to 528MB. The EIDE specification extends the size to 8GB, allows for connecting four drives, and is quite a bit faster (13.3 MBps instead of 3.3 MBps).

EIDE is also a different type of interface technology. If you have an older IDE interface card for hooking drives to your PC, you may want to invest in a newer interface card that supports the new standard, which will give you better and faster performance.

That said, EIDE and IDE are completely compatible with each other. There really are no "EIDE hard drives"; they're all IDE drives, but they come in sizes larger than 528MB these days. You can plug an EIDE-compliant drive into an IDE interface—it'll just run more slowly and will only show you 528MB of storage space unless you use a special software driver (see "I've heard that my PC won't run drives that are bigger than 528MB. Can't I install a new 4GB drive?" later in this chapter).

Finally, our third answer: Most people use the terms IDE and EIDE interchangeably and, in fact, say "IDE interface" when they mean "EIDE interface." Don't worry about it too much; just be aware that IDE is the drive and EIDE refers to the newer interface standard.

Note: *EIDE is actually a marketing term that eventually became a popular "standard." For the most part, EIDE drives are ATA-2 drives, as explained in the following answer.*

What is ATA?

ATA, or *AT Attachment*, is the interface standard to which IDE (Integrated Drive Electronics) drives adhere. In fact, the term "IDE" is relatively meaningless today—it's a holdover from times when other hard drive types *didn't* have integrated electronics. Now they generally all do.

The ATA level of a drive, along with the electronics on the motherboard, determines the speed of the drive. The original IDE/ATA specification maxed out at about 8 MBps; ATA-2 drives ranged from 11 to over 16 MBps; ATA-3 is capable of 33 MBps.

What are "Fast" and "Ultra" ATA?

Fast ATA is a marketing term that refers to ATA-2 level drives (this is in the same general vicinity of "EIDE" drives.) *Ultra ATA* is another marketing "standard" term referring to the ATA-3 standard. If you have an Ultra-ATA drive and an Ultra-ATA hard drive interface on your motherboard (or on a separate card), you can see speeds up to 66 MBps. Ultra-ATA is also known as Ultra-DMA or UDMA.

What is ATAPI?

ATAPI is the ATA Packet Interface, which allows removable drives (CD-ROM, Zip, CD-R, DVD) to use the ATA specification. All PCs built these days include ATAPI support so that you can hook up an internal removable drive just as if it were an internal IDE hard disk.

Why are all the bays in my case called half-height?

Over the years, most PC components that use expansion bays—like floppy and hard disks—have been reduced in height by half. Hence, they now use what are known as *half-height bays*. This is something of a misnomer in the sense that you can't find a full-height bay in use anymore—they went away so long ago that no one sells cases with full-sized bays, nor does anyone sell peripherals that fit inside those monsters. Nonetheless, we refer to these bays as half-height, even though they're the only size available.

If you have a very old case, such as an IBM AT or XT, you've got full-height bays. They're the ones that are filled by those huge 5.25-inch floppy drives with the loud-clasping, overbite-type latch.

What do I do when I see "Not ready reading drive A. Abort, Retry, Fail"? How about "D:\ is not accessible"?

You can encounter this message from just about any media—CD, hard disk, or floppy. It means that the computer is having trouble reading data from the drive, and it's looking for

some direction from you. Keep in mind that DOS was never very good at distinguishing the difference between Abort and Retry, and will retry the drive about three times regardless of which option you choose. If you select Fail, DOS will ask you which new drive you'd like to read from instead—just type a new letter and press ENTER. Here are some of the most common situations in which you'll encounter this error message:

- You've tried reading from the CD-ROM, but there's no CD in the drive. Simply insert a disc in the drive and select Retry.

- You've tried reading from the CD-ROM and gotten that error message—but you know a CD is in there. The CD is probably dirty. Remove the disc and clean it gently with water and a cloth. It's also possible that the disc is scratched. If a disc is visibly scratched and your only recourse is to replace it anyway, you might want to try fixing it. See "Can I get rid of a scratch on my CD?" later in this chapter.

- You get the message while trying to read from a floppy disk. Selecting Retry sometimes works—just choose Retry a few times to see if you can get the data. You might also try removing the floppy disk and reinserting it between retries because that might realign the floppy disk with the read heads slightly. If you can't get the data after a half-dozen attempts, however, you're probably not going to get it at all. Hopefully, the data is available on another disk, or you can get a replacement from the manufacturer.

- You see the message while working with a hard disk. This is the worst case, because it probably means the hard disk has a problem. Reboot the PC and try again. You might also want to let the system cool for a few hours first—if it works then, it might be indicative of a bad power supply.

 What does it mean when I see the message, "Non-system disk or disk error"?

You've probably left a floppy disk in your PC and restarted it. Now your PC is trying to boot from a floppy that isn't bootable—in other words, it isn't a "system disk." Simply remove the disk, press ENTER, and let the PC boot from a hard disk. For more information about system disks, see the following section, "Floppy Drives."

If there's no floppy in the drive, then the message means that the PC can't boot from the hard disk—and that's a significantly bigger problem. Your PC can't find the boot sector on your hard disk, and this means your hard disk may have suffered massive failure. (This assumes that the drive hasn't been disconnected for some reason. If you've recently shipped, dropped, moved, or repaired your PC, you might check to make sure that the drive is properly connected.) You'll need to check the BIOS Setup program to verify that your battery hasn't failed. If the battery is dead, the Setup program will have lost all your settings; you'll have to replace the battery and restore your configuration (see Chapter 4).

If that doesn't solve the problem, then you may have to see if a disk utility can restore the hard disk—or you may have to simply replace it. For details, see "How do I recover from a total hard disk failure?" later in this chapter.

Tip: *If your hard disk should ever fail, contact the vendor you bought your PC or hard disk from. The disk might still be under warranty.*

WORKING WITH FLOPPY DRIVES

 Are Zip disks some new sort of floppy diskettes?

No, they're not. Although they both have hard outer casings and are similar in shape, the Zip disk is actually thicker than the floppy, and uses different internals. To a degree, these differences explain the price variance between Zip disks and floppy diskettes.

I have a lot of trouble with unreadable floppy disks. Is it the disks or the drive?

That depends on what kind of disks you buy. If you are in the habit of getting the cheapest floppies you can find, odds are good that you'll have a few bad disks in every box. If you buy quality disks, however, the read or write heads on your floppy drive may need realignment. This is particularly possible if your drive is a few years old.

You can get the drive tested and repaired at a local PC repair shop, but since floppy drives cost less than $30, you're probably better off just replacing it.

I save data to floppies on my PC, but then a friend has trouble reading them. What gives?

If this is a recent and isolated occurrence, the diskette might just have been defective. (In fact, you might have received a bad batch of floppies in one box.) Otherwise, this is probably a problem with the alignment of the read/write heads in your drive—or your friend's drive. If all your friends have the same problem with diskettes you create, then it's probably your drive. Get it checked out by a repair shop or—a better and usually cheaper idea—just replace it.

What is a "system disk"?

A *system disk* is little more than a floppy disk that you can use to boot your PC. Most floppies don't have the necessary "system files" on board to tell your PC how to boot. Instead, floppies have to be specially formatted as system disks.

How do I make a system disk?

In Windows, it's pretty simple. Just follow these steps:

1. Insert a blank floppy disk in the drive.

2. Choose Start | Settings | Control Panel. Double-click the Add/Remove Programs applet and select the Startup Disk tab:

Add/Remove Programs Properties

Install/Uninstall | Windows Setup | Startup Disk

If you have trouble starting Windows 98, you can use a startup disk to start your computer, run diagnostic programs, and fix many problems.

To create a startup disk, click Create Disk. You will need one floppy disk.

Create Disk...

OK   Cancel   Apply

3. Click the Create Disk button.

Windows may ask for the original Windows CD-ROM; then it will copy system files onto the startup disk. When it's done, you can use the floppy to boot your PC.

If you want to create a system disk in DOS, it's even easier. Restart your PC in DOS (this won't work in a DOS window) and, at the prompt type **FORMAT A: /S**. (This command assumes A: is the correct drive letter for the floppy to be formatted—if you have two floppies, it might be B.) Don't forget about the **/S**—that's what makes the floppy bootable.

Why does Windows keep trying to read my floppy drive?

You've probably read some files from a floppy disk in Windows, and then shut down your PC with the floppy still inserted. Windows thinks the floppy is still inserted and

keeps trying to read it. Or you might have saved a file to floppy from within a program like Microsoft Word. To get around it, save another file to your hard disk. Then Word (or whichever program is causing the problem) will stop checking the floppy drive.

Other things can cause this, including installations that accidentally leave a reference to the floppy drive or alterations to your system's INI files (system.ini, win.ini) or Registry entries that reference the A: drive. If the problem persists, search these files for references to the A: (or B:) drive and delete them (or alter them, if necessary.) See Chapters 13 and 14 for information on the Registry and INI files.

 Tip: *You can use the Find tool in Windows to search these files easily. Just start Find, then enter* ***.ini** *in the Named field and* **A:** *in the Containing Text field, and click Find Now.*

 ### What files do I need to have on an emergency boot disk?

That's a good question, because you need more than just the system files that make your floppy bootable. Begin by creating a startup disk, as shown under "How do I make a system disk?" a couple of questions back, and then copy these files onto the floppy as well:

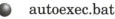 autoexec.bat

 config.sys

The autoexec.bat and config.sys files need to reference essential programs, like the CD-ROM driver. Copy this driver directly from your existing startup files on your hard disk or contact the PC manufacturer for information on exactly how the startup files should look. Delete anything that isn't essential, however. For your emergency disk, you'll want to delete references to virus checkers and other utilities that you won't run in an emergency. Make sure you invoke the mouse driver if you want access to the mouse in DOS. You can use SYSEDIT, as discussed in Chapter 2, to make changes to the startup files.

Here are other system files that should appear on your emergency disk:

- **mscdex.exe and the CDROM's ".sys" driver**   These are essential files that the config.sys file uses to drive your CD-ROM in DOS. They are usually found in your C:\DOS directory or somewhere in your C:\Windows folder. (The CD-ROM driver's name varies depending on the kind of drive you have.)

The Many Lives of the Floppy Disk

Several years ago, most floppy diskettes were 5.25 inches in diameter; the newer diskettes are 3.5 inches in diameter. Another notable difference: The 5.25-inch floppy diskette is actually floppy, while the 3.5-inch diskette comes in a hard plastic case.

From there, the density at which data is saved and how many sides of the diskette are used determine the capacities of diskettes:

- **Single-sided, single-density**   The earliest diskettes—exclusively 5.25 inch—used this technology, resulting in 180K capacities. These diskettes are tough to find and nearly impossible to read using modern equipment.

- **Double-sided, double-density**   In 5.25-inch formats, this results in 360K of disk space; for 3.5-inch diskettes, 720K. These diskettes are also often called "low-density."

- **Double-sided, high-density**   In 5.25-inch formats, this results in a 1.2MB diskette; 3.5-inch diskettes using this technology can store 1.44MB of data.

- **Extended-density (ED)**   Available exclusively in 3.5-inch formats, these diskettes can hold 2.88MB of data. Unfortunately, the disk drive mechanisms for ED format never really caught on with computer manufacturers, so both the drives and media are a bit tough to come by.

- **mouse.com** or **mouse.exe**   This is your mouse driver, usually found in C:, C:\DOS, C:\Windows, or C:\Windows\System.

- **fdisk.exe**   This program prepares a hard disk for formatting.

- **format.com**   This is the program that formats your drive.

- **edit.com**   This is a simple text editor for DOS that you can use to change the autoexec.bat and config.sys files.

Can I use a 720K disk in a high-capacity drive?

In most cases you can, although you will occasionally run into trouble with older floppy diskettes. Any high-capacity floppy drive is capable of dealing with—and even formatting—lower capacities (although the original 5.25-inch diskettes in 360K sizes can be problematic). The basic rule: If it's a 3.5-inch diskette, you can read it. If it's not a 3.5-inch diskette, consider transferring it to 3.5-inch media.

Do I want a 2.88MB floppy drive?

If it's within your budget, you might like a 2.88MB drive. A 2.88MB floppy drive is completely backward-compatible with other 3.5-inch floppy diskettes—so it can read 1.4MB and 720K floppies, too. Using special ED floppy diskettes, a 2.88MB drive can store twice as much data as a conventional HD diskette. The problem is that 2.88MB still isn't much. If you're looking to store quite a bit of data, a better move would be upgrading with a removable media drive, such as a Zip drive. In fact, that's what we recommend.

Caution: *If your system does require a power splitter, check the power supply to make sure you aren't taking it over its rated limit by installing a new drive. If you are, you may need to install a new power supply before adding the floppy drive. If you have a recent PC, this is unlikely to be an issue. However, older PCs often have low-wattage power supplies.*

Walkthrough: Removing a Floppy Drive

If you have a floppy drive that has reached the end of its useful life—or needs to be removed for repairs—then you'll want to take it out of your computer's case. If you'll be replacing it, there are definitely some important details to note. Here's how you remove a floppy drive from your computer:

1. Shut down the computer, electrically ground yourself, and remove the case.

2. Remove the drive's power cable and ribbon cable:

Ribbon
connector

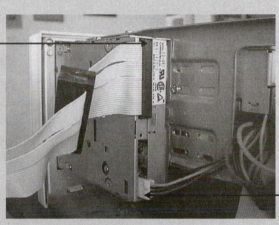

Power
connector

   When removing a cable, remember to grasp the adapter on the end and rock it back and forth, if necessary; don't tug on the cable itself.

3. Unscrew any retaining screws and slide the drive out of the front of the case. Notice if it has special rails that help it to slide in and out. If it doesn't slide at all, examine the sides of the drive—it may be screwed into the case itself. If it is, carefully remove the screws and save them for a later installation.

4. If you won't be using this drive bay anymore, cover it with a plastic bay cover. (They generally just snap into place.) If you leave the bay open and exposed, you risk disrupting the engineered airflow path inside the case and letting lots of dust in.

5. When you restart the PC, enter the BIOS setup program and find the entry for floppy drives. You'll probably need to tell the setup program that the floppy drive is no longer present.

Walkthrough:
Installing a New Floppy Drive

Whether you've had a floppy drive give out on you or you're upgrading an older system to more recent drive technology, installing a new floppy drive can be pretty straightforward, as long as you take stock of your setup and make sure you're prepared:

1. Open the case and make sure you have a free drive bay and that the floppy drive controller's ribbon cable will reach the new drive comfortably. (If you already have a floppy drive installed, notice if there's a drive bay that can accept the second floppy drive near the first one.) If the bay is too far away for the ribbon cable to reach, decide whether you're going to move the existing drive so the new one can be closer, or whether you'll get a new ribbon cable.

2. Also make sure the bay you choose for your new drive is the right size. If you're installing a 3.5-inch drive in a 5.25-inch bay, you'll need an adapter kit.

3. Next, make sure you don't need any special rails or other devices to hold your drive in place. Most drives slide into their bays from the front of the case, and are then either secured with screws or with special plastic rails that you install onto the drive itself.

4. Finally, make sure you have an available power adapter for the new drive. If not, you'll need a splitter to allow one existing power adapter to be used for two drives.

Now, with the preliminaries out of the way, you can look to the actual upgrading process:

1. Shut down the computer, electrically ground yourself, and remove the case.

2. If you're replacing a drive, remove it as explained in the Walkthrough box, "Removing a Floppy Drive." If you're not replacing an older drive, simply locate the existing floppy drive ribbon cable (it should be attached to any other floppy drives in the system), and locate an available power cable.

3. If your case requires that floppy drives use rails, install those now. Take care that you install them in the right orientation on either side of the drive. Your drive may also require a special cage or mounting kit to change it from 3.5-inch to 5.25-inch wide. Install that kit now, if necessary.

4. Remove the plastic cover from the drive bay (a coin or flat-head screwdriver can be used on one or both sides to release the cover).

5. Slide the drive into the exposed bay. Stop sliding when it's fully in and locked (using rails) or when the drive is correctly positioned and aligned with the screw holes in the case (without rails).

6. Connect the ribbon cable and the power cable to the drive. If this drive is drive A, then it should use the connector on the end of the cable; if it's drive B, it should use the connector in the middle of the ribbon cable.

    Usually, a ribbon cable can only fit one way on the drive. If you find that your cable will connect facing either way, examine the drive for little numbers at each end of the connector. The side with the low numbers should be connected to the side of the ribbon cable that has a colored stripe. Power cables only fit one way; if it doesn't seem to fit, turn it over.

7. Screw the drive into place. If it's inserted correctly, the drive will line up with a series of holes in your PC case; these accept the screws that will hold the drive in place, as shown here:

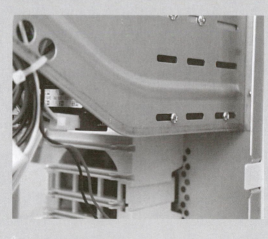

Now you're ready to test the drive. Turn on your computer and verify that the drive light for your new floppy drive comes on quickly, then extinguishes. Then, once your computer gets through the boot process, you should get one "beep" as usual, followed by the configuration table that appears along with the "Loading DOS" or "Starting Windows" message. Check to make sure that your drive is listed in the table.

My newly installed floppy drive doesn't seem to work. What should I do?

Check the symptoms of the problem. Then try these troubleshooting possibilities:

● If the drive doesn't light up or make any noise, check to make sure the power connector on the back of the drive is plugged in correctly. Also check the ribbon cable connecting the drive to the floppy drive controller. Make sure the cable is properly installed and not damaged.

● If the disk light comes on and won't turn off, check the orientation of the floppy drive ribbon cable. You may have installed it upside down.

● If the drive doesn't appear in the configuration table, you may have to change some BIOS settings so the drive is recognized by the computer (especially for 486 or older machines). Consult your computer's manual as well as Chapter 4 of this book for more on BIOS settings.

● If your drive acts strangely or doesn't appear in the configuration table, you may also have switched the ribbon cable order of the drives. Remember that drive A is connected to the ribbon connector at the very end of the cable, and drive B to the connector in the middle of the cable.

● If the ribbon cable you're using doesn't have a twist in the middle of it, you may need to set some jumpers on your new drive. Check your drive's manual for details.

WORKING WITH HARD DRIVES

 ## What is "access time"?

Access time refers to the average amount of time, in milliseconds (ms), that it takes a hard drive to find a particular piece of data on a hard disk. A hard disk's "heads" have to move quickly across the surface of the "platters" on which the data is stored, and that takes a certain number of milliseconds. That number can be used as one factor in comparing different drives. Older drives had access times of 50 ms or so, and newer drives hover around 10 ms. CD-ROM access times, by contrast, are generally measured in hundreds of milliseconds.

 ## What is the "transfer rate"?

Transfer rate refers to the amount of data that can be transferred from the hard drive to RAM once it has been found on the drive. Although this number is also used for benchmarking, it's really only useful in a general sense, as in comparing different technologies (such as EIDE and wide-SCSI).

Should I care about disk rotation speed?

Many vendors advertise the RPM of their hard disks, but for many users it's not an important issue. However, if you want to create video from your PC desktop—and by that we mean copying camcorder footage to your hard disk, editing it onscreen, and dumping the final product back out to tape—the rotation speed of the drive is critical. For video editing, you should look for a drive that rotates at no less than 7,200 RPM. These drives often come with an "AV" certification, and that's good to look for as well.

 ## My hard disk has become slower and slower over time—how come?

Over time, a disk can become fragmented, which causes the drive to spin constantly as it locates all the pieces of your files. Fragmentation can cause things to slow down considerably

About the AV Drive

Although some marketing geniuses have messed with this a bit in recent years, an AV—or *audio/visual*—hard drive has a pretty standard definition. Not only is it a drive with a high RPM speed, but specialized AV drives also write data *only* sequentially, as if they were writing the data to film or cassette tape. In this way, an AV drive can never become fragmented, which almost always results in better playback time for editing. It also makes an AV drive perfectly useless for other everyday computing tasks.

whenever the computer is forced to read data from the hard drive. See the next few answers for more on fragmentation.

 What is "defragmenting"?

Most hard drives attempt to write data sequentially on the hard drive so it can be accessed quickly and easily. This works well when a drive has been recently formatted and still has lots of unused storage space. But when you repeatedly delete and move data in the course of normal use, new data gets wedged into blank spaces between existing data and can't be stored sequentially. Your data becomes *fragmented,* with different pieces of files scattered all over the hard drive. This results in slower file access, because the hard drive's read head has to skip all over the drive looking for related bits of data.

That's why software exists to defragment your hard disk's data; "defrag" software moves the data around in such a way that information can be read sequentially, and hence more quickly.

Is a badly fragmented hard disk ever actually dangerous to the data it stores?

In general, fragmentation is a performance issue—the more fragmented your disk is, the slower it'll run. If your drive is extremely fragmented, let's say beyond 25 percent, Windows may not be able to run properly or start new programs. When this happens, you'll see an "out of memory" error—meaning that there isn't enough free memory to start a given program. Defrag the drive and your problems will go away.

A disk generally won't get badly fragmented in a short period of time unless an errant program scrambles the data on the drive. But, if you've owned or worked with a computer for a few years and have never defragmented your hard disk, now is a good time to learn how.

 ## How do I defrag my hard disk?

You can run the DOS defrag program by typing **DEFRAG** and pressing ENTER at a DOS prompt. In Windows, you can run Defrag by following these steps:

1. Open My Computer.

2. Right-click the drive you want to defrag and choose Properties.

3. Click the Tools tab:

(C:) Properties
General · **Tools** · Sharing · Norton
Error-checking status
You last checked this drive for errors 10 day(s) ago.
[Check Now...]
Backup status
Windows was unable to determine when you last backed up files on this drive.
[Backup Now...]
Defragmentation status
You last defragmented this drive 10 day(s) ago.
[Defragment Now...]
[OK] [Cancel] [Apply]

4. Click Defragment Now. Windows will check how badly fragmented the drive is, and give you one last opportunity to abort the process. (Defragging a drive can take a lot of time—hours, in fact.)

We recommend defragmenting your hard disk about once a month. If Windows reports that your drive is less than about 5 percent fragmented, you can wait until the drive is more fragmented. You won't see much performance difference until the drive is badly fragmented—over 10 percent.

How is defragmenting different from optimizing?

Certain disk utilities do what is called *optimizing,* which basically means that programs and data are rearranged not only so that they aren't fragmented, but also so that like programs and documents appear close together on the disk. This is done according to predetermined schemes that have been shown to cause the drive to seek a bit less, resulting in more immediate loading and quicker response from the drive. Feel free to optimize a drive using Norton Utilities or a similar package—you may see some improvement.

What does ScanDisk do? How often should I run it?

ScanDisk is a program that checks your hard disk for errors and corrects them. ScanDisk performs two major kinds of scans: Standard, which looks at file errors; and Thorough, which scans the surface of the hard disk for bad sectors. This is a much longer test that marks bad sectors as "out of service" so Windows doesn't try to write to them.

You can run ScanDisk from DOS by typing **SCANDISK** and pressing ENTER at a DOS prompt, or from Windows by following these steps:

1. Open My Computer.

2. Right-click the drive you want to check and choose Properties.

3. Click the Tools tab.

4. Click Check Now. The ScanDisk window will appear:

> ScanDisk - (C:)
>
> Select the drive(s) you want to check for errors:
>
> 3½ Floppy (A:)
> [C:]
> Removable Disk (D:)
>
> Type of test
> ● Standard
>   (checks files and folders for errors)
> ○ Thorough
>   (performs Standard test and scans disk surface for errors)   Options...
>
> ☐ Automatically fix errors
>
> Start   Close   Advanced...

5. Choose either the Standard or Thorough test and click the Start button.

In general, it's a good idea to run ScanDisk:

- Immediately before defragging your hard disk
- After you accidentally turn off the PC without shutting down Windows properly
- About once a month during routine Windows use

Note: *If you're using Windows 3.1, you can scan your disk running the chkdsk.exe program. Go to the DOS prompt and type* **CHKDSK,** *and than press* ENTER. *Chkdsk will round up any lost data and convert it to files, which you can then read with a text editor (to make sure nothing important is missing) or delete summarily.*

? Should I "convert lost chains to files"?

When you run ScanDisk, the program will often find fragments of data on the hard disk that it describes as *lost chains*. ScanDisk will ask what you want to do with these fragments. The option to convert lost chains to files is one that takes space reported as "in use" on the drive that doesn't belong to any application or data file and saves it as a file with a name such as file001.chk. In 99 cases out of 100, this file will never do you any good and simply takes up space on your hard disk. When ScanDisk offers you the option of saving the lost chains, as files, just say no—delete them.

? I'd like to see what's in those lost chains. How do I do it?

ScanDisk drops the CHK files into the C drive's root directory. You can load these CHK files into Notepad and investigate them—if they're data files, you can sometimes figure out what they were by reading the plain-text header information. Once you figure out what the file is supposed to be, simply rename it in DOS with the appropriate file extension and you're done.

? How often should I back up my hard disk?

How long is your comfort zone? If you work with a lot of mission-critical data, backing up daily isn't a bad idea. If you could happily live without the data you've recently saved to your hard disk, monthly backups are fine. Whatever scheme you choose, be sure to back up critical data. (You don't need to back up applications, since you can restore them from their original disks.) Specifically, be sure to back up these files:

- Critical files like the autoexec.bat, config.sys, and Windows *.ini files.

- Patches and enhancements to applications on your hard disk—anything you don't already have on CD-ROM or floppy, but need for your applications. Even if you don't back up your applications, you can use these patches to restore plain-vanilla versions of your applications to the state they were in when you had to restore.

● All your data and documents, such as files in the My Documents folder of your hard disk.

Tip: *Make a point of storing all or most of your documents in one place, such as the My Documents folder. If you save your files in the directories for their respective programs, like the Word folder or the Excel directory, then you'll have shuffle through your entire drive to back up those files.*

Alternatively, you can back up everything on your drives, but that will take more space. It's your decision.

How do I back up my hard disk?

You can back up data to a tape drive, Zip disk, or recordable CD-ROM, or you can even "mirror" your data to an identical hard disk. There are many ways to back up your data, but the key is to remember to actually do it. We recommend using a backup program that can schedule backups for you, so that you never have to remember. There are also a few backup schemes you should think about:

● **Full backup** Each time you back up your drive, you completely back up all your data.

● **Incremental backup** The first time you back up your system, you do a full backup. On subsequent backups, you simply back up what has changed since the previous session. This is a faster way to back up, because you're only recording changes, but you will need to keep track of multiple tapes, disks, or cartridges and restore them in the correct order when it's time to recover from disaster. Most people make three incremental backups then start from scratch with a full backup so they never have more than four sets of disks to worry about.

You should also have two complete sets of backup tapes or disks. If you only have one set, you might be in the process of making a backup—rendering the existing backup useless— when a catastrophic failure strikes your system. Sure, it's unlikely, but having two backup sets can prevent this from happening. If you have a small business, you might also consider keeping a recent backup at a different location so theft or fire won't rob you of your backup along with the actual in-use data.

Tip: *Windows 95 and 98 come with a program called Microsoft Backup that can help you back up your hard drive.*

I want a new hard drive. Should I remove my current one?

If your current drive is an IDE drive, then you certainly don't have to remove it. Instead, you can opt to install a second IDE drive, because nearly all hard disk controllers are capable of managing two IDE drives. (Newer EIDE controllers can handle four hard drives.) Of course, you may need to remove the existing drive if you don't have any free drive bays, or if it uses a technology older than IDE or SCSI.

If you decide to add a new IDE drive to a relatively old IDE drive, the two can be a bit finicky about one another. Unfortunately, the best advice is often to buy from the same manufacturer who made the original drive. Our other advice: Keep the receipt handy. Also, you may need to install an LBA driver—see the advice under "I've heard that my PC won't run drives that are bigger than 528MB. Can't I install a new 4GB drive?" later in this chapter.

Slave or No Slave?

If you have a PC with two EIDE connectors, it can be confusing to determine whether you need to rig your drive as a master or a slave. Keep in mind that a new drive can be either a master or a slave depending on which EIDE connector you connect it to. If you connect the drive to the same connector as the first drive using the same ribbon cable, then they have a master/slave relationship. So, you'll have to set jumpers to represent that master/slave relationship.

If you connect the drive to the other EIDE connector, however, and it's using a ribbon cable all by itself, then both drives are masters.

How do I remove my existing hard drive?

If you simply want to remove your current drive and add a new one to your system, there are some things you should consider:

- If you're going to replace the drive with a new one, is your current drive an IDE-based drive? Older drives used other interfaces, like MFM. If you have one of these very old drives (you'd probably only find them in 286 or older PCs), then you'll need to replace the hard disk controller card, too, with an IDE-capable model.

- If you'll want any data from the old drive, you'll need to save it to floppy, tape, or removable media first. Otherwise, you'll have to reconnect the old drive to get any data from it.

- If you're removing the old drive because you don't have other drive bays free (or because it's not working) then salvage any screws, rails, or other mounting hardware from the old drive. It'll make installing the new one easier.

Here's how to go about the extraction:

1. Shut down the computer, electrically ground yourself, and remove the case.

2. Remove the old drive's cables—both the power cable and the ribbon cable. Remember to remove both by grasping the adapter on the end of the cables; don't tug on the cables themselves.

3. Unscrew the drive from the case or drive cage. Notice if it has special rails that help it to slide in and out of the case, then remove the drive.

Walkthrough: Installing a Hard Disk

If you've read through the Walkthrough box, "Installing a New Floppy Drive" earlier in this chapter, then the hard drive installation may seem familiar. Aside from some jumpers that need to be set for using two IDE drives in one computer, this process is very similar to installing floppy drives.

Here are the preliminaries:

1. Open the case and make sure you have a free drive bay, and check that the hard drive controller's ribbon cable will reach the new drive comfortably. (If you already have a hard drive installed, notice whether or not there's a drive bay that can accept the second hard drive near the first one.) If the currently available bay isn't a good fit for the new drive, decide whether you're going to move the existing driver, or whether you'll get a new ribbon cable.

2. Also, make sure the bay you choose for your new drive is the right size. Any new hard drive is probably a 3.5-inch half-height drive; if you're installing a 3.5-inch drive in a 5.25-inch bay, you'll need an adapter kit. (The adapter kit includes special rails that help a thinner drive fill a wider bay—such kits are available at any computer store.)

3. Next, make sure you don't need any special rails or other devices to hold your drive in place. Most hard drives are installed in internal bays because there is no need to physically access them on a regular basis. With the hard drives in these interior bays, you'll have plenty of expansion room for removable, floppy, and CD-ROM drives.

4. If this will be the second drive in your system, determine which jumper is the "master/slave" jumper on your new drive. Set the jumper on your new drive so that it will be the "slave," which should make it drive D in your setup (assuming this is your second hard disk).

   You can make your original drive the slave drive and the new drive the master, but remember that a slave cannot be bootable,

so you'll need to be ready to install DOS or Windows from a floppy diskette right after installing the drive. You'll need to consult your older drive's manual for setting it to be the slave drive.

● Finally, make sure you have an available power adapter for the new drive. If not, you'll need a splitter (shown here) that will allow a single power adapter to be used for two drives:

If your system does require a power splitter, check the power supply to make sure you aren't taking it over its rated limit by installing a new drive. If you are, you may need to install a new power supply before adding the new drive.

Now, with the preliminaries out of the way, here's how you add a hard drive:

1. Shut down the computer, ground yourself electrically, and remove the case.

2. If you're replacing a drive, remove the original drive. If you're not replacing an older drive, simply locate the existing IDE drive ribbon cable and locate an available power cable.

3. If your case requires rails, install those now. Take care that you install them in the right orientation on either side of the hard drive.

   Your drive may also require a special cage or mounting kit to change it from 3.5-inches to 5.25-inches wide. Install that kit now, if necessary.

4. Slide the drive into the exposed bay. Stop sliding when it's fully locked in (if you're using rails) or when the drive is correctly positioned and aligned with the screw holes in the case (without rails).

5. Connect the ribbon cable and the power cable to the drive. If this drive is drive C, it should use the end connector on the ribbon; for drive D (or for any "slave" drive), use the middle connector.

   Usually, a ribbon cable can fit only one way on the drive. If you find that your cable will connect to the drive either way around, examine the drive for little numbers at each end of the connector. The side with the low numbers should be connected to the side of the ribbon cable that has a colored stripe. Your power cable will only fit one way; if it doesn't seem to fit, turn it over.

6. Screw the drive into place. If it's inserted correctly, the drive should line up with any holes in your PC that can accept screws that will hold the drive in place.

Now you're ready to test the drive. Turn on your computer. You should see both hard drives acknowledged during the boot process; if you don't, restart the PC, bring up the BIOS setup program, and enter the appropriate values for the new drive. Consult your computer's manual and Chapter 4 of this book for more on BIOS settings.

Once your computer gets through the boot process, you should get one beep as usual, followed by the configuration table that appears along with the Loading DOS or Loading Windows message. Check that your drive appears in that table.

If you've installed a new master drive, you may need to boot from a floppy diskette—either an emergency diskette or the first diskette for DOS or Windows. From there you can format and partition the drive, then install the operating system.

> **!**
>
> ***Caution:*** *Always have an emergency diskette on hand before performing any sort of hard drive installation or removal. If you don't have that diskette (or at least a boot diskette for DOS or Windows), you may not be able to boot your computer again to format, partition, or test the drive.*

I've heard that my PC won't run a hard drive bigger than 528MB. Can't I install a new 4GB drive?

Older PCs don't support Large Block Addressing (LBA), which is what lets a computer read a hard disk that's bigger than 528MB. There are two solutions:

- Buy a new hard disk controller with LBA support in hardware

- Use the LBA software that comes with most large drives

If you choose to use the LBA software, it's always possible (though unlikely) that the driver will get deleted or damaged and you won't be able to access the rest of your drive. The hardware solution is a bit safer, but obviously more expensive.

How do I tell my original hard disk that I've installed a second one?

This is done using the (unfortunately named) *master/slave jumpers* on a drive. Your "C" drive should be set to be the master, and any subsequent drives should be slaves. Note that only a master drive is bootable, so install DOS or Windows on a master drive. Consult your drive's manual for info on the correct jumper settings.

What if my newly installed drive doesn't work?

If your drive doesn't work when you boot your PC, you may need to change the BIOS setup for your hard drive. (This is especially true of 486-and-earlier computers.) Your hard drive's manual or customer support representative should be able to tell you the proper settings for a hard drive, which usually include the drive type and number of cylinders.

Why won't Windows recognize my newly installed hard disk?

It isn't unusual to install a new hard disk and have everything initially seem okay (the PC boots and BIOS displays a message that the drive has been recognized), but then in Windows the drive doesn't appear on the desktop.

What happened is that you installed the new drive as a slave—a second drive, essentially—to the original drive that was already in your PC. You will need to remove the original drive, and set the DIP switch or jumper on the underside of the drive to its master drive mode. Check the manual that came with the original drive, or call the manufacturer to determine the correct settings for the master/slave switches.

What's the easiest way to move the contents of my old drive to a new drive using Windows 95/98?

If you've recently replaced your old hard disk with a new one, it can be a pain to get all your old data, applications, and special settings on the new drive. Here's a better way than doing manually or with a tape backup:

1. Temporarily install the old drive as a slave. You'll need to set the jumpers or DIP switches on the drives so they boot properly.

2. Use the DOS XCOPY command to copy the entire contents of your old drive to the new drive, as in **XCOPY C:D:}**.

Note: *Xcopy doesn't copy the entire drive—the Registry isn't copied at all. You must perform step 3 to get a completely functional system.*

3. Reinstall Windows 95/98 on the new hard disk so that critical system files not copied with Xcopy get installed properly.

4. Remove the old drive, or reformat it so you can permanently use it as a slave.

How do I recover from a total hard disk failure?

If ever you turn on your computer and find that it simply won't load anything, there are a couple of different steps you can take to cope with the dilemma. Above all else, you can rely on the backups you've made of your data and of patches or upgrades to applications for which you have the diskettes or CD-ROM discs. More than anything else you can do,

properly backing up your hard drive is the single most effective defense against lost work and catastrophe.

But just because your hard drive will not spin does not immediately mean all your data is lost—especially if you've been working inside your computer recently:

1. Begin by taking note of any error message you receive from your computer. "HDD Failure" or "HD Controller Failure" often means that something is wrong with the hard drive, but they can also mean that there's something wrong with the hard drive controller, your I/O card, or your cable.

Tip: *If you suspect that your drive has failed due to some problem with your I/O card, you can buy an I/O card from a computer store that offers a money-back guarantee and test it with the drive. (You'll know that the I/O card might be the problem if your serial/parallel ports, other hard drives, or CD-ROM also seem to be failing.)*

2. Reboot again and use your special keystrokes to open the BIOS setup screen. Check to make sure the proper hard drive codes are entered, if necessary. If the CMOS battery in your computer is failing, these settings will sometimes be lost, making the hard drive work only intermittently after a reboot. This is only likely to happen when your computer is a few years old, but it can be a major cause of apparent catastrophic failure.

If it's neither of those problems, reboot your system using the emergency disk described earlier in this chapter. (You'll need to have created the emergency disk before this problem occurred, although you may be able to use another functional computer to create one after a problem crops up.) Run scandisk.exe by typing **SCANDISK** at the command line and pressing ENTER. You can use SCANDISK to determine whether or not your hard drive is communicating with your computer, or if it is experiencing other trouble. If the hard drive isn't responding, and you've tried a different I/O card,

then you can probably isolate the problem to your hard drive. (You can also isolate it if you notice that all other I/O devices, except the hard drive, seem to be working fine.)

Also, while booted from the A drive, you should try accessing any other partitions you may have created, like drive D, even if they're on the same hard drive that's giving you trouble. If you see a partition of the regular drive, you can be almost assured that it's a problem with the system files on the drive—not the drive mechanism itself. If you don't see the other partitions (and you definitely had them), then you're one step closer to deciding it was a mechanical problem.

If you loaded CD-ROM drivers on your emergency disk, you may be able to use the CD-ROM drive to run Norton Utilities or a similar disk recovery program to see if the boot sector of your disk has been corrupted. If this is the case, Norton Utilities may be able to salvage data on the disk or even rewrite the boot sector and get things up and running.

If all this fails, you have a decision to make. If your backups are completely in order, then you may want to format the drive and attempt to install DOS and/or Windows again.

Otherwise, you can take the computer in for service or remove the drive and take it in by itself to have it serviced. If you have good backups (and it was about time to upgrade anyway) you can purchase a new drive, then install DOS/Windows, your applications, and your backed-up data. If your original drive comes back from the shop, just add it back to the mix.

Caution: *If your hard disk has failed as the result of a boot-sector or "random formatting" problem, we recommend that you run a virus checking program on the drive to see if any traces of a virus are found. While viruses aren't something we generally scare people about, the malicious viruses tend to go for the FORMAT command or the boot sector when they do hit.*

I give up! I'm going to format my hard drive and install Windows from scratch. How do I go about it?

If you've had your primary hard disk die—the one that boots and starts Windows—you'll need to conduct major surgery to restore your system. This is one of the most nerve-racking procedures you can possibly perform, because until your system is restored, you can't even run Windows.

Of course, the first thing you need to do is make sure it's really a complete drive failure; this would be a good time to try some of the other recovery procedures in this chapter. You may find that you can recover to some degree, even if it seems that your drive is gone. You may get an emergency diskette to boot, for instance, and give you access to your files—and from there, maybe you can fix the underlying problem.

Caution: *Review this section before disaster strikes, so you'll know what you need to have on hand. If you're missing key elements when your hard disk fails, it will be too late to create them.*

If you do find the drive is dead, though, here's what you should do:

1. Install a new hard disk using the procedure discussed earlier in this chapter.

2. Insert a system floppy in your floppy drive that has emergency programs like FDISK, FORMAT, and your CD-ROM drivers.

3. Start your PC and let the system boot from the floppy.

4. Run FDISK and create a Primary DOS Partition. Exit FDISK—your PC will reboot. Leave the floppy in the drive, because you'll boot from it again.

5. After the PC has booted, format the drive with the command **FORMAT C: /S**.

6. Insert your Windows 95/98 CD in the drive and run Setup from the DOS prompt. Windows should install, and you've pretty much recovered. Now all you need to worry about is restoring applications and data, and returning Windows to all the personal settings you used to enjoy.

Note: *Your new hard disk will likely be formatted, and will probably even have Windows preinstalled. This can save you a lot of grief, so make sure before you buy that your vendor has done this tedious work for you.*

 ### Should I partition my hard disk to save space?

If you have a Windows version older than Windows 95 Service Release 2 (also called OSR2), you might want to divide your drive into partitions to take advantage of smaller cluster sizes. Consider this: If you have a single 2GB drive, each cluster is using 32K. That means any file, no matter how small, will take up 32K—even a file with only 2K of data wastes an additional 30K. So, as much as 40 percent of the space on your drive may be wasted. If you partition your drive into four separate 500MB virtual drives, each "drive" on your system now uses 16K clusters, for about 11 percent wasted space. See Table 8-1 for a breakdown of how each increment in partition size affects the wasted space on your system.

Consider, too, your personal convenience. It's ludicrous to divide a 2GB drive into 15 separate partitions to get the tiny

Partition Size	Cluster Size	Estimated Wasted Space
0–15MB	4K	6%
16–127MB	2K	3%
128–255MB	4K	6%
256–511MB	8K	12%
512–1,023MB	16K	24%
1,024–2,047MB	32K	48%

Table 8-1 Partition sizes and associated wasted space

4K cluster size—you couldn't keep track of that many drives, and each one would be too small to store much modern software. If you do choose to partition, follow these guidelines:

- Be careful that you make the partitions small enough to take advantage of the smaller cluster size. If you make a partition 512MB, for instance, you've got 32K clusters. Make it 511MB, on the other hand, and you get 16K clusters.

- Don't make too many partitions. You might break a 2GB drive into two 1GB partitions, for instance, because more than two drives is a pain in the neck.

- If you use DOS to reformat the drive, you'll erase all your data in the process. It's easiest to start with a fresh drive, or at least have a current backup that you can restore your data from.

What's FAT32?

DOS has always wasted a significant amount of the space on any drive. The bigger the drive, the more space wasted. That's because DOS (and Windows also, for that matter) has to increase the cluster size of your drive depending on the size of the drive. A *cluster* is the smallest amount of usable space on the drive. So if a file is 8K in size but you're using a drive that uses a 32K cluster, all 32K get used to save that 8K file. On large hard disks, half of the space on the drive can easily be wasted with empty space in huge clusters.

FAT32 is a new backward-compatible filing structure that addresses this problem. Beginning with Windows 95 Service Release 2 (called OSR2), you can format your drives as FAT32 disks and keep the cluster size at a manageable 4K for all hard drives up to 8GB in size. FAT32 has some disadvantages:

- FAT32 drives can't be read by some versions of Windows NT or OS/2, so they're often only good for DOS and Windows 95 systems.

- Many vendors shipped Windows 95 OSR2 systems formatted as FAT16 anyway, so you may need to reformat your drives to take advantage of the FAT32 filing system.

If you have Windows 98, there's a good chance your system was formatted with FAT32. You can check by opening My Computer on your desktop and right-clicking your C Drive icon. Choose Properties. On the General tab, you'll see the file system near the top; it should say FAT 32.

Caution: *FAT32 has some important differences from FAT16. The most important one is that it no longer supports dual booting. Even in Windows 98, Microsoft does not recommend trying to create a multi-boot partition that can start in older versions of Windows.*

Is there a better way to format a drive than by using FDISK?

Yes, oh yes. Only a masochist would use FDISK and FORMAT to repartition a hard disk these days. There are several utilities that put a graphical interface on the process and—even better—they don't destroy your existing data. This means that you can divide your 2GB drive into two or three partitions on the fly, or convert a FAT16 drive into a FAT32 drive, while retaining all the files that were on the disk to begin with. We recommend PowerQuest's product, PartitionMagic, for getting the job done without the pain and suffering caused by Microsoft's built-in tools.

What are the pros and cons of using compression software?

We try to discourage people from using compression software. Yes, there are advantages. In a nutshell, you get to stuff more software and documents on your hard disk, which makes it a cost-effective solution for storage space. However, these are some of the problems:

● Not all software gets along with compressed disks. Some games and multimedia software won't install or run properly from a disk that has been compressed.

● If you suffer a hard disk problem, it's more difficult to read or restore data that is compressed, since compressed data circumvents ordinary DOS file-handling protocols.

- You never know exactly how much room is left on your drive, because the numbers that Windows reports are only estimates based on assumptions about the "compressibility" of new software.

- You're adding another level of complexity to the mix. Because each compression setup is relatively unique, it's more difficult to troubleshoot a compressed hard drive by installing it in another computer or booting from an emergency disk. The data is scrambled on the disk—if something happens to your descrambling program, you've got a problem you wouldn't have with a regular hard drive.

What's the safest possible way to compress my hard disk?

We recommend compressing only certain partitions on your hard disk, if that's an option. Don't compress the boot partition or the partition that holds DOS, Windows, or any disk utility programs you may have. Only compress a less important partition—one that holds data or rarely used applications that you regularly back up, for instance.

What are the alternatives to compressing my hard disk?

You have a few options, not all of them quite as easy as disk compression:

- *Install a new hard disk.* You can find out how to install it as a second drive (or a replacement drive) elsewhere in this chapter.

- *Copy archived files to a Zip disk or other removable media.* That way you can remove programs or documents you rarely use from your hard drive, and keep them out of the way of your more immediate storage needs.

- *Use the WinZip compression scheme to compress specific individual files that you rarely use.* The downside is that you'll need to manually decompress them when you need them (and you'll need enough free space to decompress them to their original size). WinZip is shown in Figure 8-1.

"Increasing" the Size of Your Hard Disk with Compression

A variety of utilities—some actually built right into Windows—offer to increase the available storage space on your drives by means of compression schemes. They work okay, depending on your needs.

Compression software typically compresses the data on your hard disk and creates a new partition on your drive that is capable of decoding the compressed files on the fly, as requested by the operating system. That means that you never realize the files are compressed because there's a special "handler" doing the work for you in real-time.

Compression generally works by following rather complicated schemes to turn files into smaller—but unusable—versions of themselves. They're encoded so that more complicated data is represented by fewer symbols. (If we decided that the letter "z" could be substituted for "iss," and "x" for "ipp," then the word "Mississippi" could be represented as "Mzzxi" in a simple compression scheme.) Compressed data needs to be decompressed, however, before it's useful.

 Use a compression program that doesn't change the structure of the overall hard disk. Freespace, from Mijenix (**www.mijenix.com**), is a smart archiving program that compresses software and decompresses it as needed—but it doesn't compress an entire drive or create a nonstandard "host" partition in the process.

 ### What should I do about these disk errors?

Although different computers are certainly capable of reporting different things, we've collected some of the more prevalent disk errors here and tried to explain them for you—note that some of them are hard drive specific, while others can occur to floppies and removable media:

● **HDD or Controller Failure** Either the hard drive isn't working or the controller isn't working. Make sure the hard drive is plugged in snugly and correctly. Test

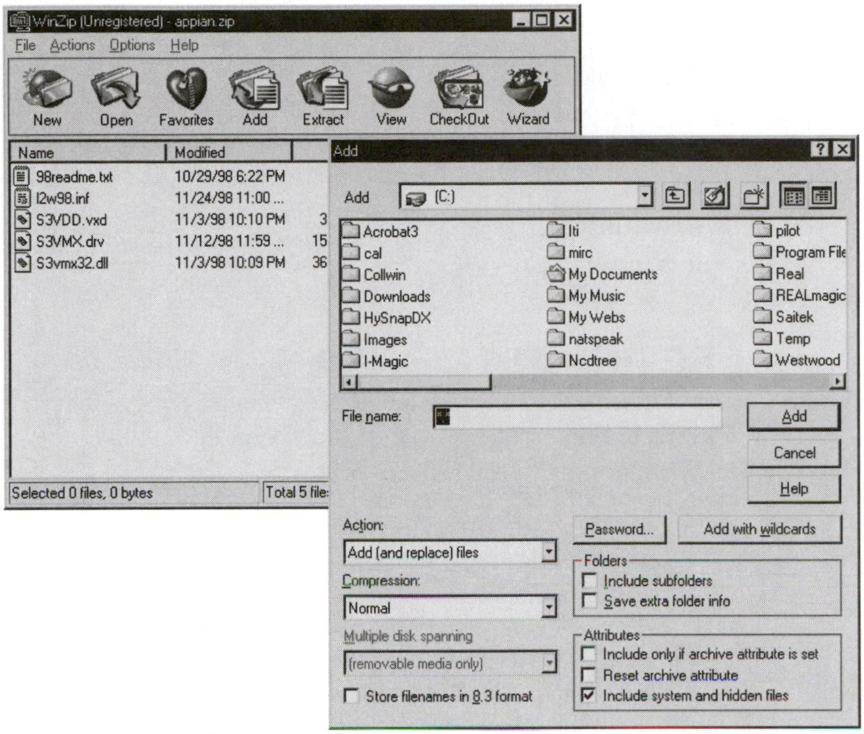

Figure 8-1   WinZip allows you to compress individual files, making more space on your drive.

the I/O controller to see if replacing it fixes the problem. You may also be having CMOS battery problems.

- **Bad or Missing Command Interpreter**   From your emergency disk, copy the file command.com to your computer. You may have wiped out the contents of drive C, deleted everything in the root directory, or deleted parts of DOS or Windows.

- **Unrecoverable Error**   Start Norton Utilities and save your data. Part of the disk has gone physically bad. If it's a floppy, toss it. If it's a hard drive, have it looked at.

- **Sector Not Found**   This disk may also be going bad. Use Norton Utilities or a similar program to rescue your data, then have it looked at. (Norton may be able to map out the bad sectors and keep them from being used, which may keep this problem from happening again.

If there are many bad sectors or if it recurs, however, something else is wrong.)

● **Disk Error** You probably have a nonbootable diskette in the drive when you boot, or your hard drive isn't correctly formatted to be a bootable system disk. If you suddenly get this error about your hard drive, boot with the emergency disk and try running Norton Utilities or a similar program.

REMOVABLE DRIVES

What are "removable" drives?

In most cases, *removable drive* is simply a shortened version of *removable media drive,* which means a high-capacity storage device that uses removable media. For instance, the Iomega Zip drive stores 100MB on each Zip disk, and the disks can be removed as easily as floppy diskettes. Such a removable media drive offers unlimited storage capacities, as long as you keep buying new media.

Of course, the downside is that you'd have trouble saving a file or folder that contained over 100MB of data on a Zip disk. Another disadvantage: You can't easily back up the data on a Zip disk unless you have a tape drive or some other backup system. Another popular removable drive is the Jaz drive, which holds a gigabyte of data on each disk. Jaz drives are commonly used to back up hard disks.

Although removable drives are also often portable, "removable" doesn't necessarily mean portable—it means only that the media can be removed and replaced.

What's the difference between Zip and LS120?

A Zip drive (see Figure 8-2) is a proprietary drive using a standard for storage that was developed and is owned by the Iomega Corporation. Although it has many competitors, Zip is by far the most popular standard as a potential replacement for the current 1.44MB floppy diskette. Many manufacturers install both 3.5-inch floppy drives and Iomega Zip drives in new PCs. The original Iomega Zip drive stores 100MB of

Figure 8-2 The Iomega Zip drive

data; a new higher-capacity Zip 250 standard stores 250MB of data.

 Note: *In reality, it takes overhead of a few megabytes for your zip drive to store the formatting and disk catalog information, so you'll usually see free space of about 95MB on an "empty" 100MB disk.*

The LS120 is a competing standard for removable storage that has a few things going for it. First, it stores 120MB of data—a little more than the standard Zip disk. Second, the LS120 specification is a standard agreed upon by an industry consortium, meaning it isn't owned and controlled by one company. Third, an LS120 drive is backward compatible with 1.44MB floppy drives, making it possible for the LS120 to replace a 3.5-inch floppy drive in a typical PC.

> **!**   ***Caution:***   *The only strike against LS120 is that it isn't terribly popular among users or manufacturers—and unpopular standards tend to vanish from the market, even if they are superior. For now, Zip is by far the most popular way to store and transfer tens of megabytes of data between PCs.*

Should I get the parallel, SCSI, or USB version of a removable drive?

Everyone has a theory on this one. Most removable parallel devices come with a pass-through connector that shouldn't affect your ability to print while using the drive. However, adding a SCSI card is relatively painless and gives you some other advanced options for adding fast hard drives or high-end peripherals.

Here's the breakdown:

- If you just want a quick and dirty removable solution— or you want one you can use with more than one PC—choose parallel.

- If you want faster performance or think you might want other SCSI devices in the future, choose SCSI.

- If you have USB ports on your PC, seriously consider a USB drive. They're hot-swappable and offer no pass-through problems and few configuration headaches. The only downside: They're a little slower than SCSI and may be a little more expensive than parallel versions.

Does it make sense to use an internal removable media drive?

It can, since the drive itself may be a few bucks cheaper. Remember, though, that you'll have to opt for an IDE or SCSI version, since a parallel or USB version is designed to be external. Buying an internal version of a Zip or Jaz type of drive is a great idea if you have a mini-tower or tower case, but remember that you'll sacrifice portability as well.

Minimize Your SCSI Nightmares

If you choose to install a SCSI internal disk, you're getting the cutting edge in speed and performance—but it's a lot harder to manage than an IDE drive, too. Here are some of the most important steps for installing a SCSI driver:

- Set the SCSI ID. A SCSI card can address up to seven devices, and each device must have its own unique number. The card is usually set to 7, and we suggest leaving it that way. Set the SCSI hard disk to 0. If you have two SCSI drives, set the second one to 1. There will generally be DIP switches on the drive to set the ID, unless it's an external drive—then you'll have a dial or microswitch.

- Install the SCSI card and connect the devices to the card via SCSI cables. If you have more than one SCSI device, they get "chained" together in a series, with the last device being terminated.

- Terminate your SCSI chain. If you have no external SCSI devices, enable the termination both on the card and the last device in the chain—probably your hard disk, at least for the time being. The terminator will be a DIP switch on an internal device and a special terminator plug on external devices. If you have external and internal devices, the card doesn't get terminated because it isn't at the end of the chain.

- Turn the system on and allow Windows to install the necessary drivers.

 Tape backup drives are cheap—why not choose tape instead of Zip or LS120?

The main reason to shy away from a tape drive is that all tape storage mechanisms are, by definition, sequential. Just like it's easier to find a song on a CD than it is on a cassette tape, it's easier to find data or a program on a Zip disk than it

is to find it on a tape cartridge. In fact, a major advantage of most removable storage over tape is the ability to use the removable storage device exactly as you would a hard drive. Most tape backup drives, on the other hand, use a completely different file format and require a special program for writing and retrieving data. On the other hand, if you need to back up very large hard disks often, a tape backup is the only practical way to do it.

The main advantage of tape drives and tape cartridges is that they are usually pretty cheap. The media is much cheaper than removable media, even for storing similar amounts of data.

CD-ROMS AND RECORDABLE CDS

How fast should my CD-ROM drive be?

CD-ROMs vary in speed from about 4x to 24x and beyond—as fast as 32x. These numbers compare the speed of a CD-ROM drive to the speed of the original CD speed of 150 KBps. A 4x drive, then, transfers 300 KBps. Keep in mind that all CDs spin back down to 1x to play audio CD, and very fast drives (24x and beyond) only achieve their top speed at the outside edge. The inner tracks run at a more modest 12x or less.

Also, keep in mind that most applications are optimized for a certain speed, such as 4x or 8x. A 32x drive won't improve performance of those applications; the faster speed is only good for reading raw data off the CD, such as when you install new software.

With all that said, the point is pretty much moot. It's hard to find slower CD-ROM drives in stores these days, and even fast 24x drives cost between $50 and $100. Get one of those and you'll be fine.

What are CD-R and CD-RW?

CD-R (*CD-Recordable*) and CD-RW (*CD-Rewritable*) are standards that allow you to copy data files to CD media. With a special CD-R drive, you can create your own CDs—both audio and data—for backup and archiving purposes. Plus, the fact that you're creating a CD makes it possible for you to share data with nearly any computer user, since most modern PCs have CD-ROM drives that can read the CDs.

CD-R discs can only be written to once; after you've filled a CD-R with data, it can't be erased. This is still useful for archiving, backing up, and sharing data, but it means you'll have to buy a lot of discs if you use the drive often. Fortunately, the discs are reasonably inexpensive.

CD-RW discs can be erased and written to again. This makes them more like Zip or similar removable drives, and useful for the same applications. CD-RW media is more expensive than CD-R media, but it can be bought at reasonable prices in bulk. CD-RW media is not always compatible with the oldest CD-ROM drives, so it's less useful for sharing with colleagues or friends who have aging PCs. CD-RW is compatible with most newer CD-ROM drives, though.

If there's a downside to both types of recordable CD, it's the fact that creating the CD (copying data to it) is generally more tedious and slower-going than copying files to a Zip or LS120 disk. With CDs, you'll often use special "burner" software that requires a lot of the computer's resources to organize and write the data to the disk. In other cases you can get special software that allows you to copy files from Windows Explorer straight to the CD-R/CD-RW media, but it's still a much slower process than copying to a removable disk.

I have a CD-RW drive, and I often waste discs because the copy doesn't work right. What's wrong?

If you get halfway into a disc copy only to have it fail, it's probably that your PC is getting bogged down doing too many things at once. Don't try to work while a disc is copied in the background. In fact, it's a good idea to disable your screen blanker and e-mail checking, especially if you have a slower PC.

What is DVD?

Digital video (or *versatile*, depending on whom you ask) disk is the technological successor to CD. Instead of CD's 500-700MB of storage, DVD packs about 4GB on each disc and is designed to play high-resolution movies (laser disc quality), audio (beyond

CD quality), and computer applications. DVD drives can even be recordable—called DVD-RAM drives, they allow you to save data from your hard disk to a special recordable DVD. This is great for backup and archiving purposes, as well as a way to share data with friends of colleagues who have DVD drives.

 ### Should I buy DVD?

DVD drives play CD-ROM discs just fine, so if you upgrade to DVD, you won't lose out on older stuff. However, there's no reason to get a DVD drive until there's enough software to justify the purchase. When that killer application comes along that only runs on DVD that's when it's time to upgrade.

Why does my CD-ROM drive work in Windows, but not in DOS?

You probably don't have the CD-ROM drivers loaded in your config.sys and autoexec.bat files (see Figure 8-3). You need to make sure mscdex.exe is available, and that the correct entry for your drive has been entered in the autoexec.bat file. You'll also need a cdrom.sys entry in your config.sys file—consult your CD-ROM drives manual for the exact entries. (Mscdex.exe can usually be found in the C: directory).

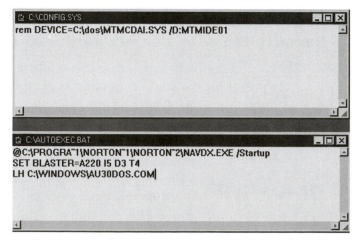

Figure 8-3 Typical config.sys and autoexec.bat files for CD-ROM access

If you can find your CD-ROM setup floppy diskette, it should have a program that prepares the autoexec and config files for you. If not, contact the PC manufacturer or visit their Web site for the specifics.

If you start DOS using Start | Shut Down | Restart in DOS Mode, then things are a bit different—Windows ignores the autoexec.bat file, but instead relies on the dosstart.bat file found in the Windows folder. Make sure you invoke the CD-ROM driver (and mouse driver, for that matter) in the dosstart file just as if it were the autoexec.bat file.

Make sure that your emergency boot disk has the CD-enabled startup files on it, or you won't be able to access the CD-ROM in an emergency. And guess what? You're going to need your CD to reinstall Windows!

You might also want to have two different sets of startup files on your system. Use your normal autoexec and config files when ordinarily starting Windows 95/98, and switch to the ones that refer to the CD-ROM when booting directly to DOS. (When you first installed an update to Windows 3.1, Windows created the files config.dos and autoexec.dos, which are unchanged from your old setup. You can use these files on a boot disk to start your CD-ROM drive and your other drivers when booting directly into DOS.)

Should I buy an IDE CD-ROM, a SCSI CD-ROM, or a proprietary model?

For most folks, IDE is the way to go—especially if your computer is reasonably new (with enough IDE ports available that you can add a CD-ROM). If you think you may want to include other SCSI devices in your computer in the future (or if you already have some), then SCSI is a decent option. We'd recommend against proprietary cards, since they tend to waste an expansion slot without being much help. However, some cards combining CD-ROM drive and sound card functions include proprietary interfaces. If you get a deal that's too good to be true, we won't hate you for choosing a proprietary CD-ROM.

Walkthrough: Installing a CD-ROM Drive

Because virtually all CD-ROM drives use IDE connections these days, they're a snap to install. In fact, the procedure is a lot like installing a hard disk. Simply follow these steps:

1. Shut down the computer, electrically ground yourself, and remove the case.

2. Locate the empty bay into which you're placing the drive, an IDE drive ribbon cable, and an available power cable. Make sure they reach the bay—you may need to move things around a bit to get it all to reach.

3. Slide the drive into the exposed bay. Stop sliding when the drive is correctly positioned and aligned with the screw holes in the case.

4. Connect the ribbon cable and the power cable to the drive.

    Usually, a ribbon cables can only fit one way on the drive. If you find that your cable will connect to the drive either way around, examine the drive for little numbers at each end of the connector. The side with the low numbers should be connected to the side of the ribbon cable that has a colored stripe. Your power cable will only fit one way; if it doesn't seem to fit, turn it over.

5. Connect the audio cable from your sound card to the CD-ROM drive.

6. Screw the drive into place. If it's inserted correctly, the drive should line up with holes in the case of your PC that can accept screws and will hold the drive in place.

7. Turn your PC on. You should see a message that the BIOS recognizes a CD-ROM—it will appear along with the hard disk message. After Windows starts, you may need to run a setup disk so Windows recognizes the drive.

 My CD-ROM has trouble reading my CDs. Can I fix it?

If your drive has trouble with more than one CD, it's probably the drive's fault, not the CD's. Try cleaning the read head in the

CD-ROM drive, either using the manufacturer's instructions or using a CD head cleaner from a music store. Also check to make sure the cable is fully engaged in the back of the drive, particularly if you recently did any work under the hood of your PC. If that doesn't solve the problem, we recommend that you replace the drive—they are not easily repairable.

 ## Can I get rid of a scratch on my CD?

If you're sure that there's a scratch on your CD that is impeding your disc from being read, you have nothing to lose by trying the following procedure.

Here's what to do:

1. Look on the read side (the bottom) of the CD-ROM disc. Look for the scratch that is affecting the CD's performance.

2. Buff the scratched region vigorously with a cotton cloth in swirling motions. Then test the disc; if it still doesn't work, continue.

3. Dab some white toothpaste onto your fingertip and apply it on the scratch.

4. Use your finger to rub it into the platter. Make swirling motions. Since toothpaste is slightly abrasive, the goal is to take the edge off the scratch so that the laser doesn't skip when it hits the problem area. Don't rub too hard, and try to avoid straying too far from the scratch.

5. Rinse the CD with some water, dry it with a cloth, and try to run the disc in your CD-ROM drive.

If this doesn't work, give up and get another copy of the CD.

 Caution: *The toothpaste procedure might further damage your CD, so you should try it only when you know that a scratch is keeping data from being read properly and you can't get a replacement in a timely manner.*

Chapter 9

Networking

Answer Topics!

Networking @ a Glance

Assembling a PC network is often considered one of the few
remaining forms of black magic left in the computing world. Not only
are network cards notoriously finicky, but the terms you'll encounter
are intimidating—IPX, routers, Ethernet. This chapter debunks the
myth that networking is hard—understand the basics, and
everything will fall into place.

● The most common kind of network for the home and small office
is an Ethernet network. Ethernet moves data at 10 or 100 Mbps
and comes in either coaxial or twisted-pair cabling variations.
Whichever you choose, the underlying principles are the same.
In this chapter, we'll discuss how to choose your network—
including cables and hubs.

● After you've physically installed a network, you may be
concerned about privacy and security issues or how to expand a
small set of PCs. Read on to see how.

● Don't want to commit to a full-fledged Ethernet network? That's
okay; Windows 95 and 98 come with a rudimentary networking
scheme called Direct Cable Connection. Using a parallel or serial
cable, you can attach two PCs together in minutes, and share
data and applications.

THE BASICS OF COMPUTER NETWORKING

❓ What exactly is a "network"?

A *network* is a collection of computers and peripherals—such as printers and scanners—that are connected enabling everyone to share applications, data, and equipment. If you connect two laptops so that they can use data on each other's hard disks, you've made a network.

❓ Does a network make sense for my home office?

If you have more than one PC—perhaps two desktops, or a desktop and a notebook—then you should consider a network for your home. Hooking up a network is often considered a scary or intimidating upgrade, but the reality is that modern network kits are inexpensive and usually straightforward to install. Yes, they often have more installation trauma than many other kinds of upgrades, but we think they're worth it. Here's what a network can offer:

- *Gain access to the content of all your PC hard disks from any computer in the house or office.* That means you can start writing a document in Microsoft Word on one machine, and finish it on another without transferring the document via a floppy or Zip disk.

- *Print from any computer.* Without a network, you can't easily make a single printer available to two, three, or more computers without manually rearranging cables. With a network, you just click the print button.

- *Play multiplayer games.* Sure, it may sound decadent, but you'll appreciate the ability to play a wide variety of games head to head with your friends, kids, and neighbors. Most games are multiplayer enabled these days, and they're a lot more fun when played against real people. A network is, in many ways, the cheapest entertainment upgrade you can make.

If you don't want to go all the way—at least right now—check out the section "Direct Cable Connections" later in this chapter.

? How much will a network cost me?

Complete network solutions for a pair of PCs will run you about $100. And because networks are modular, you can expand to three or more PCs for a low additional cost. Linksys, for instance, sells a product called Fast Ethernet 10/100 Network in a Box that we've had great success with. It has everything you need to connect two PCs. To add additional computers to your network, you simply need an additional Ethernet card (available for less than $50) and the proper amount of cable to reach the new computer. If you're using Windows 95 or Windows 98, you already have all the software you need to make it work.

Tip: *Don't want to add PCI cards? You can also add Ethernet using a USB-to-Ethernet adapter. It's an external connection that's easy to make and the adapters aren't much more expensive than internal cards.*

? What's a "server"? What's a "client"? Will I need them in my network?

They're both components of a *hierarchical network*. In a hierarchical network—like a Windows NT system—a number of *client computers* rely on the resources of another computer (called the *server*) to manage the network, share information, and host all needed peripherals:

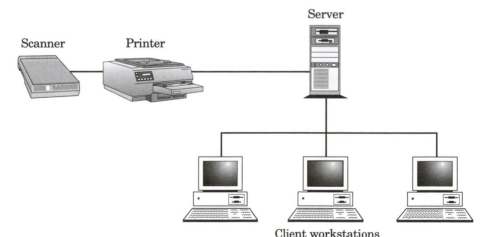

Client workstations

In your own office or home, odds are good that you'll use Windows to set up your network, and that it will not be hierarchical. In this kind of network, which is called *peer-to-peer*, each computer takes an equal role in managing system resources:

A peer-to-peer configuration is easier to assemble and administer, but with large networks it is generally not as effective as the hierarchical structure.

What's the difference between a LAN and a WAN?

A *local area network* (LAN) is what you normally create when you bind two or three (or a hundred) PCs together in an office. A *wide area network* (WAN) is the result of connecting two or more LANs together into a super-network. The Internet, for instance, is the world's largest WAN. On a smaller scale, many businesses that operate multiple LANs (one for each branch office, perhaps) network these LANs together into a WAN so everyone in the company can communicate.

What is Ethernet?

Based on a networking protocol developed in the mid-70s, *Ethernet* is one of the most common kinds of networking in existence today. It uses *coaxial, twisted-pair,* and *fiber-optic cable* to transmit data, and it employs CSMA/CD (*Carrier Sense Multiple Access with Collision Detection*) to regulate network activity.

That's the jargon-filled explanation—for more details, check out the answer to the CSMA/CD question later in this chapter. For our purposes, it suffices to say that Ethernet is a practical and inexpensive way of networking PCs and peripherals together. To make it all work, you need the following:

- Ethernet adapters for each computer
- Coaxial (10Base2) or fiber optic (10BaseT, twisted-pair) cabling
- A hub, if you're using twisted-pair cable
- Network software, such as Windows 95, Windows 98, or Windows NT

What's a "hub"?

A *hub* is a small box used in networks that are connected via twisted-pair cable. Unlike coaxial cable, which is strung directly from one PC to another, twisted-pair cable is arranged in an orbital pattern:

Hub

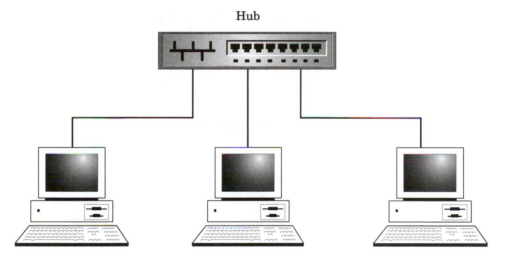

Each PC is wired directly to the hub, which serves as a central I/O station, or concentrator, for the network. If you attempt to use twisted-pair cable without a hub, the network will fail.

Tip: *You can connect two—and only two—PCs together using twisted pair cable if you get a specially marked "crossover" cable designed for that purpose. The special cable essentially reverses the wiring so that two PCs can communicate without a hub.*

 ## What's a "router"?

A *router* is used in some networks, but typically not in the sort of small LANs used in a home offices. Routers are hardware devices that automatically choose the most efficient route for transmitting information. When a router sends *data packets*—which are the basic components of e-mail, Web pages, and video—from a Web server to your PC, there's no human intervention; indeed, the route may never be the same twice. A router is a sophisticated device that analyzes network outages, capacity, and data paths in order to identify the most efficient path for the data to take.

 ## What is IPX?

Internetwork Packet Exchange (IPX) is the transport protocol originally developed for Novell Netware networks that is used to move data over most PC-based Ethernet networks. You generally won't need to care much about IPX, but the IPX protocol will have to be installed before your network will operate. You'll find that many computer games require an "IPX network." It's a very popular protocol for Ethernet LANs.

How much cable should we use in our network?

A standard Ethernet network will be fine for pretty much any small office or home environment. The maximum length of cable you can use in a LAN is determined by whether you choose coaxial or twisted-pair cable. Here's the guideline:

Cable	Designation	Maximum Length
Coaxial	10Base-2	650 feet
Twisted-pair	10Base-T	328 feet

 ## Our system has been wacking out ever since we rearranged the office. Is it possible to put PCs in a network too close together?

Yes. To eliminate interference, you should make sure that PCs are never closer than about 1.5 feet.

CHOOSING A NETWORK DESIGN

 If I connect two PCs now, can I add to the network later?

Sure! You can scale an Ethernet network at any time. Start with two PCs, and you'll later be able to access additional computers at a fairly low cost.

One common solution is to have a basic two- or three-PC network in a small office and leave empty hub connections for notebook PCs. If someone uses a notebook that has an Ethernet PC Card, you can temporarily add that portable PC to the network and remove it when you're done. It's very easy to scale a network in this way—the system recognizes the new PC and adjusts accordingly.

If we install a network, do we need to buy a "network printer"?

Nope. A *network printer* is a special kind of printer that includes its own Ethernet card. You connect such a printer to the network using a coaxial or twisted-pair cable, and it becomes an independent network device. You don't need a network printer for a small office, however. Any printer that you already have can easily be made accessible to your network in Windows 95 or Windows 98.

There are two principal advantages to using a real network printer:

- It performs faster than a printer connected to a PC on the network.

- It can be used all the time—a printer connected to a PC can't be used if the PC to which it's connected is turned off.

We don't think that either of those advantages amounts to much for a small home office, however. The performance difference is small, and to avoid the second problem simply keep the printer connected to the PC that you use most often.

> ***Tip:*** *If you're shopping for a new printer, look for one that can accept an add-on Ethernet expansion card in the future. That way, if you decide you want a dedicated network printer, you'll have an easy option for upgrading your current printer instead of buying a new one.*

What's the difference between CSMA/CD and "token passing"? Do I care?

Apparently, you've been reading too many articles about networking. In a nutshell, these are the two principal ways that different network protocols allow computers to pass information from one system to another.

In *token passing*, computers may send data over the network only when they hold the *token*, or a special authority to transmit. Only one PC at a time can have the token, so that's how token-passing networks (such as Token Ring) maintain control over the client computers.

Other networks (such as Ethernet) use the CSMA/CD protocol. This protocol doesn't use any kind of token to determine when PCs can and can't communicate over the network. Instead, each PC has the authority to transmit whenever it wants—but it waits until it hears "silence" over the network. If two PCs choose the same opportunity to send data, that is detected as a collision, and both PCs reset for a short, random amount of time before attempting to resend the data. It may sound like a form of digital anarchy, but it works very well, particularly for smaller networks.

Keep in mind that these protocols are completely transparent to the user. You really don't need to care whether you have a token-passing network or a CSMA/CD network. All you know is that you can communicate with the PC on the other side of the room, seemingly at the speed of light, but in reality, probably only at about 10 megabits per second (Mbps).

What's the best kind of cable for an Ethernet network?

You have a choice of either coaxial or twisted-pair cabling for your network:

Twisted-pair cable

Coaxial cable

Coaxial cable is often called 10Base-2, and it is often easier to set up than twisted-pair—and cheaper, to boot. Twisted-pair cable looks like phone wire except that the connector, an RJ-45 jack, is larger than a telephone's RJ-11.

When you are trying to decide which to use, consider these pros and cons:

- Coaxial cable networks are cheaper than twisted-pair, because the cable itself costs less and you don't need a hub to connect your PCs.

- Twisted-pair is easier to use in modular offices, because you can wire the baseboard of each office or cubicle to accept RJ-45 connectors, much like phone lines are set up.

- Twisted-pair performs better than coaxial because it can send and receive data simultaneously; coaxial cable can only do one or the other.

- Twisted-pair will let you add notebook PCs to your network (PC Cards often only accept RJ-45 connectors).

Which do we suggest? These days, 10Base-T is more common, so you'll find the cabling more readily available in office supply stores, wholesale stores, and so on. But 10Base-T cabling is also necessary if you want to take advantage of the latest 100-Mbps Ethernet cards and connections. So if you're buying new, that's the direction we'd point you in.

 Tip: *The entire network doesn't need to be 10Base-T to connect a notebook; you can add a single hub to your 10Base-T network and connect your notebook there.*

❓ OK, before I go shopping, what else do I need to know about selecting cable?

It isn't always easy to decide what kind of cabling to use in a new network. You need to consider how many PCs you will have, whether you will want to include portable PCs, and even what your distance limitations are. Here's a handy guide:

Type of Cable	Network Characteristics
Coaxial	Only a few purchase
	No portable PCs that require RJ-45 connections
Twisted-pair	Fewer than 16 PCs within 328 feet of each other
	Allows for portable PCs with RJ-45 connections
Twisted-pair, with multiple hubs connected via coaxial	More than 16 purchase
	Separated by 328 feet or more

❓ Our office may upgrade to a Fast Ethernet network someday. Can we use the same cabling we've got now?

If you plan to upgrade to a 100-Mbps network at some point, you should start your network with a grade of cabling that can support that high data rate or you'll end up replacing it all down the road. Twisted-pair cabling—10Base-T—is "graded" for certain applications. While Grade 3 is fine for ordinary 10-Mbps networks, you need to use Grade 5 for 100-Mbps networks. You can't use coaxial cable for 100-Mbps networks—sorry.

❓ Can we use both coaxial and twisted-pair cables in the same network?

Yes. In fact, you can purchase inexpensive hubs that have both a coaxial port and between two and eight twisted-pair RJ-45 connectors (see Figure 9-1). In that way, you can start with coaxial cable and scale up with twisted-pair as needed.

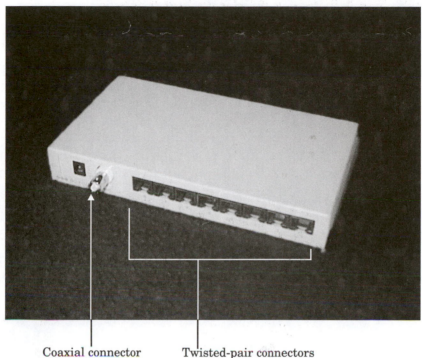

Coaxial connector   Twisted-pair connectors

Figure 9-1 An Ethernet hub

 ## Can I use my USB ports for a direct connection?

Yes, if you buy special connectors and cabling to stretch between them. USB actually offers a little more bandwidth than standard Ethernet; 12 Mbps vs. 10 Mbps, respectively. That said, you may be using USB for other devices, too, and they all need to share that connection. A heavily used network may affect your other USB peripherals.

Also, USB networking is only reliable on Windows 98. If you're running Windows 95, we highly encourage you to upgrade your operating system before installing a USB network.

Walkthrough: Installing a Windows-Based Network

Installing a network is a multi-step process that you need to perform not just for one PC, but for each computer involved. To reduce confusion and simplify any troubleshooting, start with only two computers and perform all the steps just on them. Once you have your network working as expected, you can go back and add the other PCs.

Here's the procedure:

1. Shut off the power to your system.

2. Remove the cover of your PC and locate an empty slot. If you're installing a PCI network card, remember that it may need a bus master slot; install it in one of those if possible. Make sure that the card is fully seated, and screw it into place:

Replace the cover of the PC.

3. Install the network card in the second PC following the instructions in steps 1 and 2.

4. Attach the two network cards using the appropriate cabling:

   ● If you're using 10Base-2 coaxial cable, connect the two PCs using T-connectors:

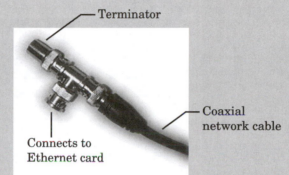

Terminator

Coaxial network cable

Connects to Ethernet card

   Both PCs should have terminators on the ends of the T-connectors so that the chain is composed of a terminator, PC, PC, and another terminator.

   ● If you're using 10Base-T twisted-pair cabling, situate the hub between the two PCs and plug in its power cord. Connect the 10Base-T cable to one PC's Ethernet card, then into a port on the hub. Then connect the other PC's Ethernet card to another empty port on the hub.

5. After the two systems are connected, start one of the PCs.

6. Windows should detect the new network card. Follow the manufacturer's instructions to install the appropriate driver software for the card and restart the PC.

Now it's time to install the appropriate network drivers and protocols so your LAN can function. Follow these steps:

1. Choose Start | Settings | Control Panel and open the Network applet:

2. Make sure that the following entries are listed in the Configuration tab:

- Client for Microsoft Networks
- IPX/SPX Compatible Protocol
- NetBEUI
- TCP/IP
- An entry for the network card you just installed

You should also see an entry for each of the following: IPX/SPX, NetBEUI, and TCP/IP, in which an arrow points to your network card driver. If any of these items are missing, add them by clicking the Add button and choosing Protocol | Microsoft.

You may need your Windows CD-ROM to complete the next part of the setup. If Windows asks to restart, wait until later; we'll do it all at once.

1. On the Configuration tab of the Network applet, make sure that the Primary Network Logon is set to Windows Logon.

2. Click the File and Printer Sharing button and enable file sharing.

3. Click the Identification tab:

```
┌─────────────────────────────────────────────────────┐
│ Network                                    ? X       │
├─────────────────────────────────────────────────────┤
│ Configuration │ Identification │ Access Control │    │
│                                                       │
│   ┌──┐   Windows uses the following information to    │
│   │  │   identify your computer on the network.       │
│   └──┘   Please type a name for this computer, the    │
│          workgroup it will appear in, and a short     │
│          description of the computer.                 │
│                                                       │
│   Computer name:  │Dell            │                  │
│                                                       │
│   Workgroup:      │Johnson         │                  │
│                                                       │
│   Computer        │                │                  │
│   Description:     │I               │                 │
│                                                       │
│                                                       │
│                                                       │
│                         │  OK  │  │ Cancel │          │
└─────────────────────────────────────────────────────┘
```

4. Name the computer (any name you want) and create a name for the workgroup. Every PC on your LAN will have to have the same name in the Workgroup box. The computer description is optional, because Windows doesn't do anything with that entry.

5. Click OK to close the Network applet.

You're done with that PC. Now start your other PC, install the network card drivers, and follow the previous instructions to configure the network controls. When you've finished, reboot both systems. They may ask you for a username and password: While you have to provide a username, a password is optional. We recommend leaving the password blank, because the security it provides is minimal anyway.

After both PCs have fully booted, wait about 30 seconds and open the My Neighborhood icon on the desktop. You should see entries for both PCs. You're done!

 ### What if I don't want to use an Ethernet network? What are my alternatives?

You're in luck. In the last year, a number of "home networking" initiatives have resulted in good alternatives to Ethernet. For the most part, they're easy to set up and use, and offer good performance. Here are some options from which to choose:

Network	What It Does	Brand-name Example
USB	Connects your PCs together using only the USB ports on the outside of your case.	Belkin USB Direct Connect Adapter
AC Power	Connects your PC's parallel port into an AC power outlet, then transmits your network throughout the house using your internal electrical wiring.	Interlogis Passport
Phone Line	Plugs into your standard phone line and transmits the network throughout your house using phone lines. Doesn't interfere with regular phone calls.	Diamond HomeFree Phoneline

Network	What It Does	Brand-name Example
Wireless	Connects your PC to a wireless transmitter and network without wires for distances up to about 500 feet.	Symphony Proxim

 There are so many choices! What network solution is best for me?

With so many new kinds of networks, choosing the right one can be a challenge. Here's a handy chart you can use to help narrow the field:

If you want to...	Try this solution
Share files with someone at another PC in the same room	An Ethernet or USB network
Share files with a PC running Windows 3.x	An ISA-based Ethernet kit
Share files with someone who works in a different part of the house	An AC Power or Phone Line network
Work on a notebook in the yard while remaining connected to the network	Wireless
Share a printer or scanner with several computers	Any network solution
Share the files on my PC with a Macintosh	In general, only Ethernet will work.
Play network computer games	Almost any solution will work; we recommend Ethernet or USB.

USING THE NETWORK EFFECTIVELY

 Can we use ordinary phone cables to connect our network?

You can't use regular phone cables for an Ethernet network. What looks like ordinary telephone twisted-pair is actually a special kind of Ethernet cable. It has eight wires instead of the phone cable's ordinary four wires. In addition, the jack at each end of the wire is called an RJ-45 connector, and it's somewhat bigger than a typical RJ-11 telephone jack.

This twisted-pair cable is called 10Base-T and is available at most larger computer stores in standard lengths (such as 25 feet, 50 feet, and 100 feet). A newer variation on this twisted-pair cable is called 100Base-T. Unlike 10Base-T's 10 Mbps limitation, 100Base-T can move network data at 100 Mbps.

On the other hand, remember that there's a standard out there called *phone line networking*. It involves a special kind of adapter card that plugs into a regular phone jack, and it isn't compatible with Ethernet.

When should we use a hub?

You'll need a hub if you use 10Base-T or 100Base-T twisted-pair cabling that terminates in RJ-45 connectors. Unlike coaxial Ethernet cable that can "daisy chain" from one PC to another, twisted-pair travels from each PC to a central hub, then back out to other PCs.

A hub increases the cost of a small network, because it's an additional piece of hardware you need to buy, but it allows you to connect laptop computers to a LAN. That's because notebooks invariably have LAN cards that only accept twisted-pair inputs, which require a hub to connect (see Figure 9-2).

How do we protect the data on our network?

Don't want everyone on your LAN to be able to read or change everything on your hard drive? There are numerous levels of protection you can implement quite easily on a Windows 95 or Windows 98 network. Here are your options:

- No one on other PCs on the network has any access to your data at all.

- Everyone on the network has complete access to your data.

In between those two extremes, you can also specify:

- **Read-only** Users can open and copy your data, but not make any changes to anything stored on your hard disk.

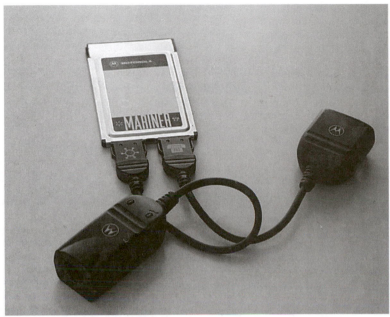

Figure 9-2 A PC Card Ethernet adapter with a 10Base-T (RJ-45) connector

- **Password for read-only access** Only the people with a password can read your data.

- **Password for complete access** Only the people with a password can change your data.

- **Some of your drives are accessible, but others are restricted** You can specify which drives are completely off-limits, while other drives are password protected.

 Note: *The default state for your network is high security, which means that file sharing is disabled.*

As you can see, there are many options. To give even minimal access to other users on the network, you need to first enable file sharing by following these steps:

1. Choose Start | Settings | Control Panel and open the Network applet:

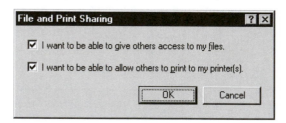

2. On the Configuration tab, click the File and Print Sharing button.

3. Make sure that there's a check mark in the box for "I want to be able to give others access to my files":

4. Click OK twice to close the Network applet.

> **Caution:** *After you enable file and printer sharing, any network connection can potentially access your resources. That includes the Internet. It is possible for a remote user to access your computer and steal data via the Internet if you haven't taken reasonable precautions to prevent that.*

After you've enabled file sharing, you can fine-tune the data access on a drive-by-drive basis. Follow these steps:

1. Open My Computer and right-click the icon for any drive, such as drive C:

   ![Screenshot of the Dell My Computer window showing drive icons and a right-click context menu with options Open, Explore, Find..., System Information, Sharing..., Add to Zip, Scan with Norton AntiVirus, Corel Versions, Format..., Create Shortcut, Properties. The left panel shows "Dell c (C:) Local Disk, Capacity: 2.04 GB, Used: 1.97 GB, Free: 74.5 MB".]

2. Choose Sharing from the drop-down menu.

3. Choose the level of protection you want to afford that drive. Click Shared As and give the drive a name you want others on the network to see:

4. Choose Read-only, Full, or Depends on Password. Using passwords, you can give specific people the ability to read your data, and others the ability to read and write to your drive.

5. Repeat this process for every drive on your system—including CD-ROM and floppy drives.

Remember that every PC on the network has these same protection privileges, so you will not be able to read a drive elsewhere on the network without someone else's permission.

? Do we need to have all the PCs in our network turned on all the time?

No, you don't. Let's suppose you have four PCs networked using Ethernet. You can turn on just one of the systems and

use it just fine with the others turned off. It's quite all right to turn other PCs on as needed and turn them off when you're done—the network dynamically adjusts to the presence or absence of computers.

There's one caveat to this rule. If you intend to print, the PC that is hosting a non-network printer must be on.

Can I access the Internet from a modem on a different PC?

Ordinarily, not with Windows 95 or 98. There are ways around this limitation, however. What you need is a special kind of program called a *proxy server.* One inexpensive proxy server, WinGate, allows you to configure all the PCs in a small LAN to use a single computer's modem for Internet activity. WinGate is free for two PCs and carries a small price tag if you network three or more PCs. Download the program from **http://www.wingate.net**.

Caution: *It isn't necessarily easy to get a WinGate network operational, and the documentation—which is apparently in a state of constant evolution—is awful. Even so, if you have some time to kill, however, it's the best available solution for sharing a single modem connection among multiple PCs.*

Windows 2000 has proxy server software built in, so you can access the Internet from any PC in a Windows 2000 network with no additional software.

Can I access a scanner that's attached to a different PC from my LAN?

Probably not. You'll need to get a scanner that has a network driver, and not all do. You can contact the manufacturer to see if one is available. If not, you can shop around for a scanner and ask for that feature explicitly. In particular, the Umax Astra scanner is a favorite of ours that comes with such a network capability.

 ## We have only two PCs, and we're using twisted-pair cable. Can we avoid the hub?

Yes, you can. Computer stores and specialty electronics stores sell an Ethernet cable, called a *crossover cable*, that makes it possible to connect two PCs without a hub, even though it's a twisted-pair connection. You can then set up Windows networking as you normally would. This is great if you have a laptop and desktop, both with Ethernet capability, and you want to move data from one to the other.

Don't connect the crossover cable to a hub, though—it's a special kind of cable with the leads switched and it won't work for a hub-based network.

I've set up a network, but one of the computers won't connect. What can I do?

There can be any number of possible reasons for your problem. Check this list for starters, in order of easiest to hardest to fix:

- If you're using coaxial cables, are there termination plugs on the first and last PCs in the network? Are they securely attached?

- If you're using a hub, is it plugged in?

- Check all the connections, such as the BNC connectors for coaxial cables and RJ-45 connectors for the twisted-pair. Make sure they're secure.

- Are any of the cables tightly coiled? If so, unwind them. This can create interference that can disrupt the network.

- Are any of the cables pinched or under something heavy? Move them—this may also be causing interference.

- Make sure you log in when Windows starts. If Windows boots without asking for a password, fine. But if you cancel the Windows Login dialog box to avoid entering a password, Windows doesn't log into the network.

- Check the protocols in the Network applet in the Control Panel. Make sure all the PCs have the same workgroup name and that they all have unique computer names. Make sure there are entries for IPX/SPX, NetBEUI, and TCP/IP as well as for your network card.

- Is the network card properly seated in the PCI or ISA slot?
- Is it in a bus master slot? If necessary, rearrange cards in your PC to find out.

Does it matter which slot I put my Ethernet card into?

Yes, it does. For best performance, get PCI-based Ethernet cards. ISA network cards can suffer from slow performance and, even worse, setup nightmares, because they may not be able to autoconfigure properly.

If you choose a PCI-based Ethernet card, be aware that it will probably want a *bus master* slot. Most PCI slots are bus masters, but not all. If you install the card and it doesn't appear to work, try moving cards around until you find which slot works.

We've outgrown our hub. What can we do?

You don't have to replace it. You can string multiple hubs together to continuously scale your network as needed. Simply connect one hub to another using a coaxial cable, and you can have a virtually unlimited number of PCs arranged in clusters, or nodes, by sharing hubs.

How do I let other computers on the network use my printer?

If you have a printer already connected to your PC when you install a network, it's easy to let all the computers have access to it. Remember, however, that your network will only be able to use the printer when the "host" system—the one to which the printer is connected—is turned on and connected to the network.

There are two steps to enabling the printer. First, you need to make sure that Windows will share your printer with the rest of the network. Then you need to visit each computer on the network and show it where the printer actually is. Here's how you do it:

1. Choose Start | Settings | Control Panel and open the Network applet.

2. On the Configuration tab, click the File and Printer Sharing button.

3. Make sure that there's a check mark in the box for "I want to be able to allow others to print to my printer(s)."

4. Click OK twice to close the Network applet.

Next, go to each computer that the printer isn't directly connected to via a parallel or serial cable and do the following:

1. Choose Start | Settings | Printers.

2. Select Add Printer and click Next.

3. Choose Network printer and click Next.

4. Click the Browse button and look for the computer with the printer attached. Click the plus sign to its left and choose the printer when it appears; then click Next.

5. Choose the appropriate printer from the list and click Next.

6. Name the printer and click Next.

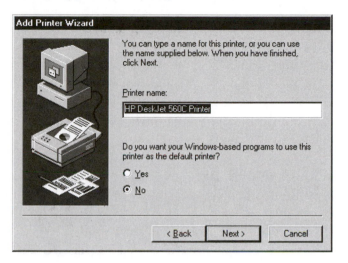

7. Click Finish to complete the printer's installation.

Now your printer can serve not just the PC it's attached to, but also the other PCs on the network.

Walkthrough: Turning an Existing Printer into a Network Printer

Often, people configure networks but already have the printer drivers installed on all the PCs. Perhaps they were used to moving the printer every time they needed to print. You can quickly turn a printer into a network printer just by choosing Start | Settings | Printers and finding the printer that is now accessible via the network. Then do this:

1. Right-click the printer and choose Properties.

2. Click the Details tab.

3. Click the drop-down menu under Print to the Following Port and choose the printer directly. If you've already made it available to the network, you'll find it here.

Click OK to close the dialog box.

 Can play a multiplayer game on my home network?

Look on the game box for certain code words that give away what the network requirements are. These are the most important terms to look for:

● You might see "LAN" or "IPX." Both of these refer to a run-of-the-mill network that you can create at home with a few Ethernet cards.

● If you see "TCP/IP," it means that you'll either need to connect through the Internet or have each computer on the LAN assigned its own TCP/IP address.

● "Direct Cable Connection" is a simple network you can rig with Windows 95 or Windows 98, using a parallel or serial cable.

DIRECT CABLE CONNECTIONS

 Can I network two PCs without adding Ethernet cards and hubs and spending lots of money?

Yes, you can. Microsoft includes a feature called the Direct Cable Connection in Windows 95 and Windows 98 so you can easily create a "poor man's network." By connecting two PCs with just a serial or parallel cable, you can allow two PCs to communicate almost as effectively as if you had installed a real Ethernet network.

 Does a Direct Cable Connection require a special kind of cable?

If you want to make the connection with a serial cable, you'll need a *null-modem* cable (also sold as a *LapLink* cable). A normal parallel cable works fine for the parallel connection.

✚ ***Tip:*** *If you buy a null-modem cable to use for Direct Cable Connections, mark it with a sticker so you can find it later. Often, there's nothing on a null-modem cable that identifies it as different from your ordinary serial cables.*

 When I connect with the Direct Cable Connection, which should I use—parallel or serial?

We recommend the parallel connection because it's faster—significantly so. If you don't want to disconnect a printer from the parallel port just to use a Direct Cable Connection, however, you can use the serial port instead. In addition, serial connections are good for longer separations than parallel can support.

 How far apart can PCs be and still use the Direct Cable Connection?

You're limited by the maximum length of parallel and serial cables:

Parallel	25 feet
Serial	200 feet

How many PCs can we network with the Direct Cable Connection?

Only two, and that's the Direct Cable Connection's major limitation. If you want to connect three PCs simultaneously, use a real Ethernet network (or another type of home network).

Walkthrough: Networking with the Direct Cable Connection

It's a simple matter to connect PCs with the Direct Cable Connection. Before you can actually connect, however, you need to configure them. Just do this:

1. With both PCs shut off, connect a parallel or null-modem serial cable to both PCs.
2. Power on both PCs.
3. On the computer that will act as "host," choose Start | Programs | Accessories | Direct Cable Connection.

4. Choose Host and click Next.

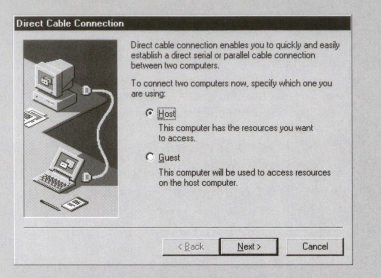

5. Choose the appropriate cable type. If you're using a serial cable, make sure you identify the correct COM port you used. Click Next.

6. If you want to use password protection, specify it now. Click Finish.

7. On the "guest" PC, start the Direct Cable Connection program and choose Guest. Click Next.

8. Select the appropriate port. Click Next.

9. Click Finish.

Once the configuration has been made (and you need only do it once), you can actually connect. Follow these steps:

1. On the computer that will act as "host," choose Start | Programs | Accessories | Direct Cable Connection.

2. Click Listen.

3. On the computer that will act as "guest," choose Start | Programs | Accessories | Direct Cable Connection.

4. Click Connect.

Both PCs should connect and you can begin sharing files—assuming you've set the PCs up for printer and file sharing. If not, see the answer to, "How do we protect the data on our network?" earlier in the chapter.

Tip: COM1 *is generally the small connector, and* COM2 *is usually the large one.*

? Can I dial into my PC with a modem and access my files?

Yes, if you have the Plus pack for Windows, Windows 95 OSR2 (see Chapter 15 for determining what version of Windows you have), or Windows 98. The Dial-Up Server is a program found in Start | Accessories (though you may need to install it on your system first) that lets you configure your PC as a server; instruct it to allow caller access and optionally to require a password. Then dial the modem's phone line with another Windows PC when you're away, and you'll have complete access to the system as if you were connected via LAN—except that it will be quite a bit slower.

Chapter 10

Electronic Imaging

Answer Topics!

Electronic Imaging @ a Glance

● Just a few years ago, scanners and digital cameras were the exclusive domain of professionals, and no one in small offices or at home even thought about them. How times change. Now one in three households with a PC also has some kind of imaging device, and as prices hit rock bottom, we can only expect those numbers to go up.

● You can take a few steps out of the image digitizing process by starting with a digital camera. Cameras store pictures internally on a RAM card, or on a tiny hard disk, and connect quickly to your PC for instant data transfers.

● Want to grab video from a camcorder or VCR and edit it on your PC? You need a video capture card, but first consider the details. What kind of hard disk should you use? What about data compression? Or should you simply get a DV camera and a FireWire card and be done with it?

SCANNERS

What does a scanner do?

Scanners create a digital image by passing a light along the surface of a piece of paper (or similar medium) while sensors follow behind the light, picking up information from the page and turning it into a binary file. Using colored light (usually three different colors: red, green, and blue), the sensors can detect the colors of the image and render that in the image file as well. (Some scanners use a fluorescent light, and the sensors separate the colors, but the result is similar.)

Pragmatically speaking, a scanner is a tool you can use to transform a printed page, photo, or something similar into a graphic file on your computer. You can then take that file and place it in other documents, edit it using photo-editing software, and so on.

I've thought about getting a scanner, but I'm not sure it's worth the money. What can I do with a scanner?

Scanners are valuable if you often find yourself needing to transfer real-world 2-D objects—like pictures, faxes, or book pages—into your PC. Not long ago, a scanner only made sense for someone who needed to do a lot of scanning, but by mid-1999 you could routinely find quality scanners for under $75. That means it's cost-effective for you to get a scanner even for occasional use.

But it's not just pictures for newsletters. You can scan any number of things—important documents, cleared checks, photos for a home inventory—and file them away digitally on your PC. And, most scanners come with some sort of Optical Character Recognition (OCR) software, making it possible to scan a document, have it recognized by your PC, then put into an editable format. Beats retyping!

I want to get a scanner. What are my options?

Most everyone is familiar with the flatbed scanner. It's good for a lot of different kinds of scanning jobs, but it may be "too much" of a scanner for some people, or just not the right fit

for your needs. Here's an overview of the kinds of scanners from which you can choose:

- **Flatbed scanner** A *flatbed* is typically a long, narrow tray on which you place your document. (It looks like the top part of a document copier.) The scanning head travels the length of the bed to create a digital image of the document. Flatbed scanners traditionally connect to your PC with an included SCSI card, but these days you can find many inexpensive scanners that connect via the parallel port or USB port. They generally make high-quality images and accept options like automatic sheet feeders—so you can copy lots of pages at once. On the downside, flatbed scanners have a big "footprint," meaning that they take up a lot of space on a desk or table, so they're harder to integrate into small offices.

- **Sheetfed scanner** This is a much smaller device that does away with the traditional moving optics and flat scanning bed. Instead, these scanners typically stand upright and pull documents through the unit—right past the stationary scanning head—to offer a compact scanning solution. Their advantages include a small size and a design that's optimized for scanning sheets of paper and photos. In fact, you can get sheetfed scanners that accept a load of 25 originals at a small fraction of the cost of a flatbed document feeder. Of course, you can't scan thick objects like books or magazines unless you first separate the pages from the source. Also, some low-grade sheetfed scanners can introduce imperfections in the scan due to the motor that pulls the page through. (A few vendors have even offered a sheetfed scanner built into a keyboard, which is an interesting space-saving option.)

- **Photo scanner** This class of scanner is designed to scan just pictures—usually 3×5-inch pictures, in fact, though some also can handle 5×7s. If all you need is the ability to convert 35mm photos into digital images, this is a good solution. (Some photo scanners fit in an empty drive bay in your PC, taking up no desk space at all.) On the other hand, these scanners are completely useless for scanning anything except small pictures or perhaps business cards.

● **Hand scanner** Handheld scanners have largely disappeared from the PC scene. In years past, they were a good alternative to flatbeds, but sheetfeds have taken over the role that hand scanners used to serve. While you may still find some hand scanners around, we don't think they're a good investment.

 ## What should I look for when shopping for a scanner?

The most important things to consider when scanner shopping are the scanner's fundamental specs. In a nutshell, you should consider resolution and color depth.

● **Resolution** Scanners are rated by the resolution at which they can convert documents into digital images. Inexpensive scanners are typically able to scan at 300 dots per inch (dpi). Often, you'll see a spec like 300×600 dpi. The first number is the optical resolution of the imaging system; the second number is the resolution of the motor that moves the scanning head across the document. Because the optical resolution is always lower than the number of discrete steps the motor can perform, the first number—the optic's actual resolution—is more important. You should use that number to compare scanners when you shop. Also, see "What resolution should I be using when I scan?" later in this chapter.

● **Color depth** As we discussed in Chapter 6, computers measure colors in terms of bits per pixel. (See Chapter 6 for a chart that relates color depth in bits to the number of colors you can see.) Some inexpensive scanners are 24-bit scanners, meaning they can digitize as many as 16.7 million colors, which also happens to be about as many colors as the human eye can see. More sophisticated scanners work at 30 or 36 bits per pixel, meaning they can distinguish billions of colors. Some scanners work this way so they have more colors to choose from when resolving dark regions, or images with lots of rapid color changes, into 24-bit images. The bottom line is that extremely

high-end color scanners can produce better images, but that's typically beyond the needs of most small office and home users.

 ### What does it mean when a scanner has 600 dpi but 9,600 dpi maximum resolution?

Many scanners can use sophisticated software routines to interpolate color changes and image information between pixels that were optically observed during the scan. That means they can render images with a higher apparent resolution—as much as 9,600 dpi. In general, we think this feature is of dubious value. You'll need a lot of memory and hard disk space to use resolutions beyond the optical resolution, and the final results may not be all that impressive anyway. Don't buy a scanner based on this feature unless you really need it—for example, you need to scan small images and render them very large in digital documents.

 ### What's the difference between a one-pass scanner and a three-pass scanner?

In the old days—a few years ago—most color scanners made three passes of every document they scanned. Each of these passes captured image information for each of the red, green, and blue color components that would eventually make the final color image. Modern scanners, almost without exception, are single-pass devices. In a single pass of the scan head, the document is sampled for all three colors simultaneously. Obviously, this makes single-pass scanners a lot faster than the old three-pass units. If you have a three-pass scanner, there's no reason to upgrade unless you really want a new, faster scanner. Just be prepared to wait a longer amount of time for documents to be digitized.

What are the advantages of a flatbed scanner?

Flatbeds are handy for scanning thick and oversized documents, like books and magazines. You can even scan three-dimensional objects with some success, depending on the object. You can scan car keys, for example.

Because flatbeds are so bulky, however, other scanners have added features to do some of the things that flatbeds are good at. You can find sheetfeds, for example, that allow you to scan open book pages, such as those from 3-ring binders.

One thing that flatbeds will always do better is provide high-quality images—flatbeds offer high resolution and color depth options that sheetfed models can never approach.

Can't I scan multiple sheets without feeding them in one page at a time?

Many flatbed scanners accept accessories such as an automatic document feeder (ADF), like the one shown in Figure 10-1. You can determine if your scanner accepts an ADF attachment by checking the manual or looking at the back of the scanner. If

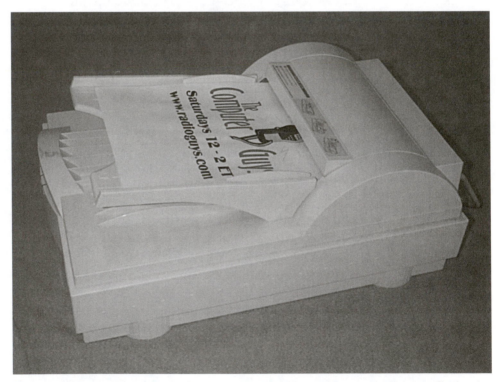

Figure 10-1   An automatic document feeder, often an option on flatbed scanners

you see a small port next to the SCSI connector, then that's probably for accessories. Call the manufacturer and see if they sell an ADF for your scanner. Keep in mind that such ADFs are often quite expensive—while the scanner might cost $300, the ADF attachment could cost an additional $400.

 ## Should I get a scanner that connects through a SCSI port?

A few years ago this question would have been irrelevant, because all scanners used SCSI. Here are some common pros and cons for the traditional SCSI port vs. a parallel port or USB scanner:

- *SCSI cards are more difficult to install.* Granted, you're armed with this book, so installing a card in your PC is a piece of cake. On the other hand, you need to have an expansion slot available, and SCSI devices aren't as portable because they're tied to a specific slot in a particular PC—to use the scanner elsewhere you'll need to transplant the SCSI card as well (or take it to another system that has a SCSI adapter installed).

- *SCSI cards are faster.* In general, you get better performance from SCSI than from a parallel port device. USB scanners are faster than parallel scanners and can hold their own against most SCSI scanners.

- *You can attach other SCSI devices to your SCSI card.* This isn't always true, however. If you use the SCSI card that comes with the scanner, it is probably certified to work with the scanner—and only with that scanner. If you want to use other SCSI devices, you'll need to call the scanner vendor and find out what third-party SCSI cards are compatible.

- *Parallel and USB scanners are easier to install and move.* Sure, all you're doing is plugging it into the printer port of your PC. That makes it easy to move around.

- *Parallel port scanners usually have a pass-through for your printer, but you can experience compatibility problems on occasion.* Not all printers are compatible with pass-throughs, so keep the receipt until you know the new scanner works with your system.

● *USB scanners are quick and hot-pluggable.* The going argument for SCSI scanners has been that they can move all of that digital data (scanned photos can be many megabytes in size) from the scanner to the PC more quickly than a parallel port scanner. USB negates some of that advantage, though, offering speeds much greater than parallel port connections. Plus, the convenience of USB makes it easy to attach a scanner even while the PC is turned on.

Walkthrough:
Installing a Scanner with a SCSI Card

Your SCSI scanners should have come with its own ISA-based SCSI cards, so you'll have everything you need in the box to perform the installation. Follow these steps:

1. Shut down your PC, ground yourself, and open the cover. Locate an empty expansion slot and remove the screw holding the slot cover in place. Remove it.

2. Take the SCSI card out of the anti-static bag, and insert the card in the empty slot. Make sure it is seated level in the slot, and screw it into place:

3. Set the scanner up on a sturdy, flat, level surface within a few feet of your PC.

4. Look for the shipping pin, which holds the optics in place when the scanner is in transit. It will be on the bottom, back, side, or even on the top of the scanner. Some shipping restraints come in the form of dials, knobs, or levers:

Refer to the manual for instructions on loosening or removing the shipping pin, and then do so. It is possible that there is no shipping pin; some inexpensive scanners are beginning to do away with them to save money.

5. Plug the scanner's SCSI cable into the scanner and the other end of the cable into the back of the PC. Unless the scanner is internally terminated, you'll need to insert the SCSI terminator into the other SCSI port on the scanner (shown here):

6. Plug the scanner's power cord in and turn it on. You should see the optics turn on and hear the motor initialize.

7. Turn on the PC. When Windows 95 or 98 starts, you'll see a New Hardware Found dialog box, and you can install the driver software as directed by the manufacturer.

Your scanner is now installed. Test the scanner to be sure everything works properly. Start some graphics software such as Adobe PhotoDeluxe or Microsoft Imaging and choose the Scan menu option.

Make sure you select the scanner from the Select Source menu the first time you use the scanner, then acquire an image. If you see the scanner control window, Windows has recognized the scanner. Go ahead and make a scan.

! ***Caution:*** *If you turn your scanner on with the shipping pin in place, the scanner will be instantly ruined. If your shipping pin can be removed completely from the scanner, be sure to save it in case you ever need to ship your scanner in the future.*

 ### If I get a parallel port scanner, can I still use my printer?

Almost all scanners that use a parallel port also include a pass-through port so you can use your printer as well. There are occasionally compatibility problems with certain combinations of PCs, scanners, and printers, but this system generally works without a snag. If in doubt, check the vendor's Web page for any reported compatibility problems.

For a list of common scanner vendors, see the answer to "My PC complains that it can't find my scanner! What do I do now?" later in this chapter.

Walkthrough: Installing a Scanner with a Parallel Connection

Instead of a SCSI card, a brand-new scanner will probably have a cable that plugs directly into your parallel port. These scanners are very easy to install—here's how to do it:

1. Shut down your PC, and unplug your printer from the parallel port.

2. Set the scanner up on a sturdy, flat, level surface within a few feet of your PC.

3. Look for the shipping pin, which holds the optics in place when the scanner is in transit. It will be on the bottom, back, or even on the top of the scanner. Some shipping restraints come in the form of dials, knobs, or levers:

Refer to the manual for instructions on loosening or removing the shipping pin, and then do so. It is possible that there is no shipping pin; some inexpensive scanners are beginning to do away with them to save money.

4. Plug the scanner's parallel cable into the scanner and the other end of the cable into the back of the PC. Then plug your printer into the pass-through port on the scanner.

5. Plug in the scanner's power cord and turn it on. You should see the optics turn on and hear the motor initialize.

6. Turn on the PC. When Windows starts, you'll see a New Hardware Found dialog box, and you can install the driver software as directed by the manufacturer.

The scanner is now installed. Test the scanner to be sure everything works properly. Start some graphics software, such as Adobe PhotoDeluxe or Microsoft Imaging, and choose the Scan menu option. Make sure you select the scanner from the Select Source menu the first time you use the scanner, then acquire an image. If you see the scanner control window, Windows has recognized the scanner. Go ahead and make a scan. You shouldn't have a problem, but if you do, unplug the printer from the scanner and reboot everything. Try to get it to work a second time. If it works now, contact the scanner vendor to find out if there's an incompatibility with your printer.

Do I need to know anything special to install my USB scanner?

Not much, except that most of the time you'll want to install your scanner software first, then plug in the scanner. That way the USB manager can find the software it needs when it detects the attached scanner. Other than that, it should be hot-pluggable; you can plug and unplug the scanner at will and Windows will recognize it.

Note: *As with any USB device, we recommend you upgrade to Windows 98 for maximum reliability and performance.*

What is TWAIN?

TWAIN stands for *technology without an important name.* Seriously. That's the meaning behind the acronym. But

what does it do? TWAIN is the standard protocol for allowing scanners and other digitizing devices to communicate with applications. Before TWAIN, every scanner came with its own proprietary drivers for each application. Now with TWAIN, you can simply install your scanner and then scan from any application that knows how to speak to scanners using TWAIN. This gives you the added advantage of being able to scan directly into most image editing software—Adobe PhotoDeluxe, Adobe PhotoShop, and CorelDRAW—without requiring you to use a scanning program first.

My PC complains that it can't find my scanner! What do I do now?

If your scanner worked when you first installed it, odds are good that the PC didn't recognize the scanner's presence when you first tried to access it in this scanning session. Some scanners need to be turned on when you boot the PC so that they are active when Windows starts—others simply need to be turned on before you first try scanning. The solution to your problem is probably to shut down your PC and restart it with the scanner already turned on.

If your scanner doesn't work at all—you just installed it and there's no response, for instance—it's possible that you need a new TWAIN driver or other software for your scanner. Contact the vendor for updates. Here are some popular vendor Web sites to help you in your search:

Pacific Image	http://www.scanace.com
Hewlett-Packard	http://www.hp.com/go/scanjet
MicroTek	http://www.microtekusa.com
Umax	http://www.umax.com
Mustek	http://www.mustek.com
Acer	http://www.acer.com
Visioneer	http://www.visioneer.com

? I get messages like "Scanner not ready" when I try to scan. What's going on?

Ah, the wonderful world of scanners. There is a wide range of problems that can cause this—here are some things you can check, in order from easiest to most difficult to fix:

● If you have a cable that is identical at both ends, check to make sure that the end with the big round lump (called a *choke*) is on the scanner end:

The choke eliminates interference that might prevent the scanner from functioning properly.

● The scanner might not have the SCSI termination block in place (SCSI scanners only). Plug the terminator into the empty SCSI port on the scanner, or into the empty port of the last SCSI device in the chain.

● The scanner might be using another device's SCSI ID number. Check the numbers used by the other SCSI devices and set the scanner to an unused number (SCSI scanners only).

● The scanner might have been turned off when the TWAIN driver tried to query the scanner. Reboot your system with the scanner on before the PC.

● The software might not be installed properly, or the drivers may be out of date—check with the manufacturer for an update.

● The SCSI or parallel cable might be bad—try replacing it.

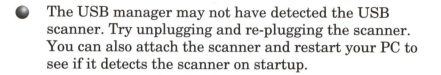

● The USB manager may not have detected the USB scanner. Try unplugging and re-plugging the scanner. You can also attach the scanner and restart your PC to see if it detects the scanner on startup.

 I already have a SCSI card in my PC for an AV hard disk. Can I use it for my scanner, too?

You'll have to call the scanner vendor and ask. Scanners are fickle SCSI devices, and they don't all work with just any SCSI card. Remember that you may need to replace the SCSI cable (or find a cable converter), because many newer SCSI cards use a small, high-density connector that won't fit the cable that came with your scanner.

I'm using a new SCSI card for my scanner, and my images have gotten very "noisy." Is this card defective?

Probably not. In the process of switching to a new SCSI card, you probably had to get a new cable, too, unless the new card has the same SCSI connector as the one that came with the scanner to begin with. If you're using a new cable, it may not be properly shielded or it might be too long. A scanner cable should never exceed six feet, and three feet is even better if your scanner is close enough to the PC.

Walkthrough: Adding a Document Feeder to Your Scanner

An automatic document feeder (ADF) can make it easy to put a stack of documents in your flatbed scanner and go to lunch while it scans. Here's how to install one:

1. Shut your scanner off. It's quite all right to leave the PC on.

2. Remove the light shield document cover from the top of the scanner. You can usually just pull it off the scanner—only two short pegs should hold it in place:

3. Take the ADF out of its packaging and insert its pegs into the same slots that the cover came from. There may be screws or some other means of securing the ADF in place.

4. Find the accessory connector cable. Plug it into the appropriate port on the back of the scanner (it's usually near the SCSI port).

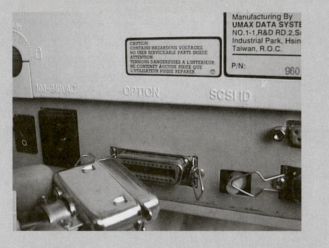

5. Turn the scanner back on.

6. Start your scanning software and look for the media type selector:

Reflective is probably already selected. Choose ADF from the list and begin scanning.

Keep in mind that the documents will probably load face up instead of face down. That way the documents will be drawn into the scanner and past the scan head face down.

? Why doesn't my document feeder do anything?

It is possible that the media type isn't set to ADF. When you select your scanning software, be sure that the media says ADF, and not some other setting like Reflective or Transmissive.

 My scanner works extremely slowly, and sometimes it crashes altogether. How can I fix this?

Many scanners come with two versions of its driver software—16-bit and 32-bit varieties. You might think that you need the 32-bit version, but if you experience problems with a particular program, use the 16-bit one instead. That will probably fix the problem. You can switch between them when you choose the Scan menu in your graphics program—select the Source option and choose the driver with a "16" in its name.

 Why do my scanned images have little marks or dots on them?

Like any optical system, you may need to clean the glass scanning bed occasionally. Use a barely damp cloth and wipe the surface of the bed, but don't spray water or cleaning solutions directly on the glass; it can leak into the mechanism through the edges of the glass.

Surprisingly, dust can accumulate on the underside of the glass (inside the mechanism) after months or years of use. You can often remove the glass to clean it, but beware—that can void the manufacturer's warranty, so check first.

 What resolution should I be using when I scan?

That depends on your goal—but don't use the scanner's highest resolution simply because it's there. Table 10-1 is a handy reference for the best resolution for various common projects.

Keep in mind that if you are going to scan only part of an image and then increase its size in print, you will need to increase the suggested resolution by the appropriate amount. That's why you might want a 600 dpi scanner even if you only use it to create Web pages—you might want to scan a small portion of an image and scale it up.

Document	Scan Resolution
Fax documents	200 dpi line art or grayscale
Optical character recognition	300 dpi line art
Pictures for Web pages	75 to 90 dpi
Color or grayscale images for print	Look up the *line screen frequency* (LSF) of your laser printer (or of the ultimate output device) and scan at twice that value. If you have a 300 dpi printer, the LSF is probably about 70. Scans for home printers are generally between 140-200 dpi.
Line art for print	Scan at the printer's resolution (for example, 300 dpi for a 300 dpi printer).

Table 10-1   Common Scan Resolutions

 I need to load some graphics onto Zip disks so I can take them to a print shop. How do I figure out how big the files will be?

File size for your graphics is an important consideration if you scan a lot or you start scanning large documents in full-color mode. You'll be amazed at how quickly your disk space will evaporate.

To determine how big your scanned images will be, you can use this equation:

$$file\ size = (resolution \times horizontal\ size) \times (resolution \times vertical\ size) \times scan\ mode$$

Where size is measured in inches, *resolution* is in dpi, and *scan mode* refers to the color depth you used in the scan:

Color Depth	Scan Mode
Line art	1/8
Grayscale	1
Color	3

Using this equation, you can see that scanning a full-color 5×7-inch image at 300 dpi will produce a 9MB file, but scanning that same image at 600 dpi will generate a file that is more than 36MB. If you're trying to carry images on a 100MB Zip drive, this formula comes in handy.

What is optical character recognition (OCR)?

OCR is a technology that lets you convert scanned text into digital text so that you can edit documents, such as faxes, in your word processor. Without the conversion that OCR software provides, a scanned page of type may look like a text file to you, but the computer will see it as a bunch of lines and dots that can only be edited with a graphics program. OCR software is often bundled with new scanners, or you might need to buy an OCR program on your own.

I often get lousy results with my OCR software. Should I upgrade to a new program?

It can often be the software's fault, but don't run out to get new software right away. Consider these factors:

- Newsprint routinely provides about 85 to 90 percent accuracy. That's 15 incorrect words per 100.

- Even laser-printed documents only offer 97 percent accuracy.

- Using different fonts can drastically affect your results. If you're trying to convert documents with odd or obscure typefaces, you're going to get awful results. The best fonts are Courier, Times New Roman, Helvetica, and Arial.

- Scanning resolution affects OCR accuracy. Scan at 300 dpi or higher and use the line art mode.

- The nontext part of the page can slow down the conversion. If your program supports it, choose which parts of the page to convert, so your program doesn't waste time and effort trying to convert pictures or photocopy noise to text.

 Should I leave my scanner on all the time or turn it off between scans?

Because most modern scanners are rated for at least 30,000 hours and often more, you can safely leave the scanner on all day when you know you'll be coming back to scan more. Turn it off at the end of the day, however, and leave it off when you don't plan to be scanning for an extended period of time.

DIGITAL CAMERAS

 What can I use a digital camera for?

Digital cameras (see Figure 10-2) are an increasingly popular alternative to scanners for digitizing needs. They're great for a number of applications:

- Getting pictures onto the Web or into digital documents quickly—because digital cameras transfer data directly to the PC, you cut out the film-developing and image-scanning steps.

- Taking pictures of three-dimensional objects, like houses and people, quickly and inexpensively.

However, they have drawbacks, too:

- Most digital cameras have limited resolution. If you want to achieve the same resolution as chemical film (such as 35mm camera film), you'll be disappointed. Most inexpensive cameras provide 640×480 or 1024×768 resolution, though more advanced cameras can double or triple that.

- Most digital cameras use about 4 AA batteries, which get quickly exhausted by the flash, optics, and LCD display. You'll use a lot of batteries and need to always carry spares. We recommend rechargeables.

Figure 10-2   A popular digital camera from Epson

 How do digital cameras compare to 35mm cameras?

The resolution of most digital cameras is vastly inferior, usually achieving just 100 or 200 dpi as compared to chemical film's thousands-of-dots-per-inch resolution. Digital cameras are usually easier to use, and they're generally lighter and smaller. Plus, you'll lose some image quality when you scan an image into your computer using a traditional scanner, so if your primary goal is getting photos into your PC, a digital camera is a good investment.

Digital Cameras and This Book

The vast majority of the photographs in this book were taken with the Olympus D-620L, and other were taken with the Kodak DC-210. The key features that you need to have for this kind of work are a good macro mode (for close-up shots), an AC adapter or rechargeable batteries, and a tripod mount. Also, ensure that the LCD display or optical viewfinder is good enough to let you see whether objects are in focus, even in low-light conditions.

What's a "megapixel" camera?

Digital cameras are divided into classes based on their image resolution. A *megapixel camera* can take pictures with a million pixels. Cheaper cameras only take 640×480-pixel images; hence they are *submegapixel*. There are also two- and three-megapixel cameras around. While the higher the resolution the better the result, keep in mind that you may not need very high resolution images. If you're taking pictures for a Web page, for instance, you don't need a two-megapixel camera. But if you're planning to frame your pictures in the living room, then more resolution is better.

 ## How will my digital camera interface with my PC?

They usually come with a serial connector to attach to your serial port. Some also have a SCSI, USB, FireWire, or infrared port, which makes transfers significantly easier.

Recently there's been a move to standardize the storage device used for digital cameras—many use CompactFlash or SmartMedia memory cards. Readers are available in parallel port and USB versions for these cards that allow you to copy data from the card to your PC quickly. Some digital cameras also have USB ports, allowing them to connect directly to a PC that has USB for copying images from the camera to your PC.

Or, you can go the Sony Mavica route—it uses standard floppy diskettes to store images. The floppy slides out of the camera and right into your PC's floppy drive.

What should I look for when I go camera shopping?

Base your decision half on specs, and half on features and ease of use. Look for these key things:

- **Storage**   Most cameras use removable data cards that store 10, 50, 100, or more images on each card (see Figure 10-3). See what the largest data card is that the camera supports. It's also possible that the camera may use internal storage only. Be sure that the camera can hold enough images, or you'll have to delete some to take new pictures when you're away from your PC.

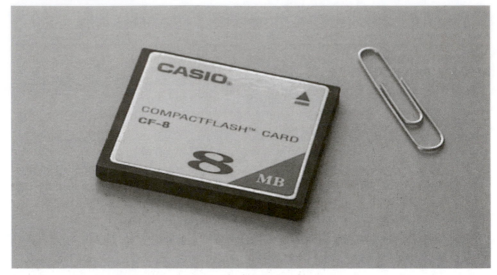

Figure 10-3 Casio's CompactFlash storage card

● **Focal length** Digital cameras compare the focal length of their lens to equivalent 35mm lenses so consumers can make an easy comparison. Be sure you get a camera that either has detachable lenses or comes with the focal length you expect to use. A 50mm equivalent lens, for instance, will do you little good if you like to photograph airshows.

● **Zoom and macro** Do you take pictures under lots of variable conditions? Then you might want a zoom or macro capability. See if the macro mode has a variable focus, or if it focuses at a fixed (and often useless) distance.

● **Through the lens viewing** Some cameras work like traditional 35mm cameras in that they show you the real image through the viewfinder, complete with through-the-lens exposure and focusing. This is a great feature, and one to look for when shopping. One example: the Olympus D-620L, used to photograph much of this book.

● **LCD display** Many digital cameras use a color LCD display so you can more easily see what you're photographing.

● **Sound and notes**   The Nikon CoolPix camera records not just audio, but handwritten notes you can jot onto the images with a pen that slides into the camera. This concept is great for journalists and other traveling photographers.

 Note: *Professional digital cameras—such as ones made by Minolta and Olympus—have actual hard drives to store images, each of which can be many megabytes in size, because they sample in very high resolutions.*

 ### Which kind of memory is better—SmartMedia or CompactFlash?

Both are commonly used in digital cameras, but they're hardly the same. We prefer CompactFlash memory, because it comes in much higher storage densities. You can get CompactFlash cards that hold as much as 96MB of memory; the largest SmartMedia cards are only 32MB. CompactFlash is also more rigid, and consequently more resilient to abuse.

VIDEO CAPTURE

I'm dying to use video on my computer! How do I get started?

To capture video, you'll want a video capture card that has inputs for video from your VCR or camcorder. There are a number on the market, so you have a lot of choices. If you want to replace your existing video card, look for a system like Matrox's Rainbow Runner. Otherwise, you can get a stand-alone video capture card that works alongside your existing video display card, like Miro's DC20.

As an alternative, you could investigate DV (digital video). DV camcorders are increasingly inexpensive, and they capture video to tape in pure digital format. You connect the camcorder to your PC using a FireWire (also known as IEEE 1394) port. The advantage is that the video stays pure digital through the whole recording, editing, and mastering process, so there's no loss of quality like you have with old analog tape.

 ## What kind of system requirements do I need for capturing video?

Capturing video is one of the most intensive, demanding tasks you can ask of your PC. The problem is that analog video—like the kind you record with your camcorder—is extremely dense with information. Because NTSC video is roughly equivalent to a 640×480 pixel display, you can see that just one frame is almost 8MB all by itself. If you then try to capture 30 frames of it per second, you're asking the processor to encode and store on a hard disk about 22MB of uncompressed video per second.

Of course, no PC hard disk in the world can hope to record that much data that fast, so the processor also has to contend with compressing the video as it is read from the video input port. That's a tall order, but a modern PC with a good video card can not only do it, but create video that looks nearly broadcast quality when you send it back out to tape.

If you want to digitize full-motion video, here's the kind of system you should have:

- At a minimum, you should have a Pentium II. Slower PCs have a hard time keeping up with the tremendous amounts of data you need to process.

- 64MB of RAM. More RAM helps, and we'd recommend 128MB for efficient video editing with the latest software.

- A fast AV SCSI hard disk or an UltraDMA hard disk. An AV drive is important, because it'll spin at 7200 RPM (faster than most hard disks) and only write data sequentially to the drive—that prevents hiccups caused by fragmentation.

In addition, look for a PCI-based video capture card that offers Motion-JPEG hardware compression and broadcast video output—or, for even better results, try DV (Digital Video).

What kind of hard disk do I need to capture video?

We recommend an AV or UltraDMA drive. (Return to Chapter 8 for more information on these drives.) Some of the

Walkthrough:
Installing a Video Capture Card

We're assuming that this video capture card works alongside your original video card; most do. If you bought an all-in-one card that replaces your old video card, then follow the instructions in Chapter 6 to replace your old video card.

Shut down your PC and remove the cover.

1. Take the capture card out of the anti-static bag and slip the card into an empty PCI slot.

2. Screw the video card in place securely.

3. Attach video and sound cables to the back of the capture card:

Don't be confused by the labels. If a port says Video In, that means you should run a cable from the Video Out connector on your camcorder or VCR into that port on the capture card.

4. Replace the cover on your PC.

5. Start your PC. Follow the plug-and-play instructions to add the new drivers for your capture card. If Windows starts but doesn't detect the new card, open the Display Properties and add the card manually.

Your card probably came with a nonlinear video editor such as
Corel Lumiere or Adobe Premiere:

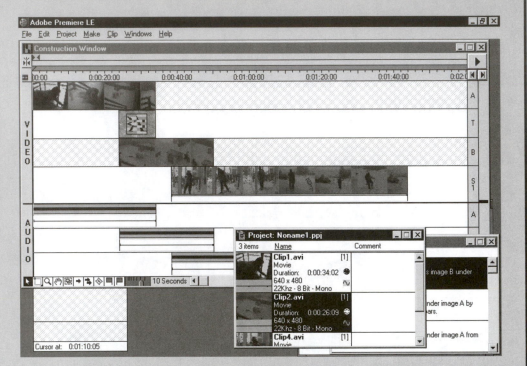

6. Start the program and test your card according to the instructions
   that came with it.

If your capture card doesn't seem to work, check for these possible
problems:

● Some cards require that you start a program that initializes the
capture card before it'll work with capture and display software.
Check to see if it's running.

● Make sure the video card is securely seated and not sticking up at
either end of the slot.

● Some video devices need to be in a "bus master" slot. Most PCI slots
are bus masters, but the one you used might not be. Try putting
the video card in a different slot, particularly one at the end of
the PCI chain.

companies that make AV drives include Western Digital Quantum, and Seagate. By and large, these drives are SCSI, so you may need to refer to Chapter 8 for details on SCSI drives.

Whatever you choose, you should be sure to only put video on the drive—don't mix it up with applications, word processing files, or other data—and defragment the drive before you work with it.

 I just got a capture card but I don't know how severely to compress my video. Are there any guidelines?

One of the advantages of Motion-JPG is that you can adjust the compression for better video quality or more efficient hard disk storage. Table 10-2 is a guide to how much to compress the video you capture.

What kinds of things can I do with the video once it's stored in my PC?

The digitizing process creates a computer file that now represents that video in digital data—ones and zeros. That makes it possible to load the video in a video editing application. Once there, you can edit the video, add titles, clean up frames, morph, animation and do whatever your skill and talent will allow you.

How do I get my edited video from the PC to my TV or VCR?

Your video digitizing card will have connectors that allow you to connect the card to a TV or VCR. This is usually accomplished

Compression Ratio	File Size for One Minute of Video	Quality
4:1	300MB	Broadcast
8:1	150MB	Professional
16:1	75MB	Consumer
25:1	48MB	Multimedia

Table 10-2   Capturing Video

using S-Video cables (which offer higher quality) or an RCA-style video cable (which offers compatibility with a wider variety of TVs and VCRs). Once these cables are hooked up, you simply play back the video on your PC, and the video is mirrored on the TV or VCR by the digitizing card. If you've hit Record on the VCR, you now have a video!

 ## What are the advantages of a DV camera?

They simplify the process of creating electronic video. A *digital video* (DV) camera is designed from the ground up to create computer files—it stores the images it sees as ones and zeros. This means that you don't actually have to digitize the video as if comes from the camera to your PC—because it's already in digital format, all you do is copy the file from the camera.

To do this you usually use a *FireWire connector*. FireWire is likely built into the camera if it's a DV camcorder. In that case, you just plug the camera into a FireWire port on your PC and copy the video to your PC as if the camera were a hard drive.

To output video, you just reverse the process—copy the edited video from your PC to the camera or a digital video deck. From there, you can play the video on TV or transfer it to videotape, if that's your goal.

What's FireWire?

FireWire is Apple Computer's trademark for a technology standard called IEEE 1394. It's essentially a new type of "serial SCSI," which allows for a USB-like connection that happens to be very fast—about 400 Mbps in its first iteration. That makes it popular for DV cameras, because video takes up a lot of storage space and a high-speed interface is useful for getting video from the camera to a computer.

In order to use FireWire, you'll need a special FireWire port (common, especially, on Sony-brand PCs) or a FireWire adapter card. The cards are installed like any other PCI adapter card, and include a FireWire port on the back of the card for connecting to your camera.

FireWire is hot-pluggable, meaning you can plug and unplug FireWire devices at any time, even while the PC is turned on. FireWire devices can also be "daisy-chained" together. If you have more than one FireWire device, one can plug into the PC, another can plug into the first device, and so on. Theoretically, FireWire supports up to 127 devices in this manner.

Ultimately, though, it's just another way (more modern, perhaps) to connect device to a PC. Like USB or parallel ports, FireWire just lets you move data from external devices to your PC. In the case of FireWire, it does it very quickly.

Tip: *If you happen to add FireWire to your PC, or if you already have it, you can buy very small, fast hard drives and other removable storage devices that connect to the FireWire port. FireWire is a self-powered bus, so devices don't need external power supplies to work with it.*

I want to set up video teleconferencing at my jobsite. What kind of camera do I need?

You certainly don't need a video capture card designed for broadcast video, but if you already have one, it'll work. In fact, you can connect a camcorder to the video card and teleconference with that. A cheaper solution, however, is one of the many "tethered cameras" now for sale for the PC (such as the Connectix QuickCam). These cameras typically connect to the always-in-demand parallel port and capture low-resolution images that are fine for the current state of Internet video broadcasting.

Where can I find video-teleconferencing software?

Much of it is free, or nearly so. You can get Microsoft's NetMeeting, which ships with Internet Explorer 5:

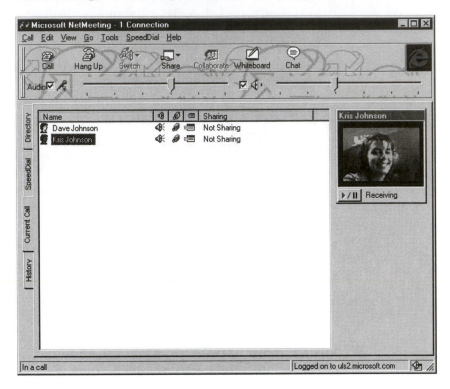

Or look into CU-SeeME from White Pine Software. Many tethered cameras come with conferencing software as well.

Chapter 11

Modems and Internet Access

Answer Topics!

Modems and Internet Access @ a Glance

Modem troubles can make you feel shipwrecked within sight of civilization. They're not always easy to troubleshoot, thanks to COM ports and conflicts with other hardware. Use this chapter as a guide to installing modems and solving conflict troubles with your modem.

Windows is both helpful and unbelievably frustrating when it comes to modems and Internet connectivity. Not only are dial-up connections difficult for beginners to figure out, but the modem software itself is found in two different parts of the operating system. This chapter helps you track down problems and get everything working properly.

Thanks to the Internet, no computer is an island anymore. But before you can get connected, you need to pick an ISP, choose a Web browser, and learn how to get a presence on this vast information network.

MODEMS

 What is a modem?

A *modem* is a device designed to modulate digital data—ones and zeros—into an analog signal that can be transmitted over the phone line (see Figure 11-1). It also demodulates analog data into digital information using universal standards that allow almost all modems to communicate with one another, even if they're rated for different maximum speeds. The name *modem* comes from the *mo*dulate/*dem*odulate functions modems perform. New kinds of modems—such as ISDN and cable modems—aren't actually modems at all, because the data is always digital. We still refer to them as modems, however, because we're recognizing the role they play (little boxes that help us get on the Internet or an online service) more than the engineering function they perform.

 What are the differences between 28.8, 33.6, and 56 Kbps modems?

The number in a modem's name refers to the maximum number of kilobits per second (Kbps) that it can transmit through a telephone line. In other words, it's a measure of the modem's speed. The commonly accepted standard in computer telephony today is 33.6 Kbps, although it's getting difficult to find plain old 33.6-Kbps modems on store shelves these days. Instead, 33.6 has been supplanted by 56 Kbps modems.

Probably the end of the line for modem technology is the 56 Kbps modem. These modems take advantage of the fact that many switching stations have digital phone lines at the sending end. That means for downstream transmissions— getting data into your PC—you can avoid the 33.6 Kbps

Figure 11-1 The flow of data across a phone line between modems

limitation and receive data at a somewhat higher 56 Kbps. Sending data from your PC to the Internet, however, is still limited to 33.6 Kbps, even with a 56-Kbps modem.

It gets even more confusing, however. Though 56 Kbps is the theoretical limit of these new modems, they're restricted by FCC regulations to 53 Kbps, so that's the most you'll ever get from these devices. And finally, while the industry has settled on a 56 Kbps standard, called v.90, there were originally two competing standards: x2 (from US Robotics) and KFlex (from Rockwell International). Newer 56-Kbps modems adhere to the v.90 standard, but some older models may need a special upgrade—a Flash ROM or firmware upgrade, before they fully recognize the new v.90 protocols.

Will I notice a difference between a 33.6 and a 56 Kbps modem?

Probably not. Because the numbers measure the *width* of the connection (otherwise referred to as *bandwidth*), there isn't actually a *speed* difference between the two. If a 2-kilobyte file were transferred between 33.6-Kbps modems and 56-Kbps modems, the speed would be the same, because such a small file doesn't fill the bandwidth of either.

Where the apparent speed difference comes is when you're downloading larger files. On the World Wide Web, most Web site designers try to keep graphics and Web pages reasonably small, so there's only the slightest advantage to a 56-Kbps modem. When you're trying to download a much larger file—a large image file, a shareware utility or a game, for example—then you may see the difference, because a 56-Kbps modem can allow more data through the pipe at once.

For that reason (along with the fact that 56-Kbps modems are rather cheap these days) we recommend purchasing a 56-Kbps modem if you need a new modem for some reason. But should you upgrade from a perfectly fine 33.6? You can, but don't expect breathtaking results—you'll spend a few dollars and see very little performance improvement in return. If it's an option, you get much better bandwidth from cable modems, ADSL, and ISDN connections. So if one of those is an option, you should consider it carefully.

 ## What's the difference between "baud" and "kilobits per second"?

In the old days, we measured modems with the term *baud*. Baud is defined as the number of transmittable events per second, which used to be roughly analogous to kilobits per second. That's no longer true—using data compression, a 2400-baud modem can actually transmit 9600 Kbps or more, so we have largely stopped describing modems in that way. Now, modems are measured strictly in kilobits per second, and if you see the term "baud" on the packaging, the modem is probably many years old (or the marketing folks have made a mistake in using the term).

Why don't I ever connect at my modem's full speed?

There are a few possible reasons:

- Your Internet Service Provider (ISP) doesn't support your modem's top speed. Your ISP might only have a 33.6-Kbps modem, for instance, limiting the usefulness of your 56 Kbps. Or you might have an older technology 56-Kbps modem (using X2 or Kflex) and your ISP only supports the v.90 protocol.

- Your phone line might be noisy. There's not a lot you can do about this; you can complain to your phone company and they might be able to fix the problem, but don't expect much in the way of results. In fact, it's fairly rare that you'll connect at the highest speed for which your modem is rated.

- You might have the wrong modem selected in your Modem settings in the Control Panel. Make sure you match the Control Panel to your modem; selecting a generic modem will cost you in performance.

- If you have an external modem, you might have an old Universal Asynchronous Receiver-Transmitter (UART) chip associated with your serial port. This chip contains the circuits required by modems being used for serial communication. Unfortunately, older UARTs (even those

found in reasonably new PCs, incidentally) can't handle modem speeds above 14.4 Kbps. They limit the connection speed between the modem and the computer, instead of between the two modems. You'll have to upgrade to a 16550 UART-based serial port at a PC repair store.

 If you have a 56-Kbps modem (using Flex, X2, or v.90), the FCC limits those modems to about 53 Kbps. And high-speed 56-Kbps connections only work if there is no more than one analog-to-digital conversion in the lines running between you and your ISP. In general, that means you'll have better luck in big cities or if you live very close to your ISP's main telephone office. One solution is to ask your ISP where in town (physically) their telephone answering centers are, then call the one closest to you. Even if all this works for you, don't be too surprised to get 42-Kbps or 44-Kbps connections—line noise simply slows modems down.

Note: *Many people will never connect at 50 Kbps. The problem is your phone line, which may be too old, too noisy, or too far away from the phone company's switches to support the theoretical speed limit of these modems.*

What is ISDN?

ISDN stands for Integrated Services Digital Network. ISDN has been around since the 1970s, but the phone company had no one to sell it to until the Internet became popular in the last few years. It provides a robust digital connection between you and the phone company, enabling high-bandwidth Internet connections. The typical home-service ISDN speed is 128 Kbps (about four times faster than a 33.6-Kbps analog modem) in both directions, but you can get higher and lower connection speeds as well.

ISDN actually requires that the lines to your house (the ones that come from out under the street) and the wiring in your home be changed to digital lines. If you use ISDN for your phones, they must be powered, because the digital line

won't keep the phones running like a typical analog line does. It's an expensive proposition, but sometimes useful.

We don't generally recommend ISDN because we consider it an interim technology. It is expensive and only generates 128 Kbps in most configurations; for the same cost or less (sometimes a lot less) you can get much higher bandwidth from solutions like cable modems or local wireless transmission. And a new crop of telephone technologies called DSL (along with the proliferation of cable modems) is starting to blow ISDN away.

How can I get IDSN?

Call your phone company. Unfortunately, not everyone can get it. You need to be located within 18,000 feet of a telephone switching station because ISDN lines have a length limitation. A telephone technician can visit your home or office and tell you if you qualify for ISDN.

You can also visit **http://www.microsoft.com/ windows/getisdn**. This excellent Web site has a wealth of information about ISDN and includes links to regional phone services for ordering ISDN.

What is DSL?

DSL stands for *Digital Subscriber Line,* and it is akin to ISDN in that it's a high speed Internet access solution provided by your phone company. Unlike ISDN, however, there are literally dozens of versions of DSL out there, and they go by names like Synchronous Digital Subscriber Line (SDSL) and Asynchronous Digital Subscriber Line (ADSL). In general, people refer to DSL as simply DSL, or perhaps xDSL.

DSL offers two main advantages—it uses the existing phone lines in your house for high-speed access, and it allows voice calls to occur at the same time that data transmissions are going on. That means you don't need a special phone line for Internet connections (as you often want with a modem) and the phone company doesn't necessarily have to tear up your street or phone poles to offer you the service (as they

might with ISDN). For these two reasons phone companies are making the switch to DSL quickly and encouraging subscribers away from modems and ISDN.

DSL bandwidth varies, depending on implementation, but it's generally at least 256 Kbps and often as fast as 1 Mbps. The technology is impressive, although you should comparison shop carefully between DSL and cable modem Internet access—there's some heavy competition out there and the price may be better on one or the other in your city.

How can I get DSL?

Like ISDN, you get DSL by calling your phone company. There are 18,000-foot restrictions from a telephone switching station, so you may not have availability in your neighborhood. Many phone companies have Web pages dedicated to DSL service; visit your local Baby Bell's (or other phone company's) Web site. You can also find DSL ISPs that do all the hassling of the phone company for you—shop the business section of your local newspaper or look for a regional computer magazine where such an ISP might advertise.

What is a "cable modem"?

Cable modems are a new alternative to traditional modem technology. Instead of using a modem to connect to the Internet, you connect with the same coaxial cable that delivers television programming to your home. These cables have incredibly high bandwidth—on the order of 27 million bits per second. But you don't get all that speed yourself—it's shared with a lot of other users also connected to the Internet. On average, cable modem users can expect to get anywhere from 500 Kbps to 1.5 million bits per second. That's as much as 40 times faster than the fastest analog modem, and yet it'll only cost around $25 to 45 a month plus a setup fee that includes the modem itself—probably about $250.

If you want a cable modem, call your local cable company and ask if they offer the service. It's likely that your cable company is beginning to offer it already, especially if you live in a metropolitan area.

What is DirecPC?

DirecPC is the first of what will surely be several satellite-based Internet provider solutions. Using the DirecTV satellite dish, you can receive Internet data at 400 Kbps, about ten times faster than analog modem access. The service is increasingly affordable but requires a satellite dish and a compatible modem for your PC. And at the time of this writing, it is a bit pricey, especially considering the fact that it's among the most limited of the high-bandwidth solutions. If you're interested in getting your Internet via satellite, visit **http://www.direcpc.com**, or call DirecPC at 1-800-DIRECPC.

If I get ISDN, satellite, or a cable modem, do I still need a regular modem?

You'll need your trusty old modem for satellite or some types of cable modem access, because both of those schemes only work in one direction. While the cable or satellite is great for getting a lot of information to you very quickly, you'll still need a plain analog modem to send e-mail, requests for Web pages, and other upstream data. On the other hand, you generally send very little information to the Internet, but get a lot back; so the fact that you're still using a slow analog modem some of the time is hardly noticeable.

It's all pretty transparent to you. As the user, you connect your analog modem the same way you always did and information comes back via another data pipe, but you don't really notice. All you do notice is that it's a lot faster.

You'll also need a modem to dial directly into network servers, to contact America Online through a dial-up number (although you can usually access it through to Internet) and to send and receive faxes, if you do that sort of thing.

What kind of modem should I buy?

If you're in the market for a new modem, you should get a 56-Kbps modem that supports the v.90 standard. The

56-Kbps modems are very inexpensive and pretty much all that's left on the market; a 33.6-Kbps modem is simply too old to worry about.

Here are some other things to consider:

● Your modem is more likely to install easily if you choose a major, nationally known brand (such as US Robotics or Supra).

● The ROM should be flash-upgradable so you can accept feature and speed improvements as they're made available.

● If you're interested in integrating the modem into your home office, you might want a modem capable of accepting voice and fax, and dealing with Caller ID signals so you can see onscreen who you is calling you (great if you use the modem as a fax or answering machine).

 ### Should I get an internal or an external modem?

We recommend that you install an internal modem because it avoids any problems with older UART chips and also saves you a serial port that you can use for other things. But if you are out of internal expansion slots, the external model might be the best choice. Keep in mind that internal modems are typically a bit cheaper than external models because you don't have to pay for the modem case and other parts. External modems also feature indicator lights built into the case, which can make them easier to troubleshoot.

How can I tell if my new modem installed properly?

You can test your installation easily. Choose Start | Settings | Control Panel and choose Modems. Click the Diagnostic tab and select your modem from the list of COM port peripherals. Click More Info. If the modem is properly installed and recognized by Windows, the dialog box will report information on the modem:

Modems Properties | ? | X

General | Diagnostics

Windows detected the following ports, and has
already installed the following devices:

Port	Installed
COM1	Sportster 28800-33600 External
COM2	No Modem Installed.

Driver | More Info... | Help

OK | Cancel

(If all didn't go as planned, you'll see an error message.)

Alternatively, you can simply try to dial out using a communication program (although that may sometimes just indicate a poorly configured communication program).

My new modem doesn't seem to work. What's wrong?

The problem could be simple or complicated. Troubleshoot your modem by checking these possibilities:

- Start by making sure there really is a dial tone at the wall jack you're using. Verify this by plugging an extension phone into the jack.

- You might have plugged the phone line into the wrong port on the modem. Try swapping them and see if that fixes the problem.

- If it's an external modem, make sure it's plugged in and turned on. (We're sorry about this one, but you'd be surprised how many people forget to do that and think the modem is broken.)

- Check for hardware conflicts. Right-click My Computer and choose Properties. Scan the System Properties for any device—like the modem or another serial device—that has a yellow warning icon next to it. If there's a conflict, move the modem to another COM port.

- Check the Diagnostic tab in the Modem Control Panel. (Open Modems from the Control Panel and click the Diagnostic tab.) Then select your modem and click the More Info button:

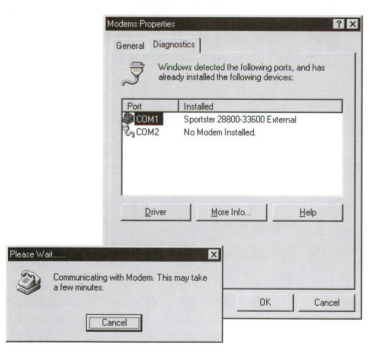

If you're not already online and the modem is working, it should report information about the modem.

- Reinstall the modem driver software and check the vendor's Web site for updated drivers.

 ## What IRQs can I use with a modem?

Internal modems can use IRQ 3, 4, 5, 7, and 9. Be sure that the IRQ you choose isn't already in use by another device.

 ## What do I do if my plug-and-play modem doesn't work?

Often, plug-and-play modems try to use the same IRQ as the sound card. You can remove the modem then change the sound card's IRQ setting in the Windows 95/98 System Properties. (Right-click My Computer and choose Properties, then choose the Device Manager tab.) Then reinstall the modem—it should be able to take the IRQ it was trying to use, and all should be well.

 ## What do I do if I can't manually change the IRQ of a device that is using the modem's IRQ?

Remove both the modem and the offending device. Enter the System Properties by right-clicking My Computer and choosing Properties. Double-click the Computer entry and choose the Reserve Resources tab. Add the IRQ your modem needs, and replace the other expansion card. It should now use an IRQ other than the reserved value. Remove the reserved IRQ from the System Properties and reinstall the modem—it should grab the proper IRQ, and everything will work properly.

 ## What if my modem doesn't come with—or I lost—the driver disk?

In most cases, your new modem will come with a disk that has Windows 95/98 drivers you can load during the plug-and-play installation. In some cases, you won't have that luxury, however. Your first alternative is to choose the modem from the list of modems in the Found New Hardware dialog box. Look for an exact match with the name of your modem. If you can't find the same modem as the one you purchased, try a similar modem from the same manufacturer.

Failing that, choose a compatible chip set. Many modems use the Rockwell chip set, for instance, so try that instead. If all else fails, use the Generic modem that most closely resembles your modem speed and capability. After you have the modem up and running, check the vendor's Web site for a driver you can download and install.

My modem seems to have hung (or crashed or gotten stuck or something). How can I reset it?

Need to get your dial tone back? An external modem is easy to reset—simply cycle the power button. Internal modems don't have power buttons, however, and can be more finicky. Try these methods to reset your modem:

- Remove the phone cord from the wall for about 30 seconds, then replace it.

- Try starting another communication program. AOL software is particularly good at resetting a hung modem.

- If all else fails, shut down and restart the entire PC.

How do I know which COM port my modem is using?

If you have an external modem, check which serial port it is plugged into on the back of the PC. Typically, the small serial port is COM1 and the larger serial port is COM2. If you only have one serial port, it's almost certainly COM1.

You can also check Windows directly. Choose Start | Settings | Control Panel and choose Modems. Click your modem on the list in the General tab and choose Properties—it will report the COM port that's in use. Alternatively, you can also click the Diagnostic tab for a list of devices using COM ports.

What do the lights on my external modem mean?

If you have an external modem, you've no doubt been mesmerized by all the lights that blink on and off while you work online. Here's a guide to what they mean. (Be aware that your modem may not have all these indicators, and that some might be combined):

Indicator Light	What Your Modem Is Doing
RI	Receiving ring signal
HS	Operating at its highest rated speed
M	Auto-answer mode is on
CD	Carrier detect signal (detected another computer or fax device)
OH	Phone is off the hook
RD	Receiving data from the remote modem
TD	Transmitting data to the remote modem
MR	Modem ready

 ## What do the two lights on the modem in the Windows System Tray mean?

While an external modem is like a sports car with a million dials and indicators, an internal modem has just a few idiot lights—displayed in Windows—that tell you the equivalent of "out of gas" and "engine overheating." You can monitor your modem's status by observing the two lights in the System Tray. The button on the left is the equivalent of TD (transmitting data) and the light on the right means RD (receiving data).

Transmitting data

Receiving data

If you try to retrieve a Web page, for example, you'll notice that the HTTP request goes out when the left light flashes; the data comes in when the right light flashes.

❓ My modem takes a really long time to connect to my Internet service provider (ISP). Is that normal?

Probably not. If you connect successfully each time, but it takes more than a few seconds to connect, then you may be trying to negotiate with extra protocols every time. Try this:

1. Choose My Computer and open the Dial-Up Networking folder.

2. Right-click your ISP's dial-up connection and choose Properties.

3. Click the Server Types tab:

```
┌─────────────────────────────────────────────────────┐
│ WantWeb analog                                ? X │
├─────────────────────────────────────────────────────┤
│  General   Server Types   Scripting   Multilink       │
│                                                       │
│   Type of Dial-Up Server:                             │
│  ┌─────────────────────────────────────────────┬──┐ │
│  │ PPP: Internet, Windows NT Server, Windows 98 │ ▼│ │
│  └─────────────────────────────────────────────┴──┘ │
│   ┌─ Advanced options: ──────────────────────────┐  │
│   │  ☑ Log on to network                         │  │
│   │  ☑ Enable software compression               │  │
│   │  ☐ Require encrypted password                │  │
│   │  ☐ Require data encryption                   │  │
│   │  ☐ Record a log file for this connection     │  │
│   └──────────────────────────────────────────────┘  │
│   ┌─ Allowed network protocols: ─────────────────┐  │
│   │  ☐ NetBEUI                                   │  │
│   │  ☐ IPX/SPX Compatible                        │  │
│   │  ☑ TCP/IP          ┌─────────────────────┐   │  │
│   │                    │  TCP/IP Settings...  │   │  │
│   │                    └─────────────────────┘   │  │
│   └──────────────────────────────────────────────┘  │
│                                                       │
│                       ┌──────┐    ┌────────┐         │
│                       │  OK  │    │ Cancel │         │
│                       └──────┘    └────────┘         │
└─────────────────────────────────────────────────────┘
```

4. Make sure that only TCP/IP is selected; deselect NetBEUI and IPX/SPX.

5. Click OK to close.

> ! *Warning:* It's best to avoid this procedure if you have America Online and you use it as your Internet Service Provider, since it uses it's own proprietary scheme for allowing your PC Internet access through the AOL software.

 ## Why does my modem disconnect when I get a call-waiting call?

Because a modem can't maintain a good connection unless it has a solid lock on the phone line. If you pick up an extension or receive another call, your modem will reset. You should disable call waiting before connecting to the Internet. (Ask your phone company for the correct code.) If your code is *70, for example, you'll want to locate the dialing entry box for your particular program and enter the code and a comma before the service provider's phone number (for example, enter ***70,555-1212**, where 555-1212 is the phone number you're trying to dial). The comma causes the modem to pause after dialing the code so the line can react with a stuttered dial tone. Then the number is dialed, as usual. You can use this trick for any codes you need to dial with your modem, including a "9" to get an outside line or a special long-distance code.

 ## Can my modem share a COM port with a mouse?

We're afraid not. Both of those devices need exclusive use of the COM port. We've seen at least one COM-starved person try to share the COM port by not moving the mouse when the modem is in use. That just might work, but the instant you jiggle the mouse when the modem is connected, your PC will probably lock up and you'll lose all your work.

What is a BBS?

A BBS—short for *Bulletin Board System*—is in many ways the forerunner of the Internet for most people. A BBS is a service that you can connect to with your modem and post messages, chat with friends, play games, and download files. Until the advent of the Internet, BBSs were the most common reason to have and use a modem. Many BBS

systems are alive and well and are an alternative to the Internet—particularly if you want to log onto a local service that is populated by people in your community or who share a common interest, such as science fiction, Windows, or board games. You'll need a terminal emulation program to use a BBS.

Can I install two modems in one PC?

Yes, you sure can. You'll need to have enough COM ports available on your PC to support both modems simultaneously, of course, and enough ISA slots and/or serial ports. You can use two modems—with two phone lines—to use your PC as a fax/answering machine, or to surf the Internet and receive voice calls at the same time. Symantec's WinFax Pro directly supports the use of two modems, for example.

You can also combine two 56-Kbps modems and effectively get 100 Kbps transfer speed. To do this, you'll need to download Dial Up Networking 1.3 from **http://www.microsoft.com**. This update to Windows allows you to group and combine up to four modems and link them for faster Internet access.

Is my modem safe in a lightning storm?

Only if you unplug it. In fact, lightning can travel through the telephone line and zap not just your modem, but your entire PC as well. That's why we recommend that you use an uninterruptible power supply (UPS) or surge suppressor that includes protected jacks for your phone line. If you route your modem's phone line through a surge suppressor, you're pretty safe. Otherwise, unplug your modem's phone cord from the wall during severe electrical storms.

CONNECTING WITH WINDOWS

What's different about a Windows modem?

Some modems are advertised as *Windows modems*. Beware of this designation if you want to use the modem in DOS; Windows modems are missing essential components that are replicated by Windows. In this way, the modem is less expensive, but is only useful in Windows. The vast majority of users won't need to use a modem in DOS, however, so it probably isn't a big issue.

Can I connect to a BBS with Windows?

Yup. Windows comes with a little-known program called HyperTerminal that allows you to emulate a terminal and connect to bulletin boards. You can also use HyperTerminal (see Figure 11-2) to connect to your ISP in shell account mode. You won't be able to run a Web browser in this mode, but you can often transfer files and change your account preferences.

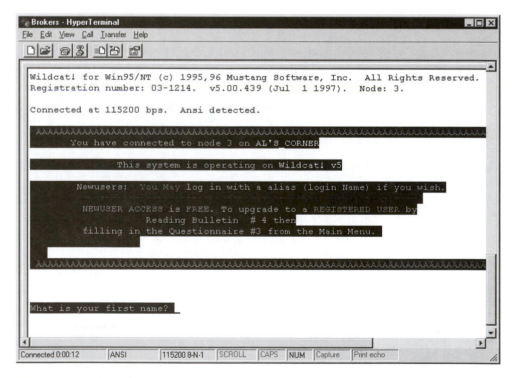

Figure 11-2 HyperTerminal is a small communication program that comes with Windows.

To use HyperTerminal, choose Start | Programs | Accessories | HyperTerminal. Start HyperTerminal and enter the name of the BBS or service you're connecting to. Then follow the Wizard and enter the phone number and country code. (If you're connecting to a BBS in the US, for instance, just find United States in the drop-down list.)

Windows won't remember my password in the dial-up connection box. How can I fix this?

This problem tends to occur fairly frequently, especially in Windows 95. You know you have a problem when you try to connect to the Internet but the Remember Password box is ghosted and you have to type in the password every time you connect. Here are a few solutions. Start with the first one, and if it doesn't solve the problem move on to the next and try again.

Note: *You must log onto Windows before the Remember Password feature will work. If you click the Cancel button when you log on to Windows, you can't save passwords. If you don't use a password and the logon dialog box therefore doesn't appear, this procedure should work properly anyway.*

- *Replace your pwl file in case it is corrupted.* Choose Start | Find | Files or Folders and search for *.pwl* (see Figure 11-3). It should be in the Windows folder and start with your username, such as djohns.pwl. Delete the file and restart Windows; Windows will create a new password file in which you can restore your passwords.

- *Make sure the PC is set to single-user mode.* Choose Start | Settings | Control Panel and choose Passwords. On the User Profiles tab, make sure you select "All users of this PC use the same preferences and desktop settings."

- *Make sure that the name of the PC is set to your logon name in Network.* Choose Start | Settings | Control Panel and choose Network. Click the Identification tab and set the computer name to your logon name.

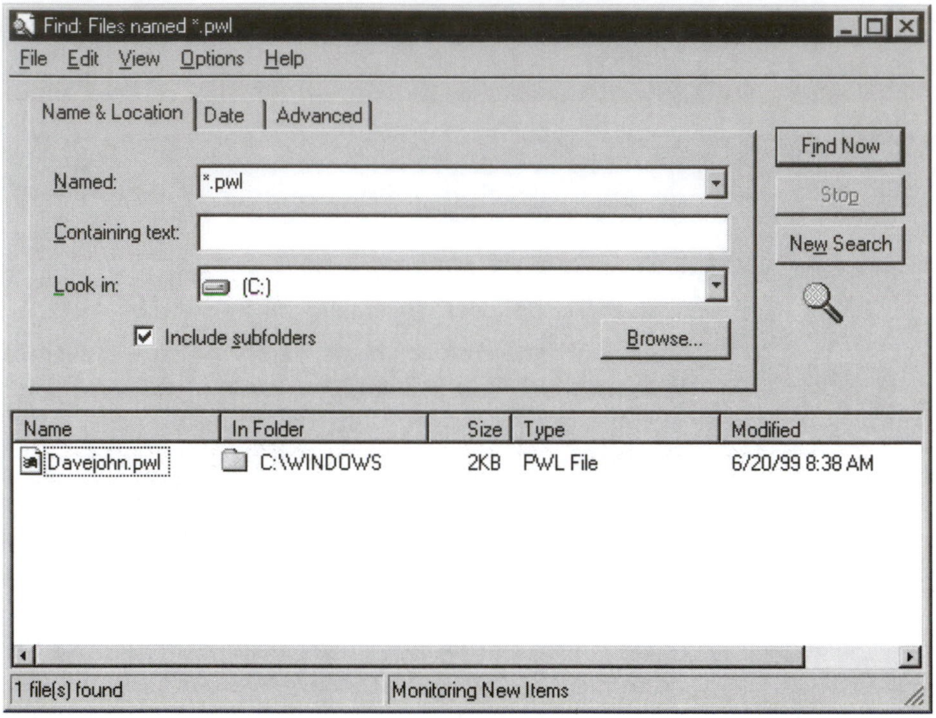

Figure 11-3 Listing .pwl files in a Find window

- *Set a password for Windows startup.* Choose Start | Settings | Control Panel and choose Passwords. On the Change Password tab, set a password for Change Windows Password.

How can I stop Internet Explorer from connecting to the Internet automatically?

If you've recently installed Internet Explorer 4 or 5 or Windows 98, you may not like the fact that it can sometimes dial into the Internet for you without your explicit permission.

You can disable Internet Explorer's ability to do that by following these steps:

1. Choose Start | Settings | Control Panel.

2. Open the Internet applet.

3. Click the Connection tab.

4. If you connect via modem, click the Settings button.

5. Make sure that the button for "Connect automatically to update subscriptions" is disabled:

Alternatively, you can prevent this unintentional connection activity by selecting "Connect to the Internet using a Local Area Network" on the Connection tab even if you use a modem.

THE INTERNET

What do I need to log onto the Internet?

It doesn't take a lot of processing power to get on the Internet and surf the Web. In its simplest form, surfing the Web is little more than downloading text documents from another computer and letting your PC assemble them into formatted pages using a rudimentary page layout language. And because it takes longer to download the documents with ordinary modems than to effectively read the documents, a slow computer is fine, as long as you're also using older Web browser applications—the newer the application, the more processing power it requires.

The real need for power comes into play when you start downloading multimedia—virtually every page you encounter uses colored backgrounds, streaming sound or video, pictures, and active components like Java and ActiveX that run programs on your desktop when you visit.

If you're interested in the Internet just for e-mail and browsing the Internet in text-only mode (disabling graphics and other advanced browser features), here's the kind of PC you need:

- A 486 PC with a 28.8-Kbps modem, Windows 3.1, 16MB of RAM, connection software provided by your ISP, and Netscape Navigator 2 or Internet Explorer 2. (In this case, we don't recommend trying to use versions 3 or higher; there's too much browser in these more recent versions for a PC of this power.)

For high-powered Web surfing, we recommend this system as a minimum:

- A Pentium 200 or better with a 56-Kbps modem, Windows 95 or 98, Internet Explorer 4 or Netscape Navigator 4, a large hard disk, and 32MB of RAM.

How do I go about choosing an Internet service provider (ISP)?

Here's a bit of trivia for you: It wasn't always possible to connect to the Internet from your home. In fact, until a few years ago, ISPs as we know them today didn't even exist. The popularity of the Internet has made ISPs as common as phone and cable TV providers.

An ISP provides you with a connection to the Internet via your phone line. If you haven't yet chosen an ISP, it pays to be selective. There are national, regional, and local Internet providers, and for the most part, they've all become fairly competitive. You can expect that many—if not most—of the ISPs serving your community will charge about $20 for anywhere between 30 hours and unlimited time each month. You can find ISPs listed in the phone book, in regional computer magazines, and on the Internet, where most maintain their own Web sites both as an advertisement and as a service to their customers.

Note: *While $19.95 a month has become a fairly common flat rate among ISPs for unlimited Internet access, some service providers are beginning to find that they can offer higher-quality service by returning to a per-hour charge. In that way, individual users don't stay connected through long periods of inactivity and those who genuinely need access stand a better chance of getting online. America Online discovered in the winter of 1996/97 the problems that can arise when 6 million subscribers have unlimited access to about 250,000 modem connections.*

One of the best reasons to choose your ISP carefully is to avoid the need to change it again several months down the line. Look at it this way: If you switch long-distance phone companies, there is no tangible effect on your phone number. If you change ISPs, on the other hand, you'll almost certainly have to change your e-mail address, which is the Internet equivalent of your phone number. It's okay to occasionally change e-mail addresses, particularly if you don't send and receive a lot of e-mail, but you don't want to change the way people contact you if you rely on e-mail for your livelihood.

 Tip: *Some ISPs are beginning to offer lifetime Internet addresses that follow you forever. Ask if your potential ISP offers this. Also, if you purchase your own domain name, your address can survive moves unscathed.*

Before you select an ISP, you should create a table of services and conditions that are important to you and call a wide variety of ISPs to compare. You might want to consider criteria like these:

Criterion	Considerations
Price	Prices vary with service, but here's a good place to start: Pay no more than $25/month, regardless of how much service you need.
Speed	Virtually all ISPs offer 33.6 Kbps lines, but what about 56 Kbps? Do they support ISDN? DSL? Make sure they can provide the access for whatever speed you want.
Local access	Is there an access number in your local calling area? And if you travel, can you connect locally from another state or country, or use an 800 number?
Ease of connection	Forget about how many phone lines or modems they claim to have. Can you actually get a connection when you need it?
Technical support	What kind of technical expertise does the staff have? How available are they?
Server space	Do they offer server space for you to publish your own Web page? Two megabytes is customary, but some ISPs offer 5 megabytes. Business pages are another animal altogether—you'll want a wide variety of services like statistics tracking, RealAudio, multiple e-mail accounts, and more.

 Tip: *Find out the ISP's connection phone numbers and experiment by calling at the time of day that you expect to use the Internet. You should get no—or virtually no—busy signals. Frequent busy signals are a sure sign of an overextended ISP.*

 ## Where do I find a list of Internet service providers (ISPs)?

You can find ISPs in the following places:

● **The phone book**   Look in your local Yellow Pages under Internet Services.

● **The Internet**   Yahoo!, for instance, has a comprehensive list of ISPs sorted in many ways, including by state. Visit **http://www.yahoo.com/Business_and_Economy/Companies/ Internet_Services**.

● **Your friends**   Find out what service others use and try it out if they recommend it.

What information do I need to configure Windows to connect to the Internet?

When you're ready to connect to the Net through a new ISP, you're going to need a few essential bits of data. When you talk to the ISP's representative on the phone, be sure to get the following information:

● **Username**   This will be some variation on your name, like "djohns" for Dave Johnson or "todds" for Todd Stauffer. You may even get to create it yourself.

● **Password**   This is some combination of numbers, letters, and other symbols that prevents others from accessing your account.

● **Access phone numbers**   There may be more than one; write them all down so you have more than one way to get on the Internet if the first line is busy.

● **Domain name server (DNS)**   The DNS is the address of the server that your computer uses to translate Web addresses into numbers (the IP, or *Internet Protocol*) that the Internet needs to locate and retrieve the address in question. The IP address is a unique set of numbers used to identify every resource on the Internet, not unlike a Social Security number for computers.

● **Mail and news server names** These are text names—like mail.usa.net and news.usa.net—that identify your mail and news servers. You may receive two mail server names; the POP mail server is for incoming mail and SMTP is for outgoing mail.

● **Logon procedure** Does the ISP support a direct dial-up via the Windows 95 dial-up connection, or will it be necessary to use a terminal window?

Tip: *If you need to use a terminal window, ask the ISP to send you a copy of the logon script for the Windows Scripting Tool. This will automate the dial-up process so you won't need to type your logon name and password every time.*

How do I configure Windows to connect to the Internet?

In order to connect to the Internet through an ISP, you'll need to create a dial-up connection profile. Microsoft, oddly enough, calls these *connectoids*. Whatever you choose to call them, when you're done, all you'll need to do is double-click one of these connection icons (stored in the Dial-Up Connection Folder in My Computer) to get on the Net. Set one up with these steps:

1. Click My Computer and open Dial-up Networking.

2. If a Make a New Connection Wizard doesn't appear, double-click the icon of the same name.

3. In the box labeled "Type a name for the computer you are dialing," name the connection anything you like.

Tip: *It's helpful to name the connection after the ISP and connection speed for easy reference, like "RMII 56."*

4. Select the appropriate modem, if you have more than one modem driver installed. If you don't have a modem configured, click Configure and let the Wizard configure one for you.

Make New Connection

Type a name for the computer you are dialing:

ISDN Connection

Select a device:

Sportster 28800-33600 External

Configure...

< Back | Next > | Cancel

5. Click Next. Enter the phone number for your ISP. Click Next and then click Finish.

You're half done: you've just created a dial-up icon in the Dial-Up Networking folder. Unfortunately, it won't do anything yet. It hasn't been fed essential information necessary to complete a connection to the Internet through your ISP.

6. Open the Dial-Up Networking folder and right-click the connection icon we just created. Select Properties. A Properties sheet appears for the connection we just made.

7. If your ISP does not require a terminal window for entering username and password (you'll need to ask the ISP to be sure), skip directly to step 9. Otherwise, click the button marked Configure.

8. Click the Option tab. Enable Bring Up Terminal Window After Dialing and click OK.

9. Click the Server Types button. Ensure the sheet is set up as follows:

- Type of Dial-Up Server: PPP
- Advanced options: "Log on to network" and "Enable software compression" are checked.

● Allowed network protocols: Only TCP/IP should be
checked:

Note: *If you leave NetBEUI and IPX/SPX Compatible*
checked, you will still connect successfully, though it may take
significantly longer.

10. Click the TCP/IP Settings box. Ensure this sheet is set
up as follows:

● Unless your ISP has assigned you a permanent IP
address, ensure that "Server assigned IP address" is
checked.

● Check "Specify name server addresses" and enter the
DNS given by the ISP in the Primary DNS box.
Enter a secondary DNS if applicable.

● Check "Use IP header compression" and "Use default
gateway on remote network":

11. Click OK on each of the three dialog boxes to exit.

That's pretty much it. You now have a dial-up connection ready to log on to the Internet. You can test your new connection by trying to connect. Do this:

1. Open My Computer and click Dial-Up Networking.

2. Find your connection icon and click it. The Connect To dialog box appears.

3. Enter your username and password, and click the button marked Connect.

4. If you had to configure your Dial-Up Networking settings to use the terminal window, it will appear automatically. Enter your username, password, and any other characters needed to proceed. You will have to click Continue or press F7 to complete the connection.

> ╋ *Tip:* *If your ISP requires you to use the terminal window to input your username and password manually, download the Scripting and SLIP Support for Dial-Up Networking Tool (if it's not already installed—you should already have it with Windows 98, for instance) from **http://www.microsoft.com/ windows95/downloads/**. This program will automate the logon process for you via a script the ISP can provide.*

❓ What Web browser should I use?

Now here's a loaded question if we've ever seen one. There's no safe way to answer it. Internet Explorer and Netscape Navigator are the market leaders—you should definitely use one or the other. We also recommend that you step up to the latest version of your browser to take advantage of the new Web features and ease-of-use tools you'll find there. After all, we're still in the horse-and-buggy days of the Internet, and features are added to Web browsers in much the same way that word processors evolved seven years ago, when PCs were still in their infancy.

If you want a browser that integrates seamlessly into the operating system so that you can display Web pages on the desktop or view the hard disk in a browser window, Internet Explorer is for you. (If you have Windows 98, you've already got IE's capabilities built in.) If you don't like that kind of encroachment, stick with Netscape.

You can download a trial version of Navigator from **http://www.netscape.com**. Internet Explorer is available from **http://www.microsoft.com/ie**.

❓ How do I create my own Web pages?

You have two choices: Learn to write HTML, or get a Web page editor that automates much of the process. HTML is a simple script language that, for the most part, is little more than a set of style "tags" that surround text for formatting purposes. For example, you would make a word bold in a sentence in this way:

```
This is an example of <b>bold</b> text.
```

You can learn the essentials of HTML in an afternoon. But like playing the guitar, learning the basics of HTML is easy. Learning to write HTML well is the hard part.

The alternative is to use one of the many programs that look and behave like page layout programs. You can enter text, drag and drop graphics, then edit and format the document's appearance with simple toolbar and menu controls. Many HTML purists don't like this method because HTML changes so quickly that a Web page made in such a program can't take advantage of the newest and most interesting innovations in Web design. Nonetheless, we recommend this method for casual Web designers who don't plan to make a living with Web design.

There are many good HTML editors on the market. Some are free and some are retail products like HotDog Pro. Here's a rundown of the editors we recommend:

Editor	Where to Find It
FrontPage 2000	http://www.microsoft.com/frontpage
HotDog Pro	http://www.sausage.com
HoTMetaL Pro 5.0	http://www.softquad.com
Netscape Communicator Suite	http://www.netscape.com

How can I get my finished Web pages onto the Internet?

The traditional method for moving finished Web pages onto the Internet is via a process known as FTP (File Transfer Protocol). You'll need to install an FTP client on your PC—one is often available from your ISP's Web site. Using FTP, you transfer the finished HTML pages to your server space, usually using an interface not unlike File Manager.

There's a newer method that avoids FTP altogether, however. If you use a Web page editor like Microsoft FrontPad or FrontPage, you can use a built-in tool that automatically uploads the pages to a destination Web server from within the program. That's a good reason to use one of these programs, because it also keeps track of which pages

change when you edit your site, and only uploads changed pages instead of the whole site every time.

Would I be better off using WebTV for my Internet browsing?

We don't think so. WebTV is a set-top box, sold by vendors like Sony, that connects to your TV and provides just enough computer hardware to let you surf the Web. WebTV is inexpensive (under $200) and frees your PC for other things. It has no internal data storage and relies on your low-resolution television for display. This is a product that is designed for people without a computer, and we don't recommend it if you already have a PC, unless you've got family members tying the PC up doing nothing but Web surfing when you've got more important things to accomplish. It's also a decent alternative for boardrooms and training rooms that need access to the Web, but don't need the full capabilities of a PC.

How can I tell how fast my Internet connection really is?

You can click your dial-up connection icon and get a dialog box that reports modem speed, but it isn't accurate. If you want to know how fast you're really connected, you can try one of these two programs:

- **Modem Wizard 4.0** Kiss software (http://www.kissco.com)

- **Net.Medic** VitalSigns Software (http://www.vitalsigns.com)

Can I find out what my IP address is, so I can play games that need an IP connection?

Unless you have a full-time connection to the Internet, such as through an ISDN connection, your ISP will assign a dynamic IP address each time you log on to the Internet, and they don't tell you what it actually is. That way, they can support more users than they actually have IP addresses for.

Some games or other Internet applications want to know your IP address, however. Windows comes with a program that tells you your IP address. Just choose Start | Run and type **winipcfg** in the dialog box. Press ENTER. A dialog box appears that tells you your current IP address.

IP Configuration	
Host Information	
Host Name	djohnson4.cos.wantweb.net
DNS Servers	207.141.62.62
Node Type	Broadcast
NetBIOS Scope Id	
IP Routing Enabled	☐ WINS Proxy Enabled ☐
NetBIOS Resolution Uses DNS	✓
Ethernet Adapter Information	PPP Adapter.
Adapter Address	44-45-53-54-00-00
IP Address	0.0.0.0
Subnet Mask	0.0.0.0
Default Gateway	
DHCP Server	255.255.255.255
Primary WINS Server	
Secondary WINS Server	
Lease Obtained	
Lease Expires	

OK   Release   Renew   Release All   Renew All

 Can you recommend a good book on using the Internet?

Sure. If you want to learn about the Internet, using Internet Explorer 4, and creating Web pages with HTML all under one cover, check out *Internet Explorer 4: Browsing and Beyond* (Osborne) by Dave Johnson. One of the best comprehensive books on using HTML is *HTML Web Publishing 6-in-1* (Que) by none other than Todd Stauffer. And we're not recommending these books just because we wrote them; we read them, too. Promise.

Chapter 12

Printing

Answer Topics!

Printing @ a Glance

It's a buyer's market. Inkjet and laser printers are so cheap you can afford to buy one of each. (Well, almost.) This chapter tells you what you need to know to make a good and informed purchase decision.

Getting to know your printer is important. Not all kinds of paper are healthy for your particular printer, for example. Need to connect more than one printer to your PC? All the answers you need are right here.

An amazing number of things can go wrong with your printer. Sometimes they just don't print at all; sometimes they print bizarre characters or blotches all over the paper. There are a lot of things that can break—the printer itself, the cable, ports, and key elements of Windows and its many drivers. Look here for troubleshooting information to help you resolve problems that might be keeping you from printing.

MAKING AN INFORMED PRINTER PURCHASE

 What should I buy—a laser printer or an inkjet?

That depends, of course. What else did you expect us to say? Nonetheless, we think most people are probably best off with a laser printer unless they plan to do a significant amount of color printing. Why is that? Here are some reasons:

- Even inexpensive laser printers are fast and generate professional-looking, high-resolution documents. Inkjet printers, on the other hand, are typically slow, and the dots in the output can bleed on many kinds of paper, diminishing the rated resolution.

- Laser printer consumables last a long time. If you get 4,000 sheets out of a typical laser toner cartridge, then you may be able to go a year without changing the toner. Inkjet cartridges are only good for a few hundred pages, so you'll change ink frequently, even if you're an occasional user.

● Laser printers are cheaper if you print a lot. That's right, in the long term a laser printer pays for itself when you consider the high cost of ink and special paper for inkjets. If a 2,000-sheet toner cartridge costs $80 and a 400-sheet inkjet cartridge costs $20, then the toner pages cost you $.04 per page and the inkjet pages cost $.05 a page. Over the life of a single laser cartridge, you'd save $20; over 10,000 pages, you'd save $100.

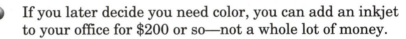

Tip: *Printer manufacturers often include a free return mailer so that you can box up the old toner cartridge and send it back to the factory. They'll recycle it instead of filling a landfill with nondegradable toxins. Take advantage of the mailer; it's free.*

● If you later decide you need color, you can add an inkjet to your office for $200 or so—not a whole lot of money.

While we think the case is strong for getting a laser printer, you might really want an inkjet because you expect to use the computer primarily for family projects. That's fine—the reverse of our theory is also true. If you later want to add a laser printer, you can do that too. There's nothing wrong with getting an inkjet.

Should I get a multifunction device?

Ever heard the phrase "jack of all trades, master of none?" That's a little of what you'll get with a multifunction device, most of which are capable of printing, scanning, faxing, and copying documents. Often you'll find that, for the device to be affordable, it'll have slightly lower print quality, scan quality, and so on, than if you bought all those components separately.

Still, they tend to take up less space and most of them these days are good enough for small business or moonlighting. We won't completely discourage you, especially if you feel like you'll be using the device for its express purposes—that is, you won't be using the printer for collating

How a Laser Printer Works

A laser printer is an interesting device. It works much like a photocopier does, but curiously enough, it actually needs to be more reliable than a photocopier, which is visited frequently by a technician on a service contract.

A laser printer has at its heart a photoconductive drum. A charging roller imposes an electrical charge on the roller that causes it to repel toner. Without any more components, this printer would simply dispense white sheets of paper. A laser, however, scans quickly across the drum to draw an image of the page that is being printed. In the process, it dissipates the charge on the electrically charged drum wherever it strikes. When the toner comes in contact with the drum via a toner roller, toner sticks to the drum wherever the laser made contact. The paper is then rolled across the treated drum, and a fuser roller melts the toner in place on the page.

huge reports (best left to a good laser printer) or for scanning high-color images (you'd want a better scanner).

Also, remember this last caveat—if part of the machine needs to go into the shop, all of it goes into the shop. It might be inconvenient to lose all or many of its capabilities if just part of it stops working and needs repair.

 ### How does the image enhancement technology in laser printers work?

Many laser printers offer higher apparent resolutions than the print engine is actually capable of delivering, by using some sort of image enhancement technology. By varying the size of the dots in graphics and text, printers can make the output smoother than the rated resolution (e.g., 300 dots per inch) would ordinarily allow (see Figure 12-1). Each manufacturer has its own name for this enhancement process, but the basic idea is the same in every case.

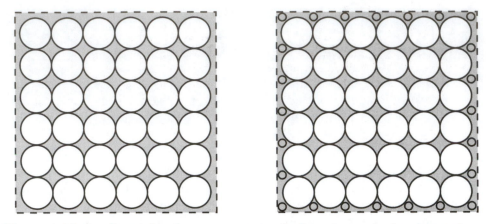

Figure 12-1 Smoother laser output results from image enhancement technology.

? Should I buy an inexpensive dot-matrix printer as a second printer?

We wouldn't. Dot-matrix printers are loud and produce noticeably inferior output—you're much better off with an inkjet printer. If you run across an old dot-matrix printer for a real steal—like free, for example, or perhaps $15 at a garage sale—we wouldn't object to hanging on to it for an emergency.

On the other hand, keep in mind that the modern world abandoned dot-matrix printers a few years ago. Replacement parts—like ribbons—are increasingly hard to come by, and some software won't work with those old printers. In particular, dot-matrix printers are awful at printing bar codes and other computer-read symbols.

The only time you should get one is when you're printing multi-part forms. If you have a good reason to use sheet-fed forms and keep a couple copies for your records, dot-matrix printers are really the only way to do that. Other printers—inkjets and lasers—don't strike the page with any force, so they don't work for multi-part forms.

Do I need a PostScript printer?

Not if you run Windows. *PostScript* is a page definition language that is popular with the Macintosh and some high-end page layout and graphics programs on both PC and Mac platforms. If you're a graphics professional, or if you want to work in Mac/PC hybrid workgroups over a network, then you should definitely consider a PostScript printer.

In general, however, you won't need PostScript, and you can save a few dollars by buying a "Windows" printer that doesn't include it. If you occasionally need to work with PostScript files such as those generated by page-layout software, you can save money by using PostScript software interpreters. However, because using software to convert PostScript into the PCL understood by most printers slows down the printing process, it's not a good solution for heavy-duty PostScript printing.

Do I need PCL?

PCL stands for Printer Control Language, and it's the standard page definition language used by the vast majority of Windows-compatible printers. Almost any printer you buy will run PCL. Those that don't will be PostScript, although most office-oriented PostScript printers also support PCL, and it will almost certainly work with Windows. Most people don't need to worry about PCL versus PostScript. Instead, they simply need to concentrate on getting the printer features they want and let Windows worry about mundane stuff like PCL.

What features should I look for when I shop for a printer?

Start with specifications. You should look for the printer's speed (measured in *pages per minute,* or *ppm*) and resolution. Slow laser printers run at 4 ppm; the fastest are around 20 ppm. Remember that inkjets print much more slowly; color is their selling point, not speed.

Resolution is measured in dots per inch (dpi), and most laser printers offer 300 dpi. Some printers offer 600 dpi, which is four times higher resolution than 300 dpi; anything higher than that approaches publication quality, and you're unlikely to need that level of quality for the home office. The sweet spot for laser printers right now is 600 dpi, so we suggest you look for a printer with that resolution; it's a great combination of price and performance. Inkjets typically print at 300 dpi, but can appear to have a higher resolution thanks to the color output. And, with the right paper, many higher-quality inkjet printers really can reach up to 1200 dpi or so, especially when printing images and color.

Also, check how easily memory can be added to the printer—it probably comes with enough RAM for most print jobs, but you might someday want to add memory for very complex documents.

After specifications, we suggest that you consider ease of use. Many printers use the capabilities of the bidirectional parallel port to tell you about the printer's status. These status monitors are handy. If you have a notebook PC, you might want to print directly to the new printer via the wireless IrDA port found in most recent portables. Few printers have IrDA support, however, so you'll have to shop around.

You should also make sure the printer is designed to accommodate any media on which you often print, such as envelopes, transparencies, and heavy card stock. Can you load a stack of envelopes at once, or do you need to buy an optional envelope feeder? To cut down on jams, look for a printer with a fairly straight paper path, meaning that the paper is pulled straight through the printer's internals, not curled up and around.

And you might consider the bevy of new features that are being added to printers these days. For instance, you can find some inexpensive laser printers that can later accept attachments that turn them into scanners, copiers, and fax machines—true multifunction devices.

Finally, trust your own eyes. Try to test a few competing printers in a PC store before making your decision. Test both text and graphics. Avoid graphics that are too dark, or that

Understanding Resolution

When we say that 600 dpi is four times the resolution of 300 dpi, what we're saying is that the print density is doubled both horizontally and vertically. That's twice the resolution in each direction, or four times the overall resolution.

lack contrast or definition; in the case of inkjets, try to determine which printers do well on plain paper, as well as on the photo-quality special paper. People are often disappointed when they discover that their new printer prints poorly on plain paper despite impressive results on expensive premium stock.

 Do I need to buy a printer with lots of fonts? How about font cartridges?

If you're a Windows user, no. Printers with lots of fonts were all the rage a few years ago when lots of people printed from DOS and used the fonts built into the printer. Windows uses TrueType fonts, however—standardized, scalable fonts that are stored on your hard disk and sent to your printer as high-resolution graphics. When you're shopping for a printer, you can disregard whatever marketing blurb they put on the box about how many fonts are included.

Printers Don't Have as Many Fonts as You Think

Many printers advertise that they have 20, 30, or even 50 fonts preinstalled. Often, that's not 50 distinct typefaces, such as Times, Arial, and Courier, but just a few typefaces in many, many different sizes and styles.

 ### What's a line printer?

Line printer is one of the oldest terms to survive the transition from mainframes to PCs. Line printers were old, Goliath printers that could print an entire line of text at a time. While no one uses line printers with PCs, the term survives. Often, people refer to whatever is connected to a computer as a *line printer*. Likewise, the parallel port is often referred to as the *LPT (line printer) port*.

Are there USB printers?

These days you can find both inkjet and laser printers that connect via USB. These printers are especially useful if you need the parallel port for something else—a scanner, camera, or some other device that uses that port. In fact, many printers support both USB and parallel connections right out of the box.

Hook up your USB printer like any other device—just plug it into a free USB port or your USB hub. Then, install the driver and use the printer!

USING YOUR PRINTER

How do I run the printer's self-test?

Every printer is a bit different; you'll need to take the printer "offline" and press the one-, two-, or three-button combination identified in your printer manual.

If you want to see if Windows is communicating with the printer, however, here's how to run a self-test:

1. Choose Start | Settings | Printers.

2. Find your printer icon in the Printers folder and right-click it. Choose Properties.

3. Click the General tab and choose Print Test Page:

If all is well, a page of text and graphics with the Windows logo should come out of your printer.

I want to install a printer, but there's no Windows driver for it. Can I use the printer?

Sure. Most printers are designed to emulate other printers. That way you can easily connect a printer and, even if it doesn't have its own set of drivers for your application or operating system, it'll understand a fairly universal set of commands used by more popular printers. Windows has eliminated the need to install printer drivers for every application on your hard disk. If you aren't old enough to remember that, it's true—in the old days, you had to install your printer separately for every program you owned!

Today, all you have to do is let Windows know what kind of printer you have. If you don't have a driver disk for your printer, try installing it with alternate drivers in this order:

- First, see if Windows has your printer listed by name in the Settings | Printers dialog box. If so, install it.

- If not, next try a similar printer from the same manufacturer. If you have an HP DeskJet 660C, for example, the 550 driver works just fine. In some cases, the driver won't support every option offered by the newer printer, but it should at least be able to accomplish basic printing in a crunch.

- See if the printer will emulate a more common printer from another vendor. If you're installing a dot matrix printer, try a driver from Epson. For a laser printer, try one from Hewlett-Packard.

- Always see if your printer's manufacturer has a Web page where you can download a new printer driver. Here is a short list of common printer manufacturers:

Manufacturer	Web Site
Brother	http://www.brother.com
Canon	http://www.ccsi.canon.com
Hewlett-Packard	http://www.hp.com
Lexmark	http://www.lexmark.com
NEC	http://www.nec.com
Panasonic	http://www.panasonic.com
Epson	http://www.epson.com
Okidata	http://www.okidata.com

!

Caution: *You can damage a printer by starting it with its packing materials (like foam or locking pins) in place. Carefully read any documentation that accompanies the printer.*

Walkthrough: Installing a Printer

Installing a printer is a simple task because it shouldn't involve opening your PC at all (unless you need to install a new parallel port). Before you get started, make sure the printer comes with an initial ink or toner supply; if not, you'll need to buy one before installing the printer. After you have all the parts at hand, here's what you need to do:

1. Locate the printer and a parallel cable. If the cable didn't come in the box with the printer, you'll need to purchase it separately.

2. Turn off your PC, because you'll be plugging something into the parallel port.

3. Remove all the packing tape from your new printer, along with any "remove before flight" stickers or other artifacts of the shipping process. Often you'll need to open the printer and take bits of foam or locking pins or tape out of the printer's insides.

4. Insert the toner cartridge (if you're installing a laser printer) or ink cartridge (if it's an inkjet):

Follow the manufacturer's warnings about not touching delicate parts and not shaking or turning anything in such a way that you spill ink or toner all over the place. Ink and toner are not fun to clean up.

5. Load some paper in the paper tray.

6. Plug the parallel cable into the printer then into the parallel port on the back of your PC. Use the tensioners to lock the cable to the printer, and screw the cable securely into the computer:

7. Plug the printer's power cable in.

8. Start your PC and power on the printer. If you're running Windows 95/98, it will probably recognize the printer and prompt you to install the printer driver. If not, wait until the PC is fully booted then choose Start | Settings | Printers and add the printer driver manually.

 Can I connect more than one printer to my computer?

Yes, you can use a simple A-B switchbox, such as the one shown here, to connect two printers to a single parallel port:

Switchboxes are inexpensive and available at most PC stores. Keep in mind, however, that some printers that rely

on the bidirectional parallel port may not work properly with a switchbox between them and the PC. Hewlett-Packard laser printers are notorious for not supporting switchboxes. (Other printer manufacturers' warranties are voided by the use of switchboxes, so check your manual before installing one.) If your printer is so affected, return the switchbox to the store and try one of these three alternatives:

- Install an I/O card to get a second parallel port.

- Purchase an active, powered switchbox. These cost around $100, so they're not an inexpensive solution.

- If you have two PCs, install a simple network (see Chapter 9) and attach a printer to each PC. If you "share" the printers in the network, you can print to either printer from either computer.

Caution: *Always power off your PC and printer before moving cables around—even to connect a switchbox.*

Can we share one printer on two computers?

This is the opposite of the previous question. There are a few ways to do this. You can either connect one printer to two computers with a custom switchbox, or you can network them together as discussed in Chapter 9 and share the printer so that either computer can print to it. (Installing a network printer is discussed in the next box, "Walkthrough: Installing a Printer on a Network.")

Can I add memory to my printer?

You'll need to check your printer's manual to be sure. Most laser printers accept memory modules that you can install yourself. If you experience data overflow errors (see "Why doesn't my printer always print all of my page?" later in this chapter), you might want to look into a memory upgrade.

Most inkjet printers don't accept memory upgrades though—while a laser printer needs memory to store at least an entire page before printing it (sometimes more), an inkjet prints the page as the computer feeds it data. So, inkjets usually only have a small *buffer* of RAM for managing the stream of incoming data.

Walkthrough:
Installing a Printer on a Network

If you've installed a local area network in your home or office, you can configure your normal printer so all the PCs in the network can print to it. There are two steps to enabling the printer. First, you need to make sure that Windows will share your printer with the rest of the network. Then you need to visit each computer on the network and show it where the printer actually is. Here's how you do it:

1. Choose Start | Settings | Control Panel and open the Network applet.

2. On the Configuration tab, click the File and Printer Sharing button.

3. Make sure that there's a check mark in the box for "I want to be able to allow others to print to my printer(s)."

4. Click OK twice to close the Network applet.

5. Now, go to each computer that isn't directly connected to the printer via a parallel or serial cable and do the following:

6. Choose Start | Settings | Printers.

7. Select Add Printer and click Next.

8. Choose Network printer and click Next.

9. Click the Browse button and look for the computer with the printer attached. Click the plus sign to its left, and choose the printer when it appears. Click Next.

10. Choose the appropriate printer from the list and click Next.

11. Name the printer and click Next.

12. Click Finish to complete the printer's installation.

Now your printer can serve not just the PC it's attached to, but also the other PCs on the network.

How many pages should I expect to print with my printer toner or ink?

You should look at the manual that came with your printer for this information. In general, you'll get a few hundred pages out of a set of color ink cartridges and a few thousand pages from a toner cartridge. In fact, that makes a laser printer very cost effective—the toner lasts quite a long time, dropping the cost per page significantly.

Most manufacturers quote toner yields based on 5 percent or 10 percent ink coverage on a page—typical coverage for text. If you print a lot of graphics, you'll use up a lot more toner or ink than the manufacturer estimates.

Tip: *When you load a new toner cartridge into your printer, keep the bag that the cartridge comes in just in case you need to ship the printer or store the cartridge for some other reason.*

Can I print on both sides of my paper?

Yes, you can. In fact, we get a lot of life out of our "draft" copies of documents by saving them and printing on the blank side. In the long run, it saves a significant amount of paper.

Walkthrough:
Replacing Toner in a Laser Printer

After a few thousand copies, your toner cartridge will wear out and you'll have very light output or streaks of white through your documents. New cartridges are easy to install yourself. Make sure you follow the instructions that accompany your replacement toner, but here is the general procedure:

1. Turn off your printer and open the access cover, as shown here:

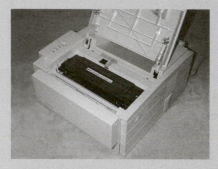

2. Remove the old cartridge:

Pull it straight out and slip it immediately into a plastic bag to prevent residual toner from messing up your office.

3. Take the new cartridge out of the sealed bag and shake it gently or rock it from side to side to distribute toner evenly inside it. Don't turn it over or you might dump impossible-to-clean toner all over your rug.

4. Find the plastic strip that seals the toner cartridge and pull it evenly, firmly, and continuously out of the unit:

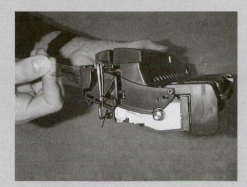

Don't jerk it or it might break—and if it does, the toner cartridge will be ruined.

5. Slip the cartridge in the space left by the old cartridge and make sure it is seated firmly in the printer. Close the access cover and turn the printer back on.

6. Run the printer self-test to be sure the toner is flowing evenly out of the cartridge.

Be sure to use quality laser paper if you intend to print on both sides of the paper. Cheaper paper will curl or crease, causing it to get stuck more often when it's fed through for a second pass.

If you create newsletters, brochures, or other documents in bulk that might benefit from a splash of color, you can print in color on one side with an inkjet printer and in black

and white—with a less costly laser printer—on the other side. Here's how we suggest you do this:

1. Start with the laser-printed side. If you are using special inkjet paper, print on the side the inkjet printer can't print on as well. If you're using plain paper, print on either side. (If you print the inkjet side first, the ink might melt in the laser printer.)

2. Take the stack of pages that have been laser printed and load them in the inkjet printer. Usually, you'll need to load the paper with the printed side up and the head of the page toward the printer. It's a good idea to print a test page in "economy ink mode" to be sure.

Caution: *Be careful if you're using special paper that is glossy on one side and absorbent on the other—if you try printing on the shiny side of some special photo papers with an inkjet printer, none of the ink will get absorbed, and you'll have a really big runny mess.*

What kind of paper should I use?

That's a good question, because there are so many kinds of paper available, particularly for inkjet printers. If you're printing on a laser printer, we recommend you use ordinary 20-pound laser or copier paper that has a brightness rating of at least 80. Decent paper shouldn't cost more than about $7 per 500-sheet ream. We'd be reluctant to buy really inexpensive paper ($3/ream or less) because loose paper fibers can slowly but surely affect the performance of your printer.

When it comes to inkjet printer paper, there are more decisions to make, because the color quality of your output is directly related to the paper you use. Use quality paper, because cheap stock can plug the ink nozzles and decrease the effective resolution of the printer. For general-purpose printing, you can use the same stock as we recommend for laser printers. When you want to get really good quality, though, you should try premium or photo-quality paper—paper designed specifically to increase the quality of inkjet output. This paper is definitely expensive, so only use it when you want fully saturated, photo-quality output.

 What should I do if I need to ship the printer off for repairs?

Make sure you remove the toner cartridge (or other removable pieces, such as the drum, combination cartridges, etc., depending on what your printer uses) before shipping it anywhere. We've actually made the mistake ourselves of mailing not just one, but two, printers to a photo studio during a magazine review, with the toner cartridge still installed. When they arrived, the printers were "toner bombed"—drenched, inside and out, with ink. Cleaning them is so expensive and troublesome that it's often a better solution to buy a new printer when that happens. Don't make the same mistake yourself.

If you need to ship the printer, you should also apply tape to any doors or moving parts that could come lose and get broken during shipping. Your best bet is to save the packing materials and shipping box that came with the printer in the first place.

TROUBLESHOOTING

 My printer isn't working at all! What can I do to get back to work?

Any number of problems might contribute to this general alarm, so let's review what you should check. Before you get too deep into this list, make sure you cycle the printer off and on again to clear its memory—that alone may fix it. Many of these tests are designed to establish where the problem actually is, because there are so many options (the printer, cable, parallel port, or Windows):

- *Try the obvious.* Make sure the printer has paper, it isn't jammed, and it's plugged in and turned on. Check the LCD display (or LED indicators) on your printer for a trouble message, and check the printer manual for an interpretation of any messages that you find.

- *Make sure the printer is online.* If you had a problem, the printer may have taken itself offline and may be waiting for you to press a button on the printer's front panel.

● *Make sure the switchbox is in the right position.* If you use a switchbox, check that it's set to the printer.

● *Run the printer's self-test.* You may need to check the printer manual to find out how to start the test, but this will determine if the printer works. If it does, the problem is elsewhere.

● *Is it Windows?* Restart your system in DOS, and try sending something to the printer. Type, for example, **type config.sys >> lpt1:** and press ENTER. If your config.sys file spits out of the printer, the printer works and the connection to your PC is fine—which means it's a Windows problem. If not, the problem is with the printer or cable.

● *Do you use a bidirectional status program in Windows?* If so, this may be the culprit. It can get corrupted and interfere with any printing from Windows. Change printer drivers to bypass this status monitor; choose a driver for an older version of your printer from Start | Settings | Printers or use an alternative driver provided by the manufacturer. Then remove the status monitor from your Startup folder, and reboot the PC. Can you print now? If so, uninstall and reinstall the status monitor.

● *Check the cable.* Make sure it's securely fastened at both ends. It is remotely possible that the cable has gone bad, so try another cable if you have one.

● *Check the parallel port.* It's even less likely that the parallel port has blown; if you suspect this is the problem, try the printer on another computer and/or test the port with another parallel device, if you have one.

Once you narrow down the problem, you can take some action. Some solutions are self-evident. If the printer fails its own self-test, for example, it needs to be repaired or replaced. If you narrow the problem down to Windows, however, you may need to remove and reinstall the printer driver.

 ### What's the difference between the printer's self-test and the Windows print test?

The self-test built into your printer is the best way to determine whether your printer works properly—the test will work even if the printer isn't connected to a computer at all.

The Windows print test, on the other hand, sends data from your PC to the printer, so if the printer's self-test works but the Windows test doesn't, you know the problem is either with the connection (the cable, port or interface on the printer) or with Windows itself. If you can print from DOS, you can eliminate the connection as a possibility, and you know the problem is with Windows itself.

Why doesn't my 8 ppm printer print at 8 ppm?

First, remember that your printer is rated by its ability to print text; if you throw a page of graphics at it, don't expect to get the speed marked on the box. If you're printing plain text and the printer is noticeably slower than the rated speed, however, try these options:

- Turn off any image enhancement technology in the printer's software control panel. This can affect print speed significantly.

- Drop your requested resolution down to the printer's base resolution (probably 300 dpi):

HP LaserJet 6P Properties

| General | Details | Sharing | Paper |
| Graphics | Fonts | Device Options |

Resolution: 600 dots per inch

- 600 dots per inch
- 300 dots per inch
- 150 dots per inch
- 75 dots per inch

Dithering

○ Fine
○ Line art
○ Error diffusion

Intensity
Darkest ——————|———— Lightest
Current intensity: 100

Graphics mode
Send high-level objects (for example, polygons) to printer
○ Use raster graphics   ⊙ Use vector graphics

Restore Defaults

OK   Cancel   Apply

- Disable the printer's power management tools.
- Check that you're using the correct printer driver for the printer.

One or more of those changes should get your printer printing at top speed—but realize that the cure may be worse than the symptoms. We'd rather enable image enhancement, for example, and sacrifice some printing speed.

Why doesn't my printer always print all of my page?

The most likely source of this problem is a *data overflow,* caused by a lack of memory in your laser printer. Other printers—such as inkjets and dot matrix printers—don't need to worry about this, because they get data in small chunks from the computer. They print as they receive data, and hence stay ahead of their small printer buffer.

Laser printers, on the other hand, fall into a class known as *page printers*. Page printers need to build an image of the entire page in memory at once, before they start printing, because the print mechanism doesn't allow for pauses in the print process while more data arrives.

So much for theory. The bottom line is that you need to have enough memory in your laser printer to handle all of the text and graphics. Usually, the amount of RAM that comes with a printer is sufficient, but you can easily send print jobs to a laser printer that overtax its capabilities. That commonly happens when you send lots of graphics, a PowerPoint presentation, for example, to a printer that doesn't have enough RAM. The problem is exacerbated by the fact that it's hard to tell exactly how much RAM you will need. Modern printers use sophisticated compression routines to do more in a limited amount of RAM. But when a particular page can't be compressed as much as the software expects, you get a data overflow and the page doesn't print.

There are two ways to solve this problem:

- *Drop down to a lower print resolution.* If you're usually printing at 600 dpi, set your printer to 300 dpi using the Start | Settings | Printers dialog box. That gets you about four times as much memory for printing. Or disable the printer's image enhancement technology, if it has any.

- *Add memory to your printer.* Contact your vendor and find out what your memory upgrade options are. You can probably add 2 or 4MB of RAM to the printer and avoid those overflow errors forevermore.

How can I prevent paper jams?

Paper jams eventually happen, but you can take some steps to minimize them:

- Don't overfill your paper tray or paper cassette.
- Fan stacks of paper before loading them, to discharge static electricity.
- Keep paper in a cool, dry place. Damp paper is more likely to jam.
- Don't print on scrap paper that has already been used on the other side. (You might choose to do this anyway to conserve paper; you'll just have to deal with occasional jamming.)
- Use good quality paper. Cheap paper is more likely to jam.
- Be sure the stock you're printing on—such as labels or transparencies—is approved for laser printers.
- When printing labels or stock heavier than 20 pounds, use the straightest paper path available. Often, that's the single-sheet accessory tray.

How can I fix a paper jam?

When clearing paper jams in laser printers, be aware that the inside of the printer is very hot. Turn the printer off and wait a few minutes for the inside of the machine to cool.

Locate the jammed paper. It might be jammed at the entryway from the paper cassette, at the rollers, or in the rear of the printer. Wherever it is, pull it straight out—not by a corner—and pull it slowly. These precautions should prevent the paper from tearing. If it does tear, make sure you remove all the shreds of paper to prevent future jams.

When the paper jam is cleared, be sure to return the printer to its online state before trying to print.

If you have a jam in an inkjet printer, allow the printer to attempt to cycle the page through first. If you must physically remove the paper, pull it slowly in the direction of the paper path. Inkjet printers tend to jam less often than laser printers do, but yanking paper out of their mechanisms can be more damaging.

 ### Why does my paper crease when it prints?

Damp paper can do that. Try to store your paper in a cool, dry place, particularly if you live in a high-humidity area.

Why does my output have big splotches of ink on it?

If you have an inkjet printer, the nozzles of your cartridges might be filled with dried ink. You can solve this easily by removing the cartridges, gently cleaning them with Q-tips dipped in alcohol, and dabbing them with a tissue. Be gentle! When you're done, simply replace the cartridges and your printing should be significantly improved.

If you are using a laser printer and you get streaks or splotches of toner on your documents, the drum might be at the end of its useful life or it might be damaged. Refer to your printer's manual to determine if the drum is a separate component or if it is integrated into the toner cartridge. If it's separate, it may cost you perhaps $200 to replace it—if not, replacing the cartridge will fix it.

 ### Why has my output suddenly turned all blank?

If your laser printer suddenly starts producing completely blank output, the charging roller (often less a roller and more of a wire) has broken. If the charging roller is contained in the toner cartridge, just replace the cartridge. If it's an integral part of the printer instead, you'll need to get the printer serviced. Check your printer manual to see which kind of printer you have.

 ### Do I ever need to use "cleaning paper" or self-tests?

Usually the manufacturer recommends that you pass a page or two of cleaning paper through your printer whenever you replace the toner or color cartridges in your printer. Don't be thrown by the term "cleaning paper"; it's usually just ordinary paper that you run through the printer when you select the printer's cleaning or self-test mode. The cleaning paper helps ensure a uniform distribution of toner or ink when you start printing for real. Check the printer manual for details.

Extending the Life of Your Toner Cartridge

If you notice that your laser toner is running low—streaks of white accompany your output—you can get another 50, 100, or more copies out of your cartridge before discarding it. Open your printer and locate the toner cartridge. It usually looks like a long, black tube that runs across the width of the printer. Pull it out and give it a few good shakes to distribute the toner across the drum. Replace the cartridge, and you should be able to print normally again for a while. This trick may even work a second time, but probably not very well after that. And whatever you do, don't go nuts when you shake the cartridge! If you flip it over or shake it up and down too vigorously, you'll spray impossible-to-clean toner all over your rug. Try to shake it from side to side.

 Someone sent me a file but it prints differently on my printer than hers. Why?

It's not a problem with your printer—it's the software. Often, word processing and graphics files that you receive from other people have been created with fonts that you don't have installed on your PC. If you try to open or print such a file, the software substitutes "similar" fonts, and the end result looks quite different from the original file on the other PC. Ask your friend to e-mail you the fonts used in the document and drag them into your Fonts folder.

> *Caution:* *In some cases, it may be a violation of the font software company's copyright for you to install your friend's fonts on your computer. In this case, you can buy and install the fonts yourself, or ask your friend to reformat the document using more typical Windows fonts.*

Can I safely store a partially used ink cartridge?

There are many reasons why you might need to do this. If you have an inkjet printer, you might have the kind of printer that uses unusual colors (like florescent and glitter inks) and swapping is the only way to use them for special projects. Or you might need to remove a toner cartridge from a laser printer if the printer is going in for repairs. Some photocopiers use toner cartridges like laser printers do, and can accept colored toner so that you can copy in blue or red. You'd need to store the black while printing in red.

The bottom line for storing toner is this: Never turn it upside down and never store it where it is exposed to light, even fluorescent office light. You should keep the opaque plastic bag that the toner comes in for storage situations like this. Tape the end of the bag shut and keep it in a drawer where you won't accidentally tip it over.

For inkjet cartridges, you don't have to worry quite so much about exposure to light or spilling ink. You should be careful to store it upright, however, and never touch the bare metal plate with electrical contacts. Many vendors provide (or sell as an accessory) special containers that hold ink carts when they're removed from the printer. We recommend you use them.

Can I recycle printer cartridges?

Yes and no. There are many commercial services that offer to refill your laser toner or inkjet color cartridges for you and resell them at a fraction of the retail cost of new ones. It can be a tempting deal, but that can void the warranty of the printer. Refurbished cartridges can rupture in your printer, damaging the printer beyond repair. You might be willing to take that chance, but anecdotally, we know of some refurbishing stories that went bad. These sorts of solutions can be cheaper up front, but you'll have no one to blame if something goes wrong and your printer is ruined. We advise against it.

Preprinted logos sometimes smear when they go through my laser printer. Can I prevent that?

It's possible that preprinted stock—like letterhead—can melt and smear in a laser printer. If this happens to you, try shutting the laser printer off for a few hours then turning it back on immediately before you print. Print the letterhead right away, before the printer has a chance to get extremely hot. The fact is that laser printers get quite hot internally; after all, they're actually melting toner onto the surface of the paper—but if left on for a very long time, they can get hot enough to damage inexpensive letterhead.

Be very careful. Some preprinted logos and letterheads are coated with plastic beads that are melted onto the paper over the ink. These will almost always melt in the fuser assembly. Once you run it through the fuser, the rollers need to be either cleaned or replaced.

 Tip: *Ask your printer or copy shop to help you create letterhead and stationery specifically designed for laser printers.*

How far from my computer can I place my printer?

If you have a parallel-port printer (and virtually all PC printers are of the parallel variety) then your parallel cable can be no longer than six feet. If you spend a bundle on a specially shielded parallel cable, you can get perhaps 12 feet, but signal degradation prevents anything longer. If your printer has a serial connection, about 200 feet is the limit.

Chapter 13

Emergency Recovery

Answer Topics!

Emergency Recovery @ a Glance

● Emergency recovery is often difficult because we don't prepare for it. A failed BIOS battery isn't a big deal, unless you never made a backup of your settings—in which case it can be quite a headache, especially on older systems whose BIOS doesn't auto-configure. Likewise, a complete hard disk failure is terrible, but it's 100 times worse if you don't have a backup of your data and an emergency rescue disk to reformat the drive. Read on to learn how to plan ahead for disaster and prevent problems.

● There are two kinds of people: those that have been hit by a computer virus and those that will be. This chapter teaches you all about viruses and how to deal with them.

● We all hate emergencies—those times when your PC doesn't respond in any meaningful way. Problems can be anything from a bad hard disk to a troublesome motherboard. But it's bound to happen eventually, so read this chapter ahead of time to know what you're up against.

● Applications in Windows offer their own fun little errors, including the standards—general protection faults, fatal exceptions, and other dangerous sounding error messages. They may not be the most helpful messages in the world, but they sometimes point you in the right direction. And if your errors focus on those ever-present DLLs, there are a couple solutions to look into.

● There are other crises that can affect you, too. The year 2000—and its problems—looms right around the corner. Will the Year 2000 problem affect your PC? (And just in case you think you've gotten past it unscathed, there might still be a little testing to do.) This is the place to find out.

GENERAL PROBLEM SOLVING

 What steps can I take to prevent problems with my PC?

You can extend the life of your PC by paying attention to your computer on a daily basis. Here are some things to watch for. (See Chapter 2 for more on routine maintenance.)

● *Limit yourself to one power up and one power down per day.* Some people turn their PC on and off repeatedly throughout the day, as if leaving it on will somehow wear it out. (This assumes you're using the PC all day—a home PC can be turned on and off once per session, if you're not using it daily.) The reality is that repeatedly turning it on and off is what will wear it out prematurely. Specifically, leave the PC on, but turn the monitor off (or use the Energy Star power-off mode), and set the BIOS to allow the hard disk to spin down if it is Energy Star compliant. You'll find these things in Windows' Power Management control panel.

● *Avoid the damage caused by power surges, spikes, brownouts, and complete power failures by using an uninterruptible power supply (UPS).* They're inexpensive—some cost less than $100. (See Chapter 2 for more information on why you should use a UPS.) Whatever you do, don't use cheap, no-name power strips, because they don't actually provide any protection from power spikes or brownouts. If you do get a power-strip surge suppressor, remember that they tend to wear out. After a year or two, they no longer provide any protection and need to be replaced.

● *Unplug your modem's phone line from the wall outlet during thunderstorms.* A power spike can kill your modem or your entire PC. If your UPS or surge suppressor has a jack for the phone line, you can avoid unplugging the modem from the wall by plugging the phone cable into the surge suppressor instead.

● *Test your hard disk with ScanDisk on a regular basis to find bad sectors and keep the drive error-free.* Also, keep your hard disk defragmented. If your hard disk gets excessively fragmented—that is, data files and

applications are scattered in tiny chunks all over the drive—software can run more slowly and, in extreme cases, can have trouble running at all. (See Chapter 8 for details on using ScanDisk and Disk Defragmenter.)

- *Use a virus checker regularly.* Your chances of contracting a computer virus are actually low, but just one virus can destroy your data permanently. And keep your virus definition files up to date. A virus checker is worthless without current definitions.

- *Don't smoke around your PC, and keep the system in a well-ventilated location.* Keep the surrounding area as dust-free as possible. And open the case of your PC every few months to remove the dust that builds up inside. Use a vacuum, not compressed air.

 ## What software will help me troubleshoot my PC?

You can use a system utility such as Norton Utilities (see Figure 13-1), Helix Nuts & Bolts, or Touchstone CheckIt to

Figure 13-1 Norton Utilities is a popular tool for keeping PCs up and running.

troubleshoot your system. Each of these programs has a suite of tools for finding and solving problems with Windows and your system hardware.

That said, let us also say that we're not big fans of this genre of software for daily use. Countless times we've been asked about problems identified by these programs that don't really exist—or at least they're insignificant in daily operation. Specifically, we've found that many diagnostic programs fail to identify real problems, yet point out phantom anomalies that have no real effect on your system. That makes it difficult to weed out the real problems from the chaff and to know how effectively these programs are working for you. We've found that real problems, such as "Windows won't fully shut down," and "I get a mysterious VxD error when Windows starts," are rarely solved by these diagnostic programs.

The bottom line? If you have a serious problem with your system, there's no harm in trying out a utility package. They tend to work very well for some basic system maintenance—things such as optimizing, defragmenting, and fixing hard drives and individual files. It's also a great idea to run file recovery or "file saver" programs that can help you undelete files in an emergency. Or you might enjoy one of these programs if you're a person who loves to tinker and tweak. Be aware that there is another level of troubleshooting that requires some logical thought and answers, such as those found in this chapter—a software diagnostic program can't do it all alone.

Can I restart my PC with the Reset button?

Only if you have no other choice. You should always shut down Windows via the Start | Shut Down menu item, if possible. The menu command allows Windows to close files, save data to the hard disk, and prepare for an orderly termination. The Reset button can cost you data even if all your applications are closed, because Windows delays writing to the hard disk to improve performance. That means you never know if all your data is saved until Windows says it's okay to shut down. If your system isn't locked up, avoid using

the Reset or Power buttons to power off your computer. Shut down Windows first, then power off.

Shut Down Windows	✕

What do you want the computer to do?

- ○ Stand by
- ● Shut down
- ○ Restart
- ○ Restart in MS-DOS mode

| OK | Cancel | Help |

If you can't get to the Shut Down command, you might still be able to recover more gracefully by pressing CTRL-ALT-DEL and forcing closed any wayward application. Then you can try again to shut down the machine.

On the other hand, there are occasions when Windows locks up enough that none of your ordinary controls (the mouse and keyboard, for instance) work properly. Your only choice in that case is to press the Reset button on your PC.

❓ What's the difference between pressing *CTRL-ALT-DEL* and using the Windows Shut Down command?

Using the Start | Shut Down menu item is the only reliable way to make sure all your files are closed and data is saved before closing Windows and turning off your PC. While long-standing PC users are familiar with using CTRL-ALT-DEL to restart the computer after a software crash, don't do that (and don't press the Reset button) unless the computer won't restart the normal way.

The CTRL-ALT-DEL key sequence has its uses in Windows, however. You can use it to selectively shut down an errant program. If a program has stopped responding to commands or is behaving oddly, you can press CTRL-ALT-DEL and choose to end the failed program. Sometimes you'll need to use CTRL-ALT-DEL and select End Task several times before the program really ends.

 Caution: Don't press CTRL-ALT-DEL several times in a row quickly, or your PC will shut down.

VIRUSES

 What exactly is a "virus"?

While computer viruses are one of the most common themes in science fiction these days, they're rarely portrayed accurately. Forget everything you think you might know about viruses—in a nutshell, a *virus* is simply defined as a "self-replicating program."

In other words, a virus makes additional copies of itself in an effort to spread itself to new locations, such as floppy disks, hard disks, the Internet, and other network stations. A virus may or may not be malicious—that is determined by the effect the virus has on your PC. Not all viruses are written to be malicious, and some are only malicious by accident, perhaps because of a bug left in the code by a sloppy programmer.

That's not to say that viruses are okay—you should make every effort to avoid getting a virus and to stamp out viruses as soon as they're detected.

What's the difference between a virus, a Trojan horse, a time bomb, and a logic bomb?

Well, for starters, they all have one thing in common—all four are often malicious and you definitely want to avoid them. But all malicious programs are not viruses. Here's a summary of what each kind of program does:

● **Virus** A *computer virus* is a program that makes copies of itself, like a real virus. Viruses may or may not be designed to destroy data, but they often do bad things regardless, even by accident. In 1999, the Melissa virus damaged many systems in an innocuous way—when it was run, it sent 50 copies of itself to names culled randomly from the owner's e-mail system. In large companies with lots of employees, Melissa managed to crash mail servers due to the load.

- **Trojan horse**   A *Trojan horse* is a program that gains access to your system by pretending to be something it's not. In 1997, for instance, there was a program called AOL4Free that was downloaded by many unsuspecting people hoping to get America Online service without paying for it. AOL4Free, however, was a Trojan horse that actually deleted the contents of your hard disk if you were unfortunate enough to try to install it.

- **Time bomb**   A *time bomb* is a malicious program that executes when a certain day or time arrives. Several famous viruses have also been time bombs, designed to activate and destroy data on specific dates such as Friday the 13th or Columbus Day.

- **Logic bomb**   A *logic bomb* is like a time bomb, except that it goes off when certain conditions are met, such as when a specific program is run or a certain name in a database is accessed. These programs are rare and few have been seen on the PC.

What does a virus infect?

There are a couple of basic types of virus, classified by the type of file they tend to infect. They include:

- **File virus**   Viruses that attach themselves to and spread via executable files such as .COM and .EXE files. Some viruses can also infect system-level files like those with .SYS, .DRV, and .BIN extensions.

- **Boot sector virus**   The *boot sector* is a part of the typical hard drive, floppy disk or removable cartridge that contains stores information that tells the computer how the disk is formatted, includes a catalog of files on that disk and includes any special hidden files necessary to boot a PC with that disk. Boot sector viruses infect this portion of the drive, making them tough to get to while it's easy for them to infect everything else. Even a reformat can't always erase these viruses.

- **Master Boot Record virus**   The Master Boot Record, located on the first physical sector of any drive, has a small program built into it. This program looks up the values in the partition table to determine how to boot the operating system (where to find it on the drive), then it tells the PC to go to that portion of the drive and execute the programs it finds there. These viruses get spread the same way boot sector viruses get spread—by booting from an infected disk. This happens most often when users leave an infected floppy in the floppy drive and restart.

Finally, some very sophisticated viruses are a combination of all three types above.

Can I get a virus through e-mail?

So far, you can't get a computer virus (or any other kind of malicious software) by reading an e-mail message. Any e-mail that claims to warn you about viruses that strike as soon as you open a message are hoaxes—don't worry about them and don't forward such messages, which are really just the e-mail equivalent of chain letters. In order for a malicious program to affect your system, it must be run, and e-mail programs don't automatically run attachments.

On the other hand, someone can send you a malicious program as an attachment, and you can trigger it by running the attachment (see Figure 13-2). There are two ways to avoid viruses in e-mail attachments:

- Only open attachments you feel secure about, such as those sent by friends or co-workers.
- Use a virus checker that scans e-mail attachments for viruses.

E-mail attachment viruses have become pretty common recently, thanks to a spate of innovation on the parts of Microsoft and virus programmers. Now, you'll find a number of strains of viruses that are able to masquerade as you, send a virus (as an attachment) to some or all the people in your address book and see if it can fool them into opening it.

The solution is two-fold: Run virus protection software and never open strange attachments. If you didn't expect an attachment from a friend, co-worker or stranger, don't open it. Write them back (or call them) and make sure they meant to send the attachment. It's considered bad "netiquette" to send an attachment without asking—this is one reason why.

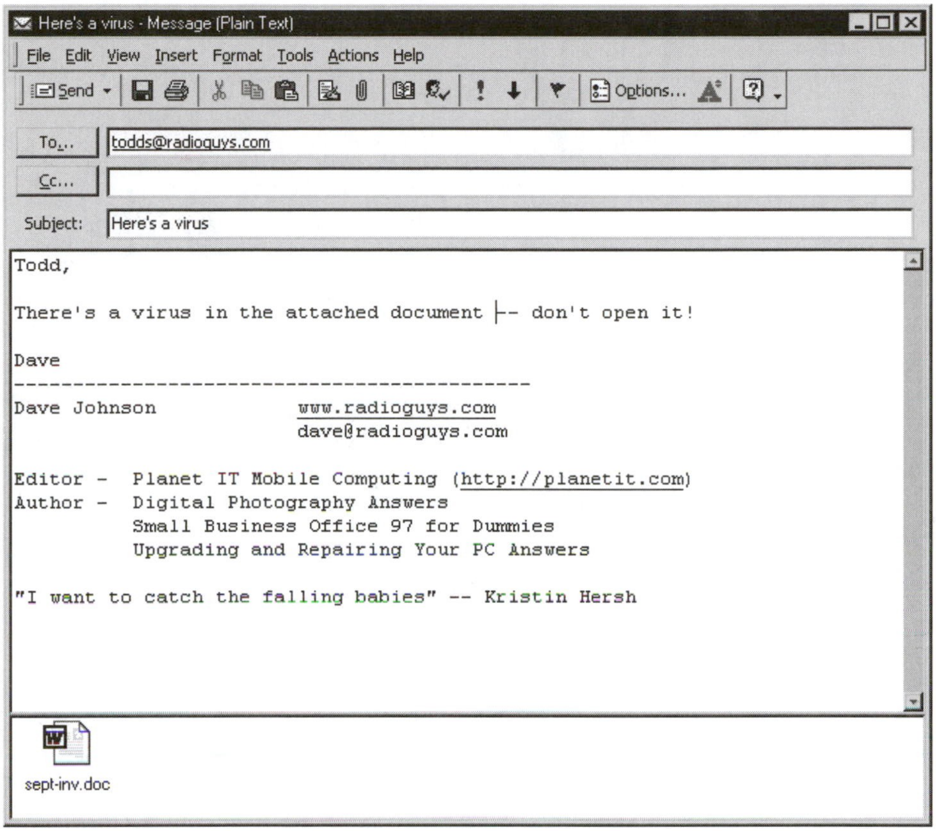

Figure 13-2   An e-mail attachment can set off a virus if you launch it.

 ## How do I know if I have a virus?

It isn't always easy to detect a virus on your PC without a virus checker. You might experience unusual behavior, such as:

- Inability to save certain kinds of files
- Inability to print
- Extra, randomized, or corrupted information in your files
- Unexpected disk activity
- Sudden loss of storage space on your hard disk
- Sudden loss of files on your hard disk

- Messages on your desktop announcing that your system is actually under the control of a malicious program (a dead giveaway)

Of course, you should absolutely be using a virus detector. Most anti-virus software is extremely accurate for flagging viruses and viral behavior as it occurs. Without such a program, you're risking all your data every day.

If you don't currently have any anti-virus software installed on your system, you can take advantage of a free service called HouseCall from Trend Micro. Visit **http://housecall.antivirus.com** to try it out. Using HouseCall, you can test suspicious files on your hard disk for viruses.

What do I do when I find a virus?

If you think a virus has infected your PC, you need to react quickly to prevent further damage to your data. If you do something wrong, even if your intentions are good, you can still lose data. Here's what you should do:

1. Stop whatever you are doing. Don't work with open applications or send any information across a network. In fact, immediately cease any network or Internet-related activities to avoid spreading the virus to co-workers, clients, or customers.

2. If you suspect that a virus is actually attacking files on your hard drive, pull the plug. Immediately. You may be able to recover some of the data later.

3. If you have a network manager, call and let him or her know that you may be infected; follow any instructions you are given. If you don't have a network expert to rely on, then you can solve the problem yourself.

4. If you have a recent copy of any open data files, leave your applications alone. If you have a lot of unsaved work that you might lose anyway, save and close the data files.

5. Scan your computer with an anti-virus program. In most cases, the virus program can eliminate the virus without destroying the underlying files.

6. If you found and killed a virus, run the virus program again, but this time change its settings so it scans all files. The default mode for many virus checkers is to ignore many types of files to save time.

7. After your PC is clean, run the virus checker on any media (such as floppies and Zip disks) that may have been exposed to the virus. E-mail friends and co-workers to advise them of the virus so they can check their own systems.

Here are a few things you shouldn't do:

● Don't format your hard disk! That's an extreme measure and is rarely (if ever) called for. Sure, you'll probably kill the virus (though some can survive being formatted), but you'll lose all your data in the process.

● Don't work with the computer anymore. The only thing worse than losing data is working on more data that you're going to lose. If you continue working in infected files—or if your continued work sets off some sort of viral response—then you'll have continued working for nothing.

● Don't e-mail or otherwise transport a copy of the virus to anyone! No one needs to get a copy of the virus—except for your network administrator or your anti-virus company, either of whom might ask for a copy.

What kind of anti-virus program should I use?

Our general advice is that you should choose nearly any anti-virus program as long as you actually use it. Despite a lot of marketing hype (this is one of the most crowded and competitive markets in PC software), there really isn't a

world of difference among leading virus checkers. Here's what you should look for:

- **Free signature file updates** A virus program is no good to anyone unless it can stay current with the latest viruses. Most companies provide a service that allows you to update the virus checking software over the Internet, via AOL, or by calling a BBS with your modem. Look for a company that offers the updates regularly—preferably monthly—and make sure they offer a way to download the update that is convenient for you. In general, the most convenient virus updates are those that transfer the files via the Internet without your direct involvement.

- **Virus checking on all the fronts you use** It's important that your virus program check for viruses in your e-mail, Internet downloads, network access, and removable drives.

- **Additional information available on CD-ROM or on the Web site** Some virus checkers have great Web sites with virus encyclopedias, hoax alerts, online virus labs, and more.

- **Automatic signature file downloads** If the program updates itself automatically, you can't forget to do it.

- **Scheduled, thorough scans** Even though these programs work in real-time, you're safest if the program checks your entire hard disk periodically (for example, once a week).

CRITICAL FAILURE

Why does my computer tell me "Bad COMMAND.COM" and stop?

You need to have a file called command.com on your hard disk (or a bootable floppy disk) in order to boot properly. It needs to be in the root directory of the bootable drive. If

command.com is missing or is somehow corrupted, your PC can't start. Copy command.com from a good system disk (it should be the same version of the OS that you have loaded on your PC) and you should be able to boot normally.

How can I recover data from a crashed hard disk?

If your hard disk has a very serious error—if, for example, it will no longer boot, and it can't be accessed when you boot from an emergency disk—then your options are quite limited. Specialized services that recover data from dead hard disks tend to be expensive (ranging from a few hundred to a few thousand dollars per drive). If you want to try it yourself, you'll need a program that can work on the drive at a lower level than common Windows utilities. One such program is Reynolds Utilities, a DOS-based program (contact Reynolds at 800-22-DRIVE or **http://www.data-recovery.com** on the Web). There are other similar programs you can try, as well.

What do I need to have on an emergency boot disk?

You should always have at least one emergency boot disk from which you can boot your PC in case of a hard disk failure. First create a startup disk (described in Chapter 8) then make sure you have these files on the disk:

- autoexec.bat
- config.sys

The only thing your autoexec.bat and config.sys files need to include are your CD-ROM and mouse drivers. The easiest way to do this is to copy your autoexec and config files from your C: drive, edit the files in Notepad, and delete everything that is not essential. If these files don't have entries for the CD-ROM or mouse, you'll need to add them manually. Many PCs come with CD-ROM utility disks that will create a set of startup files for you. Use them now—before disaster strikes—or it may be too late. Be sure to delete references to virus checkers and other utilities that you won't run in an emergency.

Make sure that you copy the appropriate CD-ROM drivers to the floppy and that the autoexec.bat file points to the mscdex.exe you just put on the A: drive, not back to the hard disk. For instance, you should have an entry that looks like this:

```
A:MSCDEX.EXE /D:MTMIDE01 /M:10
```

Likewise, your config.sys file should have an entry like this:

```
DEVICE=A:MSCDEX.SYS /D:MTMIDE01
```

(MSCDEX.EXE and MSCDEX.SYS are driver software. In this example, MTMIDE01 is simply a name for the CD-ROM drive; yours will likely differ.)

Here are other DOS files that should appear on your emergency disk:

- **mouse.com or mouse.exe**   This is your mouse driver, usually found in C: or C:/mouse/.

- **FDISK**   This program allows you to create and manage hard disk partitions.

- **Format**   This is the program that actually formats your drive.

- **Edit**   This is a simple text editor for DOS that you can use to change the autoexec.bat and config.sys files.

The Smart PC Owner's Emergency Recovery Box

Aside from an emergency startup disk, there are a number of tools you should have handy in case of emergency. If you need to do some heavy disk recovery, reinstall the operating system, or even format and start from scratch, then knowing where these disks and notes are will make the process run much more smoothly.

- Norton Utilities or its equivalent. If you have a CD-ROM drive, keep the Norton CD convenient. Armed with your boot disk's CD-ROM drivers, you'll be able to run the programs and check out an ailing drive.

- BIOS backup diskette or BIOS settings recorded on paper.

- Zip disk driver and utilities.

- Printer drivers.

- Networking drivers and a detailed list of settings.

- Modem driver (if necessary).

- Driver software for any other peripherals, such as your scanner.

- TCP/IP and Internet settings (such as DNS numbers), plus your ISP username, password, and access phone numbers.

Finally, one other note about backups. If you use an Iomega Zip drive or similar removable media drive (highly recommended), be sure to back up any updated drivers and program patches that you've downloaded for your software, printer, modem, and other peripherals. Simply drop them all onto a special Zip disk so you can easily reinstall them later.

 I've just installed a new piece of hardware, and now my computer won't start. What should I do?

Turn off the PC immediately. If you just finished installing a new expansion card, open the case back up (we recommend leaving the case open until you know you've got it working properly) and make sure the card is seated perfectly in the slot. Also, look for loose connectors and cables. It's possible you dislodged the hard drive ribbon cable or a power connector. If so, reattach it. If your PC starts now, great. If not, remove the new card and try to start the PC as it was before the installation. If it works without the new card, try installing the card in a different expansion slot. You can also try removing other cards and installing the new one by itself. (See Chapter 4 for more on expansion card troubleshooting.)

Understanding the Start-up Sequence

When you first turn on your PC, it goes through a number of important steps on the road to usability. Understanding what each of these steps does can help you troubleshoot problems with your PC. Watch for problems in the startup, and they will point you toward the solutions.

1. *When you power on your PC, the power supply feeds electricity to the various components.* You'll hear the hard disk(s) start to spin and the fan go around. If the power supply doesn't reach the proper voltage, it won't send any electricity to the rest of the system.

2. *The BIOS wakes up.* This chip stores essential details about how the PC needs to operate. It contains the genetic instincts of your PC, as opposed to the operating system and hard drives, which contain more evolved behavior.

3. *The computer performs a power-on self test (POST).* Here, it checks essential components to make sure they're present and functioning. You see this visually on the DOS screen as it performs memory tests and lets you know about the hard disks it has found. (Many newer PCs hide the process from you with a logo screen.) If something is wrong, you'll hear a series of beeps. (See the answer to "What does it mean when my PC won't start but it beeps at me?" later in this chapter.)

4. *The operating system—usually Windows—starts.* If you've left a floppy disk in the drive, this is when you'll see a "non-system disk" error (but only if the floppy isn't a system disk, of course). Or, if your hard drive has failed, this is when you'll find out about it.

5. *The autoexec.bat and config.sys files are accessed.* Any special programs or drivers you want to run right away—such as the DOS mouse driver and CD-ROM driver—are included here. If you

see lines of code being executed on the screen (and any relevant errors) you'll head to your autoexec.bat and config.sys files to troubleshoot. Press F8 at startup to execute the autoexec.bat file a line at a time.

6. *Windows finishes loading.* If all went well, you'll see the desktop. Windows has a special folder in the Start menu called Startup. Any applications in the Startup folder are automatically launched right after Windows loads the desktop, so those programs will load. As they're finishing, you gain control over your system and can begin using Windows and applications.

What does it mean when my PC won't start but it beeps at me?

You're experiencing the lowest level of error messages your PC can produce—BIOS beep codes. Unfortunately, many computer manufacturers treat these beeps as closely guarded corporate secrets. Few computer manuals detail what they mean, so we've included the most common beep codes here. You'll need to know what BIOS your PC uses because all manufacturers' beep codes are a bit different. You can find the BIOS manufacturer in the PC's startup information when the system first starts to boot. It will probably be either AMI, Phoenix, Award, or if you have a real IBM PC, IBM. If the startup screen doesn't display a BIOS copyright message, then you can even pop the cover off the PC and look for the BIOS chips themselves. Ignore video cards and disk controllers that also have BIOS labels on them—the main BIOS chips are on your motherboard.

When the PC starts, count the number of beeps and look it up on the BIOS chart for your manufacturer. This will point you in the right general direction for either solving the problem on your own or getting professional help.

AMI Beep Codes

If you have an AMI BIOS, there is a fairly short list of beeps that you can expect to hear. One beep indicates all is well; but if you hear something different, find out what the problem is in the following table.

Beep Code	Meaning
1	One beep is normal unless you see an error message. If you don't see anything on the monitor, check the obvious stuff, such as the monitor cable and power supply—the PC might be booting normally, but you can't see it. Otherwise, this is an indication of a *refresh failure*, meaning that there is a problem with memory chips or with the DMA chip. You should first make sure that your RAM is properly seated if you've recently installed new SIMMs or DIMMs or if the system has been moved, shipped or dropped. Otherwise, you'll need to get the PC serviced.
2	Some PCs beep twice when they boot normally. If nothing appears out of the ordinary (and it always beeps twice), then ignore it. If not, this is an indication of a *parity error*. This is easy to fix if one or more of your memory chips is not seated properly (particularly if you recently worked inside the PC and possibly brushed against the RAM sockets). Open the case and reinstall your RAM chips. If that doesn't solve the problem, the memory may have gone bad (you can have it tested at a computer shop) or there's a problem on the motherboard.
3	Parity error in the base 64K of memory. The solution is the same as for two beeps.
4	Timer error. Again, the problem is related to memory. Make sure the chips are seated properly and test the first pair of SIMMs in your PC for errors. If that's not the problem, you probably have a bad motherboard.
5	Processor error. The CPU has probably died. You can try reseating the CPU and memory chips. If that doesn't fix the problem, you can replace the CPU or the entire motherboard.
6	Keyboard controller error. There are a few possible solutions. First, make sure the keyboard is plugged in properly. Next, try another keyboard with your PC. If that doesn't solve the problem, you can try to reseat or replace the keyboard controller chip (unless it's actually soldered to the motherboard) or you can replace the motherboard.
7	Processor exception interrupt error. Like five beeps, this indicates a problem with the CPU. You can try reseating the CPU and memory chips. If that doesn't fix the problem, you can replace the CPU or the entire motherboard.

Beep Code	Meaning
8	Display memory failure. This indicates a problem with the video card. Try to reseat it; if that doesn't work, make sure the socketed memory on the video card is properly seated. If those fail, replace the video card.
9	ROM checksum error. Replacing the BIOS chips is just about the only solution to this problem.
10	CMOS shutdown register error. The CMOS is misbehaving; you'll probably have to replace it or the entire motherboard.
11	Cache memory bad. The cache RAM on the motherboard is experiencing problems. Try to reseat the memory chips (the cache chips—not the system memory modules). If that doesn't fix the problem, you need to replace them.

Phoenix Beep Codes

If you have a Phoenix BIOS, you've got to listen carefully, because the beep codes are a combination of long beeps, short beeps, and multiple beep patterns separated by short pauses. We listed these multiple beeps as numbers for simplicity—for example, 1-1-3, means that you hear *beep-pause-beep-pause-beep-beep-beep*.

Beep Code	Meaning
1	One beep is normal. If you don't see anything on the monitor, check the obvious stuff—for example, the monitor cable and power supply; your PC might be booting normally, but you can't see it.
2	Configuration error. In a nutshell, the BIOS has detected a mismatch between the way the computer is configured and its settings. Run the BIOS setup program and look for an invalid video card or other mismatched settings.
1-1-3	CMOS error. The motherboard can't read the information stored in the CMOS. This likely means you'll need to replace the battery on the motherboard.
1-1-4	ROM BIOS checksum error. The BIOS isn't working, and you need to replace it.
1-2-1	System timer failure. A timer chip on the motherboard has gone bad—in all likelihood, the entire motherboard needs to be replaced.
1-2-2	DMA failure. This could be a problem with an expansion card that uses DMA. If not, you may have to replace the motherboard.
1-2-3	DMA page register failure. Like 1-2-2, check DMA-using expansion cards; if not, your only recourse may be to replace the motherboard.

Beep Code	Meaning
1-3-1	RAM refresh error. You could have a problem with your memory chips, the DMA chip, or memory addressing chips on the motherboard. Try to reseat your RAM modules. If that doesn't work, you may need to replace one or more RAM modules, or you may need a new motherboard.
1-3-3	Base 64K memory error. Your memory chips may need to be reseated or tested for errors. If that doesn't solve the problem, you may have to replace the motherboard.
1-3-4	Base 64K memory odd/even logic failure. Try the same solutions as for 1-3-3.
1-4-1	Base 64K memory address line failure. Try the same solutions as for 1-3-3.
1-4-2	Base 64K memory parity failure. Your first pair of SIMMs may have come loose or gone bad. Reseat them; if that doesn't solve the problem, you may have a motherboard to replace.
2-x-x	First 64K RAM failure. Any error that begins with two beeps is an indication of a RAM failure. You should test each memory chip and replace the bad ones.
3-1-1	Slave DMA register failure. See 1-2-2.
3-1-2	Master DMA register failure. See 1-2-2.
3-1-3	Master interrupt mask register failure. The interrupt controller chip has gone bad. Replace the motherboard.
3-1-4	Slave interrupt mask register failure. The interrupt controller chip has gone bad. Replace the motherboard.
3-2-4	Keyboard controller test failure. The keyboard isn't responding properly. Look for a stuck key, a broken connector, a frayed cable. If all else fails, replace the keyboard.
3-3-4	Video initialization failure. Make sure the video card is properly seated in the slot. If that doesn't work, replace it with another card.
3-4-1	Screen retrace test failure. The video card is failing; replace it soon.
3-4-2	Screen retrace test failure. This is the same as 3-4-1. The video card is failing; replace it soon.
4-2-1	Timer tick failure. The timer chip on the motherboard has gone bad; replace the motherboard.
4-2-2	Shutdown test failure. Oddly, this can be caused by a bad keyboard or a bad motherboard. Obviously, check to see if swapping keyboards fixes the problem.
4-2-3	Gate A20 failure. This problem is solved in the same way as 4-2-2.

Beep Code	Meaning
4-2-4	Unexpected interrupt in protected mode. Most likely, a bad expansion card is causing problems. Pull them all out and replace them one at a time. Eventually, you'll find the card that causes this problem. If you get this error with no expansion cards installed, it's probably a bad motherboard.
4-3-1	RAM test address failure. The memory address logic chips on the motherboard have failed. Replace the motherboard.
4-3-2	Interval timer failure. The interval timer has gone bad; replace the motherboard.
4-3-3	Interval timer failure. The interval timer has gone bad; replace the motherboard.
4-3-4	Time of day clock failure. Most likely, you can fix this problem by replacing the CMOS battery and restoring its information. If that doesn't fix the problem, the power supply may need to be fixed. Finally, the motherboard itself may need to be replaced.
4-4-1	Serial port test failure. The I/O port may have gone bad. If your serial port is located on the motherboard, set the jumper to disable it and install an I/O card in an expansion slot.
4-4-2	Parallel port test failure. The I/O port may have gone bad. If your parallel port is located on the motherboard, set the jumper to disable it and install an I/O card in an expansion slot.
4-4-3	Math coprocessor failure. If your math coprocessor has failed, you can disable or replace it. This really only affects pre-Pentium systems, in which the coprocessor was located on the motherboard separate from the CPU.

IBM Beep Codes

Unless you have a real IBM personal computer, you're not going to need to know these beep codes—but here's a handy list of them. (L stands for a long beep; S for a short beep.)

 Note: *These codes rely on short and long beeps like some of the Phoenix codes do.*

Beep Code	Meaning
1	One beep is normal. If you don't see anything on the monitor, check the obvious solutions, such as plugging in monitor cables and power supplies—your PC might be booting normally, but you can't see it.
Constant tone or repeating short beeps	The power supply is failing. Replace it.

Beep Code	Meaning
L-S	Motherboard failure. Replace it.
L-S-S	Video card failure. Make sure the card is seated properly. If it is, you need to replace it.
L-S-S-S	Video card failure. Make sure the card is seated properly. If it is, you need to replace it.

 ## I turn my PC on and absolutely nothing happens. What's up?

First, check the obvious. Is there a power light on your PC? Make sure the power supply is plugged in to a working electrical socket. (Test it with a lamp or some other working device.) If there's power in the socket, but the computer's power supply doesn't work, see Chapter 2 for instructions on how to replace it.

If you are sure the power supply works, check the motherboard for loose chips. To make the system easier to troubleshoot, pull out any nonessential expansion cards, such as TV tuners, scanner cards, and tape backup accelerators. With just the video card in place (and a hard disk adapter, if your PC uses one in an expansion slot), try to start your system up again.

If the computer now works, sigh in relief—and then try installing your cards one at a time until you find the one that prevents the system from booting.

 ## How can I restore my BIOS settings?

We recommend that you have a backup of your BIOS handy at all times. The easiest way to back up your BIOS is to use a utility such as Norton Utilities or McAfee Office. These programs will save your BIOS settings to disk, making it easy to restore them after a battery failure.

If you don't use software, you can do it the old-fashioned way: Write it all down. Make sure you go to every screen and option on the BIOS setup and write down what all the settings are. Then, after you replace a failed battery, you can enter the BIOS setup and enter all the information manually.

Keep those settings in an easy-to-find place—for example, with this book or your computer manual.

 Tip: *Many new BIOS setups are able to auto-detect a lot of the information you need. If you have such a BIOS, it may not be absolutely necessary to write everything down. You might still want to, though, especially if you've tweaked the settings for better performance, and so on.*

What do I do if my PC can't remember the time of day or current date?

The battery on your motherboard that powers your CMOS chip has died. This happens after three to five years. You'll need to turn off your PC, open the case, and look for a small lithium watch battery on the motherboard. It's usually easy to find, but your computer manual may point you directly to it. Remove the battery and take it to the store, where you need to find a replacement. Pop the new one in your PC and close it up—you're done.

Unfortunately, you'll have lost all of your CMOS settings, so it's a good idea to keep a written record of all the CMOS data before disaster strikes. (Some PCs auto configure after a new battery is installed, so it's less of an issue.) Some utility programs (such as Norton Utilities) also save your CMOS settings to disk.

BASIC APPLICATION ERRORS

 ### I've accidentally deleted a file. Can I get it back?

Possibly. Windows keeps track of deleted files in the Recycle Bin—if you send something to the graveyard in Windows, you can retrieve the file from the Recycle Bin. Simply follow these steps:

1. Open the Recycle Bin on the desktop.
2. Scroll through the file list in search of the file you want to retrieve.

3. Right-click the file and choose Restore:

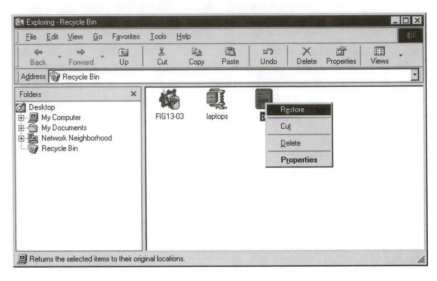

 Tip: *You should empty the Recycle Bin periodically to recapture disk space. Right-click the Recycle Bin and choose Empty Recycle Bin.*

In DOS, you don't ordinarily have the same level of protection. Some third-party utilities, such as McAfee Office or Norton Utilities, however, extend the Recycle Bin's protection to DOS. Anything you delete will be trapped by one of these programs, and you can later retrieve the file.

Keep in mind that once you empty the Recycle Bin, deleted files are gone forever. But there's yet another caveat: Many utilities (such as the ones we've already mentioned) have undelete programs that function in DOS—using these utilities, you stand some chance of recapturing the deleted file. This is less reliable than the Recycle Bin, though. Windows' Recycle Bin is little more than a folder that stores programs you've marked for deletion—they haven't really been deleted.

Undelete programs, however, take advantage of the fact that the operating system doesn't ever really delete a program. It simply erases the marker in the file allocation

table (FAT) that points to the file's location. The file exists until another file overwrites it. So, the sooner you try to undelete a file, the better, because ordinary hard disk activity can overwrite it or render it unsalvageable.

Technical Support told me to delete a DLL file from Windows, but I can't find any file with a DLL extension in the folder. What's going on?

Simple—by default, Windows hides certain kinds of files so they don't clutter up your display and so you're not inclined to delete them accidentally. To make these hidden system files visible, open My Computer and choose View | Options. Click the View tab and select Show all Files:

Click OK to close the dialog box, and now you'll see all the files that Windows used to hide.

If you use Internet Explorer 4 or 5 or Windows 98, this will work a little differently. Choose View | Folder Options

and click the View tab. Scroll down to the Hidden Files entry and choose Show all Files:

Sometimes I get the following error messages: "Fatal Exception," "General Protection Fault," and "This Application Has Stopped Responding." What is wrong?

These are all indications that the program did something it shouldn't have—usually accessing memory reserved by another program. It's not your fault, and there's virtually nothing you can do about it. These problems tend to happen infrequently, are unpredictable, and can be caused by any number of factors that are difficult to duplicate. We don't mean to sound negative about this, but the fact remains that you have no recourse but to continue using Windows if possible or reboot and try again.

On the other hand, if a particular program consistently crashes in the same manner, you've found a culprit

red-handed. Check the vendor's Web site or call them to see if there's a fix available.

Why do I get the error, "A required DLL was not found"?

The program that needs the DLL file in question can't find it. That either means the DLL was accidentally deleted, or it was never properly installed to begin with. Try to reinstall the program from the original Install or Setup program. If that doesn't work, then you should contact the vendor for technical support.

Why do I get an error that my DLL is invalid or corrupt?

In all likelihood, two programs are using DLL files that have the same name, but the files themselves are different. Contact the software vendor to see if they know about an incompatibility with other programs. If you can determine which two programs are interfering with each other, you can reinstall the first program again so that its DLL files will be restored. The vendor may have a workaround, or you may not be able to use both programs on the same PC.

THE YEAR 2000 PROBLEM

What is the Year 2000 problem?

The Year 2000 problem—also known as the *Y2K bug*—refers to the fact that a lot of computer software wasn't designed to understand the rollover from the year 1999 to 2000 (or beyond). Because this software uses two digits to hold dates, 00 implies 1900. Some software might hit the year 2000 and revert to 1980 or 1974—but whatever the particular date, it'll cause calculations to return incorrect values, and a host of other problems will result. Credit cards may read as expired, and retail databases might show products backordered for almost a hundred years.

 Will the Year 2000 problem affect me?

Yes and no. Some elements of the Year 2000 problem will no doubt affect you—after all, technology has so permeated our lives that you're bound to have at least one bad experience in the next few years with a piece of technology that fails as a result of the date.

On the other hand, the Year 2000 problem will probably not affect your PC unless you have a large collection of older software running on an older PC. Specifically, computers with old, nonflashable BIOS chips will be susceptible (and not user fixable), and old DOS software will also fall under the Year 2000 spell. And if that's the case, there are few more compelling reasons to upgrade.

How can I test my PC for the Year 2000 problem?

It is virtually impossible to completely test for and avoid a logic problem as pervasive as the Year 2000 problem, but you can get a good idea if you'll be affected by performing these checks:

1. Set your PC's clock to Dec. 31, 1999, to a few minutes before midnight. Reboot the computer. After the system restarts, watch what happens. Obviously, if it rolls over from 1999 to an earlier date, such as 1980, your operating system is not Year 2000-compliant.

2. If you passed the first test, you're not finished. Next, set the clock ahead to an arbitrary time, such as Mar. 3, 2002. Restart the PC and see if the new date holds. If it works, great. If not, it's not the operating system's fault; it's the real-time clock mounted on the motherboard. The real-time clock may only be able to hold two digits, and hence may have trouble with the date after initially making the transition to the next century.

3. Now comes the hardest part of the test: individual applications. If your applications are old, or if your applications are custom written for intense business tasks, such as accounting, order management, or factory control, it is likely you'll have at least one program that

misbehaves in the next century. Also, programs that have been written in-house or by a small publisher may be more susceptible than those that come from a large, established publisher (although this is certainly not a hard-and-fast rule). Try all your applications, one at a time. Open your data files and place an order or check the status of data that spills into the next millennium. Also, set the clock early into the next century and try working from there. See if any of the programs cause problems. In particular, keep an eye out for date comparisons and actions that occur based on the date. (For instance, consider an order tracking system that flags unpaid invoices as overdue after 30 days. If you set the clock for Dec. 31, 1999, and build the invoice, then switch the clock to Jan. 2, 2000, what happens to the invoice? How about Feb. 1, 2000? Did it work as planned?)

You can read more about the Year 2000 problem by visiting the Year 2000 Web site at **http://www.year2000.com**.

 ## How can I avoid the Year 2000 problem?

You're most likely to see problems in database applications that use MM/DD/YY data-entry formats, and in old DOS software. If you have two-digit dates hard-coded into data (such as two-digit dates in database fields), you generally have to change the way dates are entered in the program, the date field in the database to make it store four-digit years, and the existing dates in the database. Some applications can fix the problem for you automatically. If you've been hit hard by the Year 2000 problem, you may need to enlist the services of a programming consultant who specializes in Year 2000 issues.

One of the best ways to avoid the Year 2000 problem is to upgrade your hardware and software to new versions that are compliant. If you're using a 386-based PC for business purposes, it is unlikely that you'll make the transition to the year 2000 smoothly—but you can get a new PC that is Year 2000-compliant now, before the end of 1999. When you upgrade your software, your data will likely make the

transition to compliance by virtue of being upgraded to new applications.

Windows is Year 2000-compliant, as is most modern Windows software (such as Microsoft Office). Not all Windows applications are compliant very far into the future, however, so you should test your applications out to 2030, 2040, and 2050, if there's a chance you'll need to track dates that far away.

I bought this book after January 2000. Am I home free?

Nope. The Y2K problem is really a combination of bugs that will strike software before, during, and after the millennium. Some software may be affected on September 9, 1999, for instance, because the date 9-9-99 may look like an end-of-file command. October 1 marks the start of fiscal year 2000, and other bugs will crop up early in the years 2000 and 2001 as some software reaches the end of the period it was designed to work through. Your best bet? Keep your software up-to-date to avoid date compatibility problems.

Chapter 14

Troubleshooting and Upgrading Windows

Answer Topics!

Troubleshooting and Upgrading Windows @ a Glance

Windows—you either love it or hate it. But regardless of what you think about it, there's no disputing that it's a complex operating system with many subtle tricks and twists. You may think you know Windows pretty well, but in reality there are entire layers of Windows you've never seen, sort of like a digital "onion." Even if you're not having any problems with Windows, you can use these tips to improve the way you work.

You can probably handle day-to-day Windows situations pretty well, but what happens when you encounter a problem? This chapter can help you master Windows regardless of what's happening on the desktop. Look here for tips on getting better performance and more hard disk space from your Windows computer.

And if you're ready to move to another version—or add some of the capabilities—read on to learn the ins and outs of upgrading to a newer version of Windows.

GENERAL WINDOWS QUESTIONS

? What's the difference between the OK and the Apply buttons on Windows dialog boxes?

There's more confusion over these two buttons than perhaps any other part of Windows. The Apply button activates whatever feature you're working with, without closing the dialog box. It's like a preview, in a sense—you can try out different backdrop images on the desktop without reopening the dialog box each time, for example. By clicking Apply, you're saying, "Let's try this out, but stick around, because I may want to undo it or try something else."

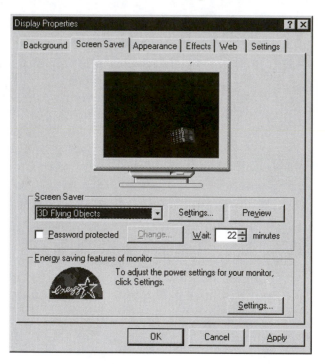

The OK button applies the feature and closes the dialog box. By clicking this button, you're saying, "I've made my decision. Let's get on with things."

The bottom line: You don't need to click Apply and OK to enable a feature. If you know what you want, just click OK.

 How can I get rid of the Windows startup sound?

Not everyone likes the sounds that Windows makes. You can change them, or disable the sounds entirely, very easily. Follow these steps:

1. Choose Start | Settings | Control Panel and open the Sounds applet.

2. Scroll down the list of Windows events until you find the one you want (such as Start Windows).

3. In the sound name drop-down menu, select another sound or [None]:

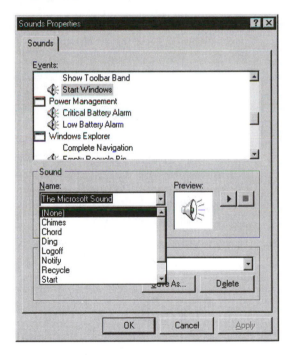

4. Click OK to close the dialog box.

 ## How can I add a background picture to the Windows desktop?

Want to show off a picture of your kids on the desktop? You don't have to stare at a plain blue or green screen all the time, you know. (Or perhaps your PC came with an advertisement for the manufacturer on the desktop, and you'd like to get rid of it.) Here's how you change it:

1. Right-click the desktop and choose Properties from the drop-down menu.

2. Click the Background tab.

3. Click the Browse button and choose a bitmap graphic stored somewhere on your hard disk. If you're using Internet Explorer 4 or Windows 98, you can also select a Web page if you want.

4. Click OK. The image will be displayed on the desktop.

How can I change the screen-saver settings?

Often, PCs come with flying cows, dancing logos, or some other screen saver selected that promotes the vendor, but it may not be what you want to look at every time you leave your PC untouched for more than a few minutes. It's easy to change:

1. Right-click the desktop and choose Properties from the drop-down menu.

2. Click the aptly named Screen Saver tab.

3. Choose the Screen Saver drop-down menu and pick a replacement. You can turn it off entirely by choosing [None].

4. Experiment with the Settings button for the screen saver you've chosen—you can vary its speed or complexity, and add a password to protect your data when you're away.

5. Click OK to close the dialog box.

How can I modify the programs in my Start menu?

When you install a new program, it invariably places an entry in the Windows Start menu for easy access. After a lot of installations, you may find that the Start menu has gotten unmanageably long or convoluted. You can reorganize the Start menu by following these steps:

1. Right-click a bare spot of the Taskbar (in a place where there isn't a program icon).

2. Choose Properties from the context-sensitive menu that appears.

3. Click the Start Menu Programs tab.

4. Click the Advanced button.

5. A window that looks like the Windows Explorer will appear. Click the plus sign next to Programs in the left pane, and a list of all the Start menu programs and folders will appear:

6. Organize the Start menu by creating new folders and dragging programs into more logical groups. You can delete, add, and rename folders just like in any Windows directory.

Tip: *Another way to open the Start menu as an Explorer window is to right-click the Start button and choose Explore.*

How can I delete programs from Windows?

Don't do it the old-fashioned way. Experienced PC users—those that are used to DOS and Windows 3.*x*—are accustomed to deleting the folder in which the offending program is stored. Sure, that gets rid of *some* of the program, but Windows 95 stores pieces of your software all over the place. You'll find DLL files and other components in the Windows directory, for example. If you delete programs manually, you'll leave lots of parts behind, and if you do this enough times, these pieces will clog up your hard disk, waste storage space, and may even conflict with other software on your system.

The correct way to delete programs from your hard disk is to choose Start | Settings | Control Panel and open the Add/Remove Programs applet (see Figure 14-1). Scroll

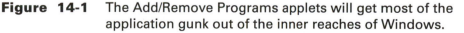

Figure 14-1   The Add/Remove Programs applets will get most of the application gunk out of the inner reaches of Windows.

through the list of programs installed on your hard disk and click the one you want to remove. Then click the Add/Remove button and follow the directions, if there are any.

You may find that some programs don't appear in the Add/Remove Programs list. Older software that wasn't written for Windows 95/98 ("16-bit applications") won't have an entry here—you'll need to delete it using the uninstall program that came with the software.

 Tip: *Windows may need to restart to finish removing some software. If you're deleting several programs at once, don't reboot until you're all done. That will save you a lot of time.*

 I need to start Windows in a hurry. Can I avoid all those programs in the StartUp folder?

Sure. When you see the desktop first appear, hold down the SHIFT key until the boot process is complete. Windows will skip any auto-start programs in the StartUp folder.

TROUBLESHOOTING WINDOWS

Where do I turn for troubleshooting help in Windows?

Depending on your specific problem, Windows may or may not be able to provide some valuable assistance. We've found some topics to be handled in an excellent manner and others—well, let's just say it's a good thing you have this book.

To get to Windows troubleshooting, click the Windows desktop and press F1. In the Contents tab, scroll down to Troubleshooting and double-click the help topic you want. Generally, these topics are built in a wizard-like style that walks you though problems in a step-by-step manner:

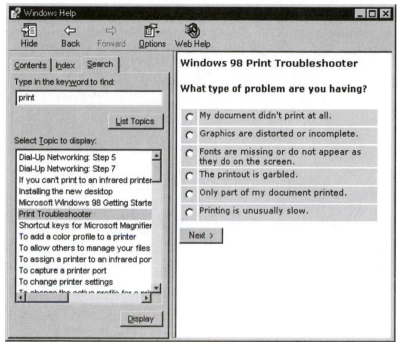

 I know my computer is going to crash if it loads Windows. How can I keep Windows from starting all the way up?

As soon as you see the message "Starting Windows," press F8. (In Windows 98, press F8 after the system beep, just as the Windows splash screen appears.) You'll get a menu of options that allow you to troubleshoot your system. Specifically, you can start your computer in Windows' Safe Mode (a no-frills version of Windows that loads almost no drivers, ensuring a reliable start despite most problems) or in DOS. To check for errors in your computer's startup sequence, you can also choose Step-by-Step Confirmation, which allows you to see the effect of every command in the autoexec.bat and config.sys files as they're executed.

 ## What can I use Windows' Safe Mode for?

If your PC experiences problems, Safe Mode may be for you. In particular, it's useful if you simply can't boot into Windows at all because of video problems, driver conflicts, or some other mysterious bug that crashes the system before you ever reach the Windows desktop. Safe Mode starts Windows in a lowest-common-denominator compatibility mode, with no network support or advanced video display capability. After you have your PC successfully running in Safe Mode, you can try to troubleshoot the problem.

 ## What is the Registry?

The Windows *Registry* is a database of settings used by Windows to manage all of your software and hardware. In Windows 3.1, these settings were maintained in part by a myriad of files that ended with an .ini extension. In more recent versions of Windows, all these old files have been combined into a comprehensive Registry database, which is even more difficult to use than the old system; it's now easier than ever to make Windows non-operable if you edit the wrong entry. Use REGEDIT—the Registry editor found in Windows—with care.

How can I back up and restore the Registry?

It's not a bad idea to make a copy of your Registry occasionally and save it to a safe location like a Zip disk, in case you need to restore the Registry after a catastrophic failure. You can back up the Registry in three different ways:

● The Registry is contained in two files called system.dat and user.dat, both found in the root of C:. If you copy them to a Zip disk or some other media, you have an up-to-the-minute backup of your Registry settings. To do

that, you'll need to change the file attributes first by following these steps:

1. Restart your PC in DOS mode. Then in DOS, switch to the Windows directory and type **attrib -h -s -r system.dat** and press ENTER. Then type **attrib -h -s -r user.dat** and press ENTER.

2. Copy the two files to another location.

3. Finally, restore the attributes for the Registry—type **attrib +h +s +r system.dat** and **attrib +h +s +r user.dat**.

● That's a fairly complex process to repeat often, so there are alternatives. You can also use a program found on the Windows 95/98 CD-ROM to back up the Registry more efficiently. Copy the program called cfgback.exe (see Figure 14-2) from the Other folder on the Windows CD-ROM to a location on your hard disk.

Configuration Backup

Use this application to create a backup of your system registry configuration or to restore a previously backed up configuration.

Selected Backup Name :
Reg 1-12

List of Previous Backups :
Reg 1-12

Date Backed Up : 1/21/98

Backup

Restore

Delete

Help

Exit

Figure 14-2   Cfgback.exe can be used to restore the Registry, but only from Windows.

> ⚠ ***Caution:*** *The disadvantage of using cfgback is that Windows must be working before you can restore a Registry; in other words, you can't run the program from DOS. This makes cfgback dangerous to rely on as your only safeguard.*

● Finally, there is a third option that is the simplest of all, and it's particularly handy for making a safe backup of the Registry, right before you edit the Registry using REGEDIT. Do this:

1. Choose Start | Run.

2. Type **REGEDIT** in the dialog box and press ENTER.

3. When the Registry Editor starts, choose Registry | Export Registry and save the file to a floppy or the hard disk.

```
Registry Editor                                    _ □ ✕
Registry  Edit  View  Help
  Import Registry File...          Name        Data
  Export Registry File...
  Connect Network Registry...
  Disconnect Network Registry...
  Print...              Ctrl+P
  Exit



Exports all or part of the registry to a text file.
```

4. When you want to restore a backup of the Registry, repeat the process but choose Registry | Import Registry instead.

? Why does Windows tell me I have a Registry error every single time I restart Windows?

Although Windows makes a backup of your Registry to prevent catastrophic loss of your Registry settings, it is sometimes possible for both the main Registry file (user.dat) and the backup (user.da0) to become corrupted more or less simultaneously. If this happens, Windows uses the corrupted backup to restore the Registry whenever you start your PC, and the cycle never ends. There are three ways to escape this loop:

● Use a diagnostic program like Norton Utilities or McAfee Office to try to fix the Registry. We don't recommend that you buy one of those programs just to solve this one problem, because the odds aren't compellingly high that they can fix it.

● If you make periodic backups of your Registry, try to import a recent copy. You may lose some settings—particularly those for hardware and software that has been installed since you made the Registry backup.

● If you don't have any Registry backups, there's one last option: Restore the original Registry settings from when Windows was first installed. You'll have to tell Windows about every hardware and software component you've added since the day you got the PC (or at least since you first installed Windows 95/98 on the PC), but at least you'll solve the Registry problem. Here's what to do:

1. The original settings are stored in a file called system.1st. Because system.1st is write-protected and hidden, we need to go to DOS and make the file writeable. At the C:\ prompt, type **attrib -h -s -r system.1st**.

2. Find system.dat, which stores the current Registry settings. You'll need to repeat step 1 on system.dat first: Type **attrib -h -s -r system.dat** at the Windows system prompt. Then delete the file.

3. Copy system.1st to your System folder (type **copy C:\system.1st C: windows\system**).

4. Rename system.1st as system.dat.

5. Restore the original file attributes by typing, in a DOS window, **attrib +h +s +r system.dat**.

 ## Windows won't shut down properly. Can I fix it?

Refer to the last questions in Chapter 1 for the answer to this question.

What should I do when a program says, "color palette not supported" or "this program works best in 256 colors"?

The program is telling you that it either won't work at all in the current color depth or video resolution you have selected, or it would prefer to work in a different resolution. You can switch the resolution of your desktop then run the program again. If you see a message that says something such as "color palette not supported" or the message shown here,

---

Living Books Player ☒

Current display driver palette too small.

[OK]

---

then you probably have a high-color mode activated while you're trying to run a program designed to work in 256 colors. Change the color depth or resolution mode by doing this:

1. Right-click the desktop and choose Properties from the context-sensitive menu.

2. Click the Settings tab.

3. Click the drop-down arrow in the Color Palette section, and choose the number of colors you want your desktop to support.

4. Click OK.

Tip: *If you don't see a monitor icon in the System Tray, click the Show Settings on the Task Bar button in the Settings tab. With that set, in the future you can just right-click the monitor icon and select a resolution and color palette directly.*

WINDOWS WORKAROUNDS

When I click an icon, it tries to start the wrong program. How can I associate it with a different program?

It's easy to change the program associated with a data file's file extension. Just find an icon that launches the wrong program, and hold down the SHIFT key as you right-click it. Choose Open With from the drop-down menu and scroll through the file list

until you find the right program. Click the box for Always Use This Program To Open This File Type then click OK.

I've run out of hard disk space. Where are some places I can free up more room?

So, you've run out of room on your hard disk. Before you dash out and buy a new hard disk, you may be able to squeeze some more life out of the drive you already have. Here are some things you can do to find more space:

- *Delete the contents of your temp folders.* Windows uses several folders to perform ordinary maintenance in the background while you work. Usually, Windows cleans up after itself. Every time you shut down your PC without exiting Windows or your system crashes unexpectedly, however, many of these temporary files get left behind and forgotten about. Look in the folders C:\TEMP and C:\Windows\Temp. You can delete anything you find there, which can sometimes add up to hundreds of megabytes.

- *Clear your browser cache.* Open Internet Explorer or Netscape Navigator and locate the option for your temporary Internet files. If you're desperate for space, deleting them can buy you a few megabytes.

- *Delete big files.* Search your hard disk for really big files that you don't need anymore, like graphics, sounds, and movies you may have created or downloaded from the Internet. (Before deleting any of these, it's a good idea to have a solid backup.)

 Tip: *You can create a list of files in a specific folder by using the Start | Find | Files or Folders command and clicking Find Now without specifying any filename at all. You'll get a list of all the files, which you can then sort by file size.*

- *Delete old files.* Search your hard disk for files dated more than a year ago. In general, if the file hasn't been

touched in a year, you may not need it. (It's a good idea to skip any Windows-specific system files, even if they are older.)

● *Delete files your system no longer needs.* Applications put useless files all over your hard disk, and you can recover lots of space by periodically eliminating them. Delete the mscreate.dir files that Microsoft uses to install applications, as well as files with extensions like .fts, .bak, and .old. If you want to recover even more space, you can delete help files (they end in .hlp), but remember that you won't be able to get online help anymore. And remember that .old and .bak files are there for your protection; if you delete them, they're gone forever.

● *Delete backup files and turn off backup options.* Some programs, like Microsoft Word, can make a backup of your work every time you save. That's good for peace of mind, but bad for storage space. If you want to, you can delete these backups and even disable the program's ability to make new backups.

● *Convert your hard disk to FAT32.* Windows 95 Service Release 2 (OSR2) and Windows 98 let you format your hard disk as a FAT32 drive and get hundreds of megabytes of space back for free if you have a gigabyte drive or bigger. See Chapter 8 for details on using OSR2 and FAT32.

● *Archive your old stuff.* If you have files that get rarely used, you can compress them in a Zip file or move them off the hard disk onto Zip disks or floppy. That way they're not hogging hard disk space, but you still have long-term access to them.

 I've downloaded a file and I don't know where I put it. How can I find the file?

Windows has a file-finding tool. Choose Start | Find | Files or Folders and enter the name—or part of the name—of the file you're looking for. Then choose to search on a specific drive, folder, or the entire PC, and click Find Now.

Tip: *Be sure to leave Search Subfolders checked, so the program will look not just in the selected folder, but in all folders nested within it.*

 ## I tried to compress my hard disk with DriveSpace, but Windows says FAT32 can't be compressed. Why?

The disk compression software that comes with Windows— called DriveSpace—predates Windows 95 Release 2 (OSR2)/Windows 98 and their FAT32 filing system. In a word, they are not compatible. In fact, Microsoft does not plan to implement a version of DriveSpace for FAT32 drives at all.

This means that if your hard disk was formatted in FAT32 (you can tell by looking at the File System description in the Properties dialog box, General tab, for your drive), you can't compress the disk. Here are your choices:

- Convert the drive back to FAT16 (and lose the advantages of having a FAT32 drive—we don't recommend this).

- Add another hard disk or removable media drive for additional storage space.

- Use another compression scheme, such as Mijenix's Free Space, that is compatible with FAT32.

Caution: *We don't recommend that you use disk compression tools like DriveSpace, because they add another layer of possible failure. Problems with DriveSpace can be catastrophic, because DriveSpace uses its own special protocols for writing files to your hard drive. This makes it more difficult to troubleshoot the drive.*

 ## How can I speed up Windows' boot process?

Windows takes a while to load, that's for sure. As you accumulate software, it tends to get even slower.

One way to speed up the boot process is to streamline the Registry. You can download RegClean from Microsoft's Web site at **http://www.microsoft.com**, which will clean up your Registry for free, or try the tools in utilities like Helix Nuts & Bolts or Norton Utilities. These programs promise to remove outdated references and compact the overall file for faster performance.

Another way to speed up the boot process is by deleting extra fonts. Because every font on your PC takes extra time to start Windows, it makes sense to keep the Fonts folder as lean as possible. Delete fonts that you never use, as long as you know that they came with a graphics program or word processor, or that you installed them yourself. Some programs need their special fonts, so if you don't know where a font came from, you shouldn't delete it.

Tip: *To preview a font, simply double-click the icon in the Fonts folder. A window appears that shows you what the font looks like.*

Finally, having more memory and more free hard disk space will reduce total startup time. You should have 32MB of RAM and no less than 60MB of free disk space on your C: drive (or wherever you have the virtual memory assigned).

How can I get rid of the Windows logon dialog box that appears every time my computer starts?

Caution: *We're assuming that you're not actually connecting to a Windows 95, 98, or NT network in an office workgroup. If you are, you may well need a password in order to gain access to the network.*

There are a few possible reasons why this box keeps popping up. Here are some things to check:

- Make sure your logon is Windows Networking. Choose Start | Settings | Control Panel and open the Network

applet. On the Configuration tab, make sure the Primary
Network Logon is Windows Logon.

Make sure you don't have a password in use. Choose
Start | Settings | Control Panel and open the Passwords
applet. Click Change Network Password and press
ENTER to make sure there is no password in use.

I have an icon in my Control Panel for a tool I no longer use. How can I get rid of it?

The Control Panel is an extensible collection of applets that
control many aspects of Windows' operation. You might
install a new device—like a scanner, for instance—that
installs an applet in the Control Panel. If you remove the
scanner, the scanner's applet in the Control Panel may not go
away at the same time. Here's the fix:

1. Make sure there isn't an uninstall program either in the
   device's folder on the hard disk or in the Add/Remove
   Programs list.

2. Find the CPL file for the device. The Control Panel's various icons are actually contained in individual files that end with a .cpl extension and are stored in the C:\Windows\System folder. Look for the CPL file that corresponds to the offending applet, and delete it.

Tip: *Before you delete the CPL file, you might want to try renaming it so that Windows won't recognize it, and then rebooting your computer. Check the Control Panel to make sure you've snagged the right file; otherwise, you might accidentally delete the wrong Control Panel icon. If you've got it right, delete the renamed file.*

I deleted a program manually from my hard disk, but the program's name remains in the Add/Remove Programs list. Can I get rid of it?

Yes, but you'll need to download a program called TweakUI from the Microsoft Web site at **http://www.microsoft.com**. It's usually included in a set of utilities called PowerToys. TweakUI lets you eliminate specific entries from the Add/Remove Programs list, but beware—it eliminates the program name, but doesn't actually uninstall the program or any of its components.

If you don't want to download PowerToys, you can still delete irrelevant entries, but you'll have to muck around in the Registry. Run REGEDIT and navigate to Hkey_Local_Machine/Software/Microsoft/Windows/CurrentVersion/Uninstall. Delete the entries that are no longer valid, and save the Registry.

Caution: *Always back up your Registry before working with it. The backup process is detailed early in this chapter.*

I can't find any entry for my program in the Add/Remove Programs list, but I want to delete it. What should I do?

If your program doesn't appear in the Control Panel's Add/Remove Programs list, try looking in the program's folder on the hard disk. You might find an uninstall utility there. If not, run the program's original install or setup software. Odds are good that there will be an option to uninstall the program there.

 Note: *If you already use a third-party uninstall utility, you might be in luck. Many of these uninstall programs catalog all of the files that other installation programs put on your hard disk, and they can automatically remove those newer programs for you. If the uninstall program wasn't on your hard disk when you first installed the program you want to delete, however, it probably won't be able to uninstall the program.*

If neither of those options pan out, contact the vendor and see if they can provide a set of uninstall directions that list every file that needs to be deleted.

Tip: *If it's a DOS program, it's okay to delete the folder—DOS programs are typically self-contained in a single directory.*

 I have deleted programs manually without using the Add/Remove Programs list. What can I do to get rid of the leftover components?

Unfortunately, it's not easy to tell what miscellaneous files scattered around your hard disk belong to specific programs. There are a few steps you can take:

- Look for shortcuts to the program on the desktop and in the Start menu, and delete them. In particular, look for an icon for the program in the Start | Programs | Startup folder—if there's one there, you'll get errors each time Windows starts, until you delete it.

- Search the hard disk for INI files that are obviously related to the deleted program, and delete them.

- If you still have the original disks, reinstall the program then delete it using the Add/Remove Programs list in the

Control Panel. Be sure that you install it in the same folder that it was in to begin with.

● Use an uninstall utility. Some of these programs are good at rooting out DLL files and other remnants of previously uninstalled programs.

 I uninstalled a program the wrong way, and now I get an error message when Windows starts. How can I make it go away?

There are two places you need to look to remove the cause of this error. First, look in Start | Programs | Startup to see if an icon for the program is there, trying to activate every time Windows loads. If so, delete it (see "How can I modify the programs in my Start menu?" earlier in this chapter).

If that folder has nothing of interest, open the win.ini file (you can get there from the SYSEDIT program, discussed in Chapter 4) and look for the "LOAD=" and "RUN=" lines. Delete any reference to the offending program and save win.ini.

 How can I make my CD-ROM drive work when I choose "Restart the computer in MS-DOS mode"?

It's unfortunate that Windows makes a secret of so many things. For instance, when you want to restart your PC in MS-DOS mode, Windows refers to a special file that looks like the autoexec.bat but that isn't stored in the root of the C: drive. Look for dosstart.bat in the C:\Windows folder and edit it. You'll find that your CD-ROM drivers may be listed, but "remarked out" (disabled with the word REM at the start of the line) so they don't run. Delete the REMs (but leave the rest of the line intact). If your drivers aren't present, add them and save the file. Of course, you can add or remove lines from dosstart.bat in the same way that you'd edit the autoexec.bat file. That means you can add a mouse driver if one isn't there or invoke a DOS program each time you restart in DOS mode.

❋ *Note:* *For more on adding your CD-ROM driver to system files, see the discussion of emergency boot disks in Chapter 13.*

Where can I look for answers to unusual problems I'm having with Windows?

Give Microsoft a try. It maintains a detailed knowledge base at **http://www.microsoft.com**. You can also check out these Web sites for advice and information:

- http://www.annoyances.org/win95
- http://www.clubwin.com
- http://www.winfiles.com
- http://www.windowscentral.com
- http://www.techweb.com
- http://www.winmag.com/win95
- http://www.winmag.com/win98

I recently installed a new hard disk, but it doesn't appear in Windows! How can I make it show up?

The Registry might be confused. Run REGEDIT and choose Edit | Find. Type **NoDrives** and press ENTER. When you find the entry, check to make sure all the numbers for NoDrives in the right pane are 0—a 1 tells Windows to ignore the drive. If any are wrong, double-click NoDrives, change them all to 0, and save the Registry.

Why does my PC run slowly, thrash the hard disk a lot, and crash rather often?

It could be a problem with the virtual memory settings in Windows. Virtual memory is hard disk space that Windows uses as if it were RAM, and you should have about twice as much virtual memory hard disk space as you do RAM (unless you have 64MB or more of real RAM—then you only need a one-to-one relationship).

If you have 16MB of RAM, but only 15 or 20MB of space left on your hard disk, you need to clear some more room for your virtual memory, or assign your virtual memory to a different drive with more available space. To change drives, right-click My Computer and choose Properties from the drop-down menu. Click the Performance tab and click the

Virtual Memory button. Choose Let Me Specify My Own Virtual Memory Settings, and select the drive you want to use. Then click OK and restart the PC.

I've heard it's a good idea to reinstall Windows occasionally. Should I?

Some people recommend this, and in reality it's not a bad idea. Here's the logic: Over time, Windows tends to fill up with incompletely uninstalled programs and unneeded software, contributing to slower operation, incompatibilities and bugs, and wasted hard disk space. You can perform a spring cleaning once or twice a year by backing up your hard disk, formatting the drive, and reinstalling everything from scratch.

The question, however, is do we recommend reinstalling Windows? If you feel really comfortable doing this kind of thing, sure. You'll need to be pretty methodical about maintaining backups and keeping patches, enhancements, and drivers for all your software on a Zip disk or some other easy-to-access media, so that it's easy to restore your data and applications.

If you aren't comfortable with the thought of taking your hard disk down and rebuilding Windows and all your software, then definitely don't do it. The payoffs are tangible, but certainly not compelling for most people. Personally, we have systems that have been running the original installation of Windows 95 for over two years and they're still quite healthy. On the other hand, we appreciate the improvement in other systems that have been reinstalled more recently.

I need to reinstall Windows, but I've lost the "key" that Microsoft asks for when installing software. What should I do?

Believe it or not, Microsoft products will often accept CD keys from other programs—so you don't have to use the exact same key as the one that came with the program. Another solution? Look at your System Properties (assuming Windows still runs on your system). Right-click My Computer and you'll find the key listed on the General tab (see Figure 14-3).

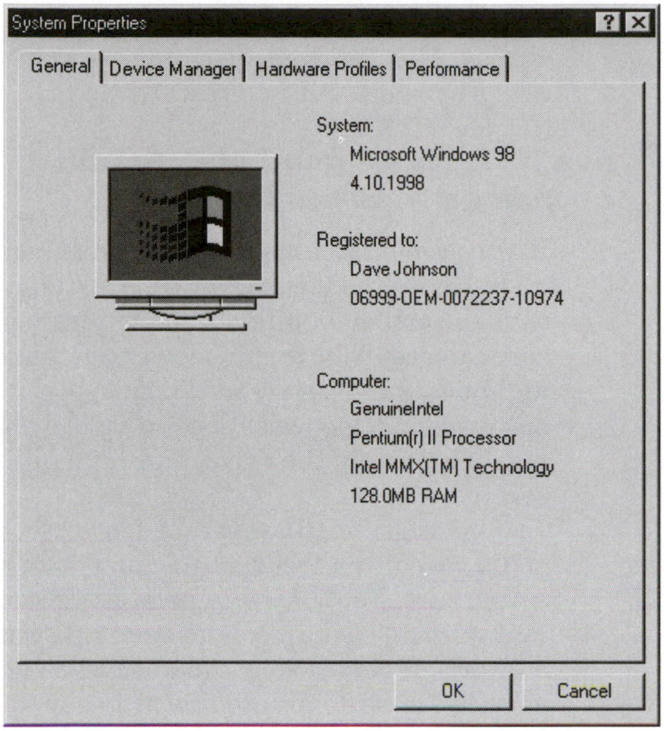

Figure 14-3 The product key for Windows can sometimes be found within Windows itself.

UPGRADING WINDOWS

 What's different in Windows 98?

Windows 98 isn't as different from Windows 95 as 95 was from Windows 3.1—it's evolutionary, not revolutionary. But it has some compelling features nonetheless. Here's what you'll find in the box:

● An integrated Web browser with Active Desktop, like the one in Internet Explorer 4.

● Multiple monitor support. Connect up to eight monitors to your PC at once for a huge desktop that spans across different displays, much like the way the Macintosh works.

- Windows Update, a tool that keeps Windows up to date by downloading new components from the Internet.

- FAT32 hard drive support, updated from Windows 95 OSR2.

- Built-in television convergence technologies, allowing you to watch TV on your PC and see channel guide and Web-related information onscreen at once.

- Instant-on technology that avoids long boot times—though this hasn't been implemented in many PCs currently on the market.

 ## Do I have to already have Windows 3.1 on my PC to install Windows 95 or 98?

No, you don't. Ordinarily, you need to install the Windows 95 or 98 upgrade over either Windows 3.1 or MS-DOS, but it's not absolutely necessary, especially if you've recently formatted the hard drive. Instead, all you really need is disk 1 of your Windows 3.1 set, in order to restore or install the Windows 95/98 upgrade.

What are the Windows Service Packs?

The *Service Packs* are updates to the Windows operating system that Microsoft makes available on its Web site for download and user installation. The existence of the Internet, in fact, makes it possible for Microsoft to allow users to update their systems without purchasing updates at a retail store. The Service Packs include bug fixes, new features, and new drivers for common hardware. The place to go for updates to all versions of Windows is **http:// www.microsoft.com/windows/downloads/default.asp**.

If you're using Windows 98, there's an even easier solution. Just choose Start | Windows Update, and Windows will take you to an update page for Windows 98. There, your hard disk will be automatically checked for any updates you might need, and the site will recommend that you install the appropriate patches. We recommend that you perform the Windows Update about once a month to check for important new fixes to Windows.

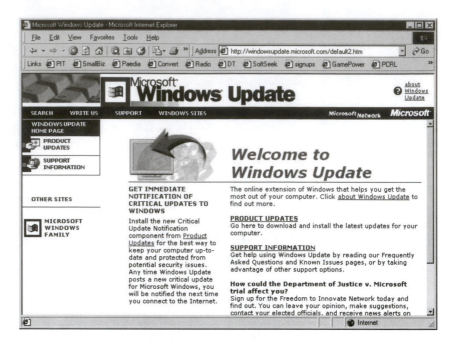

 ## How do I install Windows 95 updates?

Visit **http://www.microsoft.com/windows/downloads/ default.asp**, and follow the links to download Windows updates. You will have several major choices:

● **Service Packs**   The Service Packs are a collection of many updates and fixes, all rolled into one download.

● **Recommended Updates**   These are single-purpose fixes like Year 2000 fixes and new versions of Internet Explorer.

● **Administrative Tools**   These are program downloads intended mainly for system administrators to help them better deploy Windows on a network.

● **Toys**   Power and Kernel Toys are add-ons for Windows like TweakUI that add functionality to Windows but were never rolled into the official release of the operating system.

 ## What is Windows 95 OSR2?

Windows OSR2 is the short name for Windows Service Release 2. It has a number of major enhancements—particularly the ability to use the new FAT32 filing system and glean hundreds of megabytes of extra storage space from disk drives—but it was only available on new systems that shipped during the late part of Windows 95's reign. (These days all new PCs ship with Windows 98, which incorporates all of OSR2's improvements.) You can't purchase or download OSR2 on its own. You can tell if you have OSR2 by checking the version numbers of your copy of Windows; right-click My Computer and read the version. If it says 4.00.950b, it's OSR2.

 ## I keep hearing about CAB files. What are they?

CAB files are cabinet files—compressed data files that contain installation files for Windows or other applications. Windows 95, for instance, is composed of about two dozen CAB files that you can find on your original CD-ROM.

 Tip: *You can copy all the CAB files to your hard drive—which makes it easy to install Windows and to add components later without fishing out the CD every time. If you already have Windows on your PC, look in C:\Options. You'll probably find all the CAB files for Windows there.*

How do I know what's inside a CAB file?

Ordinarily, you can't see inside a CAB file. If you install Microsoft's PowerToys, however, you'll find the useful cabinet viewer utility, CabView, that lets you work with CAB files as if they were ordinary folders. You can peer inside and even extract specific files with the mouse. Just right-click the CAB files you want to use and choose View. A folder opens to display the contents of the CAB.

Is there a fix for the dial-up connection, so I don't have to click Connect every time I go online?

Out of the box, Windows forces you to click the Connect button to go online, even though you've just started the dial-up connection program. There are at least two ways around this problem:

- **ISDN Accelerator Pack from http://www. microsoft.com**   This isn't just for ISDN—it is an update for all modems, and allows you to bypass the Connect button.

- **Any of the third-party dial-up networking utilities**   We use Vector Development's Dunce, a handy tool that does a lot of things, including bypassing the Connect button for you.

How do I know if all my hardware is optimized for Windows?

Some of your hardware (particularly your CD-ROM) may be running on "real-mode" drivers instead of Windows-optimized, protected-mode drivers. That means you might be experiencing serious performance losses. To find out, right-click My Computer and choose Properties. Click the Performance tab. If there are any problems, you'll see them listed in the middle of this dialog box; otherwise, it will report "Your system is configured for optimal performance" (see Figure 14-4). If you see any messages, contact the vendors of any problem devices for Windows-compatible drivers.

How do I add or remove parts of Windows after installation?

Suppose that last year you performed a typical installation of Windows 95/98, but now you want to add the Direct Cable Connection drivers (discussed in Chapter 9) so you can link two PCs together. There are many parts of Windows not installed by default, but you can easily add them later. Just choose Start | Settings | Control Panel and open the Add/Remove Programs applet. Then click the Windows Setup

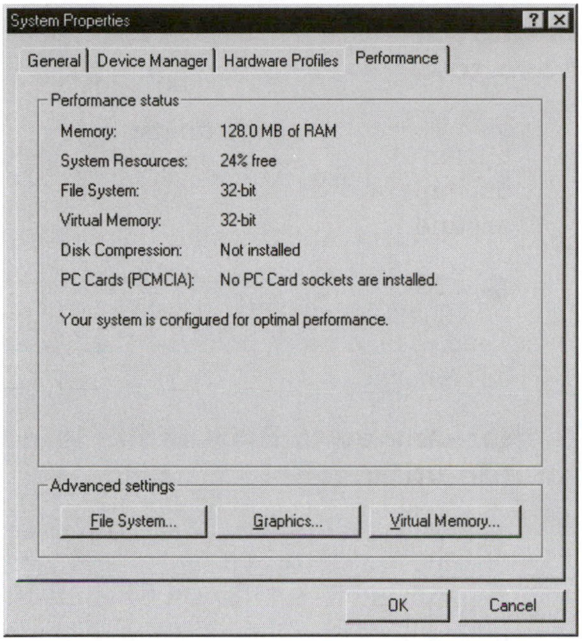

Figure 14-4 The Performance tab shows you if any devices are running in real mode.

tab. You'll see a list of categories from the Windows setup process:

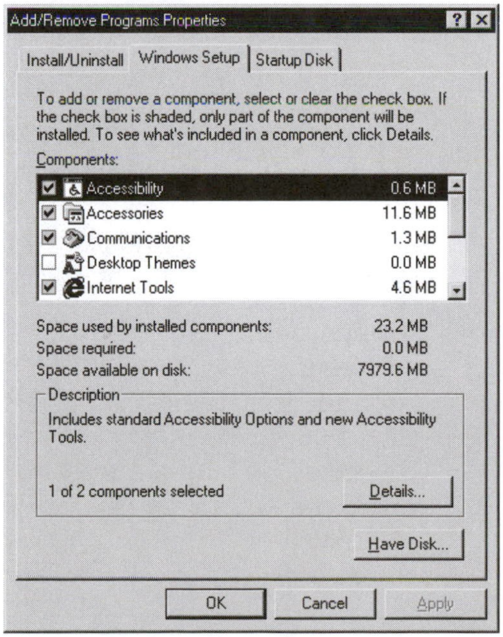

You can tell what is installed if you know the following code:

- Checked boxes are fully installed.
- Empty boxes are uninstalled.
- Gray boxes with check marks are only partially installed.

Select a category and click the Details button. You can then select the items from which you want to add or delete components. Click OK twice to accept the changes. You may need to load the Windows CD-ROM to finish the installation or removal.

Is there a way to disable the Windows startup and shutdown images?

Yes, you can disable the startup screen. But even if you could disable the shutdown screen—which you can't—we wouldn't recommend it. It tells you when it's safe to turn off your PC, after all, so disabling it would be akin to disabling traffic signals when you were driving. To disable the startup screen, you need to get TweakUI, one of the programs included with PowerToys and found on Microsoft's Web site. On the Boot tab, deselect Display Splash Screen While Booting.

Tip: *If you're really adamant about eliminating the shutdown screens, try changing them instead—see the next question.*

 ## How do I change the startup or shutdown message in Windows?

After a few years of staring at Microsoft's picture of a cheery cloud formation, you might eventually get tired of it. Believe it or not, you can not only delete this image entirely, but you can replace it with your own design. Here's how to replace the startup or shutdown images:

1. Back up the original graphics, just in case you want to restore them. There are three images:

   ● **logo.sys**   The startup image, found in the root of the C: drive

   ● **logow.sys**   The first shutdown image, found in C:\Windows

   ● **logos.sys**   The second shutdown image, found in C:\Windows

Tip: *You can look at the startup and shutdown files in a paint program by first renaming them with a .bmp extension.*

2. Create your own graphic in a graphics program, such as Microsoft Paint or Paint Shop Pro (or any other paint program of your choice). You can create a replacement for any one or all three images. You need to make sure they're 320×400 pixels and 256 colors. Save them as BMP files. No other format will work.

3. Rename these files with the filenames used by the default startup and shutdown images (logo.sys, logow.sys, and logos.sys) and save them to the appropriate locations on your hard disk (C: for the startup image and C:\Windows for the shutdown images).

Index